KIERKEGAARD

KIERKEGAARD IN THE STREET

Oil painting by LUPLAU JANSSEN

VOLUME II

Kierkegaard

WALTER LOWRIE, D.D.

Thus conscience doeth make cowards of us all;
And thus the native hue of resolution
Is sicklied o'er with the pale cast of thought.

HAMLET.

HARPER TORCHBOOKS / The Cloister Library
HARPER & BROTHERS, NEW YORK

KIERKEGAARD

Printed in the United States of America

This book was originally published in 1938 by
Oxford University Press, New York and London, and is reprinted by
arrangement with the Estate of Walter Lowrie.

First HARPER TORCHBOOK edition published 1962

TABLE OF CONTENTS

VOLUME II

CONTENTS

APPENDIXES

LIST OF ILLUSTRATIONS

See APPENDIX VI *for a discussion of S. K.'s portraits*

Volume II

KIERKEGAARD

PART FOUR
INTELLECTUAL MATURITY
1844–7

The time is out of joint: O cursed spite,
That ever I was born to set it right!

HAMLET.

NOTE

To avoid the possibility of misunderstanding, I say expressly that I am very far from meaning to affirm that S. K. attained maturity (in the fullest sense) at this time, i.e. in his early thirties; but it is clear that in this period he reached *intellectual* maturity. He himself regarded the *Concluding Unscientific Postscript to the Philosophical Scraps* as central to his literary work as a whole. The title indicates that when he wrote it he regarded it as the conclusion of his work as a writer. In fact, all the trends of his thinking find their ultimate and most adequate expression in this work, in the *Literary Review*, and in *The Book About Adler*, which all belong to this period. At this time he succeeded in formulating completely his scheme of the 'stages' of life, which he now begins to call 'the spheres of existence',[1] and he was able to state to himself exactly what Christianity is. This might well have been his last word—if circumstances had not prompted him to resort to direct communication, and to consume himself in the effort to make people understand what it means 'to become a Christian'. Intellectually he could go no farther—unless, like Hegel and his disciples, he would go beyond Christianity. For his own part he was not tempted to 'go farther', for he had made it clear that the philosophers who would advance beyond Christianity were really returning to paganism, and were not likely to get so far ahead as Socrates. He complained that the philosophers had not taken the pains to ascertain what Christianity is, before they proceeded to mediate it by speculation. That, he said, made mediation easy—but illusory. The philosophers made out that to understand what Christianity is involves such tremendous difficulties that only the highest intellects are capable of it. S. K., on the other hand, affirmed again and again that it is very easy to know what Christianity is, but exceedingly difficult to become a Christian[2]—and more difficult for the wise man than for the simple.[3] He conceived that this task was enough to occupy the remainder of his life—which proved to be only nine years after the publication of the *Postscript*, and even at that was considerably longer than he expected it to be. I would not venture to speak of S. K. as mature until he had decisively become a Christian—

which to his way of thinking was only in the last year of his life.

During the period we are here considering, S. K. lived in the great house on the Nytorv (New Market), which he inherited from his father. On October 16, 1844, he moved there from the house he had long occupied at 230 Nørregade, and on December 24, 1847, finding that there was not much left of his fortune, he sold this house, and on 'moving-day' the following April he went to live in a rented apartment on the corner of Rosenborggade and Tornebuskgade.

I. AWAY FROM SPECULATION!

1844–6

JOHANNES CLIMACUS tells us in the *Postscript* how he happened to become a writer:[1]

It is now well on to four years since the idea came into my head to try my luck as a writer. I remember it very clearly. It was on a Sunday, yes, that 's right, it was a Sunday afternoon, while I sat as usual out there at the café in the Frederiksberg Park, that wonderful park which for the child was fairyland, where the King dwelt with his Queen; that charming park which was the happy diversion of the youth in the midst of the hilarious merriment of the people; that friendly park where for the man of riper years there is such a homelike feeling of sad detachment from the world and all that is of the world, where even the *envied* glamour of the kingly dignity has faded to what it now is out there, a queen's remembrance of her deceased lord [referring to the widow of Frederick VI, who continued to reside there]. . . .

I had been a student for about ten years. Although I was never lazy, my activity was rather a glittering inactivity—a sort of occupation for which I still have a predilection, and perhaps even a congenital talent. I read a lot, and spent the remainder of the day thinking and idling, or idling and thinking, but that was all it came to; the earliest sproutings of my productivity barely sufficed for my daily use and were consumed in their first greening. . . .

So there I sat and smoked my cigar until I lapsed into thought. Among other thoughts I remember the following. 'You are gradually', I said to myself, 'getting on in years, without being anything or seriously attempting to do anything. On the other hand, wherever you look, in literature and in life, you see the admired names and figures, the precious people who enjoy acclaim, come into prominence and get themselves talked about, the benefactors of the age who know how to make themselves useful to mankind by making life easier and easier for people, some by means of railways, others by telegraphs, others by facile compendiums and succinct information about everything worth knowing, and finally, the true benefactors of the age who make spiritual existence in the medium of thought systematically easier and easier, and at the same time more and more significant. And what are you doing?'

Here my soliloquy came to an end, for my cigar was burnt out and a new one had to be lit. Then I began to smoke again, and suddenly this thought flashed through my head: 'You must do something; but since it will be impossible for you with your limited capacities to make anything easier than it has been made, you must undertake, with the same humanitarian enthusiasm that inspires the others, to make something harder.' This conceit pleased me immensely, and at the same time it held out the flattering prospect that because of my effort I should be held in singular love and esteem by the whole community. For when all combine in every way to make all things easier, there is only one possible danger, namely, that the easiness may become so great that it becomes altogether too great, and there remains only one want, though it is not yet a felt want, when men will want difficulty. Out of love for mankind, and in desperation at my embarrassing position, seeing that I had accomplished nothing and was unable to make anything easier than it had been made, and with a true interest in those who make everything easy, I conceived it to be my task to create difficulties everywhere.

We see here that Climacus was at no pains to hide the fact that he was a very 'droll fellow'. But this is not a quality which differentiates the pseudonym from S. K. himself. We have frequently had occasion to remark upon a childishly roguish trait in S. K. and a boyish humour which characterized him up to this very time. On the same day that he published his first entirely serious book, *The Concept of Dread*, he allowed Nicholas Notabene to publish the *Prefaces*, which were characterized by rollicking humour with a quality of biting satire. He remarked that 'Nicholas Notabene is a merry fellow; perhaps to divert attention from the fact that *The Concept of Dread* lectured a little'.[1] While he was writing the *Postscript*, and for some time thereafter (1844–7), he was engaged off and on with a humorous book which he proposed to call 'Specimens of Penmanship', and which was never completed.[1] Perhaps he proposed this because the *Postscript* lectured more than a little. But the *Postscript* itself, in spite of its seriousness, was so generously interlarded with humour that it did not need to be offset by a book of sheer fun; and perhaps the chief reason why the 'Specimens of Penmanship' was never finished is to be discovered in the fact that while he was writing it S. K. outgrew it, and therefore had not the heart to publish it. At all events it is a fact that this is the last playful work he ever essayed to write, although fortunately he did not lose his sense of humour. In the *Postscript* he definitely assigned to humour a place *below* religion.

But even Johannes Climacus was not a shallow humorist: he reveals a deep capacity for pathos in the long account he gives of the occasion which made clear to him his specific task as a writer, and the alert reader will discern the sharp polemic, half-hidden by the humour and the pathos.[2]

> The event in itself was simple enough. It was four years ago, on a Sunday. Here perhaps no one will believe me, because again it was a Sunday; nevertheless it is quite true that it was a Sunday, about two months after that Sunday above mentioned. It was rather late, towards evening. And the farewell of the evening to the day and to him who has experienced the day is an enigmatical greeting: its admonition is like the injunction of a careful mother to her child to come indoors betimes; but its invitation (even if the farewell itself is not to blame for such a misapprehension) seems like an inexplicable beckoning, as though repose were to be found only out of doors, in the nocturnal tryst—not with a woman, but womanly with the infinite, persuaded by the night wind which repeats itself monotonously as it scours the woodland and field and sighs as though it were seeking something, persuaded by the far-off echo of silence answering itself as though it surmised something, persuaded by the sublime peace of the heavens as though this something were found, persuaded by the audible silence of the dew as though this were the explanation and the refreshment of infinity, which is like the fruitfulness of the still night, only half understood, like the semi-transparency of nocturnal mists.

Contrary to my custom, I had gone out into the garden which is called the Garden of the Dead, where the visitor finds it doubly difficult to utter his farewell, seeing that it is meaningless to say, 'We shall meet another time', when the last time is already past, and where there is no reason to terminate the farewell which begins only when the last time is past. Already most of the people had gone home. Only a single individual vanished here and there among the trees. Ill pleased with the encounter, he avoided me, for he was there to seek the dead and not the living. And in this park it is well understood that one does not go there to see and be seen, but that each visitor is to avoid the other. And one has no need of society—least of all the society of a garrulous friend—in a place where all is eloquent, where the dead man shouts in one's ear the one word that has been inscribed upon his tomb—not like a parson who preaches diffusely upon the text, but like a silent man who utters only this one word, but utters it with such passion that it seems as if the dead man would burst his tomb. . . .

Tired of walking, I sat upon a bench, an admiring spectator of the way that proud ruler, the sun, who for thousands of years has been the hero of the day and will so remain until the end of time, how the sun in its brilliant departure cast a glamour over the whole environment, while my eye, looking over the wall which enclosed the garden, gazed upon that eternal symbol of eternity, the endless horizon. What sleep is for the body, such is a moment of repose like this for the weary soul, when it can freely breathe. At that moment I discovered to my surprise that the trees which hid me from the eyes of others hid others also from mine; for I heard a voice close beside me. It has always afflicted me with a sense of shame to be witness of an expression of feeling on the part of another man which he would only indulge in when he thought himself unobserved; for there is an inwardness of feeling which properly is kept hidden and is only revealed before God, just as a woman's beauty will be kept hidden and only revealed before the beloved. Hence I resolved to retire. But the first word I heard arrested me forcibly, and as I feared that the noise of my departure would cause more disturbance than if I sat still, I chose the latter course and became witness of a situation the solemnity of which was not profaned by my presence. Through the leaves I saw that there were two persons, an old man with snow-white hair and a child, a boy of about ten years. They were both dressed in mourning and sat beside a newly made grave, whence one could easily infer that they were engrossed in a recent bereavement. The venerable figure of the aged man became still more solemn in the twilight glow, and his voice, quiet and yet impassioned, made every word distinct, and clearly expressed the deep sincerity of the speaker, who paused now and then when his voice was stifled by a sob or his mood expressed itself in a sigh. . . . I learnt from the conversation that the small boy was the grandson of the old man, and that he whose grave they visited was the boy's father. It seemed likely that all the rest of the family was dead, inasmuch as no other names were mentioned; and this I ascertained to be the fact when on a subsequent visit I read the family name on the tombstone and the names of the many deceased. The old man was saying to the boy that he had no father any more, no one to rely upon except an old man who was far too old for him and himself longed to depart from this world, but that there is a God in heaven after whom every fatherhood in heaven and earth is named, there is one name in which there is salvation, the name of Jesus Christ. He paused an instant and then said half-aloud to himself, 'Oh, that this my one comfort should become my dismay, that this my son who is now laid in the grave should permit this consolation to slip away from him! To what end all my hope, to what end all my care, to what end all his wisdom, when now his death in the midst of his error must make a believer's soul uncertain of his son's salvation, bring my gray hairs down in sorrow to the grave, cause a believer to depart this world in anxiety, cause an old man to seek after certainty like a doubter and to regard despondently the only one that is left.' Thereupon he spoke again to the child, saying that there is a wisdom which presumes to fly beyond faith, that on the yonder side of faith there is something like a blue range of mountains, apparently a continent, which to mortal eyes looks like a certainty more lofty than the certainty of faith, but that the believer fears this mirage and shuns it as the seaman does a similar illusion, that it is a sham eternity, in which a mortal cannot exist but loses faith if he gazes upon it. He fell silent again and then said to himself,

'Oh, that my unhappy son should let himself be deceived! To what end all his learning, which he could not even make comprehensible to me so that I might talk to him about his error, because it was too high for me!' Then he stood up and led the child to the grave, and with a voice the impressiveness of which I shall never forget he said to him, 'Poor boy, you are only a child, and yet you will soon be alone in the world. Promise me by the memory of your deceased father, who if he now could speak to you would speak as I do, and who speaks indeed now with my voice—promise me by the sight of my old age and my gray hair, promise me by the solemnity of this hallowed place, by the God whose name you have learnt to call upon, by the name of Jesus Christ in which alone there is salvation—promise me that you will hold fast this faith in life and in death, that you will not suffer yourself to be deceived by any vain illusion, however the fashion of this world may change—will you promise me this?' Overwhelmed by the impression, the little one threw himself upon his knees, but the old man raised him up and pressed him to his breast.

Truth compels me to confess that this was the most moving scene I have ever witnessed. What might for an instant incline somebody to suppose that the whole is a fiction—the fact, namely, that an old man should speak in this way to a child—was just the thing that moved me most of all. The unhappy old man who remained alone in the world with a child, and had nobody he could speak to about his trouble but a child, and only one life to save, that of a child, and yet could not assume on the part of the child maturity enough to understand him, and yet dare not wait for the coming of maturity, because he was a decrepit old man....

Thereupon I went home. I was prompt to understand the old man and to appreciate his position. For in many ways my studies had led me to notice that there was a very questionable relationship between a certain modern Christian speculation and Christianity, although this had not hitherto engaged my attention in any decisive way. Now this matter acquired real importance. The venerable old man with his faith appealed to me as an absolutely justified individual whom existence had wronged in the fact that a modern speculation, like a depreciation of the currency, had rendered dubious the security of his investment in faith. I was deeply moved by the pain the old man suffered in losing his son, not only by death, but even more dreadfully (as he understood it) by speculation; and the contradiction in his situation, that he was unable to explain how the hostile power accomplished its work, was for me a decisive challenge to discover the right trail to the solution of this problem. The whole thing appealed to me like an involved criminal case where the great complication of the situation makes it difficult to apprehend the truth. That was as if made for me. I reflected as follows: 'You are by this time tired of life's diversions, tired of the girls, whom you now love merely *en passant*; you must have something that will entirely occupy your time, and here it is—to find out wherein lies the misunderstanding between Speculation and Christianity.' So this was my resolution. Honestly, I have never spoken about it to anybody, and I am certain that my landlady did not notice any change in me either that evening or the day following.

'But', said I to myself, 'as you are not a genius, and certainly have no commission to render the whole human race happy, and as you also are not under promise to anybody, you can go about this job *con amore* and follow it up quite *methodice*, as if a poet and a dialectician were watching your every step, now that you have a more precise conception of your freakish conceit of trying to make something harder.' My studies, which already in a certain way had led me towards my goal, were now pursued more methodically, but the venerable figure of the old man always flitted before my mind every time I was inclined to transform my reflections into learned disquisitions. But chiefly it was by personal reflection that I sought to trace this misunderstanding to its ultimate origin. It is not necessary to recount my many false starts; but it finally became clear to me that the error of Speculation, and the presumptive right it based upon this to reduce faith to a subordinate factor, was not something accidental, but that it lies deeper in the whole tendency of our age—must indeed be traced to the fact that with their much knowledge people had entirely forgotten what it is to EXIST and what INWARDNESS means.

When I had comprehended this, it became at the same time clear to me that, in case I wanted to communicate anything of the sort, it was of the utmost importance that my views should be presented in the *indirect* form. For if inwardness is truth, results are mere baggage which people should not burden one another with, and the desire to communicate a result implies an unnatural form of intercourse between man and man, inasmuch as every man is spirit, and truth consists precisely in the self-activity of appropriation, which a result only tends to prevent....

As I am not a philosopher, I have preferred to let Johannes Climacus tell in his own words what his book is all about. It is plain enough that S. K. was not a coldly objective thinker. Like Climacus he had a passionate reason for writing, and he was impatient of any philosophy which claimed, as Hegelianism did, to deal with vital questions objectively.[1] For him thought as well as faith was a passion. He insisted upon 'subjectivity', and by that he meant, not a disposition to ignore facts, but a vital concern about them—especially about the facts which most properly concern man.[2] His constantly reiterated assertion that 'truth is inwardness' he associated with Lessing's famous dictum [see Appendix IV, p. 608], and he meant by it that truth is really possessed only when it is acquired by 'self-activity', i.e. appropriated through reflection, not taken over as a finished product ('a result') from somebody else's hand. We may recall here the last word of *Either/Or*: 'Only the truth that edifies is truth for thee.' But this is only half the story. Truth thus appropriated by reflection proves to be a vain acquisition if it does not transform the thinker's personality and shape his 'existence'. This is what S. K. means by 'double reflection' or 'the double movement of infinity'. We must habituate ourselves to S. K.'s use of the word 'existence'. He means by it the conditions of a truly humane life. He means specifically the good life in its practical aspects, and his gravest complaint against the Hegelian system is that it 'abbreviates existence' to such a degree that it leaves out ethics.[3] It would often be far easier and more intelligible were I to use the word 'life' instead of 'existence'—and say, for example, that the truth must issue in a life conformable to it. But I adhere scrupulously to our author's terminology. 'Existence' is a far more abstract term than 'life', and I suppose that the word 'life' was eschewed because of its romantic, sentimental, and even biological associations.

Now that I have called attention to some of the words which are used in an unusual sense in the foregoing quotation from the *Postscript*, I feel free to indulge myself by continuing the same quotation, in which there occur two passages which not only tickle my sense of humour, but are well adapted to help us to understand why S. K. was so insistent upon the importance of indirect communication:[1]

> It is strange that while people are so insistent upon the 'positive' and upon direct communication of results, it never occurs to anybody to complain of God, who as the eternal Spirit, from whom all derived spirits issue, could, it would seem, put Himself into direct relationship to the derived spirits in a way which is impossible when the relationship is between spirits *essentially* alike among themselves within the common derivation from God. But no anonymous author can conceal himself more craftily than God, nor can any maieutic more cautiously avoid the direct relationship. He is in the creation, in it everywhere, but He is not there directly, and only when the individual turns in upon himself (i.e. only in the inwardness of self-activity) does he become aware of God and find himself in a condition to see Him. The direct relationship to God is sheer paganism, and only when a breach in the immediacy of the individual has taken place can there be any question of a true relationship. But this breach is precisely the first act of inwardness, the first step towards the perception that truth is inwardness. Nature, it is true, is God's work; but only the work is directly present, not God. Is not this tantamount to treating the individual man as an elusive author does when he refrains from indicating the result in large letters or apprising one of it beforehand in a preface? And why is God elusive? Just because He is the truth, and by being that would prevent man from reaching error. The observer does not attain the result directly but must concern himself independently to find it, and therewith break away from the direct relationship. But just this breach is the awakening of inwardness, the act of self-activity, the first dawning of the perception that truth is inwardness.
>
> Is it not a fact that God is so unobservable, so thoroughly concealed in his work, that it might perfectly well befall a man

to grow up, get married, attain respect and consideration as a husband, father, and master of the hounds, without discovering God in His work, without even getting any real impression of the infiniteness of the ethical, because he got along with what is analogous to the speculative confusion between ethics and world-history, that is, he got along with the use and wont of the town where he lived? As a mother admonishes a child who is about to go to a party, telling him to comport himself well and to behave as he sees other well-bred children behave—so this man could grow up and behave just as he saw the others behave. He will never do anything first and never hold any opinion until he knows first that the others hold it, for the others are his 'first'. On extraordinary occasions he would behave as one might do at a dinner-party when a dish is passed which he doesn't quite know how to eat—he will spy around to see how other people do it, &c. Such a man might perhaps know a great deal, might perhaps know the System by heart, he might perhaps live in a Christian land and know how to bow every time God's name is mentioned, might perhaps see God in nature when in the company of other folks who see God, on the whole he might be an agreeable society-man—and yet be deceived by the direct relationship to truth, to the ethical, to God. If experimentally one were to draw the picture of such a man, he would be a satire upon the human race. Really it is the God-relationship which makes a man a man, and in this he was lacking, although no one would hesitate to regard him as a real man (since the lack of inwardness cannot be directly observed), in spite of the fact that he was rather like a mario-nette figure, counterfeiting deceptively all the outward sem-blance and behaviour of a man—even to having children by his wife. At the end of his life one might say of him that one thing had escaped him—he had not taken notice of God.[1] If God could permit a direct relationship, this man would doubt-less have taken notice of God. Suppose, for example, that God should take upon Himself the form of a rare and prodigiously big green bird with a red beak, perching on a tree upon the city rampart, and perhaps chirping in a way totally unheard of—then the society-man would open his eyes wide enough, and perhaps for the first time in his life he might be 'the first'. All paganism consists in this, that God relates Himself directly to a man like the conspicuous to the astonished observer. But the spiritual relationship to God in truth—i.e. inwardness—is conditioned upon the awakening of an experience of inwardness, which corresponds in turn to the divine subtlety that God has nothing, absolutely nothing, conspicuous about Him, indeed that He is so far from being conspicuous that He is actually invisible, so that one does not notice at all that He exists, although in fact His invisibility constitutes His omnipresence. But you say that an omnipresent person is one who may be seen everywhere—like a policeman, for example. How deceptive it is therefore that an omnipresent being is recognizable precisely in the fact that he is invisible, simply and solely by that, for his visibility would do away with his omnipresence. This relationship between omnipresence and invisibility is like that between a mystery and its revelation, inasmuch as mystery is the expression of the fact that revelation is revelation in the strictest sense, so that the mystery is precisely the one and only sign by which it can be recognized, for otherwise the revelation becomes pretty much the same sort of thing as the omnipresence of the policeman.—If God would reveal Himself in human form and provide a direct relationship, as, for example, by taking upon Him the form of a man six yards tall, that master of the hounds we are experimenting with would surely take notice. But true spritual relationship, seeing that God will not deceive, requires emphatically that the form have nothing conspicuous about it, so that the society-man must say that there is absolutely nothing to be seen. . . . In paganism the direct relationship is expressed in idolatry. In Christendom every one knows, of course, that God cannot show Himself thus; but such knowledge is in itself by no means an assurance of inwardness, and it may perfectly well befall a man who knows it all by rote that he remains entirely 'without God in the world', to a degree that could hardly occur in paganism, where there was at least the untrue relationship of idolatry. Idolatry is indeed a sorry substitute, but that the category of the divine should fall out altogether is certainly a great deal worse.

The remainder of this quotation is almost continuous with the above, but as it deals with Socrates, I must call attention to the fact that the *Postscript* refers constantly to Socrates, and that the *Scraps* takes this ancient wise man as its point of departure, in order to show in what precise respect Christianity surpassed the utmost attainment possible within paganism, and that the modern effort to surpass Christianity was really a return to Socrates. S. K.'s admiration for Socrates was sincere and profound. The figure of this great and good man had engrossed him more and more since the days when he wrote his dissertation on irony, 'with constant reference to Socrates'.

> Socrates, for example, was a teacher of ethics, but he was aware that there is no direct relationship between the teacher and the pupil, because inwardness is truth, and it is just this inwardness in the two which holds them apart. Presumably it was because of this perception he was so well pleased with his advantageous exterior. In what way was it advantageous? Well, give a guess. It is true that in our time we say of a clergyman that he has an advantageous exterior, we are pleased with that, and what we mean is that he is a handsome man, that his preaching-gown is becoming to him, that he has a sonorous vocal organ, and a figure which every tailor, or I mean to say rather, every hearer must take delight in. Ah, when one is thus equipped by nature and thus clothed by his tailor, he can very well be a religious teacher and make a success of it. For there is a very great difference in the degree of success attained by religious teachers, far greater indeed than one is led to reflect upon when he hears the complaint that some ecclesiastical appointments have such big livings attached to them, whereas others are small. The difference is in fact even greater: namely that some religious teachers are crucified—although the religion is just the same. And no one bothers himself much about the question how the teaching contained in this religion is reduplicated by a repetition in the life of the teacher. The orthodox faith is expounded, and the Teacher is prettied up in pagan-aesthetical categories. Christ is described in Biblical terms. The fact that he bore the sins of the world is not apt to affect the congregation much; nevertheless the speaker proclaims that, and then to make the contrast sufficiently strong (since the contrast between innocence and guilt is not strong enough), he describes Christ's beauty, and the faithful congre-

gation is profoundly moved by this perfectly pagan conception of God in human form—his beauty.

But back to Socrates. He had not such an advantageous exterior as we have described. He was very ugly, had clumsy feet, and above all he had on his forehead and in other places a lot of protuberances, enough to convince every man that he was a thorough degenerate. This, you see, was what Socrates understood by his advantageous exterior, which he was so greatly delighted with that he would have accounted it a mean trick, meant to frustrate his ambition to be a teacher of morals, if God had given him a pleasing exterior like that of a cither-player, small feet like a dancing-master's, a languishing eye like a shepherd boy's, in short, an exterior as advantageous as one might wish to have if he were advertising for a position or had set his hope upon a private presentation to a parish. Why on earth was that ancient teacher so delighted with his advantageous exterior?—unless it was because of his perception that it might help him to keep the disciple at a distance, so that he would not be entangled in a direct relationship to the teacher, perhaps admire him, perhaps have his clothes cut in the same fashion, but might apprehend by the repulsion of contrast (a repulsion which in a higher sphere was accomplished by his irony) that the teacher is concerned essentially with himself, and that the inwardness of truth is not the comradeship of two bosom friends who walk arm in arm, but the separation by which each for himself is an existing individual in truth and reality.

Notoriously 'Socrates was a teacher of ethics'—but S. K. (or Johannes Climacus) believed he could discern in him a tendency to transcend the purely ethical by an approach to religion, not only in the sense of a relation to the absolute but in an experience of suffering and guilt—a trace of pessimism which was not essentially in conflict with humanistic idealism although it pointed beyond it. This appears in the fact that he was astonished at himself and the awful possibilities of evil he detected in himself: his wonder whether he might be something worse than the serpent Trypho, or a simpler being with a trace of the divine (Phaedrus).

On June 13, 1844, a small book was put on sale by the

bookseller Reitzel, which indicated S. K. as the editor, but Johannes Climacus as the pseudonymous author. It was called *Philosophical Scraps or A Scrap of Philosophy.*[1] This title is strange enough, but it will not seem too strange when we learn that the books involves an attack upon the Hegelian 'system'. S. K. affirmed that though 'a logical system is possible, a system of existence is impossible'—not for the divine mind, but for the individual who exists in time and space. Consequently he indicates by this title that he proposes to present only such fragments of philosophical thought as are relevant to 'existence' and intelligible to an 'exister'. He calls it moreover a mere *pièce* (pamphlet), a trifling contribution; and in fact nobody perceived that it had any importance, even when it was followed nearly two years later, February 27, 1846, by the *Postscript—Concluding Unscientific Postscript to the Philosophical Scraps*—an immense book, to which again S. K. affixed his name as editor, while he ascribed the authorship to Johannes Climacus. Only 60 copies of this great book were sold! The fact that S. K.'s own name appeared on the title-page, though he was indicated only as editor, was enough to show that the day of pseudonymous writings was past. Indeed the word 'concluding' in the title indicated that this was meant to be his last literary production. S. K. used this opportunity to review appreciatively his own works, or rather he allowed Climacus to do it, in a supplementary chapter in the midst of the book, entitled, 'Reference to a contemporary movement in Danish literature'. Climacus punctiliously refers each work to its pseudonymous author, but implies that the critics of the tea-table entertained no doubt that Magister Kierkegaard was responsible for them all. These comments are very important for the understanding of these books, and we have made abundant use of them. To make up for the fact that none of the contemporary critics was able to appraise these books justly or even to understand them, here is a reviewer who could! Appended to the *Postscript* there is a long note, called 'A First and Last Explanation', in which S. K. made formal acknowledgement of his responsibility for all these works. This was a perfunctory gesture when everybody already knew who the author was. But this note contained also the passage (discussed at length on pp. 286 ff.), in which he adjured his readers not to attribute to him the utterances of his pseudonyms. The conclusion of this note is worthy of quotation here:[2]

The importance of these books (whatever significance they may come to have in the actual world) decidedly does not lie in making any new proposal, or in founding a new party, or in the wish to 'go farther', but precisely in the opposite direction, in desiring to have no importance, in desiring—at the distance implied by the remoteness of double-reflexion—to read solo the fundamental document of the individual, humane existence-relationship, the old, well known, from the fathers handed down—to read it through once again, if possible in a more heartfelt way.

And may no half-baked thinker venture to lay a dialectical hand upon this work, but let it stand as it now stands.

Though the *Scraps* and the *Postscript* are separated by an interval of nearly two years, I cannot deal with them separately. The *Postscript* constantly refers to the *Scraps* and describes itself as 'a new attempt at the same problem'.[1] Climacus says of his earlier work:[2]

The problem presented in that booklet (without pretending to have solved it, for all that it proposed to do was to present it) was to the following effect: '*Is an historical point of departure possible for an eternal consciousness? How can such a thing have more than historical interest? Is it possible to base an eternal blessedness upon historical knowledge?*' He quotes here the words that were printed on the title-page of the *Scraps*. Christianity of course is the only historical religion which ascribes to history so essential a role. The *pièce*, however, does not mention Christianity, but represents itself as a 'thought-project', deducing the doctrines (which happen to be the essential doctrines of Christianity) from the situation which presents itself so soon as one recognizes that the Socratic refuge, the retreat backwards into eternity, is barred by the fact of sin, or by the fact that 'man is non-truth'. The book might seem to be a speculative defence of the truth of Christianity.

In order to avoid this misapprehension one must give due heed to the passage which follows closely upon the statement just quoted:[3]

Yet to avoid confusion the reminder must be made at the outset that the problem is not about the truth of Christianity, but about the individual's relationship to Christianity, and so has not to do with the zeal of the systematic individual to arrange the truths of Christianity in sections, but it has to do with the concern of the endlessly interested individual for his relationship to such a doctrine. To state the case as simply as possible (using myself for the experiment): 'I, Johannes Climacus, born here in the town, now thirty years old, just a plain man pretty much like other folks, assume that for me, as much as for a serving-girl or a professor, there is held out the expectation of a highest good which is called an eternal blessedness. I have heard that Christianity is the essential condition for attaining this blessedness.—I now ask how it may come to have a relationship to such a doctrine?

In view of this statement it is evidently unreasonable to complain of the *Scraps* that it does not seek to prove the truth of Christianity but deals with it as an hypothesis to be thought out. S. K. was scathing in his denunciation of the attempt to prove the essential truth of Christianity, the existence of God, the immortality of the soul, &c. In the First Part of the *Postscript* he deals with 'The Objective Problem of the Truth of Christianity', and especially with the historical questions involved in (1) the Scriptures, (2) the Church, (3) the witness of the centuries; but he dismisses this subject hastily, concluding that the historic proof can get no further than an approximation,[1] and that the speculative proof is still more unsatisfactory. The more proof one can produce for the object of faith (advancing from the probable to the more probable, to the highly probable, to the certain), the less room there is for faith, which is gradually exchanged for knowledge. To one whose faith is a passion the objective attitude towards essential truth must be an abomination:

People become objective, they insist upon regarding objectively the fact . . . that God was crucified.[2]

Only eternity can provide an eternal certainty, whereas existence must be content with a fighting certainty.[3]

In *The Concept of Dread* Vigilius Haufniensis equates certainty and inwardness, and to the question what this is, he answers, 'Seriousness.' In another place he says:[4]

I have no desire to use strong expressions about this age as a whole, but one who has observed the contemporary generation will hardly be inclined to deny that the chief trouble with it, and the ground of its restlessness and anxiety, lies in the fact that while in one direction truth increases in compass, in mass, and in part also in abstract clarity, certainty correspondingly diminishes. What extraordinary metaphysical and logical exertions have been made in our age to furnish a new and exhaustive proof of the immortality of the soul, an unimpeachable proof combining all earlier proofs—and, strange to say, while this is going on certainty diminishes.

The best proof of the immortality of the soul, or of God's existence, &c., is the impression of it one gets in childhood—that is to say the proof which (in contrast to the many learned and grandiloquent proofs) might be expressed thus: It is perfectly certain, for my father told me so.

This last is from the Journal (1848),[1] and elsewhere in the Journal S. K. imagines some one like Kant, who stood at the pinnacle of learning, saying about the existence of God, 'The fact is, I know nothing more about it except that my father told me it was so.' S. K. recognized that for a man like Kant to say this would involve an element of humour. But in another place he says that a learned proof of the existence of God which fails to mention this little fact has omitted the principal argument.

The preacher, he says, is courteous enough to assume that you already understand that God exists, and is not so vain as to suppose that he has discovered it.[2]

If the subjects in a land where there is a king on the throne were to set themselves down and investigate whether it was the proper thing to have a king, the monarch would surely be wroth. And it is thus people behave towards God—they forget that God exists and deliberate whether it is the most proper and acceptable thing to have a God.[3]

Far be it from me to require of S. K. a proof of the existence of God, as long as I remember the pungent saying of Climacus:[4]

The fool hath said in his heart, There is no God; but he who says in his heart or to other men, Just wait a minute and I will prove it—O, what a rare wise man is he!

One of the sections of the *Postscript* is entitled:

The eternal blessedness of the individual is decided in time, by means of a relationship to something historical, whose historical nature is so constituted as to include in its composition that which according to its nature cannot become historical, and so must become such by virtue of the absurd.

I comment here only upon the fact that S. K.'s insistence upon the historical factor in Christianity has brought the problem of time again to the attention of modern theologians. His own most characteristic expression for the decisive importance of time is 'the Instant' (*Øjebliket*)—a word which the Barthian School has heartily appropriated (unfortunately it has been translated by 'Moment'). In the *Scraps* he says of it:[1]

> And now the Instant. Such an instant has a peculiar character. It is short, indeed, and temporal, as every instant is, fleeting, as every instant is, gone like all instants, the following instant, and yet it is decisive, and yet it is full of eternity. Such an instant must have a special name, let us call it *the fullness of time*.

S. K. had already dealt with the Instant in the *Concept of Dread*,[2] where he refers this conception to Plato, and where he says of it, 'the Instant is not properly an atom of time, but an atom of eternity'. Now he expressly brings the Instant into relation with the 'leap' and the 'paradox'. 'The instant does not need to be long, for it is a leap.' 'If only the Instant is posited, the Paradox is granted.'[3] An instant, if it is only an instant in time, is 'filled with emptiness'.[4] What fills it with eternity is the apprehension of the paradox that God became man. It is then the decisive Instant of faith.

I have already run far beyond the 'objective problem' I started to speak about, and to catch up with myself I need to explain that the *Postscript* disposes of this problem as hastily as I do, devoting to it no more than 37 pages, whereas 15 times as many pages—the whole remainder of this big book—is devoted to 'The Subjective Problem: the relationship of the subject to the truth of Christianity, or the problem of becoming a Christian'. S. K. says of 'Guilty?' / 'Not Guilty?' that 'it all revolves about the forgiveness of sin'. It might be said just as aptly that in the *Postscript* all revolves about the question of faith, that is, about the subjective appropriation of Christianity. The *Scraps* concluded with a vague promise that a subsequent book would provide it with its 'historical costume'. The *Postscript* far more than fulfilled this promise, for the historical costume was provided so soon as the word 'Christianity' was mentioned. The *Postscript* did immensely more than that—far more, indeed, than I can give any idea of here. And if it had done no more than treat of the problem of faith, it would richly deserve our attention. To that subject I now propose to address myself—without pretending to treat it adequately.

As preliminary to this, however, I would anticipate an objection which, if it is not a deliberate device to escape the issue S. K. presents, may nevertheless deter the honest reader from taking so seriously as it deserves the argument here presented, and from applying it to himself. It is perfectly true that these two books refer constantly to the Hegelian philosophy and were expressly designed to counteract it. But from this it must not be inferred that they have grown antiquated along with the Hegelian philosophy which they expressly attack, and are therefore not precisely applicable to our situation. In the first place, the Hegelian philosophy is by no means so remote from us as this objection implies. Although there are few philosophers nowadays who profess dependence upon Hegel, it is very apparent that his ideas live on in the Idealistic philosophies which were regnant only yesterday and which coloured the Liberal theologies which, by reason of the notorious conservatism of religion, are influential even to-day. For a long while I puzzled over the fact that Christian Science, so called, acquired rapidly so many adherents who were drawn from various Protestant churches, and more especially over the fact that these people were not in the least aware that they were exchanging their religion for one which was radically different, inasmuch as it has no personal God, looks back to no decisive historical Incarnation, knows no present Instant of rebirth, and looks forward to no conclusive day of judgement and resurrection. In the end I understood that they were quite right in thinking that they had in fact made no violent transition, but had only progressed farther in the direction they were already going, preferring naturally enough the consistent Idealism of Christian Science to the less thoroughgoing Idealism of modern Liberal Christianity, which is still hampered by historical factors, by traces of dualistic realism, and by other incongruous elements which are vestiges of the older tradition. S. K.'s writings are so far from being antiquated that they appear rather as if they were addressed particularly to us and were meant to counteract the errors of our time. The collapse of Liberal Theology in Germany (and consequently among the higher intelligentzia of our land) was coincident with the rediscovery of S. K., and he was at least a prominent factor in bringing this débâcle about. Liberalism has found him a hard nut to crack, and Orthodoxy finds little comfort in him. The either/or which he presented to the theologians of his own day, and still presents to us, is the choice between thoroughgoing radicalism and essential Christianity. From the very beginning he has driven some men to one, and some to the other of these positions; some men to renounce Christianity altogether, and some to take refuge in Roman Catholicism. He allows no one to feel undisturbed in a mediating position. I am acquainted with no modern writer who applies so pungently the corrective our age requires, both in philosophy and in theology; and if his works are not exactly 'what the age demands', if they fill a yet unfelt want they are nevertheless just what the age most urgently needs.

> The exister who chooses the objective way to God enters upon the approximative reflection which aims at bringing God to evidence, an aim which will not be attained in all eternity, because God is Subject, and therefore exists only for subjectivity in inwardness. The exister who chooses the subjective way apprehends at that very instant the dialectical difficulty involved in the fact that he must employ some time, perhaps a long time, to find God objectively. He apprehends this difficulty in all its painfulness, because at that very instant he has urgent need of God, because every instant is wasted when he has not God. At that same instant he has God, not by virtue of any objective deliberation, but by virtue of the endless passion of his inwardness. In this way, it is true, God becomes a postulate, but not in the idle sense in which one ordinarily takes this word; rather it becomes clear that this is the only way an exister gets into relation with God, when the dialectical contradiction brings passion to despair and helps by means of 'the category of despair' (faith) to embrace God, so that the postulate, far from being arbitrary, is a necessary act of self-preservation, so that it is not God that is a postulate, but the fact that the exister postulates God is . . . a necessity.[1]

This passage from the *Postscript* is not altogether simple and easy, yet it seems to me an apt introduction to the consideration of S. K.'s idea of faith as we find it expressed at this period.

Even if I were a theologian, or a philosopher, or a professor in some other faculty, my veneration for S. K. would restrain me, I trust, from 'eating' him—as he grimly expected these gentlemen to do, and as in fact they have been doing for a long time. They masticate, digest, and assimilate his thoughts in order to expound them in terms of their own system. It may be said of them as Lord Bacon says of sheep, that the grass they eat is not returned as grass but as wool. Being what I am, and having no system of my own, I am under no temptation to spread out upon one surface all that S. K. has to say about faith, in order to arrange all these dicta neatly—or to prove triumphantly that they are not consistent and cannot be arranged. I am content to consider each new expression as it comes along in the course of a long literary production which he regarded as his own education in the process of 'becoming a Christian'. We have reason to expect that by this time he would be beyond the position he had reached when he wrote *Fear and Trembling* and expected a 'repetition' in time—though 'by virtue of the absurd' (see p. 265 f.). We shall see that in *The Sickness unto Death* he was operating with a more adequate definition of faith than he had at his disposal when he wrote the *Postscript*. Here, in the *Scraps* and the *Postscript*, we find that 'the absurd' is still prominent as a determinant of faith, but that now it is emphasized not so much in relation to apparent physical impossibility (the faith that removes mountains) as in relation to thought, the paradox, the crucifixion of the understanding. This is an intensification of the absurd as a stumbling-block to faith; and Climacus does not disguise the fact that he is intent upon making things as difficult as possible. The difficulties of every sort, and especially the difficulties for fallen and sinful men, would be insuperable were it not so vitally, so desperately necessary for men, and especially for sinful men, to get into relationship with God, to 'have' God. But the paradox of the God-Man is the most decisive expression of the fact that we cannot 'have' God as a tranquil possession, guaranteed by the immediacy of feeling and perception or by adequate rational proofs, but can only 'have' Him as having Him not, in the constant struggle to possess, the endless effort to become a Christian. In the *Postscript* it may sometimes seem as if the emphatic anti-intellectualism of Johannes Climacus stands up so straight that it leans backward—becomes an intellectualism which attaches itself to irrational propositions *about* God. But the passage last quoted makes it clear that God, God himself, is ever the object of faith, and the paradoxical form in which faith is given is a constant reminder of the terms on which we can possess faith in the unknown God.

S. K.'s notion of faith was a consequence of his pronounced tendency to voluntarism. One of the earliest entries in the Journal expresses his conviction that faith must be an expression of the will inasmuch as man is held eternally accountable for it,[1] and in 1843, among the notes for the final revision of *Fear and Trembling*, we find the affirmation that faith is not to be regarded 'as a content of the idea but as a form of the will'.[2] In the *Stages* we read, 'Will is the chief thing, even in relation to thought.'[3] That is to say, in relation even to matters historical a sort of faith is required. But religious faith is a quite different thing, occupying a sphere of its own which is not continuous with rational belief, nor to be reached by any approximations of proof and probability, but only by a 'leap'. It is characterized, however, by a certitude such as rational proof or historical evidence cannot give, for this never can amount to more than approximation to certain knowledge.[4] The Greek *pistis*, as he remarks, meant even less than scientific knowledge, for it was used for opinions founded upon insufficient proof.[5] S. K. complained of Hegel that he conceived of faith as 'immediacy' (unreflective spontaneity) and therefore felt free to treat it as a transient factor which should be superseded by philosophy. The philosopher must advance beyond faith. But S. K., inasmuch as he regarded faith as a passion, could not deny to it all trace of spontaneity and would not make it dependent exclusively upon reflection. Hence he spoke of faith as 'immediacy after reflection',[6] the immediacy of 'the new man'.[7]

There can be no doubt that Climacus expresses S. K.'s own conviction when he says in the *Scraps*[8] that 'faith is not a cognition but an act of freedom, an expression of the will', and in the *Postscript*,[9] that 'Christianity is not a doctrine'. 'Faith expresses an infinitely interested relationship',[10] and 'the important thing is not the what but the how'.[11] In the same way doubt is related to the will: 'doubt is overcome by an act of the will'.[12] On the other hand, it is stated very decisively in the *Scraps* and the *Postscript* that man is incapable of making the affirmation of faith unless the divine Teacher provides the requisite 'condition'. In the last resort faith is the gift of God, it is a 'miracle'. Otherwise we are back again in the Socratic position.

On p. 262 we referred to the confidence necessary for learning to swim, as S. K.'s favourite analogy for faith. The assurance that one is lighter than water and can float is like the confidence of faith. This was a persistent thought with him.

> If one were to say that to swim is to lie upon dry land and squirm, every one would regard him as mad. But to believe is exactly like swimming, and instead of helping a man to get his feet on land, the preacher should help him to get out into the deep. So if one were to say that to believe is to lie upon dry land and go through the motions, all the time sure of the result, he is really saying the same thing as the above, only people perhaps do not notice it. . . . For a finite being—and surely that is what man is so long as he lives in the temporal sphere (see Balle's Lesson Book)—the negative infinity is the highest attainable, and the positive is a very questionable reassurance. Spiritual existence, and the religious existence in particular, is by no means easy; the believer lies constantly out upon the deep, with 70,000 fathoms of water under him. Long as he may lie there, he gets no comfort from the expectation that little by little [because of accumulated proofs] he will find himself on land, stretched out at his ease. He may, indeed, become calmer, more accustomed, find a sense of security which enables him to take pleasure in fun and light-hearted merriment—but until the last instant he lies above a depth of 70,000 fathoms.

Thus speaks Frater Taciturnus in the *Stages*[1]—and (strangely enough) Johannes Climacus develops the same thought in the *Postscript*:[2]

> The wader feels cautiously before him with his feet, so as not to go farther than he can feel bottom. And so the man of understanding uses his understanding to feel before him after the probability, and he finds God where probability indicates, and gives thanks to him upon probability's high festivals, on which he gets a right good living with the probability of rapid

preferment, when he gets as his wife a girl who is both pretty and nice, and even Councillor of War Marcusen says that it will be a happy marriage, and that the girl has the sort of beauty that will probably last, and is so built that in all probability she will bear healthy and hearty children. To believe against the understanding is another thing—and to believe with the understanding is a sheer impossibility, since he who believes with the understanding talks only of a living, of a wife, of acres and oxen, and other such things, which are not at all the object of faith. Whereas faith *always* gives thanks to God, *always* is in the midst of mortal peril, in that conflict between the infinite and the finite which is the special peril of him who is constituted of both. Probability, therefore, is so far from being dear to the believer that he fears it most of all, knowing well that his interest in the probabilities is an indication that he is in the process of losing his faith. Faith has two tasks: to be on the lookout every instant to discover the improbable, the paradox; in order then to grasp it with the passion of inwardness. Ordinarily people conceive that the improbable, the paradox, is something that faith is related to passively, which it must put up with temporarily, and that by and by things will doubtless be better—there is even a probability of that. What a marvellous confusion with regard to faith! One must begin to believe, in the confidence that there is a probability of its becoming easier. In that way probability is smuggled in—and a man finds himself prevented from believing. In that way it is easy to understand that the fruit of having believed for a considerable time is that one ceases to believe. . . . No, faith is self-active in relation to the improbable and the paradoxical, self-active in discovering it every instant and in holding it fast.

Subjective certainty (faith) corresponds to 'objective uncertainty which is grasped with the apprehension of the most passionate inwardness. This is truth, and it is the highest truth for an exister.'[1] 'Without risk, no faith', was a maxim of S. K.'s. This is an expression of the 'martyrdom of faith'. But here is a more striking picture of it:[2]

To sit placidly on board the ship in fair weather is not a picture of what it means to believe; but when the ship has sprung a leak, then to keep it afloat by working the pump, that is a picture of it. . . . Although I am still very far from having attained a full understanding of the difficulty of Christianity (and an explanation which makes the difficulty easy is to be regarded as a temptation of faith), I can nevertheless understand that faith's struggle is not a proper subject for vaudeville-poets, and that the stress and strain of it is not meant for the diversion of *privat-docents*.

Do not tell me that what I have said about S. K.'s notion of faith is inadequate. I know that very well. How could it be adequate, seeing that S. K., without essential exaggeration, affirms that the immense literature he produced had only one theme, namely, faith; and that from beginning to end his whole effort had been to define what faith is? But inadequate as this paragraph is, I am not disposed to prolong it; for I have essayed to do here what many 'professors' have done, but what S. K. himself condemned and derided—I have arranged his teaching in sections. I let the passage stand . . . as an example of what ought not to be done. In his big book on *The Dogmatic Views of S. K.*, Professor Bohlin devotes thirty-eight pages to the discussion of S. K.'s notion of faith. Too much and yet too little. But the Professor had a reward for his unwearied pains in making S. K. dull. He was recently elevated to the episcopate.

It is clear from the above quotations that faith finds its proper object in the Paradox. The distinctive Christian paradox is the God-Man. S. K. often spoke of paradox in a broader sense, but he distinguished from this the absolute Paradox which is the special stumbling-block of Christianity:[1]

The paradox emerges when the eternal truth and the condition of existing are brought into combination, but the more the fact of existence is stressed, the paradox becomes clearer and clearer. [Here we have the broader notion of paradox.] . . . Let us now go farther, let us assume that the eternal, essential truth is itself the Paradox. How is the paradox [generally speaking] brought to light? By the fact that the eternal, essential truth and the conditions of existing are brought into combination. When therefore we combine the two in the truth itself, the truth becomes a paradox. The eternal truth has come into existence in time, this is the Paradox.

To the Paradox corresponds the notion of 'Offence'. It is a stumbling-block. It can be believed only 'by virtue of the absurd' —yet it is the only thing that can be believed, in the strictest sense of faith. We do not need Balle's Lesson Book to teach us that life is accompanied by much suffering, and religion is commonly regarded as a consolation—'only to give our joys a zest and prove our sorrows for the best'. But S. K. insists that the Christian religion is necessarily accompanied by a special suffering, 'the martyrdom of faith'. The Offence is the sign by which we can recognize the Paradox; no Offence, no Paradox. To explain the Paradox is to do away with the object of faith. When the Paradox has been 'mediated' by the philosopher (or theologian), it is no longer a paradox—and the believer is no longer a believer. To defend the Paradox in this way is 'like defending the circle by explaining that it is a quadrangle'.

S. K. has in mind Feuerbach when he says:[1]

> A scoffer attacks Christianity, and in doing so describes it with so sure a hand that one can take pleasure in reading him, and he who is at a loss to find Christianity accurately presented is almost compelled to have recourse to him.

Probably S. K. would have said the same of Nietzsche if this great scoffer had lived in his day or before him. I feel that even as an expounder of S. K. I suffer from a certain disability in the fact that I am far from being a scoffer and am pledged as a clergyman to maintain the truths of Christianity as well as to present them. It was very adroit of Magister Kierkegaard to invent such a figure as Johannes Climacus (who professed that he was not a Christian) and leave it to him to enunciate the fundamental doctrines of the Christian faith. On the other hand, when it is a question of enforcing the moral precepts of Christianity, it would be offensive to hear such exhortations from the mouth of a character who was known neither to accept nor to practise them. Therefore when it came to the writing of books for religious awakening, which solemnly enforced the obligation of imitating Christ, Magister Kierkegaard had good reason to congratulate himself upon the discovery of the pseudonym Anti-Climacus, who was pre-eminently a believer. But so far as the doctrines of the faith are concerned, an unbeliever can perfectly well understand what they are, even if he is not in a position to appraise them justly. Christianity is not an esoteric religion. In its *Hinayāna* form (the Doctrine of the Lesser Vehicle—if I may apply this Buddhistic name to Protestantism) the Bible, which is the sole rule of faith and practice, is open to all; and even in Catholicism (*Mahāyana*, or the Doctrine of the Greater Vehicle), which relies also upon Tradition, there are no secrets which are not open secrets to the profane historian. And though an outsider may be in some measure blinded by a prejudice against Christianity, its professional defenders are hampered by an impediment which in the long run and by the large is far more serious. For they are constantly under temptation to recognize in the Holy Scriptures only what they are personally prepared to believe; and the preacher suffers under an additional disability, being inhibited by a proper sense of shame from teaching as Christian truth what he personally is not prepared to practise. So it comes about that the faith is progressively reduced more and more in compass and more and more distorted. When this sort of thing goes on for generations, how could it help altering essentially the character of Christianity as it is generally preached and generally understood? It is the tendency of the preacher to make it all too simple, and of the theologian to make it too complicated. S. K. says justly that the precepts of the Gospel (even the hardest of them) are as simple and easy to understand as the remark that the weather is fair—but that this remark, if it were explained by learned commentators during the course of hundreds of years, would become perfectly incomprehensible. I have sometimes reflected that it would be more profitable if one had the opportunity of hearing Christianity expounded by a theologian who did not profess to be a believer, and more edifying to listen to a preacher who did not pretend to be a practising Christian. One may therefore be grateful to Magister Kierkegaard for providing such an opportunity in the person of Johannes Climacus.

The Protestant theologians of Continental Europe are all of them profoundly influenced by S. K., but they commonly express their chagrin at the fact that he unquestioningly held 'the Athanasian dogma'. There is no doubt about that fact, but I take exception to this way of putting it. For it is clear enough that Athanasius was not the inventor of the paradox God-Man, and it seems more honest to call it simply, as S. K. does, the Christian paradox. The Unitarian controversy in America resulted in the pacific agreement that 'the Bible is an orthodox book'. I remark that 'the Athanasian dogma' is written in all the Protestant creeds which lay claim to orthodoxy, but by the preachers especially it is commonly soft-pedalled. In the Anglican Church some priests bend the knee very low (genuflect) when in the Creed they recite the tremendous words, 'And was incarnate . . . of the Virgin Mary, and was made man'—which seems to me the least one could do who really believes it. But this is done only by Catholic Anglicans of an 'advanced' type (as they are whimsically called when they are in full retreat), and perhaps there is reason to suspect that this gesture may not mean very much, seeing that theologians of the same school are inclined to 'mediate' this paradox by explaining that God was incarnated in *humanity*—which is a notion not only highly flattering to humanity, but particularly congenial to a good pantheist. Frankly, I prefer the way Climacus (or S. K.) puts it. I believe that he has rightly understood and expounded what Christianity is. He himself says that the question whether it is true or not is quite another matter. Climacus was clearly aware that his whimsical conceit of 'making something harder for people' was accomplished by the stress he lays upon 'the Athanasian dogma'. It is chiefly by this means that he has persuaded, both in his own day and in ours, a goodly number of vague Christians to renounce Christianity, and has persuaded others to take refuge in the Roman Church. Although S. K. has made Christianity apparently more unattainable, he has made it at the same time infinitely more attractive. In this application I can very well understand what he means when he says that 'attack and defence resemble one another to a hair'. An honest exposition of Christianity may be regarded either as a defence or as an attack, it may either attract or repel—or rather it is likely to be both repellent and fascinating at the same time. To defend Christianity overtly was the last thing S. K. was inclined to do. This is very emphatically stated on the back of the title-page of that section of the *Christian Discourses* (1848) which is entitled 'Thoughts which wound from Behind—for Edification':[1]

> Christianity needs no *defence*, it is not served by any *defence*—it is aggressive; to defend it is of all misrepresentations the most unwarrantable, the most *perverse*, and the most dangerous—it is unwitting insidious betrayal. Christianity is aggressive.

Within Christendom, as a matter of course, it attacks from behind.

Both free-thinkers and Roman Catholics have expressed the pious opinion that S. K., if he had survived the martyrdom he endured in launching his attack upon Christianity as established, would have gone over to their side. This is vain speculation. In so far as the good that he did lives after him, and he himself lives on in that, it is very observable that the chief effect of his emphasis upon the decisive categories of Christianity has been to recall Protestant theologians to their own traditions, 'the old, the well-known, handed down by the fathers'.

We have been dealing here with faith as it is exemplified in what S. K. calls 'religion B'. In the *Postscript* he was still engaged with the effort to complete his formulation of the 'stages on life's road', and the last stone contributed to that construction was the distinction between religion A and religion B. By religion A he indicates the religiousness which is simply a heartfelt expression of a sense of God, or of the numinous, or of an expectation of an eternal blessedness, which is not conditioned by a definite something, but is merely heartfelt feeling itself, though in a sense it may be 'dialectical'. S. K. recognized that such religiousness may perfectly well exist in paganism. In fact this is precisely the quality of most of the religions of the world; and the great majority of those who are baptized and confirmed in the Church know no other sort. This is not to be taken as disparagement of religion A, which in its loftiest exemplifications may well be regarded as man's tip-toe reach, the most exalted attainment of humanity. S. K. recognizes that 'religion A must be present in the individual before there can be any question of his becoming aware' of religion B, which he describes as 'dialectical in the second remove, or paradoxically dialectical', inasmuch as it is conditioned by a definite something which is not included even in the deepest sensibility of the human heart. B indicates therefore specifically the Christian religiousness, possible only in Christendom, or where the historical revelation of Jesus Christ is known and believed.[1] The doctrine of the Incarnation stamps Christianity as an historical religion in a sense peculiar to it. It deals with eternity *in* time, challenging time, conflicting with time, and looking forward eschatologically to the termination of time.

Hence Christianity is essentially paradoxical. It is the only example of 'religion B'. Yet Christians are not generally aware of this peculiarity of Christianity. As children they can receive only such an impression of it as agrees with the feeling of an immediate relation to a divine environment (religion A), and as adults they do not commonly put away childish things. Though they attain so high a reach as Platonic idealism, they are still well within the limits of religion A; for the Platonic eternity is outside time and for ever parallel with it.

The importance of this distinction would not have been so generally ignored if S. K. had not drawn it so abstractly in the *Postscript*. One is justly offended by so abstract a treatment of religion. But this distinction was made very concrete in the first of the *Three Discourses on Imagined Occasions*, which was published at the same time as the *Stages*, and therefore antedates the abstract definitions of the *Postscript*. In this place we can see and feel how vitally this distinction concerned S. K.

S. K. acknowledged that he was educated by his own books. It is clear enough that the *Postscript* was his education in religion B. By writing this book he made clear to himself what 'the decisive categories of Christianity' are, and he accepted them; from this time forth all his efforts were bent upon realizing them in 'existence'. To him, therefore, the distinction between A and B was sharp and vivid. I note that many students of S. K. make light of this distinction, but I am tempted to suspect that they are disposed to ignore it only because they themselves have not got farther than religion A, and lack perhaps a certain liveliness of imagination which makes it possible to conceive of the difference which must distinguish a paradoxical religiousness. In general, I would exhort my reader not to treat slightingly the scheme of the 'existence-stages' or 'spheres' upon which S. K. spent so much time and thought. I am convinced that much of the confusion of our age is due to the neglect of such distinctions. S. K. describes many a striking instance where the religious orator at the climax of his discourse forgets his role and falls out of the religious sphere into the aesthetical—imagining that he is attaining a higher pathos. But weekly experience is enough to convince a critical observer who continues to go to church that most of our preachers have not the faintest idea how to distinguish the religious, the ethical, and the 'aesthetical'. The fact that most of the sermons we hear are sentimental is sure proof that the preacher is thinking (and perhaps living) in aesthetical categories.

I would not omit to mention that in the *Postscript* S. K. contributes another touch to the stages—just a little touch to perfect the scheme—when he finds a place for irony and humour, assigning irony to the borderland between the aesthetical and the ethical, and humour to a somewhat wider borderland between the ethical and the religious.[1] Because of the position each of them occupies, irony can serve as 'the incognito of the ethical', and humour as the 'incognito of the religious'. It is no wonder that S. K., who had to struggle so hard against his disposition to irony and preserved to the end so keen a sense of humour, who also had devoted so much time at the university to the study of these subjects, should feel the need of allotting to each its appropriate place in the scheme of existence-spheres. I am not prepared to affirm that the result he reaches is very important; but what he has to say about this subject is very interesting to one who has a disposition to irony and some sense for the comical.

I have pursued with passionate interest the study of the great religions of the world, which have provided comfort, security, and direction to countless multitudes of men who without such consolation would have been more forlorn. But I must say that S. K. has helped me more in this quest than any other thinker, for he has helped me out of the confusion into which I was plunged by the many modern studies of this subject. Perhaps he himself was saved from confusion because he had not at his disposal the superabundant apparatus which is available now, and because as a pioneer he was not distracted by conflicting schools of thought. In his day this study had not yet received a name—and that in itself was an advantage. One cannot reasonably complain that it is now called the comparative study of religion—although perhaps it is ominous that this name may be taken to imply that the task is to compare rather than to distinguish, or at least that the differences discoverable between the various religions, including Christianity, must be regarded as quantitative rather than qualitative. But another name commonly in use is more ominous, and at the same time so absurd that I hardly know whether to laugh or weep over it—it is called the study of 'comparative religion'. It is unfortunately true that a great deal of religion is only too comparative, conceived even by its votaries to be only comparatively true, or 'true up to a certain point', to use the phrase which S. K. anathematizes.[1] I am embarrassed at finding myself in a singular position when I affirm that Christianity is not a religion. I do not mean to say that Christians are not religious people, for man has been rightly defined as 'a religious animal'; but I mean that Christianity is not completely, not even essentially, defined when it is called a religion. I concede that in so far as it may be regarded as a religion, it is not unlike other religions, for religion is merely the human reaction to any intimation of the divine, or even of the diabolical. But I am of the opinion that Christianity is more properly regarded as a faith, and it is perfectly evident that if it is so regarded and is compared with other faiths, it will be seen to be radically different and entirely unique. For, to recall S. K.'s way of putting the case, it is the only religion which bases the hope of an eternal blessedness upon something historical, which moreover by its very nature cannot be historical, and so must become so by virtue of the absurd. I do not assert the truth of Christianity when I affirm this difference, but at least the difference is evident. S. K.'s discrimination between religion A and religion B is seen here to be important at the very outset of the comparative study of religion. What he says about 'mediation' in the long title to one of his passages in the *Postscript*,[1] applies exactly to this question of 'comparison' when we take the liberty of substituting merely this one word:

'The importance of a preliminary agreement with respect to what Christianity is, before there can be any question of a comparison between Christianity and other religions. The absence of such an agreement favours comparison, at the same time that it renders comparison illusory. The presence of such an agreement makes comparison impossible.'

It is inevitable, I suppose, that the learned men who pursue this interesting study of 'comparative religion' should lump Christianity indiscriminately with all the other religions, if they themselves are not only not 'existing' in the specific categories of Christianity, but are not even aware of them. And it appears that people do not commonly notice how the rabbit they pull out of the hat has been slyly put there—that is to say, that the question was begged from the beginning, that the conclusion they display to the wonderment of the crowd (that Christianity is pretty much like all other religions) was already expressed in the premiss, indeed in the very name of their study. And I am not a bit grateful to these scholars (as so many Christians are who are dubious of their own faith) when they reach the conclusion that Christianity is better than all other religions . . . comparatively. For though I cannot boast of being an exemplary Christian, I am dialectical enough to be on the alert to discover absolute differences, not satisfied with absolute relatives or relative absolutes, and am of the opinion that the confusion of our age is due not so much to false distinctions as to a prevailing vagueness about distinctions which are real. It seems very clear to me that Jesus, when he had denounced the religion of the Pharisees and then repudiated the religion of the Temple, had made a clean sweep of all the religion there was in his land. And it can hardly be said that he put another religion in its place, when all that he did in the way of establishing a new creed was to yield to his disciples' request by teaching them a few phrases of a prayer and exalting the thanksgiving at meals to a sacrament. In his commentary on the Epistle to the Romans, Barth is entirely justified in the bold act of substituting the word 'religion' where St. Paul had used 'law'; for it is clear that this Apostle was zealous to maintain that the essential characteristic of Christianity is faith rather than religion.

In the course of his deliberation about the specifically Christian S. K. was led to reflect upon religion in general, and what he has said about God as the 'unknown', as the 'limit' of the understanding, as 'the absolutely different' has had a strong repercussion upon the theology of our day; but I do not know of any one who has paid any attention to his remarks about the difficulty the understanding encounters in the effort to conceive of the 'difference', which results in what he calls the 'self-ironizing of the understanding', and accounts for the monstrous as well as for the banal and anthropomorphic conceptions of God which are so characteristic of the religions of mankind. It is a passage which exacts a good deal of reflection on the part of the reader, for it consists only of hints. S. K. was not sufficiently interested in *religion in general* to want to develop these suggestions in detail; but there is enough here to establish a new school of 'comparative religion'—perhaps several. The passage in question is taken from a chapter in the *Scraps* which Climacus entitles 'A Metaphysical Crotchet':[1]

So the paradoxical passion of the understanding constantly

stumbles against this Unknown [which in the foregoing context had been called 'God'—without any pretence that this name made the unknown known], which indeed exists, but in so far as it is unknown is non-existent. The understanding gets no farther, yet its paradoxicality is such that it cannot refrain from returning to this point and concerning itself with the Unknown; for it avails nothing to dismiss its relationship to the Unknown by affirming that it does not exist, since this very affirmation involves a relationship. But what is this Unknown? To say that it is God means to us merely that it is the Unknown. But to say that it is the Unknown, seeing that one cannot know it, and if he could know it he could not utter it, does not satisfy the passion of the understanding, even though it rightly apprehends the Unknown as the limit. And yet a limit is precisely the thing that most torments the understanding, even though at the same time it allures it. And yet the understanding cannot get any farther, whether it attacks the problem *via negationis* or *via eminentiae*.

What then is the Unknown? It is the limit which one constantly approaches, and as such (when we think in terms of rest rather than of motion) it is the Different, the absolutely Different. But the absolutely Different is something which lacks all marks of identification. When it is defined as the absolutely Different, it might appear as if it were in a fair way to be revealed; but this is not the case by any means, for the understanding cannot even think the absolutely Different, for it cannot absolutely negate itself, but makes use of itself for this end, and hence it thinks the Different in itself and in terms of itself, and so it thinks only of a certain sublimity above itself which is still thought of in terms of itself. In case the Unknown (God) does not remain merely limit, the one single thought about the Different is bewildered among the many possible thoughts about difference. The Unknown is then in a *diaspora* [scattered multiplicity], and the understanding can pick and choose at its pleasure from among what lies close at hand or what the imagination may hit upon (the monstrous, the ridiculous, &c.). [Here as usual the Hindu pantheon furnishes us readily with all the illustrations we could wish: Durga-Kālī, the monstrous, the dreadful; the monkey god Hanneman, so ridiculous and so popular, *ad infinitum*.]

But it is not possible to hold fast this difference. As often as this is done, it turns out to be essentially an arbitrary choice, and in the deepest depth of the religious consciousness there lurks a crazy caprice which is aware that it has itself produced the Deity. Since then the difference cannot be held fast because it lacks all marks of identification, the same thing occurs with difference and likeness as with all such dialectical opposites—they are identical. The difference which the understanding cannot get rid of has bewildered it, so that it does not recognize itself, and so quite naturally mistakes itself for the difference. In the matter of fantastical inventions paganism has been exceedingly rich. With reference to the last-mentioned suggestion, which is the self-ironizing of the understanding, I shall illustrate what it means with only a few strokes, irrespective of the question whether it is historical or not. So then there exists an individual, he looks just like other men, grows up like other men, gets married, earns his living, is anxious for the wants of the morrow, as a man ought to be, for it is indeed very pretty to live like the birds of the air, but it is not permissible, and if one persists in it, he must end pitiably, either by perishing of hunger, or by living at another person's expense. This man is at the same time God. How do I come to know that? Well, I do not know it exactly, for then I must know God and the difference; and I do not know the difference because the understanding has made it like unto itself wherefrom it was different. Thus God has become the most terrible deceiver—by the fact that the understanding has deceived itself. The understanding has brought God just as near as possible—and just as far.[1]

No theme in the *Postscript* has greater interest for me than S. K.'s formulation of the ethico-religious maxim: 'To comport oneself at the same time absolutely with regard to the absolute *telos* [Greek for end or aim] and relatively with regard to the relative.' I perceived rather tardily that this reflection had far-reaching consequences in S. K.'s own life. The problem which it solves was already visible to him when he wrote *Fear and Trembling* and regarded Abraham's obedience to God in preparing to slaughter Isaac as a case of 'the teleological suspension of the ethical'. What he means may be illustrated by the modern proposal to enact a law to sanction the occasional necessity of putting a beloved person to death to save him from the anguish of a hopeless disease. This proposal is perverse, because, though the individual may be justified before God in killing out of mercy, the 'universal human' is expressed in the commandment 'Thou shalt not kill', and the law is the expression of the universal human. 'Merciful killing' must be regarded as a teleological suspension of the ethical, and hence of the legal.

The problem arises in a more general form when a definite religious belief emerges to trouble an ethical norm which exemplifies 'the universal human'. But S. K. had to ponder this problem for three years before he was able to formulate it as he does in the *Postscript*. In this same book he includes 'An Edifying Diversion' which aims to show how complicated the problem is. Abstractly considered, the problem is: 'How can we manage to think the thought of God in conjunction with the finite'—even in its most trivial aspects? Concretely, Johannes Climacus considers the case of a respectable and pious citizen who purposes on a Thursday afternoon in fair weather to enjoy the innocent pleasure of an excursion with his family to the Deer Park (*Dyrhave*), a favourite resort north of Copenhagen. The more he thinks of it in connexion with God, the more impossible it seems to him to carry out such a plan with a good conscience. It is easy to misunderstand S. K. when he speaks through pseudonyms, and one might suppose that this passage betrays the fact that he himself suffered from a too scrupulous conscience. Fortunately, he happens to remark in his Journal at a much later date, 'I have never been troubled by any scruple about going to the Deer Park.'

In a long section of the *Postscript* he explains and defends the maxim mentioned above. I quote from it the following brief passage:[1]

> It is simply not true that the absolute *telos* becomes concrete in the relative *teloi*, for the absolute distinction drawn by resignation will secure the absolute *telos* at every instant from attempts to fraternize. It is true that the individual who is oriented towards the absolute *telos* remains within the relative ends; but he is not within them in such a way that the one is absorbed in the others. It is true that in the sight of God and

before the absolute *telos* we are all equal; but it is not true that, in my sight and before the single individual, God or the absolute *telos* is equal to everything else.... The phrase 'both—and' signifies that the absolute *telos* is on a line with everything else. But the absolute *telos* possesses the remarkable property of insisting every instant that it must be the absolute *telos*. So then, if the individual understood this at the instant of resignation, of reflection, of choice, this surely cannot possibly mean that the next instant he shall have forgotten it. Hence (as I expressed it) resignation stays by the individual, and the task proposed, so far from being that of mediating the absolute *telos* with every sort of 'both—and', is rather to influence the whole course of existence, which thus has the pathos of the great instant protracted.

S. K. is dealing here with the pragmatic consideration that we are living in a world of relative ends and cannot ignore the relative purposes, social and economical, which are essential to our existence. But besides these there is the absolute *telos*, 'the expectation of an eternal blessedness', which is not to be confounded with other aims and refuses to fraternize with them. How are we to behave? How are we to comport ourselves with respect to aims which are essentially different so that we shall not do injustice to either?

We are inclined, obviously, to pursue one and another of the relative ends as if it were the absolute, to pursue it for the time being whole-heartedly. In case then we recognize an end which is absolutely the absolute, how can we at the same time be whole-hearted in the pursuit of it? A common solution is to pursue the absolute end only on one day of the week, or perhaps only for one hour in church, and to pursue the relative ends all the rest of the time. Another possibility is the complete renunciation of the relative ends. This was the ideal of the early Christian hermit and of the medieval monk. S. K.'s only criticism is that it is too 'abstract'. What looks possible 'on paper' turns out to be an impossibility for the exister in the terms of existence. Or at all events it cannot be accomplished in an instant and once for all. We must wean ourselves little by little from the relative ends, and this implies suffering. Yet the deep experience of resignation admonishes us to draw and to maintain an infinite qualitative distinction between the relative ends and the absolute. The monastic ideal of renunciation is the expression of absolute respect for the absolute *telos*. The Reformation contemptuously discarded this expression of absolute respect for the absolute *telos* and abolished the infinite qualitative distinction. It 'mediated' between the claim of the absolute and the many claims of the relative by asserting that the absolute is expressed concretely in the relative. S. K. insists that the qualitative distinction must be preserved, and he seeks to preserve it by the formula: 'To comport oneself at the same time absolutely with regard to the absolute *telos* and relatively with regard to the relative.'

It is astonishing to observe that the Lutheran theologians who accept and extol this maxim of S. K.'s have not the least suspicion that it is a categorical repudiation of the most distinctive characteristic of Protestant ethics—namely, of Luther's boldest innovation, his conception of the secular 'calling' as the concrete realization of the absolute *telos*. And yet in this section of the *Postscript* it is perfectly clear that the polemic (in spite of the word 'mediated') is not against Hegel (who 'had no ethics') but against the universal Protestant conception, which here is constantly contrasted with monasticism as the Catholic ('medieval') ideal. It is absurd to accept this formula of S. K.'s and then bewail the fact that unfortunately he failed to perceive the noble significance of Luther's conception of the sanctity of the secular 'calling', of marriage, the rearing of children, &c. For S. K. consistently applied this maxim, and it accounts for much in his life and thought which is especially distasteful to the Protestant mind. Much that he says in detraction of the relative ends must be understood as an expression of respect for the absolute *telos*.

Luther's conception of the sanctity of the secular 'calling' has so permeated the whole Protestant world—indeed the western world as a whole, even including Catholic lands—that we are likely to take it as a matter of course, regarding it as an axiom, forgetting that it was a revolutionary innovation in ethics, or at least we are disposed to regard it as the noblest conception. It seems to bestow upon life a higher dignity, and any criticism of it would be regarded by most of us as sacrilege.

These considerations are not adduced here as a ground for discarding with indignation the maxim proposed by S. K. That be far from me! It is rather a reason for weighing it the more carefully, since the consequences of it are seen to be so momentous. This generation is in a measure prepared to consider it seriously, inasmuch as Max Weber in his great work on Sociology and Religion[1] has drawn attention to the ominous consequences of Luther's idea of the secular 'calling', showing that the development of this thought in Calvinism (or in what he describes more comprehensively as 'ascetical Protestantism') resulted in capitalism, our capitalistic civilization, which (whatever may be said in favour of it) cannot escape the verdict S. K. pronounced against Protestantism as a whole, that it is 'finiteness from end to end'.

Weber's thesis is not an extravagant one, and it is cautiously expressed: 'What the Reformation itself brought about in the first instance was merely that, in contrast to the Catholic conception, the moral accent and the religious *premium* attaching to the pursuit of a regular worldly calling were mightily enhanced.' He quotes from John Wesley[2] a significant passage which shows how naïvely the later development of ascetical Protestantism assumed that religion implies the profitable pursuit of a secular calling.

> 'Religion', says Wesley, 'must necessarily produce both industry and frugality, and these cannot but produce riches. But as riches increase so will pride, anger, and love of the world in all its branches. How then is it possible that Methodism, that is, a religion of the heart, though it flourishes now as a green bay-tree, should continue in this state? For the Methodists in every place grow diligent and frugal; consequently they increase in goods. Hence they proportionally increase in pride, in anger, in the desire of the flesh, the desire of the eyes, and the pride of life. So, although the form of religion remains, the spirit is swiftly vanishing away. Is there no way to prevent this—this continual decay of pure religion? We ought not to prevent people becoming diligent and frugal; and we *must* exhort all Christians to gain all they can and save all they can; that is, in effect, to grow rich. What way, then, can we take, that our money may not sink us to the nethermost hell? There is one way, and there is no other under heaven. If those who *gain* all they can, and *save* all they can, will likewise *give* all they can, then the more they gain the more they will grow in grace, and the more treasure they will lay up in heaven.'

'Man's upright posture', says S. K., 'may be conceived as an expression of absolute respect for the absolute *telos*—otherwise he goes on all fours.' 'So also the dog can be taught to walk on its hind legs for an instant—but then comes mediation, and the dog goes on all fours.'

Again and again S. K. repeated the indignant remark that 'place No. 1 has dropped out, so that place No. 2 has become the first place'. The profound pathos hidden under this prosaic expression is not so easily detected by Protestants as by Catholics, who have in mind the familiar distinction between the *consilia* and the *praecepta*. Protestantism has rejected this distinction with scorn—the distinction, that is, between 'the requirements of Christian ideality' (to use S. K.'s expression) and the minimum which the Church must exact of all its members, with the hope that by God's grace it may be accounted sufficient for salvation, but with the clear understanding that it represents 'place No. 2'. It is a proud boast of Protestantism that it has abolished such a distinction between Christians—with the aim of raising them all to the same level. But the practical outcome of it is, as S. K. said, that 'place No. 1 has dropped out' and that 'place No. 2', a bourgeois conception of Christianity, a minimum of other-worldliness which does not conflict with inner-worldly aims but rather serves to exalt them, is all that is left, and so is automatically promoted to the first place.

In the light of this reflection we can understand what S. K. meant when he insisted so trenchantly that 'the requirements of Christian idealism [the *consilia*] must be heard in every generation'. He doubtless hoped that, if they were heard, they would be followed by some, but he was far from expecting that all would seriously endeavour to follow them. He was not contradicting himself when he professed to be satisfied if the Church of Denmark would merely make the admission that the Christian observance which it exacted and exemplified [the *praecepta*] corresponded with a mildly indulgent interpretation of the Christianity of the New Testament and represented 'place No. 2'. This admission, he thought, would not only prompt men, with a poignant sense of their imperfection, to take refuge in grace, but might dispose some, as he said ironically, to be ambitious of attaining a higher degree of blessedness.

I must hasten on to another chapter, even at the cost of passing over many themes of interest and importance contained in the *Scraps* and the *Postscript*. I am consoled by the fact that the first of these two books is about to be published and the other will appear before long. But I have no space to report what S. K. says about sin and the sense of guilt,[1] or about repentance,[2] or about trial and temptation,[3] or about freedom versus necessity,[4] or about the individual as opposed to the crowd,[5] about the pros and cons of monasticism,[6] about the necessity of being 'contemporary with Christ'[7] by 'abolishing the 1800 years',[8] about 'what the age requires'[9] (namely, 'to be led by the nose'),[10] and about the deplorable misfortune that now 'all are Christians'.[11] He says of the paradox: 'One ought not to think ill of the paradox, for paradox is the passion of thought, and the thinker who is devoid of paradox is like the lover who is devoid of passion—a pretty poor sort of fellow.'[12] But S. K. was exceedingly tenacious of his favourite themes, and some of them he learnt to express more tellingly in the stress of his conflict with the Established Church, so that many themes which we are compelled to pass over at this point we shall encounter again when we come to a later period of his life which I describe as his religious maturity.

However, Climacus has a saying in the *Scraps* which encourages me not to end this chapter abruptly at this point, but to provide the reader with several long quotations. He says:[13] 'We shall not be in a hurry . . . we are not engaging in a foot race, and it is not speed that wins but correctness.' As a sequel to the last long quotation from the *Scraps* I quote the following from the *Postscript*.[14] It is one of the many scathing passages in which S. K. rebukes the presumption of attempting to prove the existence of God, which he regards as one of the symptoms of the demoralization of our age.

> Let us then rather sin out and out, seduce maidens, murder people, commit highway robbery—that is a sort of thing that can at any rate be repented of, and such a criminal God can still get hold of. But this intellectual superiority has risen to such a height that it can hardly be brought to repentance; it has an appearance of profundity which deceives. So let us rather mock God out and out as has been done before in the world—it is preferable by far to the disparaging air of importance with which people undertake to prove the existence of God. For to

prove the existence of a person who is actually in existence is the most shameless affront one can offer him, being an attempt to make him ridiculous; but the misfortune is that people have no inkling of this, that they seriously regard this as a pious undertaking. But how could it occur to a person to prove that He exists—unless because he has taken the liberty of ignoring Him, and now makes the matter all the worse by proving His existence before His very nose. A king's existence, or his presence, is commonly acknowledged by a characteristic expression of subjection and submission. What if a person in his royal presence should wish to prove that he exists? Does he prove it in this way [i.e. like the Christian apologists]? No, that would be making a fool of him; for one proves his presence by an expression of submission, which may take various forms according to the local custom—and thus it is one proves the presence of God by worship—not by proofs. A poor wretch of an author whom a later investigator drags out of the obscurity of oblivion must be awfully glad that the investigator succeeds in proving his existence—but an omnipresent being can only be brought into this ludicrous embarrassment by a thinker's pious bungling.

Then about 'the absurd' and the plausible, from an earlier section of the *Postscript*:[1]

The absurd, precisely by reason of its objective repulsion, is the dynamometer of the inwardness of faith. So here is a man who would like to have faith. Now let the comedy begin. He would like to have faith; but by the help of objective considerations and approximations to the truth he would make his position secure. What happens? By the help of approximations the absurd becomes something different, it becomes probable, it becomes more probable, it becomes perhaps exceedingly and peculiarly probable. Now he has arrived at the point where the next step is to believe it, and he may well say to himself that he does not believe like cobblers and tailors and simple folk, but only after long deliberation. Now he is about to believe it; but behold, now it has become impossible to believe it. The almost probable, the probable, the exceedingly and extraordinarily probable he can almost as good as know, exceedingly and extraordinarily nearly *know*—but to *believe* it is a thing that cannot be done; for the absurd is the proper object of faith, and the only thing that lets itself be believed. Or there is a man who says that he has faith, but now he will make his faith clear, he desires to have an understanding of himself in his faith. Now the comedy begins again. The object of faith becomes almost plausible, it becomes as good as plausible, it becomes plausible, it becomes exceedingly and peculiarly plausible. He has now completed the task, he may well say of himself that he does not believe like cobblers and tailors and other simple folk, but he has at the same time got an understanding of his faith. Strange understanding; he has on the contrary learnt to know something different about faith than he believed, he has learnt to know that he no longer believes, since he almost knows, as good as knows, exceedingly and peculiarly almost knows.

The Absurd.

Here is another passage about the absurd:[1]

The 'immediate' believer cannot apprehend the thought that the content of faith is, for the understanding and for the third person who is not a believer, the absurd, and that to remain a believer every one must remain with the absurd.

The 'immediate' believer, in so far as he is immediate, is not composite, can have no reduplication in himself, cannot contain it. With the best of intentions and with enthusiasm he, when talking to another, construes the absurd in terms of the most superlative of superlatives—and hopes that in this way he may succeed in convincing the other *directly*.

Here there is a lack of elasticity, which is dialectical: to conceive that for the understanding it is the absurd, to speak of it thus quite calmly to a third person, admitting that it is the absurd, supporting the pressure of the fact that the other must regard it as the absurd—and nevertheless to believe it. While naturally it is a matter of course that, for him who believes, it is not the absurd.

But he whose faith is immediacy cannot withdraw himself from sheer continuity with others, cannot comprehend that what for him is the most certain thing of all, an eternal blessedness, for others is and must be the absurd.

Hence the baneful confusion in talking about faith. The

believer is not dialectically consolidated as the single individual, cannot endure this double-vision—that the content of faith as seen from the other side is the negative, the absurd.

This is the tension of the life of faith, in which one must keep oneself. But everywhere there is a tendency to interpret faith as direct apprehension. An attempt in this direction is scholarly learning which proposes to understand faith.

It must not be supposed that S.K. was a Fundamentalist. He says:[1]

Zealotism of the letter, though it possessed passion, is a thing that has vanished. It was meritorious for the fact that it had passion. In another sense it was comic, and just as the age of chivalry really ended with *Don Quixote* (for the comic interpretation is always the final one), so might a poet even now make it manifest that the age of the theology of the letter is past, by immortalizing in comedy such an unfortunate servant of the letter in his tragi-comic romanticism.

And here is a longer passage about the Bible:[2]

In order that the dialectical aspect of this problem may receive its just dues, and in order that we may be able to think the thoughts through simply, without being disturbed by extraneous considerations, let us assume first the one, and then the other [i.e. that the Bible is reliable / and that it is unreliable].

So I assume that everything a learned theologian in his happiest moment has wished to prove about the Bible has been successfully proved. These books belong to the canon, and no others; they are authentic, are complete, the authors are trustworthy—one can well say that it is as if every letter were inspired (and more than this one cannot say, for inspiration is an object of faith, it is qualitatively dialectical, not to be reached by quantitative approach). Besides, there is not a trace of contradiction in the sacred books. For let us be hypothetically circumspect: as soon as there is the slightest hint of such a thing as a discrepancy, we land again in a parenthesis, and the zealous industry of philological and critical learning leads us at once into by-paths. Generally speaking, all that is needed here is a little diatetic prudence (the renunciation of every learned interpolation, which in a trice might degenerate into a parenthesis a hundred years long), so as to ensure that the affair will go easily and smoothly. Perhaps this is not so easy, and as a man is in danger wherever he goes, so is the dialectical argument always in danger—in danger of falling into a parenthesis. It is the same in small things as in great, and what makes it generally so boring for a third person to listen to a discussion is that the discussion hardly gets started before it has got into a parenthesis and then is pursued in this oblique direction more and more hotly the further it gets away from its proper topic. . . . But I discontinue these moralizing remarks intended for the public weal, wherewith I have sought to make some little atonement for my lack of historico-critical proficiency. So assuming that all is well with respect to the Holy Scriptures—what then? Has then he who had no faith come a single step nearer to faith? No, not a single one. For faith does not result from a direct scientific deliberation, and not in any case directly; on the contrary, with this objectivity one loses the infinite personal passionate interest which is the condition of faith, the *ubique et nusquam* where faith can come into being.—Has he who had faith gained anything in respect to the strength and vigour of his faith? No, nothing at all; the fact is rather that in this prolix knowledge, in this certainty which lies at faith's door and lusts after it, he is so dangerously situated that he will need immense effort, much fear and trembling, in order not to fall into temptation and mistake knowledge for faith. . . .

Now I assume the opposite, that the enemies have succeeded in proving about the Scriptures what they wish, with a certainty that surpasses the bitterest enemy's warmest wish—what then? Has the enemy abolished Christianity? Not at all. Has he hurt the believer? Not at all, not in the least. Has he gained a prescriptive right to exempt himself from the responsibility of being a believer? Not at all. For from the fact that these books are not by these authors, are not authentic, are not *integri*, are not inspired (though this cannot be disproved, since it is a matter of faith), it does not follow that these authors have not existed, and still less that Christ has not existed. So far as all this goes, the believer still finds himself just as free to accept it as before. Just as free—let us give good heed to this—for if he accepted it in virtue of some proof, he would be fairly on the way of giving up faith. If it should ever come to that point, the believer will always be to blame for it, inasmuch as he himself has invited it and began by playing the victory into the hands of unbelief by wishing to prove his faith. Here is the knot, and I am brought back again to learned theology. For whose sake is the proof adduced? Faith does not need it, indeed must regard it even as its enemy. On the other hand, when faith begins to be ashamed of itself, when it is like a woman in love who is not content with loving but begins treacherously to be ashamed of the beloved, and will have it well established that he is something remarkable, that is to say, when faith begins to lose its passion, that is to say, when faith begins to cease to be faith, then it feels the need of proof, in order to enjoy civil repute in the eyes of unbelief.

The fact that S. K. was evidently a highly intellectual man, and that he wrote in a way which is comprehensible only to intellectual people, may quite naturally suggest the presumption that he was an intellectualist, that he would construe faith intellectually, and that he would look down haughtily upon 'the cobbler, the tailor, and other simple folks', regarding them as capable of only an inferior apprehension of Christianity. In passages already quoted there are many hints which might serve to correct this misapprehension. In fact, S. K.'s position was the exact opposite of this. He never entirely dissented from the unfavourable judgement he expressed in his university years against Rationalism on the one hand and Orthodoxy on the other (that is to say, against all intellectualism in religion), and we have witnessed his growing distaste for intellectualism in philosophy. Two short passages from the *Postscript* will suffice to show that he accounted 'the wise man's' advantage over 'the simple' a very questionable one:[1]

Between the wise man and the simple man there is just this little insignificant difference, *that the simple man knows all that is essential*, the wise man little by little *is aware* that he knows it, or is aware that he doesn't know it, but that which they know is the same.

The speculative man and the simple man do not by any means know the same thing, when the simple man believes the Paradox, and the speculator knows that it is transcended. . . . If the simple wise man were to talk to a simple man about the forgiveness of sin, the simple man might well say, 'But yet I cannot comprehend the divine loving-kindness which can forgive sinners; the more lively my faith in it is, the less I can understand it.' (So the plausibility does not seem to increase in proportion as the inwardness of faith increases, but rather the contrary.) But the simple wise man surely would say, 'It is just the same with me. As you know, I have had opportunity to spend a great deal of time upon investigation and reflection, and yet the sum of it all is that at the best I can only apprehend that it cannot well be anything else but incomprehensible. You see that this difference between us is not of a sort that could dishearten you and cause you to bewail your more toilsome lot in life and perhaps your inferior talents, as if I had an invidious advantage over you. About my advantage, considering it as a fruit of study, I could as soon laugh as weep. Yet you should not despise this study, which I do not at all regret. On the contrary, it pleases me most when I smile about it, and then return with renewed enthusiasm to the exertion of thinking.'

Since I must stop somewhere (though there is no obvious reason why one should stop anywhere when quoting the *Post-script*), I conclude with two longer passages about 'dying' and 'immortality', which, if they have no other merit, serve at least to illustrate what the Greeks meant by the motto 'Know thyself'.[1]

Here are a few examples which show with all brevity how the simplest problems, by persistence in following them up, transform themselves into the most difficult, so that there is no reason for being in haste to take up astronomy, veterinary science and other such things, so long as one has not understood the simple things. The brevity with which they are treated can do no harm here, since the problems are really inexhaustible.

For example, what it means to die. In that respect I know just about what people in general know, that if I take a dose of sulphuric acid, I die, so also by jumping into the water, by sleeping in a room full of carbonic acid gas, &c.; I know that Napoleon always carried poison with him, and that Shakespeare's Juliet took poison; that the Stoics regarded suicide as a brave act, and others regard it as cowardice; that one can die of a cause so absurdly petty that the most serious-minded man cannot help laughing at his death; that one can escape certain death, &c. I know that the tragic hero dies in the fifth act, and that here death acquires endless significance and pathos, but has no such pathos when a bar-tender dies. I know that the poets vary the mood for interpreting death, even to the comical —I pledge myself to elicit in prose the same various effects of mood. I know moreover what the parsons are accustomed to say; I am acquainted with the themes generally dealt with at funerals. If there is nothing else to hinder me from going on to the study of world-history, I am quite ready for it, for I need only to buy black cloth for a parson's gown, and then I shall hold funeral orations as well as any ordinary parson; for that those who have a velvet stripe in front do it more elegantly I am quite ready to concede, but this difference is not essential, not any more so than the difference between a five- and a ten-dollar hearse. But, look you, in spite of this almost exceptional knowledge or dexterity of knowledge, I cannot by any means regard death as something I have understood. Therefore before I go on to the study of world-history (about which I am always compelled to say, God knows whether it really has anything to do with thee), it seems to me that it would be better to reflect about death, lest existence should hold me in derision if I became so learned as to forget to understand what one time shall happen to me and happen to every man. One time—but what am I saying; suppose death were to be so sly as to come to-morrow! Already this uncertainty, if it is to be understood and held fast by an exister, and just because it is an uncertainty, must be involved in everything that is thought, and hence in this resolve of mine to begin the study of world-history, so that I must make it clear to myself whether I am beginning something which is worth while beginning in case I die to-morrow—already this mere fact of uncertainty gives birth to unbelievable difficulties, which even the religious orator is unaware of when he intends to think the uncertainty of death and does not think it in and along with what he says about uncertainty, when with deep emotion he speaks movingly about the uncertainty of death and ends by exhorting his hearers to make a resolution for the whole life, and so ends by forgetting essentially death's uncertainty, for if he were consistent, his enthusiastic resolution for the whole life must be made dialectical in relation to death's uncertainty. To think this uncertainty once for all, or once a year, on New Year's morning at the midnight service, is naturally mere nonsense and is not to think it at all. In case he who thinks it thus, at the same time explains world-history, what he says about world-history may perhaps be excellent, but what he says about death is stupid. If death is always uncertain and I am mortal, this means that this uncertainty cannot possibly be understood merely in general, in case I am not just a man in general—and that I am not....

And then another question:

For example, what it means to be immortal. In that respect I know just about what people in general know; I know that some accept immortality, that others say they do not. Whether they really do not accept it, I do not know; it does not occur to me therefore to wish to combat them, for this undertaking is so dialectically difficult that I should need a year and a day before it could become dialectically clear to me, whether such a contest has any reality, whether the dialectic of communication, when it is properly understood, would approve of such a proceeding or transform it into a mere beating of the air, whether the consciousness of immortality is a subject which lends itself to instruction, and how the dialectic of instruction must be determined in relation to the pupil's presuppositions, whether these are not so essential that the instruction becomes a deception unless this is brought to consciousness, and in such a case instruction is transformed into non-instruction. Besides, I know that some have found immortality in Hegel, and others have not; I know that I have not found it in the System, where indeed it would be very unreasonable to seek it; for in a fantastic sense all systematic thinking is *sub specie aeterni*, and, in so far, immortality is there as eternity, but this immortality is not at all the one about which the question was asked, since the question was about the immortality of a mortal, for the eternal is clearly not the mortal, and the immortality of the eternal is a tautology and a misuse of words....

The question of immortality is raised in a book. The contents of the book are the answer. But (as the reader by reading the book through can assure himself) the contents of the book are the wisest and best men's notions of immortality strung on a thread. Oh, thou Great Chinese God! is this immortality? So then the question about immortality is a learned question?

All honour to learning! All honour to him who can handle learnedly the learned question of immortality! But the question about immortality is essentially not a learned question, rather it is the question of inwardness, which the subject in becoming subjective must put to itself. Objectively the question cannot be answered, because objectively it cannot even be raised, since immortality is precisely the intensification of the developed subjectivity and its very highest development. Only by really becoming subjective can the question properly emerge—how then could it be answered objectively? The question cannot be answered in social terms, for in social terms it cannot be expressed, since only the subject who desires to become subjective can conceive the question and ask rightly: 'Do *I* become, or am *I* immortal?' Unquestionably, people can combine for many things; thus several families can combine for a box at the theatre, and several single gentlemen can combine for a riding-horse, so that each one rides every third day. But it is not so with immortality, the consciousness of my immortality belongs to me entirely alone, precisely at the instant when I am convinced of my immortality I am absolutely subjective, and I cannot become immortal with two single gentlemen in turn. People who go about with a paper soliciting the endorsement of numerous men and women who feel an urge to become immortal, get no reward for their pains, for immortality is not a possession that can be extorted by a list of endorsements. Immortality cannot be proved at all systematically. The fault does not lie in the proofs, but in the fact that people will not understand that viewed systematically the whole question is nonsense, so that instead of seeking outward proofs one might better seek to become a little subjective. Immortality is the most passionate interest of subjectivity; precisely in the interest lies the proof. When one for the sake of objectivity (and quite consistently from a systematic point of view) systematically ignores the interest—God only knows in this case what immortality is, or how any one could entertain the idea of wishing to prove it, or get into his head the fixed idea of bothering himself about it. . . .

[Among the many questions which the concretely existing subjective individual must ask:] He asks how he is to manage to talk about his immortality, how he can at one and the same time talk from the standpoint of infinity and of finiteness and think these together in the one single instant, so that he does not say now the one and now the other; how language and all modes of communication are related to this effort, when all depends on being consistent in every word, lest the little heedless supplementary word, the chatty intermediate clause, intervene and mock the whole; he asks where the spot, so to speak, is; where there exists a spot appropriate for talking about immortality, for he knows perfectly well how many pulpits there are in Copenhagen, and that there are two chairs of philosophy, but where the spot is which is the unity of infinitude and finiteness, where he, at one and the same time infinite and finite, can talk in one breath of his infinitude and his finiteness, whether it is possible to find this so dialectically difficult spot, which nevertheless is so necessary. He asks how he in his existence can hold fast his consciousness of immortality, lest the metaphysical conception of immortality proceed to confuse the ethical and reduce it to an illusion; for ethically everything culminates in immortality, and metaphysically immortality swallows up existence as naught, even the 70 years of existence, and yet this naught must ethically be of infinite importance. He asks how immortality practically transforms his life, in what sense he must constantly have a present consciousness of it. . . . He asks whether it is now definitely determined that he is immortal; . . . whether this definiteness, in case he employs his life to become subjective, having this thought present to him every instant—whether then this definiteness is not rendered so dialectically difficult by the perpetual necessity of relating himself to the alternations which make up existence, that it becomes indefiniteness; and if this is the highest he attains, namely, that the definiteness becomes indefiniteness, whether it were not better to give the whole thing up, or whether he shall set his whole passion upon the indefiniteness and with endless passionateness embrace the indefiniteness of the definite, as the only way he can attain knowledge of his immortality so long as he is an exister, because as an exister he is strangely compounded, so that the definiteness of immortality can be possessed with definiteness only by the Eternal, but by an exister only with indefiniteness.—And the fact of asking about his immortality is at the same time for the existing subject who raises the question veritably a deed—which is not of course the case with absent-minded people who once in a while ask about the matter of being immortal just in general, as if immortality were something one is once in a while and the questioner himself only something in general. He asks then how he can manage to express his immortality in his existence, whether he really expresses it; and for the time being he is satisfied with this task, which surely must be enough to last for a lifetime since it is to last for an eternity. And then? Yes, then—when he has finished with this task—then comes the turn for world-history. In these days, to be sure, it is just the other way round: now people apply themselves first to world-history, and hence the ludicrous result is (as another author has remarked [Vigilius Haufniensis]) that while people prove and prove immortality quite in general, faith in immortality decreases more and more.

II. 'THE CORSAIR'
1845–6

No other external event made so deep an impression upon S. K. as the attack launched against him by *The Corsair*, the comic paper of Copenhagen, which responded romptly to his disdainful challenge by lampooning him before he vulgar, and then, when its spite was satisfied, continued the ttack for nearly a year, because the populace was willing to pay iberally for seeing one of the most distinguished men of Denmark eld up to ridicule. S. K.'s comments upon this painful subject —that is, the reflections which he confided to his Journal— ill a large volume, for he referred to this subject again and gain, almost up to the end of his life. S. K. was anything but hick-skinned, and his preoccupation with this painful subject nay be proof of a morbid sensitiveness; but it must be remem- ered that the Journal was his only confidant. To his acquain- ances he was able to pretend that the affair did not trouble him t all.

I must do my best to make this voluminous story brief. *The Corsair*, a phenomenon new to Denmark, was very ably managed y a young Jew named Goldschmidt, who in five years had aised its circulation far beyond that of any other paper in the ountry. He liked to think of it as the equivalent of the London *unch* or the Paris *Charivari*; but S. K. pointed out that whereas uch a thing might be harmless in the great capitals of Europe, it vas a devastating corruption in a land like Denmark, where 'the roportions are so small' that every one knows everybody else. 1000 prostitutes can be ignored in Paris, whereas one would be ntolerable in a provincial town.' Although *The Corsair* was not pen to the charge of blackmail, it is not unfair to compare it vith the New York *Town Topics* of unblessed memory. It was nown to pay 'a glittering honorarium'[1] to disloyal servants who vould betray the secrets of the home, and its editors protected hemselves against personal or juridical attack by hiding behind ired blackguards who were ready to suffer the penalty of the aw. All men of light and leading regarded *The Corsair* as an ntolerable scandal; nevertheless they all read it with secret

enjoyment, and none of them had the courage to protest openly
S. K. affirmed that this paper had no 'idea' behind it, that its purpos
was merely to make money by fair means or foul. Goldschmid
himself had an idea, the idea of political liberalism, but h
acknowledged that his comic paper was only a negative expressio
of it, by its tendency to level all distinctions, delivering the grea
as a prey to the vulgar, and making it apparent that the uppe
classes were not essentially superior. With the ideas of politica
liberalism as they were then being foisted upon Denmark S. K
had no sympathy, and he abhored *The Corsair* with all its works
Before this time, he said, a rabble had not existed in Denmark—
The Corsair created it. Nevertheless, for Goldschmidt himself h
had a marked liking. I get the impression that there was no othe
man to whom he felt so much drawn. Several times he did hin
the compliment of urging him to dissociate himself from *Th*
Corsair, and Goldschmidt replied with tears in his eyes, 'But yo
say nothing about my talents.'[1] There was no one in Copenhage
whose commendation Goldschmidt was so eager to have. I ma
remark here that Goldschmidt ultimately attained distinction i
Denmark, not only as a literary figure, but as a leader in th
democratic reform of the absolute monarchy. But at the tim
of which we are now speaking S. K. was the only gentlema
of distinction to converse with this Jew affably and withou
any marks of condescension. A novel he had written (nomi
nally he had merely published it), entitled *The Jew*, S. K. wa
prompt to praise. In view of this relationship between the tw
men, the conflict which arose between them appears the mor
pitiable.

Before the event I am about to record *The Corsair* had twic
uttered praise of S. K.'s pseudonymous works. In its issue o
November 14, 1845, it took occasion, in the course of a literar
review, to say: 'Lehmann [the editor of a liberal journal agains
whom in his student days S. K. had carried on a polemic] will di
and be forgotten, but Victor Eremita [S. K.'s pseudonym a
editor of *Either/Or*] will never die.' S. K.'s reaction to prais
from such a quarter was quick and sharp. He at once wrote
letter of protest to *The Corsair*, but because at that moment h
was busy with the last touches to his manuscript of the *Postscrip*
and could not afford to be interrupted by controversy, he did no
publish it.

A Prayer to *The Corsair*

Fe fi fo fum, I smell the blood of a Danish man—here its is application. O cruel and bloodthirsty Corsair, omnipotent Sultan, who holdest the lives of men as a jest in thy mighty hand and as a whim in the wrath of thy nostrils, Oh, be thou touched with compassion, cut short these sufferings—slay me, but render me not immortal: Omnipotent Sultan, consider in thy ready wisdom what the most pitiable of all thou hast slain will promptly be in a position to perceive, consider what it means to become immortal, and especially to become such by the attestation of the Corsair! Oh, what cruel favour and leniency!—to be for ever singled out as inhuman because the Corsair inhumanly had deigned to spare him! But above all let it be not this—not this, that I shall never die. Ugh! Such a life-sentence as this is unheard of. Merely to read it makes me so tired of life. What a cruel distinction I enjoy, that no one will be moved by my outcry when in womanly tones I exclaim, 'This will be the death of me, I cannot survive it'; for all will laugh and say, 'He cannot die.' Oh, be thou moved to compassion, bring thy cruel favour to an end, slay me like all the others. Be not afraid—wherefore wilt thou spare me? I have no wife who perhaps might breathe sighs against thee in sorrow for her husband whom thou slayest, no loved one who would feel the stroke more annihilating, no child whose tenderness makes the blow harder than for the father—I have no legitimately acquired distinction in civil society which I should feel the loss of with bitterness at this moment, I bear no renowned name so that a whole family would suffer from the attack upon an individual—spare rather every one who is involved with a third person that cannot but feel mortified even if the wounded one despises the attack.

Victor Eremita.

S. K. had the sort of pride which is more inclined to resent praise than criticism. He rarely replied to hostile comments upon his works, and not often to praise. However, just when he had completed the *Postscript* and was ready to deliver it to the printer—when he found himself at leisure to 'do a good deed', as he put it—he was furnished with an occasion for putting into execution his notion of attacking *The Corsair*. On or about December 22, there appeared an 'Aesthetical Annual' entitled *Gæa*, a sumptuous volume designed as a New Year's gift, prepared by P. L. Møller, and in the chapter called 'A Visit to Søro' there was supercilious criticism of Part III of the *Stages*, the part entitled 'Guilty!'/'Not Guilty?' S. K. promptly responded with a letter published in *The Fatherland* on December 27, 1845, entitled 'The Activity of an Itinerant Aesthete and how he paid for the Banquet', which was signed by 'Frater Taciturnus, chief personage of the 3rd part of the *Stages on Life's Road*'.[1] Far from being a defence of his book, the greater part of this letter was a bitter and disdainful expression of personal contempt for P. L. Møller. One gets the impression that to despise this man so deeply he must have had some intimacy with him [see p. 118 f.]. It was rare, said S. K., that this author came out into the open by publishing something over his own name, and he welcomed the opportunity to give him his deserts. Nothing could be more devastating than this attack upon P. L. Møller; and Goldschmidt, on meeting S. K. a short while after, admitted that Møller was 'annihilated' by it. I quote only the conclusion of this letter, which contains the challenge to *The Corsair* and the sting which annihilated Møller.[2]

> Would only that I might now shortly get into *The Corsair*. It is really hard on a poor author to be thus singled out in Danish literature as the only one (assuming that all we pseudonyms are one) who is not abused there. My superior, Hilarius Bookbinder [publisher of the documents contained in the *Stages*] has been flattered in *The Corsair* (if I remember correctly), and Victor Eremita has been obliged to suffer the wrong of becoming immortal—in *The Corsair*! And yet already I have been there; for *ubi spiritus*, *ibi ecclesia*—*ubi* P. L. Møller, *ibi The Corsair*. Our vagrant therefore quite properly finishes his visit in Søro by one of those disgusting Corsair attacks upon peaceable and respectable men who in honourable obscurity were attending to their several callings in the service of the state; upon distinguished men who have done much to make themselves deserving and nothing to make themselves ridiculous; for authors being public persons have to put up with many things, and among others with the imputation of kinship with people who when they have something printed are of course also authors.

The sting which 'annihilated' Møller was the divulgation of the secret that he was at that time virtual editor of *The Corsair*. This was fatal to him because at that time he was hoping to succeed the poet Oehlenschläger in the chair of aesthetics in the University. To that end he had made his recent tour of visits to the literary men outside Copenhagen and had sought to conciliate their favour by the articles he wrote for *Gæa*. He must have perceived at once that his chances for this promotion were ruined by his connexion with *The Corsair*. Nevertheless he replied to S. K. with a letter published in *The Fatherland* on December 29, in a tone 'almost deferential', as S. K. reports. 'He made his bow and disappeared.' 'I do not know whither he went, but from that moment, according to the report of my barber, there was a busy time on the dance-floor of literary despicableness in *The Corsair*.'[1]

In those days Goldschmidt approached S. K. with the hope (as S. K. understood it) that he would ask him not to reply to this attack. Naturally, S. K. would not utter that word, and on January 2 the attack was begun in force with an article by Møller entitled, 'How the itinerant philosopher found the itinerant virtual editor of *The Corsair*'. It was accompanied by several caricatures. And from that time on, for more than half a year, hardly a week passed that *The Corsair* did not produce one or more (sometimes four) articles holding up S. K. to ridicule under the names of his pseudonyms. This proved to be such a profitable line that other papers took it up. The whole country became 'ironical *en masse*'—an impossibility, as S. K. rightly affirmed—and in the whole land there was no one but 'the Master of Irony' who was unable to appreciate the joke. What chiefly delighted the populace was the constantly recurring reference to his thin legs and the unequal length of his trouser-legs. Sometimes they were both represented as too short.

S. K. published one reply—an article in *The Fatherland* of January 10, entitled, 'The Dialectical Outcome of a Literary-Political Business Concern'. But in the Journals are to be found many articles which he wrote but did not publish—attacks upon Goldschmidt and *The Corsair* which are so exquisitely witty that they ought to have seen the light in his lifetime. Barfod[2] expresses the opinion that certainly one of the reasons why they were none of them published is to be found in the fact that Goldschmidt, 'the bad boy of literature', became so ashamed of his position that on

October 2, 1846, he gave up his lucrative paper and betook himself to Germany and Italy. *The Corsair* still continued to exist, though it ceased to be a powerful tyranny, and before long P. L. Møller disappeared completely from Denmark, falling into obscurity and degradation, and dying miserably in France. Goldschmidt tells in his Memoirs[1] what prompted him to this decisive step. It was an encounter in the street with S. K., who, instead of saluting as he was accustomed to do, 'passed me with a staring embittered glance, without greeting or wishing to be greeted'. He says that he then for the first time received an impression of the lofty ideality of S. K.'s nature, 'although I had a presentiment of it'. 'It accused me and crushed me. . . . Before I had got to the end of the street on my way home it was decided that I should give up the Corsair.'

For my part I do not doubt that S. K. deliberately (and, as he said, 'prayerfully') launched his attack on *The Corsair* in the interest of public decency, doing a good deed and a brave one. But probably he did not expect to suffer an attack so devastating and so prolonged. He acknowledges that he had not anticipated that the better sort, who agreed that something must be done about this scandal, would hold back and leave him in the lurch, continuing to affirm that it was 'nothing'. He attributed this not merely to cowardice but to envy; and doubtless he was not far wrong in imagining that many people took delight in witnessing the humiliation of a great man whose melancholy aloofness they interpreted as pride. And he had not anticipated that *The Fatherland*, the editor of which was his close friend, who also had been eager for him to make this attack, would now hold aloof. But chiefly he was disconcerted by the effect this attack had upon the common people with whom he was accustomed to discourse so affably in the street. They were led to believe that he was half crazy if not worse.[2] Familiar talk with them was no longer possible. This was the part of his trial he remembered longest.[3] And, although he persisted in taking his customary walks in the streets, he could find no pleasure in them when the rabble was egged on to insult him. He recognized full well that there was no other conspicuous person in Denmark whose figure was so apt a subject for caricature. He could laugh about it with his equals, but he was unable to laugh with the crowd. It is characteristic of him that he braved it out and did not leave Copenhagen for one of his customary visits to Berlin. We can imagine that his carriage-drives in the country were a great relief to him at this time. They seem to have been more frequent then than at any other period. At least we have more numerous records of them. From February 16, 1846, to October 11, 1847, there are records of 91 days in the carriage, sometimes on excursions which lasted two or three days. But even this innocent diversion, as we shall see, was not considered blameless and did not always avail to save our hero from the attacks of vulgarity.

Considering the character of this attack and the very serious consequences it had for S. K., I cannot agree with the biographers who express their surprise that he should take it so much to heart and are disposed to regard his preoccupation with this subject as a symptom of his sickness. I am rather surprised that he could retain so much composure and was able when he wrote about *The Corsair* to consider it objectively 'as a literary phenomenon'.[1] It is true, I think, that in the year 1848 the tone of the entries in his Journal indicates a period of melancholy depression. In January of that year he wrote:[2]

> They have treated me scurvily, disgustingly, a national crime has been committed against me, a treachery by the contemporary generation. But for me it has been profitable, indescribably. For I was melancholy, infinitely melancholy—this is where I have been helped. For in my melancholy I still loved the world—now I am weaned from it.

This is the most outrageous expression he ever used—and I count that it was justified. He had then endured public ridicule for more than two years, and the jeers of the vulgar were to accompany him for the rest of his life. A little later he wrote:[3]

> What I lack is bodily strength. My spirit is calm, I have always considered that I must be sacrificed, now I have received my orders and I stand prepared for the command. I can endure it better in its daily form. But when, for example, I have sought recreation by driving three or four miles and my body has gradually become somewhat weak, partly by the drive, and partly by the sheer occupation of my spirit, when I get out of the carriage and it happens that I am met by a grinning assembly, there is sure to be some one present who is jolly enough to call me names—it has a very strong effect upon my bodily disposition.

Or when I have made a long excursion out along the lonely roads, engrossed with my thoughts, and then suddenly I meet three or four louts out there where I am entirely alone, and these then take to reviling me, then it has a strong effect upon my bodily disposition.

S. K. was constantly expecting that from mockery men would pass to physical violence. 'When they knock my hat in', he said 'then my cause will triumph.' We have seen that the ridicule started by one comic paper had infected the mob. He writes in 1848:[1]

They have infected the air for me. . . . Curiosity surrounds me everywhere. I travel five miles out to my dear forest district—ah! everywhere curiosity.

And so I am wasted upon Denmark. . . . My Christian name exists as a nickname for me which every school-boy knows. Ever more frequently the same name is now used by authors in comedies it now appears regularly, and everybody knows that it is I.[2]

The ridicule of S. K. was carried to incredible lengths in the little land upon which he was wasted. In 1847 the students of the University produced a comedy which contained a ridiculous character upon whom was bestowed the name of Søren Kirk. S. K. was surely justified in the indignation he expressed in his Journal:[3]

Mr. Hostrop writes a student-comedy—naturally with all possible inconsiderateness, using all possible licence. It would indeed show a poor spirit of comradeship if any one were to take objection to it! Good. But must it not then continue to be a student-comedy, i.e. for students? But what happens? The piece travels around the whole land, is performed finally in the Royal Theatre—and now I see to-day by the paper, that it has been played in Norway, and that the Norwegian paper calls the character which represents me, by my name, Søren Kierkegaard.

Really the thing was not quite so bad as he conceived, for Søren Kirk was not meant as a travesty of S. K. so much as of the students who were beginning to ape his style. It is a curious fact, however, that the name of Søren (from the Latin Severinus), which till then had been the commonest Christian name (as the patronymic Sørensen is still the commonest surname), passed out of use in the real world because novelists and playwrights bestowed it upon their most ridiculous characters.

Considering how generally 'infected' the air was, we cannot be surprised that S. K. sometimes suspected an affront where none was intended. Here is a case of such misapprehension:[1]

> I will adduce only one situation, but it was characteristic. It had to do with Lieutenant Bard of the Hussars. He approached with his little son. His greeting as usual was almost too deferential. He moved to one side to yield me the pavement. In case the boy did not know who I was, he must have got an impression that I was something extraordinary—but evidently the boy knew me, he was a reader of *The Corsair*. What a combination! And must not every child have great harm done him by seeing at one moment a person so treated in print that it almost looks like an invitation to school-boys as a whole to whistle after him in the street—and then at the next moment to see him treated thus by his father or to read selections of his writings in the school reader?

This was a sorry misconception. For Georg Brandes had opportunity to ask this same boy when he was grown to manhood whether he had read *The Corsair* as a child. He did not remember it, but he remembered very well that as a child he had cherished a great admiration for Søren Kierkegaard.

The entries made during the first two years of this persecution make a painful impression chiefly because of the immense mass of them. But we must remember that no one ever wrote such voluminous Journals as S. K., and at this moment he began to write them in a more methodical way, with the evident intention of clarifying his own position—for himself first of all, and then for posterity. The striking thing about the entries of this time is that they reveal no symptoms of an unwholesome state of mind. The bitterest expression is this:[2]

> It is even possible that in spite of my insignificance before God, personally humiliated for my personal transgression, I was yet 'a gift of God' to my people. They have treated me shabbily, God knows, yes, abused me as children abuse a costly present.

But to the most shameful of all the attacks of *The Corsair* (he was pictured sitting astride a young girl and beating her, and the motto was 'Frater Taciturnus chastizes his girl') his reaction was anything but extravagant:[1]

> Hear now, little Corsair! It is womanish to torment a man with his love-affair; it is a womanish thing under the impression of love disdained to continue to run after a person in the street and call him names. Be a man, hold your peace.

The few entries I am about to quote are characteristic of this time and give a fair idea of the humour with which he met the situation.

> Andersen can tell the fairy tale of 'The Lucky Galoshes', but I can tell the tale of the shoes that pinch.[2]
>
> . . . I know my exterior well, and indeed few men have so often been the object of good-natured raillery, or a little witticism, or a little banter, or a smile in passing, as I have been. And truly I have no objection to that: it is the expression of an instantaneous impression. The person in question cannot help it, and that is the atoning factor, and perhaps many who have thought too much of my talents have, as a set-off to this, got a little joy out of my legs—many a maiden who perhaps set me up too high by reason of my mental gifts has found herself reconciled to me by reason of my thin legs. And all this I find in the highest degree innocent, pardonable, and indeed enjoyable. But it is another thing when an abusive person takes the liberty of egging on the crowd to observe them.[3]
>
> In proportion as enlightenment and culture increase and requirements become greater and greater, it naturally becomes more and more difficult as a philosopher to satisfy the requirements of the age. In old times what was required was mental talent, spiritual freedom, intellectual passion. Compare the present age—now in Copenhagen it is required that a philosopher shall also have thick or at least well-shaped legs and that his clothes shall be in the fashion. It is becoming more and more difficult—unless people will be content with the last requisite alone and will assume that every one who has thick or at least well-shaped legs and whose clothes are in the fashion is a philosopher.[4]
>
> [An ale-house keeper who used to treat him with the greatest deference now shows his contempt, but the watchman

in his street is sympathetic.] My watchman's opinion about the aesthetic attack is as follows: 'If the worst comes to the worst, I could better reconcile myself to having my trousers stolen, but that somebody should draw a picture of them—that I couldn't survive.' . . . His opinion seems a strange one to me. For if somebody were to steal my trousers and I had no others to put on, then perhaps I might not survive it, supposing that I was compelled to go out without them and presumably would catch a cold. On the other hand when I am allowed to keep them on I get a profit and joy out of my trousers such as no one else in the whole realm has—I have them on (that is what I share in common with all who wear trousers), and the whole town has joy in seeing that I have them on—joy and perhaps also profit. Well, to be sure, I once thought of being able to do a little something for the individual man by my literary effort. Sheer conceit and vanity! It may be that I have merely mistaken the means and still can succeed in being of some use all the same. And the means of profiting people is discovered, it is constantly with me as I walk—it is my trousers. My biggest works have not made so much sensation. One might think that 'what the age requires' is my trousers. Then I will wish that its every requirement might be as innocent—for the requirement is that I should wear them, and at the best that I should some day bequeath them to the city. . . . I conclude that some element of enchantment is involved in this case. Just as Aladdin's lamp was entirely inconspicuous, so is it also with my trousers, which are just as inconspicuous and as little glaring as possible. If they were red with a green stripe or green with a red stripe! But again how ungrateful it was of me to regard these trousers as a thing of no importance whatever, merely giving order to the tailor to cut them out of the customary grey cashmere—and now it is just by the help of these trousers that I am becoming almost a person of importance. . . . Pretty nearly everybody has read the paper (in spite of the fact that they dare not confess that to one another—it is all part of the game)—a countless multitude of gentlemen and ladies have personally convinced themselves by inspection that I have the trousers on and that they correspond to the description. In order to meet the requirement of the age, I have given a frank answer to every one who has asked me whether these 'really' were the famous trousers, so that they could definitely say that they themselves had seen them. . . .[1]

[The umbrella figures in many of the caricatures. S. K. was abnormally sensitive to heat and carried this as a parasol.] When one is a student here in Copenhagen, a candidate for a degree, but nothing more, a copyist plenipotentiary in the Royal Exchequer, a shop-clerk, a pupil in the art academy, but nothing more—then, although it is not customary to walk with an umbrella as a protection against the sun, one can do it with perfect freedom—but in case I, for example, am bold enough to do it, then it is pride.[2]

Copenhagen is the most agreeable place to live in that can be imagined, for one who is nothing or still less. . . . When I was a young man and was nothing, then I enjoyed my freedom, then I could live as I liked, drive alone in my carriage, have the window closed in public places—it did not occur to any one to take notice of it. But now—now envy watches my every step, to say, 'It is haughtiness, it is pride, it is vanity.' . . . 'Why should he be allowed to drive alone?' says the smart-looking merchant's clerk. 'I could perfectly well drive with him; but this is pride.' Why it is I live as I do, it naturally does not occur to anybody to consider.[3]

And, considering the provocation, does this which follows seem too extravagant a complaint?[4]

To let oneself be trampled to death by geese is a slow way of dying. . . . Such a galling sort of abuse is about the most torturing experience. Everything else has an end, but this never ceases. To sit in a church and there find a couple of louts impudent enough to sit beside one, continually staring at one's trousers and scoffing at one in their conversation, which is carried on in a voice loud enough for one to hear every word. But I am now accustomed to such things. . . .

No wonder that a torment which never ceased became harder to bear with every year it lasted—impossible to bear without divine consolation:[5]

I feel no bitterness at all at the thought of all the insults I have suffered, or all the treachery that has been shown me; it does not occur to me to escape from all this, with one stroke, as it were. Oh, if in eterinty there is time and place for jest, I am certain that the thought of my thin legs and my scorned trousers will be a blessed amusement. And it is blessed to have boldness to say: God knows that what I have suffered in this respect I have suffered in a good cause and because (humanly speaking) I did a good deed with truly disinterested self-sacrifice. This I am bold to say directly to God—and I know more certainly than I know that I exist, more certainly than anything, because I already feel it, that he will answer: Yes, my dear child, you are right there; and he adds: Whereinsoever you have sinned, on the other hand, and have not been in the right, this is forgiven you for Jesus Christ's sake.

During the trying years 1846 and 1847 S. K. made several visits to King Christian VIII which he did not record in his Journal until 1849.[1] The favour of the king was clearly a relief from the scorn of the vulgar and the 'treachery' of the aristocrats who were thus furnished with 'a little difficulty to bite on'. Nevertheless he was reluctant to make these visits, and he did not go so often as the king wished. He held himself a little aloof because he knew that the king was inclined to offer him a sinecure, as a token of appreciation of him as a writer, and as a writer who steadily supported the monarchy. To S. K.'s surprise he found that King Christian knew about the bold part he had taken as a student in dissolving a meeting which threatened to end in a liberal demonstration [see p. 90 f.]. S. K. adroitly hinted that he could be serviceable only so long as he was independent; and he added characteristically, 'I have the honour to serve a higher Power, to the service of which my life is devoted.' Except on this delicate subject he was very frank and easy in his talks with the king. It goes without saying that he was humorous.

I have often reflected how a king ought to be. First of all he had better be ugly; next he should be deaf and blind, or at least give himself out to be, for it abridges many difficulties—a rash or untimely speech which acquires a certain importance from the fact that it is addressed to the king had best be disposed of by an 'Excuse me?' as an indication that His Majesty has not heard. Finally a king must not say much; he should have some set phrase to use on every occasion, which consequently says nothing. He laughed and said, A charming description of a king! Then I said, Yes, there is one thing

> more—a king must take care to be ill every now and then, it arouses sympathy. Thereupon he burst out in an exclamation almost of joy and jubilation: Ah, it is for this reason you talk so much about your ill health. You would make yourself interesting.

His last word on this subject is:

> On the whole, Christian VIII has enriched me with many psychological observations. Perhaps psychologists ought to pay particular attention to kings, and especially to absolute kings, for the freer a man is . . . the better can he be known.

We shall see in the next chapter that these years of persecution were years of intense intellectual labour. This was always S. K.'s refuge from melancholy within and vexation without:[1]

> Only when I am engaged in literary production do I feel well. Then I forget all the vexations of life, all suffering, then I am at home with my thoughts and happy. I have only to leave it off for a few days, and at once I become ill, distraught, cast down, my head heavy and overcharged. Such an urge, so inexhaustible, which after holding out now day after day for five or six years still gushes just as richly—such an urge is also surely a divine call. Were this—the whole wealth of thought which is stored up in my soul—to be repressed, it would be a torment, a torture, and I of no use at all. And why should it be repressed? Just because I have formed the idea that I should torture myself penitentially by forcing myself into a position . . . I am not fitted for. No, God forbid it. [He is here repudiating the idea of retiring to a country parish.]

I conclude this chapter with a passage[2] which shows how the memory of such painful experiences was mellowed in retrospect. In 1854, hardly a year before he died, S. K. told his story 'metaphorically' in the following entry. It is a curious fact that while Hans Christian Andersen was telling the story of his life in the fable of *The Ugly Duckling*, S. K. was recording a substantial piece of his autobiography in

THE WILD GOOSE

A Metaphor

> Everybody who knows even a little bit about life in the bird world is aware that between the wild goose and the tame geese,

different as they are, there is a sort of understanding. When the flight of the wild geese is heard in the air and there are tame geese on the ground below—the latter are aware of it at once, up to a certain point they have an understanding of what it means; so they too get under way, flapping their wings and cackling as they follow along the ground for a short distance—then it is over.

Once upon a time there was a wild goose. In the autumnal season when the time for the migration was near he took notice of some tame geese. He conceived an affection for them, it seemed to him a sin to fly away from them, he hoped to win them to his side so that they might resolve to follow when the flock took flight.

To this end he sought in every way to get in touch with them, trying to allure them to rise a little higher, and then again a little higher, with the hope that they might possibly be able to follow the flock, liberated from this pitiable life of mediocrity, waddling on the ground like respectable tame geese.

In the beginning the tame geese thought this very entertaining, they liked the wild goose. But soon they became tired of him, then they gave him sharp words and rebuked him as a fantastical fool, without experience and without wisdom. Alas, the wild goose had so deeply committed himself to the tame geese that they had power over him, their words counted with him—the end of the story was that the wild goose became a tame goose.

It can be said in a certain sense that what the wild goose wanted to do was very pretty, yet for all that it was an error, for—this is the rule—a tame goose never becomes a wild goose, but a wild goose can very well become a tame goose.

If what the wild goose did could in any way be accounted praiseworthy, he must above all have attended to one thing—self-preservation. As soon as he observed that the tame geese were acquiring power over him in any way—then off, off with the flock!

This applies to a genius—the rule is that a tame goose never becomes a wild goose, but a wild goose on the other hand may very well become a tame goose—therefore be on the watch!

With respect to Christianity this rule does not apply.

Doubtless the true Christian, over whom the Spirit broods, is as different from other men as the wild goose is from the tame geese. But the thing Christianity teaches is what a man may *become* in life. . . . Here then there is hope that a tame goose may become a wild goose. Therefore remain with them, occupied only with one, to win the individual to transformation—but for the love of God in heaven, take good care of this: so soon as you observe that the tame geese are beginning to acquire power over you, then off, off and away with the flock! lest it end in your becoming a tame goose blissfully content with a pitiable condition.

Although this story was written eight years after 'the attacks of vulgarity' began, it faithfully reflects the first positive effect of this experience. The negative effect upon S. K. was the painful reminder that he was 'different' from other men, heterogeneous (*uensartet*), an exception to the universal human—it opened wide the wound which had been his torment from childhood, which in his youth had prompted him to plunge into the activities and dissipations of student life as a way of attaining likeness to other men, which explains his desperate attempt in early manhood to 'realize the universal human' by marriage, which subsequently thrust him into a career of authorship for six years at a stretch, and which now led him to caress the purpose of retiring to a country parsonage as a way of conforming to custom. We can understand very well that the attack of *The Corsair* and the ridicule of the whole world in which he lived must have been peculiarly painful to S. K. because it opened wide the old wound which he had so sedulously sought to close. It would seem as if this experience might have crushed him. But his polemical disposition enabled him to react to this experience with a positive resolution which had far-reaching effects. He would no longer endeavour to escape from his singularity and isolation, he would not become a tame goose. He learnt to think of himself as 'separated' (*aphorismos*) in a religious sense (Gal. 1 : 15), and to regard his 'difference' as an indication that he was called upon (though not directly commissioned by a divine call) to perform in behalf of Christianity what only an extraordinary individual could do. Therefore he rejected the idea of the country parish as well as the career of authorship, in the worldly understanding of that occupation, and devoted himself henceforth to religious writing exclusively. He began to recognize at this time that the thoughts he had been seeking to communicate to his generation—and of course still more the thoughts which then began to engross his attention, such as the strange thoughts which he associated with the 'case of Adler' (e.g. 'Has a man a right to let himself be put to death for the truth?')—that these thoughts 'hovered as it were directly above the head of the contemporary age', and that if they were to make any impression at all, 'it must be like the beating of the wings of wild fowl when it is heard over the heads of the tame of the same species which live secure under dependable conditions, prompting them involuntarily to flap their wings, because this beating of the wings is not simply alarming but is at the same time alluring'.[1]

The next chapter will reveal how deep and wide-reaching were the positive effects of 'the attacks of vulgarity'.

III. A NEW STRING TO HIS INSTRUMENT
1846–8

IT is an instance of God's grace to a man when precisely in the experience of adversities he shows that he is so fortunately constituted that like a rare musical instrument the strings not only remain intact through every new adversity but he acquires in addition a new string on the string-board.

So wrote S. K. in 1847.[1] Two years later he recurred again to this figure:[2]

> It was the tension of reality which put a new string in my instrument.
>
> As an author I have acquired a new string to my instrument, have become capable of producing tones I otherwise never would have dreamt of.

It is obvious here that the 'new string' does not mean merely a new thought. The attack of vulgarity did in fact suggest several new thoughts to S. K.; but what he here has in mind is a new capacity, a deeper tone, and a broader compass. From 'the tension of reality' in this experience he learnt to know how bad the world is, and in a great measure he was weaned from it. His wealth and independence had hitherto protected him from such knowledge as he now gained. Now he received his '2nd education', and he reflected that the 1st education men get is imparted in 'the medium of imagination'.[3]

If there was any specifically new thought prompted by this experience, it was the thought of the baneful influence of the press, which he held accountable for the demoralization of society. The entries he made about journalists and the press would fill a large volume. What he most complained of was the irresponsibility of journalistic writing and the absurd pretension that the anonymous writer represents an immense number of people, if not the vast majority. For a single individual to be in possession of so disproportionate a means of communication constitutes a danger which the police must control or suppress as they do the use of fire-arms. To such reflections he was led by 'considering *The Corsair* as a phenomenon'. But these new thoughts were closely linked to his older positions, to the fundamental place he assigned to the single individual as opposed to the crowd, the mob, 'the public', to his contempt for majority rule, and especially for the notion that the truth, the right, can be ascertained by balloting—even in the Church! The notion that 'the voice of the people is the voice of God' was for him completely discredited by the fact that the people cried, 'Away with him, Crucify him, and release Barabbas!' The levelling process which he saw going on was hateful to him because it was not a levelling *up*. Every man is potentially a 'single individual', but he loses the distinction of this high calling when he loses himself in the crowd, he is not treated as an 'individual' when he is simply counted and his personality disappears in 'the numerical'. S. K.'s essential democracy was expressed in his conviction that 'every individual, positively every one' is capable of attaining the height which is man's chief end. But he saw clearly that there was no equality among men with respect to physical qualities and mental endowments, and he trenchantly expressed his conviction that by political means equality could not be brought about. Equality among men is made possible only by religion, when every individual stands alone 'before God', where at the same moment he is abased and exalted—but in that position there is revealed an equality which is essential and absolute.

These thoughts found expression not only in the Journals but in the latter part of a little book which he called *A Literary Review*, published in 1846. This fortunately has already been translated into English and will soon be published. In view of the fact that it was written nearly a century ago, it suggests that this essentially solitary man, who in his time was blamed for taking no part in the stirring political events which agitated his country, perceived the deeper trends and foresaw the demoralizing consequences of the doctrines of political liberalism which have culminated in our day and provoked the reaction of Sovietism, Fascism, Nazism, and older forms of dictatorship. S. K.'s prognostications have been punctually realized in the general demoralization which is now frankly acknowledged by the states repudiating the doctrines of political liberalism, or is tacitly acknowledged (in the English-speaking world) by the corruption of the vote and the manipulation of office-bearers in the interest of the class which is capable of ruling or able to neutralize the majority by means of its economic advantage. To-day S. K. might say, 'I told you so.' But this would be of no comfort to him in view of the fact that the right divine of majorities to govern wrong is still unchallenged in the Churches—at least in the Protestant Churches—wherever the totalitarian state does not interfere with them. And that is precisely the field where the doctrines of political liberalism most obviously do not apply—as a means of discovering what the will of God is—what is the voice of the Holy Ghost! We shall see that S. K. was at this time profoundly concerned with the question (as we now phrase it) of the seat of authority in religion, and though I can find in his writings no conclusive answer, I perceive that he was seeking it in the right direction—not in the vote of the many but in the voice of the single individual before God.

The very title of the '*Concluding* Unscientific Postscript' indicates that with this work S. K. intended to terminate his activity as a writer. Consequently he then took occasion (in a note attached to this book) to enumerate all of his pseudonymous writings and publicly declare himself the author of them. To this corresponds the determination to carry out his original intention of becoming a parson. With proud humility he would renounce the glittering prospects of fame as an author and retire to the obscurity of a country parish.[1] Such was his thought at the moment when the *Postscript* was ready for the printer. But 'the tension of reality' (the attack of *The Corsair*) halted both purposes.

On January 20, 1847, S. K. wrote in his journal:[2]

> The wish to be a priest out in the country has always attracted me and remained in the background of my soul. It attracted me both as an idyllic wish in contrast with a strenuous existence, and also religiously, in order to find time and repose to sorrow justly for sins I personally may have committed. I supposed then that as an author I was about to achieve *success*, and hence I considered that to end in this way was the right thing to do. However it seems clear enough that *the situation here at home is becoming more and more confused*. The question now is—in so far as it is true (as I am confident enough to sustain before the judgement-seat of God) that the literary and social and political situation requires an exceptional individual—the question is whether there is any one in the realm who is

fitted for this task except me. . . . The tasks proposed to me as a country parson are not essentially in my line. Therefore my thought has constantly been merely to express the universal, and the ethical significance of this step would lie in the fact that I preferred this to glittering success. But now and from now on my career as an author is truly not glittering. It is clear enough that I am becoming a sacrifice.

Four days later[1] the notion of retiring to a country parish was very emphatically discarded:

God be praised that all this attack of vulgarity has fallen upon me. I now have had occasion to learn inwardly and to convince myself that it was after all a melancholy idea to wish to live far away in a country parsonage in order to do penance in remoteness and oblivion. Now I stand far more resolutely than ever on the spot. And if this deluge of derision had not fallen upon me, this melancholy idea would have continued to pursue me. . . .

S. K. rightly apprehended that this notion of retiring to a country parsonage was 'a melancholy idea'—by which he means an idea prompted by his melancholy disposition. We can see that it was connected with the very root of his melancholy, his morbid insistence upon the necessity of living a life of penance because of his father's sin and his own. Because he had not yet triumphed over this melancholy (had not drawn out, as he expresses it, his thorn in the flesh), the entry we have just now quoted appears more decisive than it was. The resolution was decisive for the time being, but the thought of taking a country parish was to recur again in a different light, and an entry made in 1849,[2] emphasized with NB five times repeated, sounds as if the question were still unresolved. I quote it here because in part it actually does contemplate the situation we are now dealing with, and because in this way I would indicate the fact that I have omitted innumerable passages dealing with this fixed idea and arguing about it pro and contra. It is true, as S. K. recognized, that reflection by itself can never lead to action. But it must be confessed that where certain fixed ideas or 'compulsions' were involved S. K. was an example of the 'perfectly balanced mind', in the meaning which Lewis Carroll attached to this phrase when he used as illustration the case of the man who sits on the fence and cannot make up his mind to get down on either side. We shall see several instances of this, but I intend in every case to abbreviate the agony for the reader. The reader will be less inclined to be impatient with S. K. on the score of his long and painful struggles to make up his mind, when he apprehends that in reality this was a fight against his fundamental melancholy and that in the end it was a victorious fight.

> It is very true that my original intention has constantly been to seek a little post in the country. But at that time I rather thought of it as a contrast to making a success in the world as a reward for my strenuous efforts. Now the circumstances are not precisely the same, my situation is so ungrateful that until further notice it is exactly suitable for a penitent to remain on the spot. . . .
>
> It is true also that I have constantly said that the place is vacant—the place for an author who knows how to desist. All right. But up to the thought which I have described as 'An effort to introduce Christianity into Christendom', but all this done poetically and without authority (i.e. not to turn myself into a missionary)—so far as that I had to go. That has now been carried out. [He has in mind the *Two Short Ethico-Religious Essays* and *The Sickness unto Death*, about which he was then desperately debating whether he should make bold to publish them or leave them to be read after his death.] . . .
>
> Finally there is one thing that must be remembered. What I speak of as my original thought must be subjected to control of some sort. For how often I have said that a man-of-war receives its orders after it has put out to sea, and that therefore it can perfectly well be in order that I go farther as an author than I originally conceived, especially as I have become an author in a totally different sense. For originally I conceived of authorship as an escape from, a temporary postponement of, this thing of going out into the country as a priest. But is not my position here essentially changed in the fact that I as an author reach the point of working for a religious aim? First I intended to desist immediately after *Either/Or*. That was really the original thought. But productivity laid hold of me. Then I would have left off with the *Concluding Postscript*. But what happened? I was involved in all the persecution of

vulgarity, and just this brought it about that I remained on the spot. Now, said I to myself, now there can be no question of a glittering career; no, now the situation is appropriate for a penitent. Then I would have ended with the *Christian Discourses* and gone on a journey, but I did not make the journey after all—and in '48 I attained my richest productivity. Thus has Governance held me in the saddle. I put the question to myself: Do you believe that in a parsonage you would have been in a condition to write three such religious books as the three which followed the *Concluding Postscript*? And I must answer, No! It was the tension of reality which put a new string in my instrument. And so also in '48.

This retrospective passage reveals a fact we were prepared to expect, that the resolution to 'remain on the spot' (i.e. not to seek a country parish) involved continuation of authorship, but that henceforth this was to be a totally different kind of authorship, devoted expressly to a religious aim. Aesthetic and philosophic production was definitely left behind. There was, however, one exception: *The Crisis and a Crisis in the life of an Actress*, signed 'Inter et Inter', which he wrote in the summer of 1847 but which he could not muster up courage to publish (in four numbers of *The Fatherland*) until 1848, after a long and excruciating debate about the propriety of interjecting such a note in the midst of his religious production. In fact he wrote also, the following year, an appreciation of the actor Phister, who dwelt in the same house with him; but this he had no intention of publishing, he purposed only to present it to the subject of his eulogy, and we have no assurance that he went even so far as that. The actress in question was the wife of Heiberg, the celebrated aesthetic critic. The fact that Heiberg republished it in book form after S. K.'s death is proof that it gave pleasure in those high quarters. And S. K. was afterwards inclined to make much of the fact that this little aesthetic work refuted the assumption that he had turned to religion only when he was too old to appreciate the aesthetic.

The production of these years (1846–7) consisted chiefly of 'Discourses': *Edifying Discourses in Various Spirits*; *The Works of Love* (which he described as 'Some Christian reflections in the form of discourses'); and *Christian Discourses*. These titles themselves suggest that there was a new string on his instrument. Religiously they mark a striking advance beyond the *Edifying Discourses*,[1] and they begin to express what S. K. regarded as 'the specifically Christian'. He said that the expression 'for edification' 'is not my category—it is the category of the missionary'. Nevertheless, he welcomed an excuse for using this category when he entitled Part III of *Christian Discourses* 'Thoughts which Wound from Behind—for Edification'; and when he published *The Sickness unto Death* in 1849, he ascribed to Anti-Climacus the presumption of calling it 'for edification'. In 1848 he described *Lilies of the Field, &c.* as 'godly discourses'. All of these discourses were properly called Christian, but many of them were within the limits of 'religion A'. One who reads these discourses to-day may well be astonished at this distinction, for we rarely hear sermons so distinctively Christian as these. And still more astonished at the distinctions S. K. draws between the three parts of *Edifying Discourses in Various Spirits*,[2] describing them respectively as 'aesthetical, ethical, religious'. It is not easy for us to think of Part I as 'aesthetical', since it is devoted exclusively to the solemn penitential sermon which defines pureness of heart as the readiness 'to will one thing'. We get an inkling of his meaning when we read:

> The plan is essentially ethico-ironic, and hence edifying Socratic.
>
> The most ironic category (which, be it observed, is at the same time the absolutely moral) is individual personality, 'that single individual' (*hiin Enkelte*). For in point of fact 'the invididual' can be used to indicate every man, and in an eminent sense it indicates every one who in moral ideality aspires to the highest. The situation is not such that anybody is excluded by some invidious difference from being the single individual in an eminent sense, and yet it is certainly true in point of fact that there is no such thing as 'the individual' in the ideal sense. This is the relationship (a moral and ethical relationship just as much as it is an ironical one) between matter of fact and ideality.
>
> The individual as a category is quite as ironical as it is moral and it is both of these things absolutely, and then again it is absolutely edifying (in the religiousness of immanence) in the

fact that it does away with differences as an illusion and establishes the essential equality of eternity.

He says that the colouring of the first part sometimes verges on the comical, and he describes the second part (about the lilies and the birds) as humorous. He expects therefore that people will be offended and declare that this is not 'seriousness'. Very likely. But it is clear enough that the aim is not trivial, and though S. K. uses the form of fable, he uses it very seriously—'with ironical pathos'. I quote as an example the story of the horse that walked alone. It acquires a particular pathos when we recognize that it describes first of all S. K. himself, who beside being a regular church-goer was diligent in reading Mynster's sermons and other books of edification:[1]

> Suppose it were so that dumb animals could have thoughts and could communicate them to one another, although we are not able to understand them—let us suppose it. It almost looks that way, in summer-time when the farmer's horse stands in the meadow and tosses or shakes its head—true, no one can know definitely what it means—or take the two which go through life side by side pulling an equal yoke, when in the freedom of the evening they approach one another as if in confidence, when they embrace one another as it were, caress one another, fondle one another with a movement of the head; or when the free horses call to one another so that the woods echo, when they collect on the plain in great herds as if for some assembly—suppose that they really could communicate with one another. But there was one horse that kept by himself. Then when it heard the call, when it saw the herd gathered together in the evening and understood that it would hold an assembly—then it too came trotting up for the purpose of learning something about life and life's conditions. It paid strict attention to what the elders expounded—how no horse might count itself fortunate before it was dead, how no life of any creature was so exposed to sorrowful vicissitudes as that of the horse; and then the elders recounted the manifold sufferings—sufferings from hunger and cold, from being worked almost to death, from being kicked by a cruel driver, abused by injudicious masters whom it was impossible to content, who blame and punish the horse for their own want of

> judgement, and finally in old age the turning out in winter to the naked forest. Thereupon the assembly broke up, and that horse which had come trotting gladly to it went away in distress, 'by sorrow of heart its breathing became heavy' (Prov. 15: 13). It had understood what was expounded, but not a word was whispered about its particular suffering. Yet every time it heard the call and noticed that the other horses hastened to the assembly it came trotting gladly up, constantly hoping that now something would be said about it; and every time it had heard what was said it went away distressed. It understood better and better what the others talked about, but itself it understood less and less, just because the others seemed to exclude it, although it was actually in their company.—Oh, thou sufferer [here follows the word of comfort to the solitary and afflicted soul which he knew so well how to administer].

'This comical colouring', says S. K., 'is absolutely appropriate' to the first part, and 'if one is inclined to laugh, he will find that he is laughing ironically'. On the other hand, he says of the second part: 'The form of presentation is edifying, softened by a humorous trait of touching jest and jesting earnestness. In many places the reader will be inclined to smile, never to laugh, never to laugh ironically. The fairy tale, which might rather be called a parable, of the troubled lily is absolutely humorous.' This parable occurs in Part III, which is entitled, 'What is to be learnt from the lilies of the field and the birds of the air'. The title of the discourse which it illustrates is 'To be content with being a man'.[1]

> Once upon a time there was a lily which stood in a secluded spot beside a little purling stream and was well known to some nettles and a few other tiny flowers in the neighbourhood. The lily, according to the veracious description of the Gospel, was arrayed more beautifully than Solomon in all his glory and was as care-free and glad as the day was long. Time slipped by blissfully and unobserved, like the running stream which murmurs and vanishes. But it happened now that a little bird came one day and paid a visit to the lily, it came again the next day, then remained away for many days before it came back again, which to the lily seemed strange and inexplicable—inexplicable that the bird did not remain in the same place like the

tiny flowers, and strange that the bird could be so capricious. But as it often happens, so it happened also to the lily, that just for this reason it fell more and more in love with the bird because it was so capricious.

This little bird was a naughty bird. Instead of putting itself in the lily's place, instead of rejoicing in its loveliness and rejoicing in its innocent blissfulness, the bird wanted to give itself an air of importance by feeling its freedom and letting the lily feel its bondage. And not only this, but the little bird was at the same time chatty and reported all sorts of things, true and untrue, about other places where lilies far more splendid were to be found in great abundance, where there was an atmosphere of peace and gaiety, a fragrance, a splendour of colour, a chorus of birds, surpassing all description. So the bird reported, and every one of its reports ended with the remark, deeply humiliating to the lily, that in comparison with such glory it looked like nothing at all, indeed that it was so insignificant that it was questionable what right it had to be called a lily.

Then the lily became troubled. The more it heard the bird say, the more troubled it became. It no longer slept quietly by night, nor awakened with gladness in the morning. It felt itself bound and imprisoned, it found the murmur of the stream tiresome and the day long. It began now to be concerned with itself and the conditions of its life, in self-commiseration—so long were the days. 'It may be all very well', it said to itself, 'to hear the brook murmur now and then by way of variety—but to hear the same thing eternally day in and day out is too tiresome.' 'It might be agreeable enough', it said to itself, 'to be once in a while in a secluded place and alone, but to be forgotten in this way a whole life long, to be without any other society but the society of stinging-nettles, which surely are not proper society for a lily—it is not to be endured.' 'And then to make so poor an appearance as I do', said the lily to itself, 'to be so insignificant as the little bird says I am —Oh, why did I not come into being under other conditions? Oh, why did I not become a crown imperial?' For the little bird had related to it that among all lilies the crown imperial was regarded as the most beautiful and was the envy of all other lilies. The lily noticed that unfortunately its trouble was increasing, but then it talked to itself reasonably—alas, not so reasonably as to banish trouble from its mind, but in such a way as to persuade itself that its trouble was reasonable. 'For', it said, 'my wish is surely not an unreasonable wish, I do not require to be something I am not, like a bird, for example; my wish is merely to be a splendid lily, or, I might say, even the most splendid.'

All this time the little bird flew back and forth, and with every visit it made, and with every intervening absence, the lily's restlessness increased. At last it confided itself entirely to the bird. One evening they agreed that a change should be brought about next morning and an end be put to its distress. Early the next morning came the little bird; with its beak it cut the soil away from the lily's root so that it might be free. When this had been accomplished the bird took the lily under its wing and flew away. The plan was for the bird to fly off with the lily to the place where the splendid lilies bloomed, there to help it to get planted, to see if with the change of place and the new environment the lily might not succeed in becoming a splendid lily in company with the many, or perhaps even a crown imperial envied by all the others.

Alas, on the way the lily withered. If the troubled lily had been content with being a lily, then it would not have become troubled; if it had not become troubled, then it would have remained where it stood—where it stood in all its loveliness; if it had stayed there, it would have been the very lily the parson talked about on Sunday when he repeated the words of the Gospel: 'Consider the lilies; I say unto you that even Solomon in all his glory was not arrayed like one of these.' . . .

The lily is man. The naughty little bird is the restless thought of comparison which roves far and wide, unstable and capricious, and culls unwholesome knowledge about invidious differences. . . . The little bird is the poet, the seducer, or the poetical and the seductive in man. The poetical is like the bird's discourse, true and untrue, poesy and truth. For it is true that differences exist and that a great deal may be said about them; but the poetical representation is to the effect that difference passionately felt, in exultation or in despair, is the highest thing; and this is eternally untrue. In the distress of comparison the troubled person may go at last so far that in view of the difference he forgets that he is a man, so that in despair he conceives himself so different from other men that he even conceives he is different from what is meant by being a man, just as the little bird thought that the lily was so inconspicuous that it was questionable if it was really a lily.

Perhaps it is capricious of me to select these lighter passages from S. K.'s Discourses. I wanted to show that even when he was smarting most under the attack of vulgarity he was capable of writing in so genial a spirit. There can be no question about the seriousness of the third part of this volume. S. K. can well describe it as religious: here and in the very title he makes bold for the first time to call his discourses 'Religious Discourses'. The last of these discourses may be thought to reflect his own immediate experience: 'The joyfulness of the thought that courage enables the sufferer to overcome the world, and that there is a victory which transforms insult into honour and defeat into triumph.'

Nor can there be any question about the seriousness of the volume entitled *The Works of Love*, in ten chapters, which S. K. describes as 'Some Christian Reflections in the Form of Discourses'. With respect to the doctrine of 'works' S. K. was clearly not in sympathy with the position characteristic of the Reformers, notwithstanding that he was emphatic in rejecting the notion that any merit can attach to man's works before God. Incidentally we have seen that his insistence upon freedom made it impossible for him to accept the doctrine of predestination; and the reader has had abundant opportunity to observe other fundamental traits of his thinking which must have compelled him to discard Luther's characteristic assertion that salvation is 'by faith alone'. In view of his insistence upon 'double reflection', the reduplication of thought in 'existence', it must have seemed to him that 'faith *alone*' was not only monstrous but impossible, equivalent to 'faith without works'. A clear enough sign of this tendency is his predilection for the Epistle of St. James, which Luther scornfully rejected as 'a straw epistle', but in which S. K. found the texts he liked best to preach upon. But because S. K. was an 'existential thinker' he was not directly interested in the formulation of theology and would have repudiated especially the pretension of formulating a *systematic* theology. The task he felt called upon to perform was not to reform the dogmatic tradition of his Church but to insist upon its being practised. He assumed that the dogma was all right, and rather than attack the points which were objectionable to him he simply ignored them. He engaged in no controversy against the central Protestant doctrine of 'faith alone', but without any show of hostility, and without any possibility of rebuttal, he could insist that *love* must prove its reality by its works, that we cannot have love *alone*, or love without works. In these 'Christian reflections' S. K. dwells very properly upon the most immaterial, the least conspicuous, the most unobservable 'works' of love, whereby every man, even the weakest and the poorest, can discover, for himself at least, the reality of his love. But he had reason to think that Mynster was offended,[1] and he was grateful when he had proof that the bishop overlooked the offence.

The volume entitled *Christian Discourses* (written in 1847 but not published until 1848) is made up of four unlike parts. The first two parts ('The Anxieties of the Heathen' and 'Exultant Notes in the Conflict of Suffering') are not unlike the discourses we have already reviewed; but the third part ('Thoughts which Wound from Behind—for Edification') is the first expression in S. K.'s published writings of the polemic, which later was to become predominant, against established and self-satisfied Christianity. The motto on the back of the title-page expresses a polemical spirit when it asserts that 'Christianity is not served by any defence, it is aggressive, . . . it attacks—and as a matter of course within Christendom it attacks from behind'. Some notion of the polemical character of these discourses may be got from the titles. I quote only four of the seven: 'Watch thy foot when thou goest into the house of the Lord!'; 'Behold, we have left all and followed thee; what shall we have therefore? (Mt. 19: 27)—and what shall *we* have?'; 'All things must work together for our good—*when* we love God'; 'The resurrection of the dead is at hand, of the just—and of the unjust'. The passage with which this last discourse begins may suffice to give a notion of the character of these 'thoughts which wound from behind' and to show that they can justly claim to be 'for edification':[2]

For immortality is the judgement. Immortality is not a prolonged life, such a life as is prolonged into eternity, but immortality is the eternal separation between the just and the unjust. Immortality is not a prolongation which follows as a matter of course, but it is a separation which follows as a consequence of the past.

What has given occasion for the whole error about immortality is the fact that people have completely altered the statement of the case, that they have made a question out of immortality, made out of a task a question, out of a task for action, a question for thought. Would not that be the most depraved age which completely transformed its 'duties' into problems for thought? For what is duty? Duty is what one *shall do*. There must not be any question about duty, but there must be question only whether I do my duty. There must be no question about immortality, as to whether it is, but the question must be whether I live as my immortality requires of me. There must be no question about immortality, as to whether it is, but as to what my immortality requires of me, as to my immense responsibility in the fact that I am immortal.

That is to say: immortality and the judgement are one and the same. We can speak rightly of immortality only when we speak of the judgement; and naturally when we speak of the judgement we speak of immortality. Hence Felix was afraid when he heard Paul's discourse about immortality; for Paul would not speak of it except in speaking about the judgement, about the separation between the just and the unjust. Had Paul been willing to speak differently, to follow the new fashion of separating the judgement and immortality from one another, had he talked (or twaddled) about immortality without interjecting a word about the judgement, talked about immortality and let it be assumed that there is no judgement—then indeed Felix would certainly not have been afraid, he surely would have listened with the attention of a cultured man and remarked afterwards, 'It is quite entertaining to hear the man, but it is a kind of fanaticism, although it is capable of delighting one as long as he hears it; it has something in common with fireworks.'

Immortality is the judgement. There is not a word more to be said about immortality. . . . Thou shalt not labour to prove by many reasons that it is more than likely thou art immortal. No, from this inconvenience God has completely exempted thee, thou art immortal, and thou shalt give account unto God how thou hast lived—O thou immortal.

It was not possible for any man of S. K.'s generation—'especially in Protestantism, and more especially in Denmark'—to conceive more sharply and appropriate more thoroughly the eschatology of the New Testament. The Gospel notion of the resurrection of the dead and the last judgement had long been supplanted by the Platonic (Socratic) doctrine of the immortality of the soul—which Plato was not presumptuous enough to proclaim as a dogma but regarded as a 'very pretty risk' (*kalos kindunos*)—and yet this devout admirer of Socrates was the only man of his time who was not beguiled by it.

S. K. was in an agony of apprehension about publishing these discourses, fearing again that they might offend Bishop Mynster, the Primate of the Danish Church, for whom he still treasured a deep affection. At the moment when his polemic against the Church was openly launched many were surprised at it; but now that we have his Journals and can see how long it was brewing we have reason rather to wonder that it was so long repressed. He had it in mind[1] to match the 'Thoughts which Wound' with another work entitled 'Thoughts which Heal Radically—Christian Medication'; and although this plan was never carried out, something else was done to soften the effect of this first essay at 'introducing Christianity into Christendom': it was followed by the 'Seven Discourses at the Communion on Fridays' which constitute Part Four of the same volume. We learn from the Journal[2] that he thought of this as the conclusion of his work as an author. When S. K. published two addresses with the same title in 1851 he remarked in the preface with deep satisfaction that his work as an author had there found its 'definite point of rest at the foot of the altar'. He calls attention to the fact that two of the Friday Addresses of 1848 had actually been delivered by him in the Church of our Lady, remarking that the reader could easily perceive that they were 'delivered addresses'. Evidently he recognized that the closely woven thought of all his other addresses could be followed more easily by a reader than by a hearer. The Church of our Lady is the Cathedral of Copenhagen, which is rendered illustrious by Thorwaldsen's statue of Christ. S. K., as he stood before it addressing a small group in the chancel, escribed this statue, perhaps pointed to it, when he said of Christ, 'He spreads out his arms here at the altar and says, "Come unto ne"; he bows his head towards thee in benediction.'

In view of the immense religious production of the year 1847, ıcluding 1,100 pages of Discourses, S. K. was evidently justified ı conceiving that he might be allowed to continue his work as an ıthor, no longer as a mere poet, but in a form 'useful and well-leasing to God'.[1] In August he proposed to write 'a strictly :ientific work on spiritual eloquence with constant reference to .ristotle's Rhetoric'.[2] This was one of his many books that was ever written. He was evidently hunting for a subject which 'ould be 'useful' and remote from the poetical.

Parenthetically it must be remarked somewhere that on November 3, 1847, Regina was married to Schlegel, and that n December 23 Goldschmidt, having returned to Denmark, rought out the first issue of *North and South*, a monthly review f high character which he conducted ably.

But this was by no means the only serious writing S. K. ccomplished during the years 1846–7. In the first place, the eluge of ridicule that overwhelmed him—the grin of vulgarity nd the sneaking betrayal of 'superior' persons—made him for ıe first time acutely conscious, not only that he was misunder-ood, but that no one was capable of understanding the works e had been so diligent in writing. This fact is perhaps not so isparaging to Denmark, and not so much due to its small pro-ortions, as S. K. was inclined to think. For even when his works 'ere translated into the better-known languages of Europe the reat world has been slow to understand what he had to teach ıem. Indeed it is hardly conceivable that he would be compre-ensible to us to-day if his literary production had concluded with ıe *Postscript*, as he intended, and if we were not in possession of is Journals—that is to say, if we were in the same position as his ontemporaries at the period we are now considering. It appears ıat the human mind is not alert enough to appropriate, without ıe aid of revelation, communication so indirect as S. K. had ddressed to his readers up to that time. It is evident that he egan now to have an inkling of this, and though he was not eady to admit that his tactics had hitherto been at fault, he found imself compelled to reflect whether a more direct method of ommunication might not be advisable. Both his argument and

his example suffice to persuade me that there is a place for i
direct communication, and that we should do well to learn it fro
S. K. Yet it is plain to us now that his theory was an attempt
rationalize a practice to which he was compelled by a morb
reserve which was a specific product of his melancholy and w
attached in some way to the deepest root of it, namely, his sen
of sin (his father's as well as his own) which, though God mig
forgive, the sinner dare not forget—because God could not fo
get it. For this reason direct communication was impossible
S. K., even when he had come to recognize the need of it. H
could not use it freely until he had in a measure overcome h
melancholy, and that of course involved a protracted confli
delayed by many reverses. In the end he was so far successf
that he could speak with terrible directness on any subject exce
about himself; and it is so normal a thing for a man to be retice
in speaking about himself that this last vestige of S. K.'s reser
was perhaps not altogether morbid.

In the period we are now concerned with we see only the sig
of his struggle in the direction of freedom, but they are indub
able signs. In the first place, since he was always frank with hi
self and suffered from no inhibition in this respect, we witne
now the beginning of a more methodical and more comple
self-revelation in his Journals, we may even say the inception o
new sort of Journal. While S. K. was still jotting down his cu
tomary aphoristic entries in a volume which he had begun in M
1842 and which he distinguished by the sign JJ, he began
March 9, 1846, what he called 'Report', which subsequently
inserted in the Journal which he designated as NB—the fi
volume of a series of NB Journals which in the nine years th
remained of his life reached the prodigious figure of NB^{36}. Wh
the JJ Journal was full (presumably in September 1846) the ne
Journal became the repository of his customary entries on
sorts of topics, but from time to time these were accompanied
carefully thought-out statements entitled 'Report', 'Report-
Result', or 'Accounting', which makes it clear enough that
was intent upon explaining himself to posterity—for he suffer
from no inhibition against direct communication to posterit
Out of these many carefully worded passages there grew t
touching and illuminating confession which he called '*The Point
View for my Work as an Author*. A Direct Communicatio

.eport to History', which he composed in 1849 but, after excru-
iating debates with himself, preferred not to give to the public
uring his lifetime. The NB Journals give evidence that they
ere written with an eye to publication; for instead of using the
bbreviations common in the earlier Journals, the words are for
ie most part written in full, and an entry of the year 1849 pro-
oses 'The Book of the Judge' as the title that might be used for
ie Journals if ever they were published. Doubtless this entry had
i view chiefly the NB Journals, but an entry of August 1847
eveals that he had begun the revision of his earlier diaries.

Another and a more surprising result of S. K.'s uneasy appre-
ension that he was not understood was the plan he formed of
elivering a course of public lectures.[1] Needless to say, they were
ever delivered. He got only so far as to write copious notes
or a series of lectures on 'The Dialectic of Ethical and Ethico-
Religious Communication', which was meant as a preface to
welve lectures on 'Love, Friendship, and Charity'. It is interest-
ng to note that as a way of explaining his works to his contem-
oraries he proposed to explain what indirect communication is
nd aims at. He had begun to question whether at least the
heory of indirect communication might not be directly communi-
ated. This was a compromise which came very far short of the
irect communication of his fundamental thoughts. But this
vas his last formal defence of the tactic of indirect communica-
ion. In many subsequent entries[2] he recognizes that his em-
loyment of it stood in relation to his 'heterogeneity', that to
nake a right to use it one must be 'more than human', and that as
etween man and man it betrayed a daimonia.

S. K.'s sense of the need of making himself understood, or at
east of ensuring that he should not be totally misunderstood after
is death, prompted him a little later (in 1849) to 'draw' to him
Rasmus Nielsen, Professor of Philosophy in the University. In
act, the Professor had already showed that he was eager to be
lrawn, and in the end he justified S. K.'s saying that a disciple is
he greatest of all calamities. This relation to Rasmus Nielsen
constitutes an interesting episode in S. K.'s life, and I regret
hat I have to dismiss the subject with so brief a notice. It was on
he whole profitable to S. K.'s cause, for though the Professor
vas inclined to strut a little because of the honour accorded him,
ind though he vexed his master by divulging in his own name

thoughts which were not his own, it was fortunate that whe S. K. died in the midst of his attack on the Church there was on man at hand who could explain to the bewildered nation what all meant.

I have postponed to the last place a subject which might hav come first in this chapter were it not that it serves as a transitio to the next, being an interest which continued to absorb S. K more and more up to the end of his life.

After his return from a short visit to Berlin in the spring 1846 he bought three books by Magister A. P. Adler, and befor long his collection was enriched by four more books which th same author published all at once. S. K. was intensely occupie with these books for the space of nearly two years. Adler wa a pastor in the Danish Church who had lately been deposed fo the fact that he represented in the preface to his first book tha it was written under divine inspiration—in fact at the dictatio of Jesus Christ. His awkward retraction of this claim did not ad dignity to his fall. It showed rather, as S. K. pointed out, that h was not acquainted with the Biblical terminology, and therefor confounded the promptings of a lively mind awakened by a ne religious experience with the Scriptural conception of revelation The immediate result of S. K.'s intense study of this case wa 'the great book about Adler'.

To understand why he was so much preoccupied with 'th case of Adler' we must revert to the considerations presented i the concluding paragraph of the preceding chapter. The attac of vulgarity, which made him smart more than even under th sense of his 'heterogeneity', prompted him at the same time t accept it finally as an indication that God had a singular work fo him to perform as an exceptional individual. We have seen tha even in his youth there were adumbrations of this thought, an in *Either/Or* he contemplated the possibility that the fault exception to the universal human might eventually become excep tional in a good sense. With this thought in view he found him self compelled not only to make himself intelligible to others bu to attain an understanding of himself and of his exceptional task In several passages he has remarked that if he had not been s dialectical he might have become an extravagant enthusiast, lik Adler or many others who boast of 'new light', special guidanc

eculiar spiritual gifts, or an immediate divine call. His reflec-
ons on this subject may well serve to save from such delusions
thers who lack his unusual power of self-defence.

How can a man who recognizes himself as an extraordinary
ase think soberly of himself? When he has accepted his singu-
arity as a sign that God has appointed him to perform a singular
ask, how can he contrive not to regard himself as the singularly
lect vessel of God's grace? In fact S. K. was well defended at
is point, for the doctrine of election was exceedingly abhorrent
 him because it implied the preterition of the non-elect, and
othing was more dear to him than the belief that every single
ndividual was equally the object of God's love. From the very
eginning of his literary career he had used repeatedly and with
mphasis (as in the prefaces to the *Edifying Discourses*) the expres-
on 'without authority'; and now, with a deeper understanding,
e recurs to this sober phrase and insists upon it as his category.
 few years later he began to dwell upon the prophet as the
xample of authority in religion, but at this time he thinks only
f the apostle. The apostle is the paradigm of authority in the
hurch—the man who has an express mandate from Christ. He
und that upon the question of authority in religion his contem-
oraries were completely at sea. Just as his reflections upon *The
orsair* as a phenomenon revealed to him that his age was com-
letely confused with regard to the question of civil authority, so
ow in the case of Adler he discovers that it is equally confused
ith regard to the question of religious authority. The title he at
ne time proposed to give to this book shows that it was this
eneral confusion that concerned him, not Adler personally:[1]

THE RELIGIOUS CONFUSION OF THE PRESENT TIME
illustrated by Mag. Adler as a phenomenon
By Petrus Minor
Edited by S. Kierkegaard

He recognized that Adler had a certain sort of genius—'a con-
used genius which can be essentially described as dizziness'.
This dizzy experience of exaltation Adler himself confounded
ith revelation, and his contemporaries were no better able to
istinguish between a genius and an apostle. They conceived that
ey were exalting St. Paul when they described him as a genius,

extolled the profundity of his thought, and wondered at his dialec tical ability. Mere aesthetical categories! One might as well exto his talent as a tent-maker and affirm that there never was nor woul be an upholsterer capable of doing such wonderful work. If a so obeys his father, not because he is his father, but because he i so wonderfully clever and profound, he has turned everythin upside down. Religious authority is specifically paradoxical be cause it is related to transcendence. The root of the confusio lies in the fact that men have lost all sense of the qualitative di ference between God and man. 'If I, as some people think, ar a bit of a genius, I say, A fig for it. But an apostle is as differen from me as from the greatest genius that ever lived and th stupidest man that has lived.'

It can hardly be said that this confusion which S. K. strov to clarify no longer prevails in our generation, when men thin that even Christ is exalted when they extol him as a 'religiou genius'.

Adler was a person of no importance and would long ago hav been forgotten were it not for the interest S. K. took in his cas But as 'an epigram upon present-day Christianity' he has sign ficance:[1]

> So Mag. Adler was born, brought up and confirmed as native in geographical Christendom—thus he was a Christia (just as all the others are Christians); he became a theologic licentiate—and was a Christian (just as all the others ar Christians); he became a Christian priest and then for the fir time the curious chance befell him that through a profoun impression made upon his life he came into serious touch wit the decisive experience of what it means to become a Christian Just at this point, when by being religiously moved he undeni ably comes nearer to the experience of what it means to becom a Christian than he had come during all the time he was Christian—just at this point he is deposed. And his depositio is quite justified because the State Church only now has th opportunity to ascertain how the matter stands with regard t his Christianity. But all the same the epigrammatical applica tion still remains—that as a heathen he became a Christia priest, and when he had got somewhat nearer to the experienc of becoming a Christian he was deposed.

This passage gives an idea of the polemic against established Christianity which pervades this book. Many of the themes which afterwards were prominent in the public attack are already emphasized here—'geographical Christendom', 'we are all Christians', 'the 1800 years', &c. This is surely one of the reasons why S. K. did not publish this book. He was not yet ready to begin a frontal attack and preferred for the time being to wound from behind. But there was another reason; he was too magnanimous to strike a man when he was down. For all that, the thought of publishing recurred again and again. He took the pains to rewrite the book twice, and at one time he proposed to include it with other writings under the title of 'The Minor Works of S. Kierkegaard'. For he recognized that it expressed presuppositions which the readers of his later Discourses ought to be made acquainted with. Even now *The Book about Adler* is not published among S. K.'s *Works* in the Danish edition, but only among the *Papers* (vols. vii and viii). Fortunately it has been translated into German by Haecker, who calls it (not very happily) 'The Concept of God's Elect'.

S. K. transformed the book about Adler into a 'cycle' of essays; but in the end he contented himself with publishing in 1849 *Two Minor Ethico-Religious Treatises*, one of which—'The difference between a genius and an apostle'—was taken from this book; whereas the other—'Has a man a right to let himself be put to death for the truth?'—deals with a theme which was beginning to concern him more and more. No one can understand S. K. without knowing this 'treatise'. As a victim of the grins of the populace he reflected upon the possibility of martyrdom at the hands of the crowd. His judgement then was that a man (a mere man) has no right to do anything (even for the cause of truth) that would involve other men in the guilt of murder. In the last days of his life, however, he reversed his opinion and expected that as a consequence of his open attack upon the Church he would suffer martyrdom as 'a witness for the truth'.

In his Journal[1] S. K. significantly remarked, 'For the Apostles I always keep a separate account.' In fact he not only took pains to distinguish an Apostle from a genius but was scrupulous about keeping this category separate in every respect. To his mind the Apostle was qualitatively distinguished by the fact that he had a direct, immediate, and explicit commission from Jesus

Christ Himself while He was still visible on earth. This therefor represented an authority which could not be exactly repeated i the Church. But S. K. also kept a separate account of anothe extraordinary ministry in the Church, namely, that of the Prophe The authority of the Prophet also was direct and 'immediate but it had not a commission so ostensible. Perhaps S. K. was th only Protestant of his time to have an eye open to the poss bility of the recurrence of this extraordinary ministry. But h conceived of the ordinary ministry of the Church after the analog of the Apostolic authority. It was too explicit and ostensible, ye it was qualitatively different for the fact that it was not direct an 'immediate'; it was *derived* through ordination, which was it ostensible token—though not an infallible one. S. K. affirme again and again that the priest received his 'authority' throug ordination, which he seems therefore to have regarded as a sacra ment *ex opere operato*—which does not necessarily conflict wit his diatribe against the parsons of Denmark and his refusal t receive the viaticum from a 'royal official'. Such notions ar decidedly not Lutheran. The emphasis upon the Apostles an upon ordination might have been derived from Calvin, were not for the fact that S. K. had strangely little interest in th Reformed Church and no knowledge of its theology. On th whole we have here evidently a Catholic view of the ministry which is retained in the Anglican Communion, unaltered b the Reformation, and in some respects over-emphasized in th polemic against Rome and her 'traditions'. It should be remem bered that the Church of Denmark, though it has bishops neither has nor claims to have an episcopal succession. S. K seems to have taken no notice of this fact. At all events it di not disturb him. Ordination still remained an ostensible sign o authority, as a delegation, not from a congregation, neither fro the Church as a whole, but from Christ, however indirectly.

For the oft repeated assertion that he himself was 'withou authority' he had another reason which he thus expresses in hi Journal:[1]

'Without Authority'

That I have constantly talked about having no authorit has its ground in the fact that I myself have felt that ther was too much of the poetical in me, moreover in the fact th I feel myself assisted by a higher Power, moreover in th fact that I am built topsy-turvy; but also in the fact that I understand how my life's suffering as well as my guilt cause me to have need of Christianity on so great a scale, whereas I am constantly apprehensive of making it too heavy for some one, since he perhaps has no need of so great a scale. Such a concern, of course, neither the God-Man, nor an Apostle, could have—but I am only a poor human.

Although his physical frailty naturally reminded him constantly of the probability of an early death, the expectation of martyrdom evidently was (as he himself sometimes reflected) a product of his melancholy. A more normal religious experience is expressed by the phrase which at this time he began to use with emphasis: 'before God'. It means that, in spite of the 'distance' implied by the qualitative difference between God and man, God is ever near. At this time S. K. sometimes thought of God as menacingly near:

That a bird can live is a thing I can conceive very well: it has no notion at all that it exists before God—and I can well conceive that a man can endure the experience of existing before God when he himself does not know it. But to know that one exists before God—and then to be able to live!

Only when in 1848 he attained the experience that his sin was not only forgiven but *forgotten* by God did the phrase 'before God' become an expression of childlike confidence. But an entry of August 16, 1847, is an anticipation of this experience and may serve as a transition to the next chapter:[1]

[He resists the impulse to make a short visit to Berlin and resolves instead to take a bath-cure, which is so distasteful to him that he can be sure it is no weak foible.] That I remain at home has a far deeper reason, and I feel impelled to it. Some time I must begin to accustom myself to do without such strong diversions. . . . I feel now impelled to come to myself in a deeper sense by coming nearer to God in the understanding of myself. I must remain on the spot *and be renewed inwardly*. . . . I must try to get a better hold upon my melancholy. Hitherto it has reposed in the deepest recesses, and my prodigious mental exertion has helped to hold it down. That I have profited others by my work and that God has approved it and has helped me in every way is perfectly certain.

I thank Him again and again that He has done for me infinitely more than I had expected. Sure as it is that no man has any merit before God, yet it is my comfort that He has been well pleased to see my endeavour, that in my frightful sufferings I have endured to the utmost by His aid. I know within myself before God that my labour as an author, my readiness to obey His signal, to sacrifice every earthly and worldly consideration, will mitigate for me the impression of the evil I personally have committed. Just because I began my work as an author with a troubled conscience I have striven with the utmost care to make it so pure that it might be a little abatement of my debt. This purity, disinterestedness, diligence, is what appears in the eyes of the world to be madness. That God regards it differently I know—without implying that in His eyes it might be so pure that before Him I can dare to boast of it.

But now God will have it differently. There moves in me something that indicates a metamorphosis. Just for this cause I did not dare to take the trip to Berlin—for that would be a way to produce an abortion. I shall therefore keep myself quiet, not exert myself too much in any way, indeed hardly at all, not begin a new book, but try to come to myself, *to think thoroughly the thought of my melancholy together with God on the spot.* In that way my melancholy must be relieved and *Christianity come closer to me.* Hitherto I have defended myself against my melancholy by intellectual labour which keeps it at a distance—now I must see what can be done . . ., with faith that God in forgiving has forgotten what guilt there is, in forgetting it oneself, but not any distraction, not any aloofness from it, but in God, that in thinking of God I must think that He has forgotten it, and so learn to dare to forget it myself in forgiveness.

KIERKEGAARD AT HIS HIGH DESK

Oil painting by LUPLAU JANSSEN

PART FIVE
BECOMING A CHRISTIAN
1848–52

And that should teach us
There's a divinity that shapes our ends,
Rough-hew them how we will.

HAMLET.

I. METAMORPHOSIS
1848

KIERKEGAARD completed his 35th year on May 5, 1848. It is difficult to think of him as so young a man, yet he was young enough to be converted again, to experience a change in his whole nature, to become a new man, incredibly older, in a sense, because he had become spirit, and yet eternally young. These are his own expressions. Ten years had passed since his first conversion (the experience of 'an indescribable joy'), and within this interval of time we have noted several occasions which marked new progress in his apprehension of Christianity. Before the completion of his 35th year he had written 15 religious books (75 Discourses in all) over his own name, besides 5 'aesthetical' works which had a religious aim, and 2 philosophical works which had the effect of throwing into sharpest relief the distinctive categories of Christianity. When I describe him now as 'becoming a Christian' I do not mean to disparage or to stamp as unchristian the quality of his life and activity before this final conversion. I simply use the expression which S. K. persisted in using about himself, more emphatically after this new conversion than before it, and continued to use to the end of his life. He assumed that it was appropriate as a description of 'Christians' in general, and it might be profitable for us to consider whether we might not well apply it to ourselves. St. Paul gave expression to the same thought when he said, 'not as though I had already attained'. This phrase which S. K. used with reference to his life as a whole is particularly appropriate here where his progress in Christianity was most manifest and most decisive.

And of course I do not mean to imply that the period of intellectual maturity was passed before he attained to spiritual maturity. Dying in his 42nd year he did not reach the age when one might expect to observe signs of senility, and in fact his extraordinary powers suffered no eclipse, no slightest obscuration, up to the end of his life. We shall see that his attack upon the Church gives us no reason to suspect that illness had by that time obscured the power of his intellect or shaken the balance of his moral judgement.

Professor Hirsch[1] says that 'the year 1848 represents the climax of Kierkegaard's intellectual productiveness'. He affirms that '*The Sickness unto Death* and *Training in Christianity* (his two masterpieces as a Christian author) and *The Point of View* (a religious autobiography so unique that it has no parallel in the whole literature of the world) have more prospect than any other Christian theological productions of the nineteenth century of finding a place among the imperishable writings of the Christian Church'.

S. K. himself says in an entry of September 1849:[2]

Concerning the year 1848

1848 potentiated me in one sense, in another sense it broke me, that is to say, religiously it broke me, or, as I put it in my language, God had run me to a standstill. He has suffered me to undertake a task which even in reliance upon Him I could not lift in a higher form, I must take it up in a lower form. And hence this thing has become really my own religious or more inwardly religious education in an inverse fashion. In a certain sense I would be so glad to venture [he is thinking of the danger involved in making an attack upon the established order]; my imagination lures and incites me; but I must just learn to be good enough to venture in a lower form [i.e. pseudonymously]. It [*The Sickness unto Death*] is certainly the truest and most perfect thing I have written; but my relation to it must not be such as to make it seem as if it is I that come down upon all the others with an almost damning judgement—no, I must myself first of all be educated by it; there is perhaps no one that has a right to be so deeply humbled by it as I before I have a right to publish it.

Economic anxieties come upon me suddenly and all too near. Two such heterogeneous weights as the opposition of the world and anxiety about my subsistence I am unable to lift at the same time. Then the confusion suddenly breaks loose. For a few months the situation was such that to-morrow I might perhaps own nothing at all but be actually in financial need. That went hard with me. All the more powerfully did my spirit react. I produced more powerfully than ever before, but more than ever before like a dying man. [He confidently expected to die within that year.] In the direction of Christianity it is the highest yet accorded me, that is true. But in another sense it is too high for me to assume responsibility for it in my lifetime and step out openly in this role. That is the deeper significance of the new pseudonym [Anti-Climacus] who is higher than I am.

In another place he says of the year 1848[1]: 'It was beyond all comparison the richest and most fruitful year I have experienced as an author.' The long passage quoted above suggests more topics than we can deal with in this place, and I have introduced it here as a programme, not of this chapter only, but of the fifth part as a whole. But here I need to explain that the 'confusion' which threatened S. K. with penury was the war with Germany which began in March 1848 and the great revolution which compelled the king to grant parliamentary government to Denmark. S. K. complained pathetically that his faithful man-servant was conscripted just when he most needed his help in moving away from his old home on the Nytorv—'they took my Anders from me'. Everybody's fortune was imperilled by the revolution, and S. K. actually lost a good part of the price he received for the sale of his house, having invested it in 'royal bonds', which subsequently fell in value. He blamed himself for making so bad an investment, but doubtless he was prompted to do it by the recollection that in the critical year 1813 his father had greatly increased his fortune by investing the whole of it in this same security.

The works which S. K. produced so abundantly in 1848 were none of them published until the following year—some of them not until after his death. I shall give an account of these works in the next chapter, and in the chapter following that I shall describe the grievous embarrassment he was in about publishing them. This present chapter deals with the religious conversion which occurred in Holy Week 1848. This experience cannot be briefly described, because, sudden as it was, it was evidently a crystallizing point up to which the reflections of 1847 were leading, and from which the resolutions of 1849 derived. Although S. K. had the psychic disposition characteristic of twice-born men, as is shown by the sudden transformations he underwent, yet his voluminous Journals enable us to perceive how gradual was the labour of reflection which led up to these changes, and also to trace the permanent effects they had upon his life. The quotation with which we concluded the last chapter is one of the amazing instances of anticipation which the Journals not infrequently reveal. The thought that God forgets as well as forgives, which was the liberating idea in his new experience, was clearly expressed eight months before the date of his conversion. We must understand, however, that it was not yet realized, and that even as a thought he did not hold it securely in his possession. All this long interval of time and the exercise of laborious reflection was required before he could make it his own.

To measure the distance that had to be travelled I quote the confession of faith which S. K. made at the end of 1847 in 'Thoughts which Wound from Behind'.[1] He found himself obliged by the context to make a personal confession of faith. For in preaching on the text, 'He was believed on in the world' (1 Tim. 3: 16), he argues that if no single individual has the courage to say openly, '*I* have believed on Him', there is no knowing if ever He was believed on in the world. There can be no doubt that he expresses here his own belief, but because he had not yet become bold enough to use direct communication, he ascribes this confession to a hypothetical 'individual':

> I have believed much in the world which trustworthy men related to me about things which I myself have neither heard nor seen, I have believed the testimony of history; in daily life I have in such manifold ways believed others. Among the things I have thus believed there is much that is unimportant and is forgotten the next day, much that has occupied me for a considerable time, much that I have transformed into my soul's possession and accepted as my necessary task—but yet, supposing that the whole sum of this were untrue, it is a loss I could put up with. But I have believed on Him—if in this too I am deceived, I am not only of all men most miserable, but then my life is nullified in its deepest root, so that nothing can either help or hurt me any more. For I have not held time at arm's length year after year, waiting for new and ever new security in order to dare to believe; no, by an eternal decision I have secured my life by believing on Him—if He is a delusion, my life is lost. But this is not so, for I *believe*. I have already encountered, therefore, and sustained the temptation involved in staking all upon uncertainty, which is what believing is. But

faith has conquered, I believe on Him. Will any one say to me, 'But *if!*', that is a thing I no longer understand. I understood it once in the instant of decision, now I understand it no more. Will any one be anxious and fearful on my account, that because of an 'if' or in spite of an 'if' I risked my life so far out—let him not bewail me but rather himself. I do not live by any 'if'. I am stoutly against an 'if', in dread of this 'if'. I ventured out so far (that is what properly is venturing), now I believe. But that word 'if' which must be understood in the first instance when one is grasping faith, is again the word and the thing which faith understands least of all.

So might the individual speak. And I allow him to speak on so that he may interpret this clause in the Scriptural text, which elsewhere is never interpreted.

'I have admired what has been produced among men in the way of the noble, the great, the glorious. I do not mean that I am acquainted with it all, but I know that in relation to what I am acquainted with my soul is not a stranger to the delight of admiration, its blissful joy. . . . To take an example which, humanly speaking, stands absolutely alone and which people are accustomed to bring into closest relation to Christianity, I have admired that noble, simple wise man of ancient times [Socrates], my heart too has beat violently as did that of the young man [Alcibiades] when he conversed with him; the thought of him has been the enthusiasm of my youth and filled my soul to overflowing. . . . I have admired his wisdom, that in wisdom he remained simple so that he could catch the shrewd! That in wisdom he remained simple, so that without having many thoughts and without using many words he could sacrifice his life in the service of truth—Oh, touching simplicity! That with death before his eyes he talked about himself, the condemned man, just as simply as ever he did in the market-place with a passer-by about the most commonplace subject; that with the goblet of poison in his hand he preserved a festive air and talked just as simply as ever he did at a banquet—Oh, sublime simplicity!—But I have never believed on him, that has never occurred to me. I count it also neither wise nor profound to institute a comparison between him, the simple wise man, and Him on whom I believe—that I count blasphemy. Whenever

I reflect upon the matter of my salvation, then is he, the simple wise man, a highly indifferent person, an insignificance, a naught. I could not at all, could not possibly get it into my head or into my heart or across my lips to make answer to the blasphemous question, to which of these two I owe most—the simple wise man or Him on whom I believe. But on the other hand I can truly make answer to the question to whom I owe most, most of all, most beyond all comparison—Him, namely, on whom I have believed, Him who has given his life also for me, staked his life, not as one man can do for another to *preserve* his life, no, rather to *give* me life. For without Him it is indifferent whether I live or die, it is an empty phrase that some one has saved my life when this life he saved means only to be dead. But He is life, to Him eternally I owe life, Him on whom I believe.

With the very feeling with which I am conscious of being myself I cling tightly in filial devotion to the man to whom I owe life—but I crave to be dispensed from answering the question, to which of these I owe most, him the father, or Him on whom I have believed. In case it were required of me, that is, in case He were to require it of me, I will not hesitate to wound myself more feelingly than any man could wound me, to relinquish a son's love—out of love to Him on whom I believe. . . .

As a confession of faith this is of course more intensive than extensive. But it is clearly a Christian confession, a personal appropriation of Christ as Saviour. 'Also for me' is an echo of one of his earliest independent religious perceptions (p. 163). There is nothing in this passage to betray the fact that this very positive expression of faith was not an all-inclusive faith. But in fact S. K. was still troubled by a profound incredulity. Not only had he failed as yet to appropriate the thought that God can forget as well as forgive, but (in close connexion with this) he was incredulous of the power of God to help him temporally when He saved him eternally. It was the more difficult for him to overcome these incredulities because he had succeeded in disguising them as an expression of pious humility. Innumerable passages could be quoted to illustrate the incredulity which still possessed him, but I prefer to cite an entry written after his conversion, because, while it starts far back with a review of his earlier condition, it carries us up to and through this critical experience. Incidentally this passage has a particular interest to me because it shows with what entire abandon S. K. could reveal himself when he was not explicitly speaking of himself but of an indefinite individual, 'one'. I imagine that such entries must have slipped from his pen with the ease of automatic writing. The spirit 'control' was obviously enough S. K. himself. In *The Point of View* he gives some account of the spontaneity of his writing, of the thoughts which welled up so abundantly that they needed to be controlled by divine governance. That of course is the specific quality of genius. It is observable in very many of his writings, and though the simple passage I am about to quote has no poetical colour, it is one of the many entries in the Journal which, to use his own expression, seem to have been written with 'a guided pen—though not in this case guided by God'.[1]

The majority of men (if they find that from the earliest age it is their lot to bear one suffering or another, one cross or another, one of those sorrowful limitations of the soul) begin by hoping, or, as they say, believing, that it may yet go better, that God will make it up to them, &c., and then at length when no change occurs they come little by little to rely upon the help of eternity, i.e. they resign themselves and find strength in contenting themselves with the eternal.—The deeper nature, or he whom God has fashioned on a more eternal plan, begins at once to understand that this is a thing he must bear as long as he has to live, he dare not require of God such an extraordinary paradoxical help. But in this case God is love just the same, nothing is more certain to him. So he is resigned, and inasmuch as the eternal lies close to him he thus finds repose, blessedly assured all the while that God is love. But the suffering he must put up with. Then in the course of time, when he becomes more concrete in the actuality of life, comes more and more to himself as a temporal being, when time and its succession exercises its power over him, when in spite of all his effort it becomes so difficult to live on with the assistance only of the eternal, when he becomes in a more humble sense a human being or learns what it means to be human (for in his resignation he is still too ideal or too abstract, for which reason also

there is something of despair in such resignation)—then the
possibility of faith presents itself to him in this form: whether
he will believe by virtue of the absurd that God will help him
temporally. (Here lie all the paradoxes.) So the forgiveness of
sin also means to be helped temporally, otherwise it is mere
resignation, which can endure to bear the punishment, though
still convinced that God is love. But belief in the forgiveness
of sins is to believe that here in time the sin is forgotten by
God, that it is really true that God forgets.

I could point to many earlier reflections in the Journals which
led almost up to this point. The approach was gradual. But why
was it so very hard for S. K. to believe fully in the forgiveness of
his sins, or to believe that they were fully forgiven? How many
take it as a matter of course! Heine on his 'mattress grave'
satirized the easy-going 'faith' of his age when in response to the
query whether he trusted in God's forgiveness he responded
lightly, 'Oh, he'll forgive me—that's what he's for—*c'est son
métier*.' And how many there are who have the knack of forgiving
themselves! No wonder that S. K.'s persistent incredulity i
regarded by many as a symptom of morbidity. It is true enough
that it had to do with his melancholy, indeed with the deepest
root of it, but we shall find reason to think that the fixed idea of hi
own and his father's sin was not so much the effect of his melan
choly as its cause. The entry I am about to quote is a classica
expression of the normal Christian experience:[1]

Something about the forgiveness of sins

Just as the first expression of a true and deep experience o
human love is the feeling of one's own personal unworthiness
so the longing after the forgiveness of sins is the evident sig
that a man loves God. But no man by himself can hit upon th
thought that God loves him. It must be proclaimed to mar
This is the Gospel, Revelation. But just because no man o
himself can hit upon the thought that God loves him, just fo
this reason can no man of himself conceive how great a sinne
he is. The Augsburg Confession consistently teaches that
must be revealed to a man how great a sinner he is. For with
out a divine scale to measure with no one is the great sinne
(that he is only . . . before God).

But both sides correspond to one another: when a man do

not conceive how great a sinner he is, he cannot love God; and when (in response to the proclamation how highly God loves him) he does not love God, he cannot conceive how great a sinner he is. The inwardness of the consciousness of sin is just the passion of love. For it is true that the Law makes one a sinner—but love makes one a far greater sinner. It is true that one who fears God and trembles feels himself a sinner, but he who truly loves feels himself a still greater sinner.

If S. K., while believing in forgiveness of sin in general, found it peculiarly difficult to believe in the complete forgiveness of his own sin, this was at least partly due to the sense he had of being a 'single individual' pricked out from the crowd, deprived of the security one feels in the companionship of men, and standing directly under the eye of God. He felt to the full how intolerable this position is to any man, let alone to a sinner. I have already quoted what he says of the difficulty of living 'before God' (see p. 387).

He says in another place:[1]

> But to be thus before God, however blessed it may be, when viewed from the other side is prodigiously exacting.

It is at this time that the expression 'before God' begins to be used with peculiar emphasis. We encounter it constantly in the Journals, and it emerges in *The Sickness unto Death* as a decisive category. One chapter of the book is devoted to this subject, regarding it as the 'decisive qualification' of man as a self having full consciousness of selfhood:[2]

> The gradation in the consciousness of self which up to this point we have been concerned with lies within the definition of the human self, or the self whose measure is man. But this self acquires a new quality and qualification by the fact that it is the self in direct apposition to God. This self is no longer the merely human self, but it is what I should call (hoping not to be misunderstood) the theological self, the self in direct apposition to God.

Perhaps the meaning of this might be better expressed by saying 'face to face with God'. It implies the 'I-and-Thou relationship' with God which Martin Buber has emphasized.

> Where then is the possibility of offence? It lies in the fact that a man should have a realization of being a *single individual* person in direct apposition to God; and then (what follows in turn from this), that a man's sin should be a matter of concern to God. This notion of the single individual man 'before God' is something that speculation never can get into its head; all it does is to universalize the individual man fantastically in the race.

This is as much as to say, as in other places S. K. does say expressly, that the forgiveness of sin is a paradox—no less paradoxical than the God-Man—and hence can be accepted only by faith, 'by virtue of the absurd'.

In view of this qualification, 'before God', it is not to be wondered at that S. K. was slow in appropriating with full confidence the forgiveness of his own sin. *The Sickness unto Death* was written before his last conversion, but it was revised during the two months immediately following it. In this case it is not possible to discern between cause and effect, to distinguish what was written before the decisive moment of conversion and what was added or altered after it. And fortunately it is not important to make such a distinction; for the fundamental concepts of this book afford the clearest proof of the fact that through a process of reflection S. K. had reached a position closely approximating to the conviction which suddenly surged up into the clear field of consciousness at the moment when the following entries were made:[1]

NB NB

Wednesday April 19 [Wednesday in Holy Week 1848]

My whole nature is changed. My closeness and reservedness are broken—I must speak.

Great God, grant me grace!

That is indeed a true word my father said about me: 'Nothing will come of you so long as you have money.' He spoke prophetically. He supposed that I should drink and revel. But not that exactly. No, but what with my mental acumen and my melancholy and my money—oh, what a favourable condition for developing the torments of self-torture in my heart!

Such a strange coincidence: just when I had decided to speak, my physician comes in. However, I did not speak to him, it seemed to me too sudden. But my resolution to speak holds firm.

Maundy Thursday and Good Friday have become true holy days for me. [*Appended as a note to the above.*]

Alas, she was unable to break the silence of my melancholy. . . . Now by God's help I shall become myself, I believe now that Christ will help me to triumph over my melancholy, and then I shall become a priest.

In this melancholy I have still loved the world, for I have loved my melancholy. Everything has helped to key up my relationship higher: her suffering, all my exertion, and finally that I have lived as an object of derision, has by God's help, now at the end when I am brought to the pass of needing to be anxious about my subsistence, conduced to prompt me to break through.

The reader may be surprised to observe that this explosive entry has nothing to say about the forgiveness of sins. Hence he may doubt the relevancy of the factors we have adduced to explain this new conversion. But it must be observed that this entry deals not at all with causes but only with effects ('my whole nature is changed')—really only with one effect ('I must speak'). Here it is clear that 'I must' implies *I can*. For the first time he felt that his tongue was loosed, as by a miracle. This is the theme of the whole passage. 'I did not *speak* to my physician, but my resolution to *speak* holds firm.' This new-found freedom reminds him sorrowfully of the critical moment of his life when he could not speak (could not make himself 'manifest' to Regina) and so could not marry—'Alas, she was unable to break the silence of my melancholy'. Knowing as we do that this secretiveness, closeness, morbid reserve was the most specific effect of his melancholy, the thraldom he has so long groaned under, the 'chain which rattles with every step I take', we can understand how he could exclaim exultantly, 'My whole nature is changed.' But this freedom could not have been won before the 'thorn in the flesh' was removed, his 'fundamental misery' relieved, the 'dark spot' erased, his own and his father's guilt *forgotten*, and with that the sombre thought annulled that he was condemned to do penance all the days of his life for a sin forgiven but not forgotten. 'A darling child has many names', is a proverb S. K. often quotes, and it can be aptly applied in this connexion. He was unable to 'pull out' the thorn, and was even unwilling to do it, until he understood it as a commandment, 'Thou shalt'.[1]

> Essentially this is the everlastingly comforting thing about the doctrine of the forgiveness of sins: Thou shalt believe it. For when the anxious conscience begins to employ itself with heavy thoughts and it seems to one as if in all eternity it would be impossible to forget—then the word is, Thou shalt forget, thou *shalt* stop thinking about thy sin, thou hast not only a right to stop, it is not merely that thou mayest make bold to pray to God for permission to dare to forget it; no, thou shalt forget, for thou shalt believe that thy sin is forgiven.

This was the thought that 'heals radically', the 'Christian medical art' about which he at this time proposed to write. We may remember that in his youth he had shrunk from Christianity with the perception that it must be 'a radical cure'. He had learnt in the meantime that to welcome such a radical cure one must know that one is a sinner.

The cure was radical, as we shall see in the sequel, but it was not at once complete, not so prompt as S. K. at first supposed. A few days later he made this disconsolate entry:[2]

> NB NB
>
> Monday after Easter.
>
> No, no, my reservedness cannot be eliminated, at least not yet. The thought of eliminating it by force of will has the effect of preoccupying me so much that it only gets more and more firmly fixed.
>
> It comforts me, however, that I have spoken to my physician. . . .
>
> I believe indeed in the forgiveness of sins, but I understand it as I have hitherto, in the sense that I must bear my punishment as long as life lasts by remaining in the painful imprisonment of this morbid reserve, remote in a deeper sense from community with men—yet with mitigation in the thought that God has forgiven me. I cannot yet achieve such confidence of faith as to believe this painful recollection away. But by believing I defend myself against despair, contrive to bear the painful punishment of morbid reserve—and am so indescribably

happy or blessed in the activity of spirit which God has so graciously granted me.

This marks indeed a serious relapse, and yet it does not describe the case as altogether hopeless. He says, 'at least not yet', and he had mustered up courage to speak to his physician. 'And what in effect did the physician have to say? Nothing. But for me it has its importance that I have shown deference to the human tribunal.' We have reason to expect that with so reflective a disposition S. K. would require some time to chew the cud and assimilate the fruit of his experience. And if we are disposed to be impatient with him, we should remember that it was not an ordinary conflict he was engaged in but the most stubborn sort psychologists have described—the attempt to overcome a 'compulsion idea'. He had not given up the conflict, but he was shrewd enough to recognize that the tactics he at first sought to employ were worse than futile. The last sentence in this entry reads: 'The determination to eliminate a morbid reserve by thinking constantly about eliminating it leads directly to the opposite result.' The very next entry (written perhaps on the same day) shows how far he was from giving up the conflict. It comments upon the one story in the Gospels which associates forgiveness of sin with the recovery of psychical and bodily freedom:[1]

> It was a miracle when Christ said to the paralytic, Thy sins are forgiven thee, arise and walk. But if this miracle does not now happen to me—what a miraculous boldness of faith is involved in believing that the sin is entirely forgotten so that the remainder of it has no anguish, in believing that one has become a new man so that one hardly can recognize oneself again!

And on a loose leaf we find this:[2]

> When one has thus verily experienced and experiences what it is to believe in the forgiveness of sins, he has surely become another man; all is forgotten—yet with him it is not as with a child which when it is forgiven becomes the same child again. No, he has become an eternity older, for he has now become spirit, the whole of immediacy with its selfish clinging to the world and to itself is lost. Humanly speaking, he is now old, prodigiously old, but eternally he is young.

The next following was written immediately after the entry of May 11 (see p. 397) which I had reason to quote out of its chronological order and before the entry about Wednesday in Holy Week:[1]

> And now [after he has recited the story of his ineffectual struggle with melancholy], now that in many ways I am brought to extremities, now (ever since last Easter, though with intermissions), now there is awakened a hope in my soul that God might be willing to relieve that fundamental misery of mine, that is to say, now I am dealing with faith in the strictest sense. Faith is immediacy after reflection. As a poet and thinker I have depicted everything in the medium of imagination, while I myself was living in resignation. Now life comes closer to me, or I am coming closer to myself, coming to myself.—To God all things are possible. This thought is now in the deepest sense my solution, it has acquired a significance for me which I have never before reflected upon. That because I do not see any way out, I must not for an instant be so presumptuous as to say that there could be no way for God. For this is despair and presumption, to confound one's bit of imagination with the possibility God disposes of.

In an entry of 1848 S. K. compares himself to a leaky boat[2]:

> I ventured out upon life with a fundamental leak from the earliest time—precisely because of the immense effort at the pumps which was required to keep my existence afloat I developed an eminently intellectual existence.

He means the same thing when he speaks of the thorn in the flesh:[3]

> From the earliest time I have winced at a thorn in the flesh, to which also a consciousness of sin and guilt associated itself. I have felt myself heterogeneous. This pain, this heterogeneousness of mine, I have understood as my God-relationship.
>
> My life is completely arranged with a thorn in the flesh—to attain what I never would have dreamed. But the question which I must raise now and then is, whether I ought not to direct my attention to getting the thorn out of the flesh if

possible. Have I a right to attempt such a thing, even in case it were possible, which I doubt—in my earlier youth I made an effort in this direction.

The earlier occasion when he thought of 'repairing the leak' and drawing out the thorn was when he was engaged to Regina—and at that time he concluded that it was hopeless: 'I broke my engagement because I could not believe that God would relieve my fundamental misery, take away my almost crazy melancholy.' At that time too he consulted his physician:[1]

> Although no friend of confidants, although absolutely disinclined to talk with others about my most inward interests, I believe and have always believed that it is a man's duty not to ignore the court of first resort, which is the counsel one can receive from another man—if only this is not a silly familiarity but a serious and official communication. Therefore I spoke with my physician, to learn whether he thought that the discordancy between the bodily and the psychical in my constitution could be removed so that I might realize the universal. This he doubted. I asked him whether he thought that by the exercise of the will the mind might be capable of transforming such a fundamental discordancy. He doubted it. He would not even counsel me to put to the test the whole power of my will, of which he had a conception, since I might explode the whole thing.

This entry has occasioned an immense amount of speculation. To me it seems plausible to suppose that, as in the later instance, the thing that most concerned S. K. was his morbid reserve, but that at the earlier date it was impossible for him to 'speak' because he conceived that he was bound to make open confession of his secret sin. And if this was the case, I cannot wonder that the physician, knowing his physical frailness, would not take the responsibility of counselling him to do what would cost him exquisite anguish and perhaps his life. We must remember that this took place nearly a century ago, when von Feuchtersleben's epoch-making little book on the hygiene of the heart (*Diätetik der Seele*) had only just been published (1838) and Kant's letters on 'The Power of the Mind by a Mere Resolution to Master the Feeling of Sickness' were known only to a few. And even to-day when such notions have been popularized a physician might well hesitate to advise a man so frail as S. K. to exert the full power of his will in the way that he proposed.

Having in mind the fact that S. K. had at one time so seriously reflected upon the grim necessity of making a public confession of his sin, it would not be unnatural to suppose that now his exclamation 'I must speak!' implied a recurrence of that thought. But in fact that thought was banished when once he was convinced that God had forgotten. He felt no need any longer to make a confession of his sin, but he felt all the more need to make a confession of his faith. We can be sure it was not a confession of sin he made to his physician—that was not a competent 'tribunal' for such a case. The sequel instructs us what he meant by 'I must speak'. He was recurring to the generic idea of confession expressed in the dictum of the Judge, that 'it is the duty of every man to be manifest'. He had ignored this maxim for a long time, having succeeded in suppressing it below the threshold of consciousness because it was an ideal which he was not able to realize. He had set up a defensive mechanism against its recurrence by stressing the importance of 'double reflection', 'indirect communication', 'hidden inwardness', 'religion A with humour as incognito', &c. Whatever may be said in favour of these notions, it is evident that they are the polar opposite of the Judge's maxim; and when S. K. reverted to this earlier ideal he implicitly repudiated the concepts he had been dealing with for so long a time. He could truly say, 'My whole nature is changed.' The use of pseudonyms, as they had hitherto been employed, was discarded. For though the pseudonym Anti-Climacus was the new invention of this period, it did not make it doubtful that S. K. was speaking in his own person. Though he did not expressly repudiate the method of indirect communication, which he still held to be appropriate at certain times, yet he began to suspect in it a particular daimonia, he was ready to learn from Solomon that 'there is a time to speak', and he recognized that for him the time to speak out had come. In 1851[1] he remarked that though he had begun with indirect communication, with the aim of compelling people to take notice of Christianity, he had no right to end with it. It is true that Christ employed it up to the last. As the paradoxical God-Man he could do no other. Socrates also cannot be condemned for using it up to the last. 'It is the highest form of communication, but it is appropriate only to supermen. Hence I have never ventured to use it at all over my own name. On the contrary, I have poetically produced imaginary persons with an ideal consistency which is more than human.'

For a long while after the experience of Easter 1848 the entries in the Journal are largely concerned with reflections about the forgiveness of sins, but the other theme which emerges prominently is the question of direct communication. His reflections upon this subject were endless, but it is a proof of radical healing that his deeds had not to wait upon the termination of his reflections. He began at once to plan the outspoken books which he was to write during the course of this year. The themes of two of them occurred to him precisely at the time of his conversion. The first concept of the Discourses about the Lilies and the Birds is registered in the entry[1] immediately preceding the ejaculation 'I must speak'; and the theme 'Come hither' (which was developed in the first part of *Training in Christianity*) was jotted down on Easter Even. We learn subsequently that the specific answer to the question what it was he felt compelled (and empowered) to 'speak' is to be found in *The Point of View for my Work as an Author* and the other self-revealing writings which accompanied it. Recognizing that the great literary works he had produced with so much labour had not been understood because of the employment of the method of indirect communication, and that the serious purpose they had would never be understood so long as he (through his own fault) was completely misunderstood, he felt it incumbent upon him to drop his incognito and explain himself, if not to his contemporaries, at least to the generations that were to follow them—to explain himself so far as was necessary for the understanding of the serious purpose of his books, and above all to assert that from first to last he was a Christian writer. Hence the significance of the words he attached to the title: 'A Direct Communication, A Report to History.'

'The religion of hidden inwardness' which had for so long been his pet virtue was soon to become his pet aversion and the object of his most bitter satire. Already in *The Works of Love* the polemic against it was begun. He had begun to suspect that the commonest and the greatest danger was a religion that was all too hidden, that the claim to the possession of Christianity in hidden inwardness might be only a subterfuge, a cloak intended to hide the fact that there was nothing beneath it. From henceforth he wanted no incognito for himself and would not tolerate it in others. So thoroughly was his nature changed! But at the moment of his 'conversion' the change was only potential. We shall see in the following chapters how long he had to struggle before he could acquire boldness to step out openly in the character of his role.

II. BACK TO CHRISTIANITY!

1848–9

MINDFUL of the fact that I have described the tendency of S. K.'s first great works as 'Away from the Aesthetical!', and the works ascribed to Johannes Climacus as 'Away from Speculation!', I use here the title 'Back to Christianity!' to indicate the character and tendency not only of the works ascribed to Anti-Climacus but of the whole production of 1848. It is to be understood, however, that this was emphatically the tendency of all the works which followed and that it could be used as well for a description of the pamphleteering attack upon the Church. This chapter essays to describe briefly the works which were written in 1848, most of which were published the following year. But even this chapter is in a measure biographical, because all of S. K.'s works reflect his personal progress. It is very evident that all the works produced during this year reflect the religious 'metamorphosis' which culminated at Easter.

But before speaking of the works which actually were written, I mention several which were merely proposed. At the beginning of 1848 (in January) S. K. proposed to offer to subscribers 'a course of lectures on the organizing tendency of my whole literary work',[1] and an entry of the same month proposed a fortnightly publication for subscribers entitled 'Edifying Readings'.[2] Although these plans went no further than the Journal, it is highly significant that S. K. thought of resorting even to lectures as a means of getting his ideas across. He was painfully aware that no one even suspected there was an organic unity in his work, and to explain it he was ready now to employ the most direct methods of communication.

The Sickness unto Death was the first work produced in 1848, and S. K. was justified in regarding it as the greatest of his religious works. It shows how profoundly he was influenced by Luther at this time. Luther had dwelt upon the dreadfulness of the sin of doubting the forgiveness of sin. Essentially it is not a pseudonymous work, in spite of the fact that when it came to be published it was ascribed to Anti-Climacus. Clearly it is S. K.

who is speaking in his own person all the way through. We have already had occasion to make a few quotations from this book, a few more will be produced here, and a synopsis of the themes it deals with is presented in Appendix IV. But this is not the sort of a book one can get an idea of without reading it and without reading it more than once. One may not at first realize the importance of the problems it handles. The first impression is baffling because there is nothing in the literature of the world with which it can be compared. To this one exception must be made. This later work of S. K.'s is essentially so like his earlier work on *The Concept of Dread* that it might almost be regarded as a very much expanded edition of it—understanding that the expansion is in the direction of depth as well as of breadth. Both books are properly described in the title as 'psychological' studies, and both deal (essentially, if not formally) with the same subjects: sin and faith. And yet in a sense they are like concentric circles which touch one another at no point, or rather they are like two ellipses described from the same foci, sin and faith. 'Despair' is formally indicated as the principal theme of the latter book, but the whole importance of despair, which in itself is the sickness unto death, lies in the fact that instead of plunging a man into more outrageous sin, it may prompt him to seek healing through faith. Here S. K. is operating with a more profound definition of faith than he had at his disposal when he wrote the earlier work. I quote the definition as it is given in the concluding words of the book:[1]

> The formula for the state or condition where there is no despair at all: By relating itself to itself and by willing to be itself, the self is grounded transparently in the Power which posited it. Which formula again, as has been often pointed out, is the definition of faith.

Perhaps these last words of the book may sound more intelligible after one has read the words with which the book begins—I say only 'perhaps':[2]

> Despair is a sickness in the spirit, in the self, and so can assume one of three forms: in despair at not being conscious of having a self (improperly called despair); in despair at not willing to be one's self; in despair at willing to be one's self. [This is printed in heavy type as a title.]

Man is spirit. But what is spirit? Spirit is the self. But what is the self? The self is a relationship which relates itself to itself, or is that in the relationship which accounts for the fact that the relationship relates itself to itself; the self is not the relationship but lies in the fact that the relationship relates itself to itself. Man is a synthesis of infinitude and finiteness, of the temporal and the eternal, of freedom and necessity—a synthesis in short. A synthesis is a relationship between two. Regarded in this way, man is not yet a self.

In the relationship between two, the relationship itself is the third factor, which constitutes a negative unity, and the two relate themselves to the relationship and in the relationship to the relationship—such a relationship is the relationship between soul and body, when nothing higher than the concept of soul is considered. On the other hand, if the relationship relates itself to itself, then this relationship is the positive third factor, and this is the self.

If any one is inclined to complain that this is not perfectly clear, let him try his own hand at defining what spirit is—a problem which no one nowadays ventures to deal with, either because it is supposed to be impossible, or because it is assumed that spirit does not exist—or even soul, for that matter. S. K. was well aware that he could not write this book in such a way that it would be intelligible to all. He says in the Preface:[1]

Many will perhaps consider this 'treatment' strange; it will seem to them too strictly exact to be edifying, and too edifying to be strictly scientific. So far as the last statement is concerned, I have no opinion to express. On the other hand, concerning the first statement, it does not express my opinion; and if it were the case that it is too strictly exact to be edifying, that according to my conception is a fault. It is one thing to assert that it cannot be edifying to every one, seeing that not every one has the requisite qualification for following it; it is another thing to assert that it has the character of edification. In a Christian interest everything, positively everything, ought to serve for edification. The sort of scientific treatment which in the end is not edifying is for that very reason unchristian. All presentations of Christianity must have a likeness to the physician's discourse beside the sick-bed; although only one

> who is versed in medicine can understand it, it should not b
> forgotten that it is pronounced beside the sick-bed. . . .
>
> In one sense, therefore, this little work is such as a seminar
> student could write; yet in another sense, perhaps, it is such a
> not every professor could write.

It cannot seem a trifling thing to ignore the existence of spiri
when we perceive that with this is involved the existence of a self
Speaking of the fantastic despair which is due to 'lack of finiteness'
S. K. has this to say:[1]

> But because a man has become so fantastical and hence i
> fallen into despair, which in most cases becomes manifest, h
> may, nevertheless, be perfectly able to live on, be a man to al
> appearance, engage in temporal affairs, marry, beget children
> enjoy honour and repute—and no one perhaps notices that in
> deeper sense he lacks a self. Not much ado is made in th
> world about such a thing; for a self is the last thing to be in
> quired about in the world, and to let it be noticed that one ha
> such a thing is exceedingly dangerous. The greatest possibl
> danger, that of losing one's 'self', can pass as quietly as if i
> were nothing. No loss can pass so quietly; every other loss
> that of an arm, a leg, $5, a wife, is sure to be noticed.

We plunge deeper (yet not too deep for edification) when w
hearken to what S. K. has to say about sin. This is the point wher
he broke decisively with 'the simple wise man of ancient time
whom he so heartily admired:[2]

> Hence Socrates does not indicate sin definitely—whic
> surely is a flaw in a definition of sin. If sin is ignorance, si
> does not exist, for properly sin is consciousness. . . . Wha
> definite factor does Socrates lack for the definition of sin? It i
> the will, the defiant will. Greek intellectuality was too happ
> too naïve, too aesthetical, too ironical, too witty . . . to be abl
> sinfully to get it into its head that one could knowingly om
> to do the good, or knowingly, that is conscious of what i
> right, do what was not right. The Greek spirit posits an inte
> lectual categorical imperative.

In terms which the reader of this work becomes familiar with
S. K. defines sin:

> Sin is—after being enlightened by a revelation from God a

to what sin is—sin is before God in despair not to will to be one's self, or in despair to will to be one's self.

. . . . . .

This is the expression of the fact that sin is a position [not a negation]; this fact that it is *before God* is precisely the positive element in it. [This appears especially paradoxical in Christianity.] Christianity first proceeds to fix sin so firmly as a position that the human understanding can never grasp it; and then that same doctrine undertakes to abolish this position in a way which the human understanding can never grasp. Speculation which prattles itself free from the paradoxes pares off a little from both sides, and so it goes easier—it does not make sin by any means so positive . . . and yet in spite of this it can never get it into its head that sin might be entirely forgotten. But Christianity, which is the first discoverer of the paradoxes, is in this place also as paradoxical as possible; it works as it were against itself by fixing sin so firmly as a position that it now seems to be perfectly impossible ever to get rid of it again—and then it is precisely Christianity which by means of the atonement would abolish sin so utterly that it is as if drowned in the sea.

In another place[1] S. K. points out that the contrast Christianity has in mind is not that between sin and virtue but between sin and faith.

I introduce another quotation which, though it is not particularly characteristic of this book, is generally characteristic of S. K., both before and after this time:[2]

But a parson ought surely to be a believer. A believer! But surely a believer is a lover—indeed he who of all lovers was the most in love is in the matter of enthusiasm a mere stripling in comparison with a believer. Consider now the case of a lover. He will be capable, will he not, of talking day in and day out about his love, as long as the day lasts and the night as well. But do you believe it could occur to him, do you believe it would be possible for him, do you not believe it would be abhorrent to him to talk in such a way or to strive by the help of three reasons to prove that after all there was something in this thing of being in love—just about as when the parson proves by the help of three reasons that it is profitable to pray, showing that this thing of prayer has sunk so low in price that three reasons must be adduced to raise it a little bit in repute? Or as when the parson (and this is the same thing, only still more ridiculous) proves by three reasons that to pray is a blessedness which surpasses all understanding, proves by three reasons (!) which if they have any force at all certainly do not surpass the understanding and on the contrary must make it evident to the understanding that this blessedness does not by any means surpass the understanding, for 'reasons' obviously lie within the compass of the understanding. No, as for what surpasses the understanding, and for him who believes in it, three reasons signify no more than three bottles or three deer.—And then further, do you believe it would occur to a lover to produce a defence for his being in love, that is to say, that for him it was not the absolute, unconditionally the absolute, but that he thought of it in connexion with objections which might be raised against it and which prompt him to defend it? That is to say, do you believe he could or would concede that he was not in love, denounce himself as one who was not really in love? And in case one should propose to a lover that he talk in this manner, do you not believe that he would think him mad? And in case the lover, beside being in love, was a bit of an observer, do you not believe that he would have a suspicion that he who proposed such a thing never had known what it is to be in love, or else wanted to betray him to deny his love . . . by defending it? Is it not indeed plain that he who really is in love would never think of wanting to prove his love by three reasons or to defend it, since he himself is what is more than all reasons and every defence—he is a lover? And he who does such a thing is not a lover; he merely gives himself out to be such, and unfortunately—or fortunately—does it so stupidly that he merely shows himself not to be such.

But this is just the way Christianity is talked about . . . by believing parsons. One either 'defends' Christianity, or one transforms it into 'reasons', or at the same time dabbles speculatively at 'understanding' it. That is called preaching, and in Christendom it is regarded as already a mighty big thing that this sort of preaching is done and that some hear it. And just for this reason (here is the proof of it) Christendom is so far from being what it calls itself that the life of most men, Christianly understood, is far too spiritless to be called sin in the strictly Christian sense.

Disclaiming the presumptuous thought of giving in brief compass an adequate notion of this book, I conclude with a passage which has a poignant biographical interest. It is clear that this is S. K.'s psychological analysis of himself in the light of the experience of Easter 1848. Although it is thoroughly in keeping with the character of this book, he was at a loss to discover a place where it could be aptly introduced. He introduced it finally as a transition from the first to the second section:[1]

> Although in this section, and least of all in part A [where this passage is interpolated], there is no room or place for a psychological description; nevertheless, here, at the most dialectical border, between despair and sin, there must be introduced what might be called a poet-existence in the direction of the religious, an existence which has something in common with the despair of resignation, except that the conception of God is a component of it. Such a poet-existence will be (as the conjunction and the position of the categories shows) the most eminent poet-existence. Christianly conceived (in spite of aesthetics) every poet-existence is sin, the sin—to poetize instead of to be, to be related to the Good and the True through the medium of imagination instead of being it, that is, existentially striving to be it. The poet-existence here contemplated differs from despair in the fact that it has the conception of God as a component, or is before God; but it is prodigiously dialectical, and there is an impenetrable dialectical confusion as to the question how far it is itself obscurely aware of being sin. Such a poet can have a very deep religious urge, and the conception of God is included in his despair. He loves God above all, God who is his only comfort in his torment, and yet he loves the torment, he will not let it go. He would so willingly be his own self before God, but not with regard to the fixed point where the ego suffers, there he wills despairingly not to be himself; he hopes that eternity will remove it, he cannot resolve to assume it as his own, to humble himself under it in faith. And still he continues to hold fast to God, and this is his only blessedness; it would be the greatest horror to him to

be obliged to do without God, 'it would be enough to drive one to despair'; and yet he permits himself, perhaps unconsciously, to poetize God a little bit other than He is, a little more à la kindly father who is all too ready to fulfil the child's . . . special wish. As one who was unhappy in love and thereby became a poet is able to sing sublimely the praises of happy love, so he became the poet of religiousness. He was unhappy in religiousness, he understood darkly that it was required of him to let go this torment, that is, in faith to humble himself under it and to assume it as belonging to the self—for he would hold it away from him, and just by that means he holds it tight, although he really means to let it go in so far as it may be humanly possible—for every word of a man who is in despair is true backwardly and so should be read reversed. But to accept it in faith is a thing he cannot do, that is to say, in the last resort he will not do it, or here his ego ends in darkness. But like that poet's description of love, so has this poet's description of religion a charm, a lyrical lilt such as the married man and his reverence cannot match. What he says is by no means untrue, not at all; it is the impersonation of his happier, his better ego. In relation to the religious he is an unhappy lover, that is, he is not in the strictest sense a believer; he has only the first element of faith, despair, and with that an ardent desire after the religious. His collision properly is this: Is he the especially called? Is the thorn in the flesh an expression of the fact that he shall be used as the extraordinary? Is it before God perfectly in order with respect to the extraordinary he has become? or is the thorn in the flesh the thing he must humble himself under in order to attain the universal human?

Very many entries in the Journal reveal acute dissatisfaction with the 'poet-existence'. I quote one which was written in January 1849:[1]

> . . . What is it to be a poet? It is to have one's personal life, one's actuality, in categories entirely different from the poetical productions, that is, to relate one's self to the ideal only in imagination, so that one's own personal way of living is more or less a satire upon the poetical or upon one's self.

And here are two, written in April and May of the same year, in which S. K. is even more bitter against himself:[2]

Only one humiliation must I as a writer accept from God's hand, from Whom I receive all (and personally I have always been deeply humbled): it is that I may not presume to express in the world of reality what I portray and in the measure in which I portray it, as if I myself were the ideal. I have in this respect to make the admission that I am predominantly a poet and thinker. Melancholy and impatience and sorrow have nearly driven me too far out, which would have ended in my being broken. There was also—as I early became aware, but not so clearly as now—a misunderstanding of all my qualifications. It would have been a superhuman task, such perhaps as has never been accomplished—with my build, my imagination, my sense for literary production, to desire *at the same time* to be all this existentially. Ordinarily the hero comes first, or the ethical character, and then the poet—I wanted to be both, at the same time when I needed the 'poet's' repose and detachment from life and the thinker's repose, at that same time I wanted in the midst of real life to be what the poet and the thinker depict. . . . I remain the unsuccessful lover with respect to *being* myself the ideal of a Christian, hence I become its poet. . . . As in the poet's song there echoes a sigh from his own unhappy love, so will all my enthusiastic discourse about the ideal of being a Christian echo the sigh: Alas, I am not that, I am only a Christian poet and thinker.

Oh, and that I could be so melancholy that by reason of fear before God, of fear lest I might be taking too much upon me, I would be . . . a poet. A poet! Now, of all times, one poet more —that is just as crazy as if a man were to avail himself of just that moment to get married, just that moment when a conflagration was raging in the house where he dwelt. Just now, a poet! Now when what is needed is, if it were possible, martyrs by the thousand, the real fire-brigade. Yet I have been fearful of wishing to do something too high, then in my impotency doing some harm. But that is melancholy.

Such thoughts were frequent in 1849. S. K. could be satisfied for a while with the formula 'Christian poet and thinker'—he was not merely a poet, but a thinker and 'a prodigiously passionate thinker'.[1] 'Yet understanding and reflection are also gifts from God. What shall one do with them, and what make of them, if one must not use them?'[1] 'What I have said often enough I cannot often enough repeat: I am a poet, but of a very peculiar sort; for the dialectical is my soul's natural qualification, and dialectic is commonly quite a stranger to poets.'[2] But he was not long satisfied with this provisional solution; he preferred to think of himself as 'a writer in God's service', and this definition served for a while as an answer to the disquieting thought that he ought to give up being an author in order to *be* in reality what he knew so well how to say. But he was never deeply satisfied until he had fought his way through to the resolution 'to adventure in reliance upon God', that is, to make his writings a deed, which to his great danger he did when he launched his open attack upon the Church. But with that he ceased to be an 'author' and became a pamphleteer.

But this victory over himself involved a fight which seems to us incredibly long. Again and again he slew the same adversary, which was always able to rise up again and confront him. And this fight began a long way back. In 1847 he seemed to be further advanced than he often appeared to be three years later:[3]

> I am that last stage of a poet-formation bordering on that of being a sort of reformer in a small way. . . . There are certain things which must be impressed upon the recollection, otherwise the measuring-rod is lost. It is like the flight of the wild bird over the head of the tame ones when a reminder is given of such definitions of the Christian life as require the utmost.

And early in 1848 such reflections did in fact issue in a deed—S. K. resolved to write no more as a poet, or rather to write just one more poetical work, his most poetical, and finish with that. This resolution is recorded in the entry made immediately after his conversion (probably on Easter Even) in which he outlines a plan for 'new discourses about the lilies and the birds':[4]

> The purpose of these discourses therefore will be to make evident the conflict between poetry and Christianity. How Christianity in a certain sense when compared to poetry (which is wishful, infatuating, benumbing, transforming life's reality into an oriental dream, as when a young girl could wish to lie all day upon a sofa and let herself be enchanted)—how Christianity in comparison with this is prose—and yet it is precisely the poetry of eternity. Consequently the lilies and the birds

(i.e. the description of nature) will on this occasion receive a more poetical colouring and splendour of hue, just to show that the poetical shall be given up. For when poetry really must fall (not before the rant of a glum and sullen parson) it must wear its festal dress.

I quote from one of these Discourses enough to show that this programme was carried out:[1]

'Behold the birds of the air, behold the lilies of the field.'

But thou wilt say perhaps with the 'poet', and thou art immensely pleased when the poet talks thus: Oh, would I were a bird, or would I were like a bird, like a free bird which gratifies its *Wanderlust* by flying far, far away over sea and land, so near to heaven, unto distant climes—ah, poor me, who feel only too much bound to the spot, bound and nailed there, where I am the mark for daily cares and sufferings and adversities, compelled to dwell there, and for the whole duration of my life! Oh, would I were a bird, or would I were like a bird which rises into the air lighter than the air itself, Oh, would I were like the airy bird which when it lacks a footing can build its nest upon the surface of the sea—while I, alas, with every slightest movement, even when I merely turn on my bed, feel how gravity weighs me down! Oh, would I were a bird, or would I were like a bird free from all concern, like the little song-bird that sings so humbly, notwithstanding no one listens, or which sings . . . so proudly, notwithstanding no one listens—while I, alas, have not an instant to myself but am distracted by a thousand concerns! Oh, would I were a flower, or would I were like the flower of the field happily in love with myself, and with that enough said—alas for me, who feel in my own heart also the all-too-human-hearted discord, neither to be able in self-love to break with all else, nor to be able in love to sacrifice all.

Thus the poet. Cursorily hearing this it sounds almost as if he said what the Gospel says, when he employs the strongest expressions to extol the happiness of birds and lilies. But hear him further. Hence it is not far from being a cruelty on the part of the Gospel to extol the lilies and the birds and say, Thou shalt be such as these—alas for me, in whom this wish is so real, so real, so real—Oh, would I were like a bird of the air or like a

> lily of the field. But that I should become such a thing is indeed an impossibility; just for this reason is the wish so hearty in me, so tenderly sad and so ardent. How cruel then of the Gospel to talk to me thus, it is as though it would compel me to go out of my senses, by saying that I *must* be that which I am not and cannot be. I cannot understand the Gospel; between us there is a difference of language which if I could understand it would kill me. . . .
>
> So it is always with the poet in relation to the Gospel. . . . But if one of you should say to him in accordance with the Gospel: This is seriously meant, it is solemn earnestness that the bird in all seriousness is the teacher, then the poet might laugh—then he makes a jest about the birds and the lilies, so witty that it causes all to laugh, even the most serious man that ever lived; but he does not affect the Gospel in that way.

I cite this passage for the sake of making it clear once for all that S. K.'s Christianity was not 'the religion of a literary man'—to use an expression I heard from a teacher of mine at the time when Matthew Arnold was the religious guide of many and when the literary clique of *The Outlook* in Dr. Abbott's day exemplified the theology of America. Inasmuch as S. K. preached often about the lilies and the birds, it might be expected that he, like everybody else, would talk sentimentally about them. But no, not even in these Discourses, which contain so much poetry, such glowing descriptions of nature. The passage continues as follows:

> From the lilies and the birds as teachers let us learn
>
> *Silence* or *to hold our peace.*
>
> For no doubt it is speech which distinguishes man from the beast, and hence, if one so will, distinguishes him very far from the lily. But because it is an advantage to be able to speak, it does not follow that to be able to keep silent is no art or that this is a humble art. On the contrary, just because a man is able to speak, it is an art to be able to keep silent; and just because this advantage of man so readily tempts him, it is a great art to be able to keep silent. But this we can learn from the silent teachers, the lilies and the birds.
>
> '*Seek ye first God's kingdom and his righteousness.*'

But what does this mean, what have I to do, or what sort of effort is it that can be said to seek or pursue the kingdom of God? Shall I try to get a job suitable to my talents and powers in order to exert an influence thereby? No, thou shalt *first* seek God's kingdom. Shall I then give all my fortune to the poor? No, thou shalt *first* seek God's kingdom. Shall I then go out to proclaim this teaching in the world? No, thou shalt *first* seek God's kingdom. But then in a certain sense it is nothing I shall do. Yes, certainly, it is in a certain sense nothing; thou shalt in the deepest sense make thyself nothing, become nothing before God, learn to keep silent. In this silence is the beginning, which is, *first* to seek God's kingdom.

In this wise, a godly wise, one gets to the beginning by going, in a sense, backwards. The beginning is not that with which one begins, but at which one arrives, and one arrives at the beginning backwards. The beginning is this art of *becoming* silent; for to be silent, as nature is, is not an art. And to become thus silent in the deepest sense, silent right before God, is the beginning of godly fear, for as the fear of God is the beginning of wisdom, so is silence the beginning of godly fear. And as the fear of God is more than the beginning of wisdom, or rather is wisdom, so is silence more than the beginning of godly fear, it is godly fear. In this silence the many thoughts of wish and desire are rendered mute by godly fear, in this silence the prolix eloquence of thanksgiving is rendered mute by godly fear.

It is man's superiority over the beast to be able to speak; but in relation to God it can easily become the ruin of man who is able to speak that he is too willing to speak. God is in heaven, man upon earth—therefore they cannot well talk together. . . . Only in much fear and trembling can a man talk with God; in much fear and trembling. But to talk in much fear and trembling is difficult for a further reason; for as a sense of dread causes the bodily voice to fail, so also does much fear and trembling render speech mute in silence. This the true man of prayer knows well, and he who was not the true man of prayer perhaps learned just this by praying. There was something that lay so close to his heart, a matter of such consequence to him, it was so important that he should make God understand him, he was afraid that in his prayer he might forget something, ah, and if he had forgotten it, he was afraid God might not of Himself remember it—therefore he would collect himself to pray right earnestly. And what happened then?—in case he did indeed pray right earnestly. The surprising happened to him. In proportion as he became more and more earnest in prayer, he had less and less to say, and in the end he became quite silent. He became silent—indeed, what is if possible still more expressly the opposite of speaking, he became a hearer. He had supposed that to pray is to speak; he learnt that to pray is not merely to be silent but to hear. And so it is: to pray is not to hear oneself speak, but it is to be silent, and to remain silently waiting until one hears God speak.

This quotation is already too long, and yet it is so hard to break off here where the passage evidently does not end. Again and again I have caused myself this distress, for the sake of making the reader feel that S. K.'s works *must* be published in English, to make him feel that it is a scandal they are not available. Of the Discourses at least it cannot be said that they would interest only theologians or professors or philosophers or suchlike. And here I say aloud, as I have often felt like saying when I brought to an end a quotation which was hardly begun, *praeterea censeo* . . . that S. K. must be translated. And like Cato I shall say it again.

The three discourses about *The High Priest* [i.e. Jesus Christ], *The Publican*, *The Woman that was a Sinner* I must pass by, as so often I am constrained to do, without making a single quotation. But not without making one comment, which applies as well to others of S. K.'s discourses which deal with the story of the Gospel. If I were writing a commentary upon the Gospels, I should look first of all to S. K. for instruction how to understand sayings which have been so often 'explained' through many generations that now they are generally understood to be merely the obvious dicta of common sense—notwithstanding that they are unfortunately expressed in the exaggerated form which was characteristic of the 'oriental mind', and therefore must be taken with a grain of salt. It has often been said in disparagement of S. K.—and, who knows? perhaps as a way of escaping from the consequences of his rigorous argument—that he had an entirely 'abstract idea' of Jesus Christ. Perhaps Johannes Climacus is responsible for this misapprehension. For in the *Scraps* he makes this astonishing statement:[1]

> Even if the contemporary generation had left no other tradition than this saying: 'We have believed that in the year so and so God showed himself in the form of a humble servant, lived and taught among us and thereupon died'—that would be more than enough.

But as a matter of fact there is hardly a passage in the Synoptic Gospels which S. K. has not reflected upon profoundly, and profoundly illuminated either in his books or his journals. One of the projects which he proposed to himself, but did not carry out, was a 'Life of Christ'. But really he has written it; and there could hardly be a better way of writing such a work now than by gathering together all his scattered reflections on the subject.

In connexion with *The Book on Adler* mention was made (p. 385) of the *Two Minor Treatises* which were not published until 1849. More particular notice must be taken of them here. But inasmuch as Mr. Dru has translated the whole of the treatise which deals with 'The Difference between a Genius and an Apostle', I quote from it only the first paragraph, with the aim of showing that the distinction it draws, so far from being vain, is vital to Christianity:[2]

> What is it that erroneous exegesis and speculation have done to confound Christianity? and whereby have they confounded it? Briefly stated and with categorical precision it is thus: They have withdrawn the paradox-religious sphere into the aesthetical and thereby gained the advantage that every Christian term, which in its own sphere is qualitatively categorical, can now in reduced circumstances do humble service as a *spirituelle* expression signifying pretty much anything. Now when the paradox sphere is done away with or expounded back into the aesthetical, an apostle becomes nothing more or less than a genius—and then, good-night, Christianity! The Spiritual and the Spirituelle, revelation and spontaneous originality, a call of God and human talent, an apostle and a genius—all of them come to pretty much the same thing in the end.

I quote here also the Preface—perhaps the shortest ever written: 'These two minor treatises will no doubt be of interest essentially only to theologians.' This is hardly true, for they interested Th. Haecker and evidently they interest Mr. Dru. In a footnote which refers to the first sentence quoted above S. K. says: 'Moreover, this error is not merely that of heterodoxy but of hyperorthodoxy and generally of thoughtlessness.' I expect that this treatise interests a Catholic layman like Mr. Dru more particularly because it reveals the 'thoughtlessness' of so many Protestant theologians.

The other treatise, entitled 'Has a man a right to let himself be put to death for the truth?' begins with the story of a child's first impression of the picture of the Crucifixion, which we quoted in full on p. 42 f. The significance of that story is plain enough; but as for what follows, S. K. in another short preface (dated 'at the end of 1847') recognizes that not even theologians can be interested in it unless they are ready to lay aside their customary way of thinking:

> This preface contains nothing more than an adjuration tha the reader will first exercise himself in putting off from him his customary mode of thought. For otherwise the problem which is here presented will have no existence for him at all—an that for the curious reason that he has already solved it long ago, but in an inverted way.

That is true, and yet the passage I am about to quote (from the beginning of Section B) shows that S. K. succeeded in makin it fairly plain that a serious Christian cannot lightly put aside th thought, not of loss and suffering only, but even of the possibilit of martyrdom for the sake of Christ:[1]

> It is true, the parson (collectively understood) preache about those glorious ones who sacrificed their lives for th truth. As a rule the parson can very well assume that there i nobody present in the church who could entertain any notio of adventuring such a thing. When he is sufficiently assure of this by reason of the knowledge he has of his congregatio as its pastor, he preaches without embarrassment, he declaim vigorously and wipes the sweat from his brow. If the followin day there came to see the parson at his home one of thos resolute men who do not declaim, a quiet, modest, perhap plain-looking man, announcing himself as one who had bee carried away by the parson's eloquence so that now he ha

resolved to offer his life for the truth—what then? Then the parson would reply to him good-humouredly as follows: 'Why! Merciful Father in Heaven! How did you get such an idea into your head? Travel a bit, you need diversion, take a laxative.' And suppose the plain-looking man, his tranquillity unaltered, modestly fixed his eye upon him and continued, with this glance steadily fixed upon him, to talk about his resolution, but with the modest expressions which a resolute man always uses—this parson would surely say to himself, 'Would that this man were far away!'

We have already noticed that the plan of Part I of *Training in Christianity*, that is, the part entitled 'Come hither', occurred to S. K. a few days after his last conversion.[1] I need not quote from this part, since the whole of it is available to English readers in Dr. Hollander's translation.[2] The other two parts were subsequently made to match it. Part I dwells upon the scandal necessarily provoked by the lowliness of Christ's appearance, insisting that, in spite of the 1,800 years which have intervened, in spite of the proof of His divinity which 'the effects of His life' are supposed to afford, and in spite of our knowledge that He is now exalted, we must put ourselves in the place of His contemporaries, become ourselves 'contemporary' with Him—and then we shall not only be able to understand but we shall keenly feel the offence of His lowliness, we shall know what it is to believe in spite of appearance, that is, really to *believe*. Part II considers the three possibilities of 'offence' in the humble figure of Jesus Christ. Part III (five discourses on the text 'And I, if I be lifted up, will draw all men unto me') contemplates Jesus as the exalted Lord, yet as the same Lord that appeared in lowliness and in lowliness uttered these very words and all others we can attribute to Him.

The theme of the whole work is the imitation of Christ. The sting of it lies in the insistent affirmation that Christ can be imitated only in His lowliness, in suffering, in death. In a sense, the treatment is narrow, inasmuch as it envisages almost exclusively the suffering involved in witnessing for the truth. But for this reason it is the more intense. This was the question most personal to S. K., and we can see plainly enough that if he was in any way called to imitate Christ through suffering, it was in this way, as a witness for the truth. The necessity of the *imitatio*

Christi was sternly pressed by S. K., but not fanatically, not with the confusion we have witnessed in our day, when the question 'What would Jesus do?' was asked without reflecting how far a disciple can imitate the Master, a mere man can be like the God-Man, a sinner who is saved can emulate the Saviour of the world. S. K. was well aware of these distinctions, but he was also not blind to the distinction between an 'admirer' and a 'follower'; and from the Gospels he could furnish convincing proof that it was not admirers or worshippers Christ wanted. To be a disciple of Christ does not mean merely to know the truth but to do it—or, still more fundamental, to *be* the truth, as Christ in His own person was the Truth and was also the Way. In Christianity, at all events, truth is not the goal but the way. Although S. K. had to admit with shame that he was a poet and thinker, he could nevertheless say of himself that he was 'quantitatively more' than that, in the fact that he was really trying to be what he poetized and thought—'not qualitatively more, for that describes the witness for the truth, the martyr, which I am not'.[1]

The notion that the Church is already triumphant here on earth is the devil's invention to hinder men from even thinking that it might be required of them to be followers of Christ in His humility, and to render them content with being His admirers and worshippers. 'So long as this world lasts and the Church within it, it is a militant Church.' But it is not the Church as a body that strives and wages war against the world while the individual remains secure in its bosom; rather it is incumbent upon every individual to fight at his own peril. And this warfare is waged not only without but within. Neither the individual nor the Church is in secure possession of the truth but must continually strive to possess it. S. K. recognized that in our day the fight is not waged against a frankly hostile world, but against the very idea of Christendom, the delusion that all are Christians as a matter of course, that Christianity has triumphed, that the world (or at least 'Christendom') is Christianized. He understood that for the individual, and for himself in particular, to be militant in this sense was 'to live dangerously'—to use Nietzsche's expression. But we do not need to use this expression, seeing that S. K. had a better one, 'to venture far out in reliance upon God'. This we must understand as a version of his earlier saying about 'lying above 70,000 fathoms of water and still trusting in God'. This expresses the feeling that in launching his attack upon the established order he was venturing far out upon the water as a lonely swimmer—so far out that there was no possibility of return to the secure conditions of life on dry land. Particularly at this moment when he was confronted with the prospect of penury he felt that he was cutting himself off from the possibility of assuring for himself a livelihood by procuring a post in the Established Church, which in his little country, under the conditions then prevailing, was the only way such a man as he might hope to earn a living. Such was the danger necessarily involved in being the truth. His whole nature, and the Gospel as he understood it, was passionately opposed to the temperate maxim *ne quid nimis*, never too much, no excess. For he was living consciously on the verge of eternity—that is, he was living eschatologically.

It is perfectly true that S. K. had no interest in the fantastic apocalyptic imagery, which is prominent in the Gospels, but was already a vanishing element there, and is only a particular embellishment of eschatology. But it cannot be denied that S. K. had a vivid sense of 'the hereafter' (*hisset*) as opposed to the 'here', of the impending judgement of the last day, of the resurrection of the dead, 'both of the just and of . . . the unjust', and that in this light (that is, in the light of other-worldliness) he understood the beatitudes of the Gospels and the requirements of discipleship. But this is the essence of Christian eschatology. Even the 'thoroughgoing eschatology' with which Albert Schweitzer has made us familiar was in some singular respects anticipated by S. K. In spite of his reliance upon the report of the Fourth Gospel that Christ openly proclaimed Himself to be God, S. K. understood that in the days of His flesh He was completely unrecognizable as God and preserved 'the strictest incognito'.[1] And the whole period, however long it may be, which extends from Christ's earthly life to His return in glory, he regarded as a 'parenthesis', a time of testing for man, which prescribes a sort of behaviour (Schweitzer's 'interim ethics') which cannot be simply deduced by common sense from the conditions in which we find ourselves in this world.

From this time forth S. K.'s polemic was ever more and more sharply directed against *det Bestaaende*—the existing Church, Christianity in its all-too-established form. This word cannot be satisfactorily translated. I shall call it simply 'the established', with the warning that it does not indicate exclusively the State Church which is established by law. Eventually S. K. had much to say in reproach of the State Church as such, but in the first instance he did not think at all of the special dangers the Church is exposed to as a state establishment, and he was emphatic in affirming that he was not proposing any change in respect to outward forms. Least of all was he inclined to champion sectarian conventicles or 'Free Church' movements, although he was ready to concede that schismatic movements, even when they were hopelessly astray, had the eminent advantage of being genuine and spontaneous. It was the lack of spontaneous enthusiasm which seemed to him deplorable in the Church as it was, so complacently settled as it was, so definitely established. He regarded the Protestant Reformation in its first phase as a necessary 'corrective', but he perceived that the situation was rendered absurd when the corrective came to be regarded as the norm. Protestantism, he affirmed, could not exist except as a corrective. The first sign that the Church was about to deify itself he saw in the tendency to conceive that 'the outward was commensurable with the inward', that there was perfect 'congruence' between them. And 'the deification of the Church is nothing but permanent rebellion against God'. 'It is 1800 since Christ lived, then He is forgotten—only His teaching survives [as the possession of the Church], that is to say, Christianity has been abolished.'

Inasmuch as we have no established Church in America, we may be complacent enough to think that we can side-step his attack. But complacency is just what he was attacking. Many of the Protestant sects in America had at the beginning a genuine passion, perhaps a creditable zeal, for reform—before they became 'established' and respectable. S. K.'s polemic is not levelled against Methodists and Baptists, for example, in their first phase. But when they spend a million dollars on parish churches they must be understood to be very thoroughly 'established' in his sense—quite as much established as the 'prelatical' Churches which spend many millions on cathedrals. But here we are not talking of Roger Williams or John Wesley or their disciples, but about the third and fourth generation from them that feared God. (This expression cannot surely be regarded as offensive to anybody in this age, when the notion is so generally repudiated that men ought to fear God.)

S. K. would have been very ready to accept Karl Barth's affirmation that 'God is not only in the Church but over it'. This is the fulcrum for every reformation in the Church. To S. K.'s mind it justified the single individual before God in declaring even to the Church that he must obey God rather than man. It not only justifies, it compels him; and it constitutes the standing possibility of revival in the Church. The more the Church is secularized (that is, the more it is 'established'), the more obvious this right and duty become. Now, when the Creed and 'canon law' are determined by the ballot, and so are quite frankly understood to represent the will of the majority rather than the will of God or the truth, the right of maintaining another opinion is too obvious to be denied.

'The fundamental misfortune of Christianity', said S. K., 'is Christendom.'[1] In his criticism of 'established' Christianity in Denmark and northern Europe ('especially in Protestantism, and more especially in Denmark', as he was accustomed to say) he found occasion to compare it to its disadvantage, not only with the Christianity of the middle ages, but even with paganism. In *The Sickness unto Death* he says:[2]

> Is it not very epigrammatical that profane swearing was not customary in paganism but is quite at home in Christendom; that paganism generally uttered the name of God with a certain awe, with a dread of the mysterious, whereas in Christendom God's name is the word which occurs most frequently in daily speech and to which altogether the least significance is attached, because the revealed God, poor fellow (because he was so lacking in shrewdness and foresight that he became revealed instead of keeping himself hidden as superior persons always do), is the one personage out of the whole population who has become all too well known, upon whom one confers an exorbitant favour when one goes to church once in a while, where one gets praised for this by the parson, who thanks one on behalf of God for the courtesy of the visit, honours one with the title of pious, and takes occasion to sneer a bit at the man who never shows God the courtesy of going to church.

As an example of comparison with the middle ages I quote one of S. K.'s many remarks about the celibacy of the clergy:[3]

> The middle ages fell into error and believed that it was a

sacred shame for a priest to marry. Then came Luther . . . and got married. Now it is regarded as a shame when a priest doesn't marry. One cannot well be a parson when one is not married. The congregation will not have entire confidence in him when he is not married. . . . Verily the world has gone ahead spiritually! In the middle ages they had most confidence in an unmarried man, they conceived that they had a guarantee in his unmarried state—this is the syllogism of the spirit. Now they have most confidence in the married man, they conceive that in the fact that he is married they have a guarantee that he will not seduce one's wife and daughter—this is the syllogism of the flesh.

What I have said here, briefly combining S. K.'s most characteristic utterances, may serve as an introduction to the whole campaign of which the works of 1848 were only a tentative beginning, although it was boldly enough announced at this time that his task was nothing less than that of 'introducing Christianity into Christendom'. The very title implies as much, for it properly means 'training *into* Christianity'. I have registered here the *motifs* which were heard in the overture and which were to recur in the writings of the next six years with ever-increasing fullness and emphasis.

The few longer quotations I can give from *Training in Christianity*, though important passages, are far from giving an adequate idea of the book. It is more illuminating to observe that just as *The Sickness unto Death* was in a sense a re-edition of *The Concept of Dread*, so is *Training in Christianity* a maturer edition of the *Scraps* and the *Postscript*. Like the earlier works it seeks to define the fundamental concepts of Christianity. But it is far more intense, the polemical note is more apparent, the incognito of humour has been laid aside and it is evidently written by a believer, a convinced believer to whom this book was his education, not in Christian faith but in Christian practice.

The first quotation has to do with the claim that Christianity has been abolished:[1]

Christianity is literally dethroned in Christendom; but if that is so, then it is also abolished. A king has not ceased to exist because the country in which he lived made itself a republic and made him its president; but Christianity is abolished so soon as it is hurled from the throne. Christianity is the unconditional, it has only one mode of being, unconditional being; if it is not unconditional, it is abolished; in relation to Christianity either/or applies unconditionally. For a long enough time we have heard the impudent talk about going farther, about not being satisfied with Christianity as it is, with mere faith, with the simple thing, with obedience, with the 'Thou shalt'. . . . Hence for obedience there was substituted 'reasons', the notion of believing for three reasons; for people were annoyed at having to obey. Hence leniency was substituted for severity; for men did not presume to command and they were reluctant to be commanded—those who ought to command became cowardly, and those who ought to obey became impudent. Thus it came about that Christianity was abolished in Christendom . . . by leniency. In shabby second-hand clothing Christianity slinks about in Christendom, and one does not know whether to take off one's hat to it, or whether it is not *it* that ought to bow to one, whether it is the pity of Christianity we need, or whether it needs our pity.

But for us there is only one salvation—Christianity. And for Christianity verily there is only one salvation—severity. By the help of leniency it cannot be saved—that is to say, Christianity neither can nor should be saved thus, for this thought is the crime of *lèse-majesté* against it; but by severity it must be re-enthroned as sovereign. And though I myself sink under the weight of the standard I proclaim, though I should be the first to succumb to its condemnation, or though I should be the only one—I can do no other. I know well what I am doing; I know also what I have suffered in fear and trembling, pursued by temptation, as I ventured so far out, concerned alone by day and by night with such thoughts, and for so long a time concerned therewith in loneliness, with an effort ever more highly strained; alone in spite of the fact that I live in Christendom, where indeed all are Christians, but where I have never heard a discourse or sermon about which, if it was before God the question were put to me, I could say unconditionally that it was Christian—for even the most Christian sermons I have heard had yet always a suspicious admixture of 'reasons', a smack of human pity and whimper, a discordant note of ingratiation. I have no monastery where

I could take refuge and find an environment in any way corresponding to my preoccupation. I chose the only way out that was still left to me in Christendom—that of seeming to be the most light-minded of all, to 'become a fool in the world', in order to preserve if possible what lay hidden in my inward man, a bit of real seriousness, and in order that the protection of this inwardness might allow the peace which resides in lonely reserve to grow up in quietness. By means of this life I learnt inwardly what one perhaps through knowledge of man's unreasoning lightness of mind and complacency in error can learn better than in the desert and from the stillness of the night; by means of this life in the midst of swarming human activity, by this, if one will, false life of mine—for it is true enough that I have kept something different hidden in my inward man, but what I hid was the best part of me. I have never, never deceived in such a way as to make myself out better than I was—by means of this life in the midst of swarming human activity I have learnt with frightful realism to understand that severity is the only thing that can help.

That I have employed. But I have no might, neither soldiers, nor any other might; I have no powerful connexions, have no influence or power over the fate of others; I am of all men the most lonely, in a worldly sense the most impotent. The employment of severity may inflame men to wrath; hence he who would employ severity is accustomed first to assure himself of power. I neither can nor will employ severity thus; for I would not rule, I would only serve the truth, or, what is the same thing, serve Christianity.

How exquisitely personal this whole passage is! Although this book was ultimately ascribed to a pseudonym, such was not the original intention, and every word of it can be taken as S. K.'s own. This passage in particular is as intimate a revelation of himself as any we can find in the Journal. It shows what progress he had made in the way of direct communication—but when it came to publishing he retired behind a pseudonym.

The complaint that in this 'serious world' he was the only person supposed to lack seriousness because he had no official post and was doing nothing to earn a living is often heard in the Journal, and here is an amusing expression of it:[1]

'Had the Apostle Paul any regular job?' No, he had no regular job. 'Had he then a salary?' No, he had no salary. 'Did he earn much money then in other ways?' No, he did not make money in any way. 'But at any rate he was married, was he not?' No, he was not married. 'But then Paul was not a serious man!' No, Paul was not a serious man—every tradesman especially will easily understand that.

I quote again from *Training in Christianity*, the conclusion of Part II.[1]

> Verily the 18 centuries have not contributed so much as a tittle to prove the truth of Christianity, on the contrary they have contributed with a steadily increasing force to abolish Christianity. It certainly has not turned out as one might reasonably expect when one does homage to the proof of the 18 centuries, that now in the 19th century people are more entirely convinced of the truth of Christianity than they were in the first and second generation—it has turned out rather (as something of a satire upon the votaries and worshippers of this proof) that just in proportion as the proof increased in power . . . fewer and fewer are convinced. . . . Now that it has been *proved*, and on a prodigious scale, that Christianity is the truth—no one is found, or next to no one, who will make any sacrifice for the sake of it. At a time when they—shall I say 'only'—believed its truth they were ready to offer life and blood. Oh, fearful infatuation! Oh that (like that pagan who burnt the libraries) they would do away with these 18 centuries—if they cannot do that, then Christianity is abolished. Oh, would that they could take these many orators who prove the truth of Christianity by the 1,800 years, that they could take them and make them understand, terrible as it is, that they are betraying, denying, abolishing Christianity—if they cannot do that, then Christianity is abolished.

This passage throws some light upon the meaning of S. K.'s contention that the disciple of to-day must be 'contemporary' with Christ. This is the contention of the whole book. We see here that it was not meant in a mystical sense.

Although S. K. eventually ascribed this work to a pseudonym, his own name appeared as 'editor', and although the Editor's Preface was printed only once, the Second and Third Parts had each a page for the Preface where a note referred the reader to the Preface of Part I. In this way attention was called very emphatically to this preface, and it is in fact very important to read it if one would understand the spirit in which this book was written—or in which it was made public. I quote the whole of it:[1]

> In this work the pseudonym has strained to the utmost the requirement for being a Christian.
>
> Yet certainly the requirement ought to be uttered, presented, heard; there ought, Christianly, to be no paring down of the requirement, let alone a tacit agreement to ignore it—instead of making on one's own behalf admission and confession.
>
> The requirement ought to be heard; and I understand what is here said as said to me alone—that I might learn not only to flee to 'grace' but to flee to it with intention of making use of 'grace'.

This thought of an 'admission', viz. that the claims of Christianity were not being met, was to play a conspicuous role. S. K. required that Bishop Mynster as Primate of the Church in Denmark should make the admission that the Church as 'established' did not represent the claims Christ made upon his disciples—and he professed that with this admission he would be satisfied. The word 'grace' is used here with quotation marks because it was about 'grace' people were constantly talking, and it was a word they were using in vain so long as they had no intention of making use of it except as a dispensation to sin.[2] He had it in mind, moreover, that people were commonly replying to his stern admonitions by an appeal to 'grace'. But indeed S. K. could be mild as well as severe; he was most severe with himself, yet when his own heart condemned him he was ready to flee to grace. He thought at one time of putting the following motto upon the title-page of the book we are now dealing with:[3]

> I do not feel myself yet strong enough to imitate Thee in such wise as to die for Thee or for Thy cause; I content myself with the lesser thing, with thanking Thee adoringly that Thou wert willing to die for me.

A very singular and a very important feature of this book is 'The Moral', which stands at the conclusion of Part I. The importance of it is evident from the fact that when the 'admission' he required was not made by the Church, and when he had resolved upon a trenchant attack, his first overt act of war was to 'withdraw' the Moral and the Preface. He conceived that without these mitigating elements the book would appear evidently to be an open attack upon the 'established' on a line with the offensive he was about to launch. But I do not understand this action as an indication of a radical change of mind. S. K. was never inclined to press ruthlessly upon others the supreme ideal of Christianity, and he never felt himself so far advanced that he did not need to flee to grace. But he saw that the Church required the most trenchant and direct communication if it was to be aroused from its lethargy and self-contentment, and he perceived that 'The Moral' was likely to be abused as a dispensation from the necessity of admitting the imperfection of the Church and its members.

The Moral[1]

And what does all this mean? It means that every one for himself, in quiet inwardness before God, shall humble himself under what it means in the strictest sense to be a Christian, admit candidly before God how it stands with him, so that he might yet accept the grace that is offered to every one who is imperfect, that is, to every one. And then no further; then for the rest let him attend to his work, be glad in it, love his wife, be glad in her, bring up his children with joyfulness, love his fellow men, rejoice in life. If anything further is required of him, God will surely let him understand, and in such case will also help him further, for the terrible language of the Law is so terrifying because it seems as if it were left to man to hold fast to Christ by his own power, whereas in the language of love it is Christ that holds him fast. So if anything further is required of him, God will surely let him understand; but this is required of every one, that before God he shall candidly humble himself beneath the requirements of ideality. And therefore these should be heard, be heard again and again in their infinite significance. To be a Christian has become a thing of naught, mere tomfoolery, something which every one is as a matter of course, something one slips into more easily than into the most insignificant trick of dexterity.

'But if the Christian life is something so terrible and frightful, how in the world can a person get the idea of accepting it?' Quite simply, and, if you want that too, quite in a Lutheran way: only the consciousness of sin can force one into this dreadful situation—the force on the other side being grace. And in that very instant the Christian life transforms itself and is sheer gentleness, grace, loving-kindness and compassion. Looked at from any other point of view Christianity is and must be a sort of madness or the greatest horror. Only through the consciousness of sin is there entrance to it, and the wish to enter in by any other way is the crime of *lèse-majesté* against Christianity.

. . . .

Only the consciousness of sin is the expression of absolute respect, and just for this reason, i.e. because Christianity requires absolute respect, it must and will display itself as madness or horror, in order that the qualitative infinite emphasis may fall upon the fact that only the consciousness of sin is the way of entrance, is the vision, which by being absolute respect, can see the gentleness, loving-kindness, and compassion of Christianity.

The simple man who humbly confesses himself to be a sinner—himself personally (the individual)—does not need at all to become aware of all the difficulties which emerge when one is neither simple nor humble. But where this is lacking, this humble consciousness of being personally a sinner (the individual)—yea, if such a one possessed all human wisdom and shrewdness along with all human talents, it would profit him little. Christianity shall in a degree corresponding to his superiority erect itself dreadfully against him and transform itself into madness and terror, until he learns either to give up Christianity, or else by the help of what is very far remote from scientific propaedeutic, apologetic, &c.—that is, by the help of the torments of a contrite heart (just in proportion to *his* need of it) learns to enter by the narrow way, through the consciousness of sin, into Christianity.

Since *Training in Christianity* was written almost 100 years have passed; we can now count 1,900 years and more; and yet it cannot be said that this book is not as appropriate to our age as it was a century ago. The situation has not changed very greatly either in Denmark or in the world at large—except for the fact that the Churches do not appear to be so securely and self-confidently 'established', that it is no longer lightly assumed that everybody in Christendom is a Christian, and that people here and there are beginning to perceive that 'this world' is pretty much the same old world, the antagonist of the truth and a field for Christian adventure. All this S. K. would surely have rejoiced to see. Yet it did not come about through the force of his polemic, nor as a result of a penitent admission on the part of any Church, and it remains to be seen whether the Churches will learn from the situation which is developing that their task is 'to introduce Christianity into Christendom'—and first of all into the Churches.

The Point of View for My Work as an Author is an intimate and sincere revelation of S. K. at the moment when from the height of his intellectual and religious maturity he looked back upon the work already performed and began to look forward to a literary work of an entirely different character. I should feel compelled to quote largely from it here in this chapter, were it not that so much has already been quoted (on pp. 47 ff., 173, 184, 248, 263 f.) and that, even when no express reference has been made to it, it has furnished the clue we have followed in interpreting S. K. as an author.

Ever since Easter S. K. had been venturing ever farther and farther out in the direction of 'direct communication', and with this book he reached the goal he contemplated in the entry which recorded his Easter experience: 'I must speak!' He recognized with profound satisfaction that he had succeeded in breaking at last his morbid reserve; by writing such a book about himself he had triumphed—but at the thought of publishing he drew back appalled. The book was not made known to his generation but was left to be published after his death as 'a report to history'.

It was the most difficult task he had as yet performed; but the difficulty was not due, as we might suppose, to reluctance before the necessity of making a public confession of his sin such as he contemplated at an earlier period; for after Easter he no longer conceived of such a necessity, and the purpose of this book was simply to illuminate the character of his work as an author. Consequently he did not feel obliged to make any reference to his *vita ante acta*, except in so far as this might be necessary to explain the character of his literary production. What he says here about his personal history before he became a writer is quoted on pp. 47 f. and 173. This book was a revelation of himself, but it is a sort of self-revelation we are not accustomed to associate with the word 'confession'; it was a confession how *good* he was—and for this reason he did not feel free to publish it. Surely it was a rare doubt, a characteristically Kierkegaardian scruple, which tormented him: 'whether a man has a right to seem as good as he is':[1]

> But some one says: In case a man is inwardly so pious, in such a degree devoted to the good, then let him say it outright, and if it is God's will that he shall be honoured and esteemed for it, let him accept it, this is the simplest thing.
>
> But then reflection discovers that to serve God in truth is to avoid the appearance of doing it so as to have advantage therefrom. This is the self-denial which reflection discovers and which immediacy (even if accompanied by a modicum of reflection) essentially does not recognize, for self-denial is a reflection. . . .
>
> So then one is better than he seems to be. But then one must be pure. Suppose now that there was a man who in one respect perhaps, humanly speaking, was noble and disinterested and understood reflectively that the true course was to avoid seeming to be this. But suppose now that the same man was in other respects a greater sinner than many others—when now in obedience to reflection he hides or avoids the appearance of being as good and disinterested as he is, but does not attend to the other side or cannot bring himself to make the other side evident, here again there is a falsehood.
>
> The self-denial of avoiding the appearance of being as good as one is, is too high a perfection, it is too highly strung for humanity, there is a sort of daimonia in it—it is not for sinners. A sinner must never imagine that he is so good that it would be dangerous for the world or mankind that they should get a notion how good he was. Instead of this heathen thought of avoiding the appearance, Christianity proposes something else, confession of sin. If a man will be quite candid in this respect, it can never be dangerous for the world to get to know how good he is.

Here the case was adjourned for the time being. But at all events the book *must* be written—at least *written*.

Communication of Christian truth must end at last in 'witnessing'. In this connexion he took satisfaction in the thought that at least the Discourses had been direct communication.

It is certainly the right thing to give my contemporaries once for all a definite and non-reduplicated impression of what I declare myself to be, what I purpose, &c.

So the book was written—and he wrote with the expectation that he would die before there would be time to publish it, so that this, along with the other works of 1848, would not be read until after his death. Just before September 1 he wrote in the Journal:[1]

Now I find myself in a position to write an account, as short and serious as possible, about my foregoing works, which needs to be done before the transition to the next phase. And why do I find myself now in a position to do this? Just because I am now clear about direct communication in relation to decisive Christian truth. Just for this reason I am now able to illuminate and explain indirect communication. Earlier I was constantly unclear about it. For one must always be beyond what one would explain. Earlier there remained an uncertainty with regard to the whole matter because I was not myself clear, and as a matter of fact I was engaged in indirect communication. This relationship would have ruined absolutely the whole presentation.

In spite of the difficulty S. K. experienced in writing it, *The Point of View* was completed in little more than a month. We must remember that the material for it was already at hand, had already been written and rewritten, carefully formed and polished, in the numerous passages in the NB Journals which were entitled 'The Accounting', &c. Perhaps the book could never have been written if it had not first been written substantially in the Journal; for it was easy for S. K. to write such things in his Journal, and difficult only when he had in mind a possible reader. Every time he approached this task and recognized the necessity of it he was inclined to sheer off from it. Three of the entries which sound most resolute end in this way:[2] 'But now is not the moment, and besides at this time I am rather over-taxed. I had more need of bodily recreation'; 'It is firmly settled that I shall communicate definitely and directly an explanation how I understand my authorship. And now I need recreation and repose'; 'A poet am I—travel I must.'

The difficulty S. K. most expressly remarks upon was that of reviewing the whole of his immense literary production and attaining a point of view from which the unity in such extraordinary variety could be perceived and explained. The result of such a review astonished him. He perceived that even his most spontaneous outpourings were co-operant to an end which he himself had not devised and could not ascribe to himself as his own conscious plan. He could ascribe it only to 'Governance'—'a Divinity which shapes our ends, rough-hew them how we will'. The difficulty he experienced in reviewing these works was due primarily to the fact that they were not altogether his own.[1]

S. K. characterizes 'the total thought' of his many works by the phrase he so often used, 'to become a Christian',[2] and a whole chapter is devoted to the illustration of the fact that his polemic was directed predominantly against the assumption that 'all are Christians', against the very idea of 'Christendom, as a prodigious illusion'. The very much abbreviated 'Accounting', which S. K was brave enough to publish in 1851 with the title *About M Work as an Author*, shows clearly that what he had most at hear to affirm was the fact that from first to last he was a religiou writer, and that the maieutic method of indirect communicatio properly came first. This brief accounting concluded with th following words printed in large characters:[3]

> '*Without authority*' to **draw attention** to the religious, th Christian, is the category for my work as an author regarde as a whole. . . .
>
> 'Before God', religiously, when I talk to myself, I call m whole work as an author my own education, and that not in th sense that I count myself already perfect or entirely beyon needing education and development.

Just before this he says:[4]

> The movement described by the authorship is: **from** th 'poet' (from the aesthetical), **from** the 'philosopher' (fro speculation) **to** the most inward definitions of the Christia . . . This movement is traced or described *uno tenore*, in on breath, if I may speak thus, so that the authorship regarded a a *whole* is religious from first to last.
>
> . . . .
>
> And this also is the **Christian** *movement*. Christianly, it not the simple from which one starts out, in order then t become interesting, witty, profound, poet, philosopher, &

No, exactly the contrary; it is *here* one begins and becomes more and more simple, *arriving at* the simple. This is the Christian movement of reflection in 'Christendom'; one does not reflect himself into Christianity, but one reflects himself out of something else and becomes more and more simple. . . .

The only long passage I shall quote here from *The Point of View* is the beginning of Part II, Chapter III.[1]

The Share Governance had in my Writings

What I have written up to this point has not been dear to me to write nor pleasant; there is something painful in having to talk so much about oneself. . . . But now, God be praised, I breathe freely, now I actually feel a longing to speak, now I am on a subject about which to think or to speak is an indescribable blessedness. In a life which in many ways has been an unhappy and a troubled one, this relationship of mine to God is the experience of a happy lover, and although this love-story (if I dare call it such) has the essential characteristic of all true love-stories that only one person can entirely understand it, and complete joy is experienced only in relating it to one alone, the Beloved, by whom in this instance one is also loved—yet it is also a happy thing to talk to others about it.

For that I needed God's aid, and how constantly, year after year, I needed God's aid—to recall that to mind and to repeat the experience precisely I do not need to seek the help of memory or recollection or journals or diaries, nor to compare the one with the other—I live through it again so vividly, so actually, at the present moment. What was not this pen capable of producing, if it were a question of audacity, of enthusiasm, of fanaticism nearly to the verge of madness! And now that I must speak about my relationship to God; about that which is every day repeated in my prayer which gives thanks to him for the indescribable things he has done for me, so infinitely much more than I had ever expected; about that which taught me to be amazed, to be amazed at God, at his love and at what man's impotence is capable of performing with his aid; about what has taught me to long for eternity and not to be afraid of finding it tedious, since it is just the situation I have need of so as to have nothing else to do but give thanks—now that I must speak about this, a poetical impatience awakens in my soul. I would,

more resolute than that king who shouted, 'My kingdom for
horse!', and more blessedly resolute than he, I would give al
and my life along with it, in order to find what thought ha
more blessedness in finding than the lover in finding hi
beloved namely, 'the expression', so as to die with this expres
sion on my lips. And behold! they well up, these thought
as enchanting as the fruits in the garden of a fairy-tale, s
satisfying to the impulse of gratitude within me, so refreshin
to my hot desire—it seems as though if I had a winged pe
indeed if I had ten of them, I still should not be capable
keeping pace with the wealth which offers itself. But once
take my pen in hand I cannot for the instant move it, just as or
speaks of not being able to stir hand or foot; and in this co
dition not a line concerning this relationship gets put down c
paper. It seems as if I heard a voice which said to me: Sil
fellow, what does he imagine? does he not know that obed
ence is dearer to God than the fat of rams? Do it all simply
a prescribed task. Then I become entirely calm, then there
time to write each letter with my slower pen quite carefull
And if the poet-passion stirs in me again for an instant,
seems as if I heard a voice speaking to me as a teacher spea
to a boy when he says: Now merely hold your pen properly ar
write every letter with equal precision. And then I can do
then I dare not do anything else, then I write every wor
every line, hardly knowing what the next word and the ne
line is to be. And then when I read this over again it satisfi
me in quite a different way. For even if it were the case th
one or another glowing expression escaped me, the productic
is a different one, it is the expression not of the passion of po
or thinker but of godly fear, and for me it is an expression
divine worship.

But what I now at this instant live through again or ha
just lived through has been constantly experienced during n
whole activity as an author. It is said of the 'poet' that
invokes the muse in order to obtain thoughts. This has hard
been the case with me, my individuality also prohibits me fro
understanding it; but on the contrary I have needed God eve
day to protect me against the wealth of thoughts. Give a m
such a capacity for production and therewith a health so fr
as mine, and verily he will learn to pray. This is a *tour de for*

I have been able at any instant to perform, and I can perform it yet: I could sit down and keep on writing uninterruptedly day and night, and again a day and a night, for there was wealth enough. If I had done it, it would have been the end of me. Oh, even the least dietetic imprudence and I am in peril of my life. But then when I learn obedience, do this work as a prescribed task, hold the pen properly, write each letter carefully, then I can do it. And thus many and many a time I have had more joy in the relationship of obedience to God than in thoughts I produced.—This, as one can easily see, is the expression of the fact that I have no immediate relationship with God to boast of, that I am neither able nor bold enough to say that it is He that immediately puts thoughts into my mind, but that my relationship is a relationship through reflection, inwardness in reflection, as reflection is the predominant characteristic of my individuality, wherefore also in prayer my forte is thanksgiving.

. . . . . .

And now as to details; it would be in vain for me to try to relate how I have been sensible of God's aid. It is so inexplicable to me, this that has so often happened, that when I did something I could not tell why, or in relation to which it did not occur to me to ask why, when as a mere individual I followed the promptings of my natural inclination, that when this which for me had a purely personal significance on the verge of the fortuitous, that this then should show itself to have an entirely different, a purely ideal significance when it was viewed in retrospect as a factor in my literary activity, that much which I have done in a purely personal interest was, strangely enough, exactly what I should have done in my capacity as an author. It has been inexplicable to me how so often minor incidents in my life which seemed quite accidental (though it is true that with my imagination they became something much more) have brought me into certain situations where I did not understand myself and became melancholy—and behold, there then developed from this a mood which was just what I found serviceable in relation to the work I was occupied with at that time, and just at the right place. For there has not been the least let-up in production; what was wanted for use has always been at hand just at the instant when it needed to be used. In a sense my whole production has been

as even and uninterrupted as if I had nothing to do but to cop
every day a certain passage from a printed book.

This is not the end, but I break off—with my *praeterea censeo* . . . However, the 'Conclusion' of the Epilogue reflects the sam dependence upon Governance:[1]

Conclusion

I have nothing more to say, only in conclusion I will le another speak—my poet, who when he comes will allot me place among those who have suffered for an idea, and will say 'The martyrdom this author suffered can be briefly de scribed in these words: He suffered from being a genius in provincial market-town. The scale he applied with regard t talents, industry, disinterestedness, self-sacrifice, absolutenes in the definition of thoughts, &c., was very much too great a a measure for his contemporaries, it screwed up the price to terribly high and reduced their price too terribly low— almost made it seem as if the market-town and the majorit within the same did not possess *absolutum dominium*, but th there was a God in existence.

. . . . . .

'Yet verily he found also here in this world what he sought— if no one else, then he himself was "that individual" whom h sought, and he became that more and more. It was the cause Christianity he served, his life from childhood up being ma vellously adapted to this end. So he brought to completion h work of reflection, the task of exhibiting what Christianity i what it is to become a Christian, entirely in and through refle tion. His purity of heart was "to will only one thing"; what i his lifetime was the complaint his contemporaries made again him, that he would not abate the price, would not compromis precisely this same thing is his eulogy in the mouth of the fo lowing generation, that he did not abate the price, did n compromise. But he was not infatuated by the immense unde taking; whereas dialectically as an author he had a survey of th whole, he understood Christianly that the whole of it signifie for him that he himself was being educated in Christianity. Th dialectical structure which he brought to completion, the singl parts of which were works in themselves, he could not ascrib to any man, and still less would he ascribe it to himself; if h could have ascribed it to any one, it would have been Governance, to whom in fact, day by day, year after year, it was ascribed by the author, who historically died of a mortal illness, but poetically died of longing for eternity so as to have nothing else to do uninterruptedly but give God thanks.'

This is in fact the end of the book, yet it is only a small part I have quoted—and again I say, *praeterea censeo*. . . .

Hardly less important than *The Point of View* is its Supplement entitled ' "The Individual"—Two "Notes" concerning my work as an author'. In compass it comes to about a quarter of the whole book. 'The single individual' is here regarded as 'the Christian category', 'the category of spirit and of spiritual awakening'. S. K. remarks upon the double meaning of this term: 'The individual can signify the unique, and it can signify every one.' The proud meaning angers some people, and the humble meaning repels others. The pseudonym may seem to use the word in the first sense, corresponding to 'the superior man' of Confucius, but the Discourses manifestly dwell upon the humble sense. S. K. calls the attention of politicians to the fact that human equality is not to be attained by political measures; but 'in case the politician really loves humanity and loves men, he may, by reading these works, become observant of the fact that the religious is the realization of all that in his happiest moments he has ever conceived. For if every one really loved his neighbour as himself, perfect human equality would absolutely be obtained—and the mere fact that the individual recognizes this as a duty shows that he recognizes human equality.' This is an 'age of disintegration'—reflection upon the individual discloses the fact, but it also suggests the cure. The individual is the opposite of the 'crowd', which is always 'non-truth'; the individual therefore must stand out as a 'witness for the truth'; and 'the Missionary' who is to come to introduce Christianity into Christendom will surely make use of this category.

One might wish that S. K. had included in the admirable Introduction to *The Point of View* a long passage which occurred to him as an afterthought and which now is printed in the *Papers*.[1] It plainly expresses the thought that when once he had produced his 'accounting' for the whole of his foregoing works he would be free to go on to the adventure of direct communication:

To speak out—just as distinctly, as directly, as openly, a conciliatorily, as peaceably as possible. Now that I regard i religiously as my duty to speak, I shall by God's help speak in that spirit candidly, and for the rest, as well as I know how My heart is enlarged—not that it has ever been narrowly con stricted in my breast, but the inwardness which has been my life and which I thought would be my death has now found vent, the dialectical band is broken, I dare to speak directly.

Inasmuch as this passage was not included, there is no clea expression in the book of the fact that it deals with a chapter in S. K.'s life which was already closed, and looks forward to a entirely new style of production exemplified in the works of 1848 But S. K. had it in mind to write an addendum which would account in advance for the new venture in direct communication He called it 'Armed Neutrality'. This work was never finished but part of it was carefully written and is preserved in the *Papers*. The title had occurred to him ten years previously, as we se from a jotting in the Journal:[2] 'My standpoint is armed neutra lity.' At one time he proposed to publish a religious periodica with that name, which should display the ideal picture of th Christian.[3] The book as he planned it had in view his future pro duction (including the production of 1848 which was not ye published), and it sought to emphasize chiefly two things: th necessity of displaying constantly the ideal picture of the Chris tian; and the fact that he did not claim to be himself the ideal h portrayed:[4]

Certainly it is of the utmost importance that in every genera tion the ideal picture of the Christian should be held up pro minently, and illuminated precisely with a view to the error of the time being; but he who draws this picture must abov all things guard against mistaking himself for it—so as to gai a group of adherents, get himself idolized, and then pass judge ment upon Christendom with a passion earthly and worldly No, the relation must be kept purely ideal. He who present the picture must be the first to humble himself under it, t admit that though he also strives within himself to realize thi picture, he is still very far from being the picture; he mus admit that actually he is related poetically or as a poet to th *presentation* of this picture, that whereas he associates himsel

Christianly in his own person with the picture which is presented (this being his difference from the poet as he is commonly conceived), yet it is only as a poet he is ahead of others in the presentation of the picture.

So there remains no danger of fanaticism; the poet, or rather the poet-dialectician, does not represent himself as the ideal, and still less does he pass judgement upon any single man. But he holds up the ideal, so that now every one if he likes can in tranquil solitude compare his life with the ideal. The presentation of the ideal cannot but be polemical to a certain degree, but it is not polemical against any individual person, it is not finitely polemical against something finite, but only infinitely polemical to illuminate the ideal, it has no practical proposal to advance, does not aim at any decision in outward affairs, in the worldly sphere. This was and is my idea of a reformation, which, whether it now succeeds or not, and how far it succeeds or not, in any case will come about by itself without international congresses, synods, balloting, in short, without any profanation.

An entry in the Journal of a date a little earlier than the above shows how decisive was the transition from indirect communication to direct, to the duty of 'witnessing':[1]

Yet the communication of Christian truth must end at last in 'witnessing'; maieutic cannot be the last form. For, Christianly understood, the truth does not reside in the subject (as Socrates understood it) but is a revelation which must be proclaimed.

The maieutic method can perfectly well be used in Christendom, just because the majority actually live in the illusion that they are Christians. But since Christianity is after all Christianity, the maieutic teacher must become the witness.

But however clearly, however trenchantly, S. K. bore witness from this time on to the truth of Christianity, he was very far from the spirit of puritanical severity. His position is revealed clearly enough in the three extracts from the Journal with which I conclude this chapter. He did not exact of others that they should 'venture so far out' as he himself felt compelled to venture.

No, I am a memento—as far as possible from exacting of others that they shall live as I do, as far as possible from finding anything meritorious in my life. But I am a memento for the age, that they may be so kind as to appreciate thankfully the fact that for them it is possible and also permissible to have this alleviation of occupying themselves with finite aims, and also that they may be ashamed if they impudently invert the relation and regard this mitigation as the highest seriousness and as the loftiest thing of all. This has been more and more forgotten since Luther, whom they have taken in vain—and here I come in.

But reassurance is to be found in the fact that (especially in the beginning) it was in an all-too-frightful measure I was existentially compelled to become attentive (and thereby also enabled to make others attentive) to the sterner side of religious existence—by the fact, namely, that by suffering and under compulsion I am put outside the universal.

The pain and the torture, especially in the beginning, have been frightful—and just for that reason I have had something quite different to think about than to become self-important by reason of the 'meritorious' or to be busy about forming imitators.[1]

(Severity/Leniency.)

In my presentation severity is a dialectical moment in Christianity, but leniency is just as strongly represented. The first is represented poetically by the pseudonyms; the second personally by myself. So the matter must be presented to this age which has taken Christianity in vain. But it is quite a different thing when a man in despair has nothing else to say about Christianity but that it is the cruellest self-torture. To put an end to coquetry I had to introduce severity—introduced just for the sake of giving impetus in the direction of the leniency of Christianity. So it is I have understood Christianity and my task. If I had only understood its frightful severity—then I should have kept silent. This is a point to which Johannes de silentio has already called attention: that under such circumstances one must keep silent, or at least show that one loves other men . . . by keeping silent. For a merely negative result, especially so terrible a negative result one must not communicate. Such a thing is not communication, it is assault, betrayal, weakness of character which would have at least some satisfaction in the sorry pleasure of making others just as unhappy and confused as one is oneself.[1]

The Requirement/Indulgence.

The requirement is the universal, that which applies to all, and is the scale by which every one shall be measured. The requirement, therefore, is the thing that must be proclaimed; the teacher has to proclaim the requirement and thus provoke uneasiness; he dare not reduce the requirement.

Indulgence must not be proclaimed. Not by any means must it be proclaimed, for it is the entirely particular, corresponding to the particularity of the individuals, and it is their inmost private understanding with God.

The proclamation of the requirement shall drive men to God and Christ with the intent of finding what indulgence they need, what they dare pray for in the sight of God by way of indulgence, while the proclamation of the requirement at the same time holds them to God.

But the relation has been inverted. The teachers (the parsons) do not proclaim the requirement but indulgence. Instead of regarding the indulgence as the deepest secret of the conscience before God in the face of the requirement, they have inverted the relation and proclaim, with mutual contentment and edification, simply and solely indulgence; they entirely leave out the requirement, or they may say of it that it was only for the Apostles; and so with high enthusiasm the one man proclaims to the others indulgence—indulgence, which however is one of the prerogatives of God's glory, so that only by Him can it be bestowed upon the individual, that is, upon every individual, but to each man severally.[2]

III. VENTURING FAR OUT

1849–52

THE year 1849 is memorable for the fact that gold was discovered in California. Something very different was going on in Denmark, where S. K. was embarrassed by finding himself in possession of a more precious treasure and did not know what to do with it. He found that it was one thing to write books which exemplified direct communication and quite another thing to publish them. The endless debate whether to publish or not to publish began as early as the middle of 1848 while he was still busily writing, and it was not entirely concluded until the middle of 1852. The Journals for this period, occupied predominantly with this subject, are now printed in four and a half big volumes comprising 2,000 pages, reproducing twenty manuscript books, from NB^6 to NB^{25}. Most of the students of S. K. become impatient with him at this point. It seems to me that they might at least preserve the tolerant attitude of the physician dealing with his patient. For my part I am inclined rather to dwell upon the fact that in the end S. K. triumphed over a thousand fears and scruples, 'venturing himself far out where God could get a hold of him'. I propose to spare the reader a detailed account of the many relapses and repetitions, recommending that he should measure the triumph by the difficulty and recognize that this was the first great victory S. K. had won over the melancholy which made his life so tragic and inhibited frankness of speech.

At the beginning of 1849 he was facing the second peril involved in what he called 'the duplex danger of being a Christian':[1]

> First, all the sufferings of inwardness involved in becoming a Christian: parting with one's understanding and being crucified upon the paradox—here belongs the Concluding Postscript, which presents this as ideally as possible.
>
> Then the danger that the Christian must live in the world of worldliness and in it express the fact that he is a Christian. Here belong all the later productions which I have ready.

Of course the danger of being a Christian was not reduced by S. K. to the mere question of publishing certain books, but this question was for him inseparably involved with the necessity of *expressing* himself as a Christian in this world of worldliness. For this reason the debate was so difficult and so long drawn out. We have already had occasion to notice that S. K. was commonly very slow in making up his mind. This may be regarded as a symptom of his malady. He himself ascribed it to 'melancholy'. But we must not overlook the fact that in general it is characteristic of a highly reflective mind. To account for his slow motion, S. K. remarked that he was 'heavily armed'; and a more amusing analogy occurred to him when he observed how great a disparity there is between birds with respect to their promptitude in taking flight. In fact the crow furnishes a good analogy to S. K.'s helpless efforts to leave the branch:

> Others (the heavier and more sluggish, like the crow) make a great fuss when they start to fly: they let go with one foot, but then grab it again, so that no flight results; then they labour with their wings while they still continue to hold fast with their feet; . . .[1]

The question of publishing the last books was very seriously complicated by the thought of taking a parish, which again had entered his mind. It naturally astonishes us to see this thought coming to the front again after it had been so definitely rejected. But this, as he said, 'was my original thought', and S. K. was exceedingly tenacious of his original thoughts. Moreover, in the entry which records his Easter experience there is a sentence surprising enough to arrest the attention of the reader, although I made no remark about it at that place: 'And then I shall become a parson.' This thought, as I understand it, was very naturally suggested by the experience that he was at last able to 'speak'. When once his melancholy reserve was broken, it must occur to him that now he was in a position to 'realize the universal' by engaging in that calling which was his father's ambition for him, his original intention, and perhaps the only profession he was in any way fitted for. However, we hear no more about this resolution for many months, and no steps whatever were taken to put it into effect—until his economic situation became so pressing that he was compelled to think of some way of earning a living. Already in 1848 he began to reflect that the publication of his latest works with their 'judgement upon Christendom' might hinder him from obtaining a benefice in the Established Church:[2]

The next step in publication will be very decisive for my outward existence. I have steadily had in view a remote possibility of being able to seek appointment to a parish when things came to the worst with respect to my livelihood. Now when I publish these last books it is quite possible that they would refuse it to me even if I should ask for it, so that the difficulty is not as heretofore whether I dare accept it, but that they will not give it to me.

The solution which first presented itself was to get the parish first and *then* publish. This was a shrewd plan, and in a way it was natural to S. K.'s 'intriguing pate'. He could boast that his mind was fertile in shrewd plans—and that habitually he scorned to follow them. Eventually this plan was rejected with the strongest expressions of disgust and self-reproach:[1]

Monday, June 25 [1849].

Fie, Fie!

So I have been willing (or at least had the thought) to act shrewdly in order to assure myself first of a position and then publish the works pseudonymously. A capital interpretation of 'Seek first God's kingdom'!

In the 7th number of *The Instant* (August 31, 1855) there occurs one of the most devastating satires S. K. ever penned, and I am told that in Denmark it is familiar to every young man who is preparing for holy orders:[2]

'First God's Kingdom'

A sort of novel.

The theological candidate Ludwig From [*From* means pious]—seeks. And when one hears that a 'theological' candidate seeks, one does not need a vivid power of imagination to understand that what he seeks is naturally God's kingdom, which indeed one ought to seek *first*.

No, not exactly that. What he seeks is a living as a parson in the royal establishment; and a great deal happened *first*, before he got even so far as that—as I shall indicate with a few strokes.

These few strokes describe first the artificiality of the whole course of scholastic training. Then after eight years of such training the young candidate begins in earnest to seek—*first* a wife (at least he assures himself of her by becoming engaged); then, 'running from Herod to Pilate', he seeks appointment to a good living. He gets it—but discovers to his dismay that it does not bring in nearly so much as he expected. He tries in vain to draw back. The dean (who knows the whole story) preaches the ordination sermon on the words of the Apostle Peter, 'Lo, we have left all and followed thee'; and the young ordinand preaches on the text, 'Seek ye first the kingdom of God.'

Is it not shocking that S. K. could so soon forget that this was precisely his own case, or at least that he had dallied with such a possibility? The entry last quoted assures us that he had by no means forgotten, and the name of Ludwig wherever it occurs is an indication that he is thinking of himself. This is the disarming trait in S. K.'s criticism, that he was often satirizing himself, or at least the possibilities which he had entertained. He spoke the truth when he affirmed that he regarded his later writings as addressed first of all to himself, and his concluding satire upon established Christianity, exaggerated as it was, was unanswerable, because it was written from within the Church, by a man who knew in his own person, at least in the form of possibility, everything he was talking about.

But the shrewd plan S. K. excogitated was not by any means so crass as it might seem. At the first mention of it (some six months before it was so scornfully rejected) he reflected that the humble thing for him to do was first to accept a position as parochial parson in order that he might be eventually included under the condemnation he was pronouncing:[1]

> . . . On the other hand, if I have first procured a position in the Established Church, then my form of existence will obviate all misunderstanding [that I conceive myself to be something like an apostle]. . . . The 'judgement', if one will call it such, which is contained in these works, the judgement upon Christendom, I myself like every one else shall be subjected to by the fact that I am so situated.

At this time he did not seriously purpose to publish his last works pseudonymously, but he intended to print on the title-page of each of them:[2]

'Poetically', to indicate that I do not give myself out to be an extraordinary Christian or to be what I describe. 'Without authority', to indicate that I do not bind others or judge others. 'For revival in inwardness', to show that I have nothing to do with changes in outward things or with reformation of that sort.

The employment of a pseudonym made this precaution unnecessary. But it must be understood that S. K. never for a moment thought of concealing the fact that he was the author. The pseudonym he chose would have given him away, even if he had not put his own name on the title-page as editor, and both the substance and the form were so characteristic of S. K. that no one could be for a moment in doubt about the author. We may remember that he expressed strong contempt for anonymous writing.

S. K. had sagacity enough to recognize that it was hypochondria which suggested to him the fear that the authorities might be unwilling to appoint him to a country parish; for he perceived that Bishop Mynster would feel greatly relieved at seeing so dangerous a person removed from the capital to the country. But by this time the idea of a country parish had ceased to attract him. Acquaintance with country parsons had made him aware that it was far from being the idyllic life he had fancied. He now thought rather of a post in the Pastoral Seminary, as more consonant with his tastes and with his intellectual preparation. He said that he had worked for a long time intensively and could work in the seminary more extensively. On the occasion of one of his many visits to Bishop Mynster he 'let drop a word' about appointment to the Pastoral Seminary.[1] He was glad he had done this, to prove to himself that he was not held back by pride from seeking an appointment. But at the same time he knew himself well enough to understand that 'in case it was offered to me, it would hardly tempt me'. He recognized that difficulty and opposition might be dangerous for him, because they might incite his polemical nature and prompt him to do what in his heart of hearts he was resolved not to do, i.e. end the long debate by actually procuring an ecclesiastical benefice. As a matter of fact, his polemical nature was aroused, by the slight rebuffs he received, to do just the contrary—to publish his books.[2] When he broached again this subject of the seminary the wily bishop replied, 'Why don't you found one of your own?' It was a good answer; for however helpful S. K. might have been to the students, he would surely have been a devastating element in the faculty.

Singular as his character was, I cannot help thinking that in one respect he was rarely fitted to be a teacher of young men. It is tragic to think that though once in a while he preached on a Friday in a church, he was regularly in church as a hearer—so regularly that he never voluntarily was absent on a day of obligation and missed no sermon of Mynster's but his last. He said of himself very truly:[1]

> What is it essentially that has made me a religious speaker? It is the fact that I am a hearer. That is to say, my life has been so complicated and strenuous that I truly felt an urgent *need* of hearing a guiding and instructive word. I heard and heard—but if what I heard was Christianity, I should be beyond helping. So I became myself a speaker. Hence it is that I know definitely (what certainly our parsons seldom know) that there is one who has profit from these discourses—myself. I am exactly the opposite of the other speakers—they are busy talking to others—I talk to myself.

To tell the truth, it has often occurred to me that a preacher who is not primarily talking to himself is not likely to be very profitable to others.

A decision about the publication of the works which were lying ready in his desk could not be postponed indefinitely, owing to the fact that a second edition of *Either/Or* was impending. The public had long been clamouring for it, and S. K. at last yielded reluctantly. He felt that this book, which was appropriate as the beginning of his literary production, was incongruous with the stage he had now reached and with the serious books he had lately been writing. It was clear to him, therefore, that it must be 'accompanied'. His first thought was to accompany it with the 'Cycle of Ethico-Religious Treatises' (which included the *Two Minor Treatises* eventually published).[2] A second suggestion was the 'Two Notes', which appear now as an addendum to the *Point of View*.[3] But finally he resolved to accompany it with the 'Three Godly Discourses about the Lilies and the Birds', which were as if written expressly for this purpose. In fact, they were written at this time, although I found it convenient to mention them in the preceding chapter. So this poetical farewell to poetry, a poem to end poetry, was published on the same day (May 14, 1849) as the second edition of the first aesthetic work.

But the solution of this problem still left unsolved the fate of all the writings which caused him so much uneasiness. After a tremendous struggle the decision was made to publish *The Sickness unto Death*. It appeared on July 30, 1849. But *Training in Christianity* was a more drastic attack on the 'established', and another year or more elapsed before S. K. could make up his mind to publish it—on September 27, 1850. Still another year of debate was needed before he finally decided *not* to publish *The Point of View* but to substitute for it the brief explanation *On my Work as an Author*, which was published near the middle of 1851. It is not necessary to quote many of the entries which register this long debate.[1] One must do for all, and I quote from that only a part:[2]

> Contemplating my own personal life, am I a Christian in that sense? or is not this personal existence of mine a mere poet-existence, though with a trait of daimonia? The logical thing to do would be to venture on so prodigious a scale and bring upon myself such misfortune that I should then be in a situation to become really a Christian. But have I a right to do it dramatically, so that the Christianity of the whole land is involved in the game? Is there not something of desperation in all this—as though one were treacherously to start a conflagration in order to cast oneself into the arms of God?—Perhaps, for perhaps it might turn out that I do not become a Christian.
>
> . . . . .
>
> I must bewail the fact and reproach myself for it that in several of the foregoing entries which are registered in this Journal there actually is to be found an attempt to exalt myself † for which God forgive me.
>
> Till now I am a poet, absolutely nothing more, and it is a desperate struggle to will to go out beyond my limits.
>
> The work on Training in Christianity has for me great significance—does it follow from this that I must at once make it public? Perhaps I am one of the few who need such strong measures. And instead of profiting by it and beginning myself

quite seriously to become a Christian, I would first make it public. Fantastical!

This work and the others are actually in existence; the time may perhaps come when it is appropriate and I have strength to do it and it is right for me to do it.

It is true in many ways that the whole productivity is my education.—Very well, does that mean that I, instead of making serious work of becoming a Christian, should become a phenomenon in the world?

So THEN *now* Sickness unto Death is coming out pseudonymously with me as editor. It is called 'for edification'—that is more than my category, the poetical category, 'edifying'.

As the river Guadalquivir (this occurred to me earlier and is to be found somewhere in the Journal) plunges underground at one place, so there is a stretch (the edifying) which bears my name. There is something lower (the aesthetical), which is pseudonymous, and something higher, which also is pseudonymous because my personality does not correspond with it.

The pseudonym is called Johannes Anti-Climacus in contrast to Johannes Climacus who said he was not a Christian. Anti-Climacus is the opposite extreme, that of being a Christian in an extraordinary degree—whereas I manage only to be quite a simple Christian.

In the same way Training in Christianity can be published, but there is no haste about it.

But nothing about my author-person. It is falsehood to anticipate in one's lifetime, which means only to convert oneself into the interesting.

Generally speaking, it is in quite a different direction I must now venture. I must venture to believe that I can be saved by Christ from the power of melancholy in which I have lived, and I must venture to try to be more economical.

S. K. was delighted with the discovery of Anti-Climacus as a pseudonym. It exactly suited his roguish disposition. It seemed to him to solve his present difficulty, and in later entries he looked back with complacency upon this solution, although sometimes he perceived clearly enough that it really made no difference at all whether he published the books over his own name or attributed them to a pseudonym.[1]

We can discern in the passage just quoted, and more clearly in others, that this question of publishing was in reality a far more serious one for S. K. than we at first had any reason to suppose. S. K. regarded this as the first step in a venture which would take him very far out, for it meant (to use his own expression) 'stepping forth in character'.[1]

> The power to awaken lies in the fact that God has given me strength to be able to live as an enigma—but now no more of that, lest the awakening end in confusion.
>
> The thing to do now is with a resonant voice to assume responsibility for the foregoing maieutic works and then step out decisively and straightforwardly in character as one whose will has been and is to serve the cause of Christianity.

But the reflective mind sees also the other side:[2]

> Yet all too near lies the way of error, the will to reform and awaken the whole world . . . instead of oneself—and this is just the path for restless heads with much imagination.
>
> That is a fault I have a disposition to—to compel myself almost daimoniacally to be stronger than I am. As a man of sanguine humour is required to hate himself, so perhaps it is required of me that I should love myself and renounce the melancholy hatred of myself which in a melancholy man can be almost a pleasure.
>
> This is also the way with me, that I constantly accompany myself poetically and now require of myself almost in desperation that I shall act so as to be in character.

And yet again, if he did not explain his work,[3]

> It is as if one possessed a great treasure and kept it safely hid by throwing away the key. The thought that troubles me is whether I have a right to do that, whether it is permissible with respect to a productivity which is so infinitely indebted to Him for its meaning, to let it remain an enigma and for many a mere curiosity.

We must bear in mind that in 1849 S. K. already clearly envisaged the necessity of the dramatic attack upon easy-going Christianity which five years later he actually launched. His contemporaries were astonished at the unexpected outburst, but we who can read his Journals have rather reason to be astonished that he held in so long, waiting for courage to face the ordeal and for a signal that the time for it was come. In an entry of February 1849[1] he imagines himself preaching in the most elegant and fashionable church in the capital, before a distinguished congregation which included the king and the queen. Taking for his text the driving out of the business-sharks from the Temple, he begins with the declaration that in such an environment Christianity cannot be preached. It can only be preached in a situation that is real. 'I am in your hands, a lone man, but now I will speak —and so this is reality. An attack upon the elegant church and the elegant congregation. Christ was not an elegant man who preached in an elegant church to an elegant assembly about the fact that the truth suffers—it was *reality* that he was spat upon.... Behold, there was an awakening!'

This entry was immediately preceded by three which have the rare distinction of being introduced by a triple sign of the cross. They deal profoundly with the dialectical aspects of Christ as our pattern and our atonement, with the duty of imitation and the blessedness of adoration:[2]

> So it is not just a matter of course that Christ is the pattern and I must be willing to imitate Him. In the first place, I need His help in order to imitate Him; and in the second place, in so far as He is the Saviour and Redeemer of the race, I cannot imitate Him.

One who knows S. K. will see that these reflections were forced upon him by the thought of the necessity of martyrdom. He could think of no other imitation of Christ but the imitation of His suffering and death. And indeed the Gospels speak of no other sort of imitation. S. K. was once prompted 'unaccountably' to say to his fiancée that even in childhood he had had the thought that 'in every generation some individual is chosen to suffer for the others'. And he says in *The Point of View*:[3]

> Very far back in my recollection stretches the thought that in every generation there are two or three who are sacrificed for the others, are used in order to discover in frightful sufferings what redounds to the benefit of the others. So in my melancholy I understood that I was marked out for this.

When he reflected how urgently martyrs were needed to stay

the dissolution of Christendom, and how strangely he had been prepared from his youth up to play a singular role, he could not but understand it as a call for him to stand out as a 'witness for the truth', and he anticipated with fear and joy that his open attack upon Christianity as established would involve martyrdom at the hands of the crowd. We cannot wonder then that he hesitated about publishing his latest works when he regarded this as the first step along such a path. Though the thought of martyrdom was the product of a vivid and melancholy imagination, the fear it prompted was no less real. Reading his impatient critics I am compelled to suppose that they would feel no hesitation about going to the stake as witnesses for the truth.

> They say that the Good lends strength. And that is quite true, but it is a very fine and delicate sort of strength . . . a sort of strength that doesn't make much show in the world.[1]
>
> It has come to my ears that some of the strict Christians here at home find that my presentation of Christianity is exaggerated, too high, superhuman. Capital! A capital proof that my judgement upon Christendom is justified! I testify before God that I am conscious of having abated 30%, often 50%, of the Gospel's own presentation—and then 'the strict Christians' find that my presentation is too ideal.[2]

The publication of these 'last works' was the more momentous for S. K. because he regarded them as literally the last he would ever produce as an 'author'—before he stepped out in character with a pronouncement so blunt and plain, that to regard it as a 'literary' production would be almost as impertinent as to judge the Ten Commandments by the standard of belles-lettres. He prided himself upon the fact that he was the only author to have resolution enough to 'let up', i.e. cease to write. 'That place', he said, 'is vacant.' Actually, because the moment for decisive action was long deferred, several more writings followed: two small volumes of Discourses (pronounced 'at the foot of the altar' where it seemed fitting he should end); and *For Self-Examination*, which may be regarded as the beginning of the open attack. The sequel to it, *Judge for Yourself*, was not published during his lifetime because he thought it too 'direct'. When we think of the prodigious productivity he displayed during the seven years which preceded 1849, and reckon how little was produced during the next five years, it must be admitted that he did 'let up'.

We may well be astonished to discover that in S. K.'s mind there was still another complication which inhibited the prompt publication of his last works. He was fearful that the scandal created by his open attack, and perhaps even by the preliminary skirmish, would distress Regina. He had hoped that his renown as an author would accrue to her—but the direction his writing had taken was likely to involve him (and 'her') in a notoriety the very opposite of renown. When at the end he stepped out decisively in character, it was a great relief to him to know that his 'little governess' was already far away from Denmark, following her husband as Governor of the Virgin Islands; and at that time he managed adroitly to have his favourite nieces sent away from Copenhagen on a long visit to Paris. I may remark, in passing, that on my visit to the Virgin Islands I found that Fritz Schlegel was still remembered as the best governor they had ever had.

It cannot surprise us, of course, that S. K. who was so tenacious of his loyalties still remembered Regina affectionately; but we may well be surprised to discover that in 1849 he had already begun to think of the possibility of a *rapprochement* with Madame Schlegel. But I can see how this might be a consequence of his Easter experience, for it is to be remembered that he mentions 'her' in the entry which records this experience. His exultation at the conviction that his reserve was broken was dampened at once by the reflection that this liberation had come too late to permit him to marry Regina. It cannot seem strange that he should begin after a while to think of the possibility of establishing a friendly relation with her, receiving her forgiveness after he had disclosed to her the reasons which compelled him to break the engagement and practise so cruel a deceit—not without reflecting anxiously upon the consequences a disclosure of his constant love might have for her as a married woman. But for the moment, so long as Councillor Olsen lived, the thought of making it up with 'her' was not practical. S. K. had always cherished a profound esteem for his near-father-in-law. But an attempt he had made in 1848 to engage the offended father in conversation (it is an amazing story) was enough to convince him that the Councillor was an implacable enemy.

Councillor Olsen died on the night of June 25–6, 1849. It

happened that S. K. just at that time had formed the resolution to publish *The Sickness unto Death*. The evening of the 25th, after a vain attempt to see Bishop Mynster and the Cultus Minister Madvig, he wrote to ask his printer whether he was free to begin promptly to print the book, which he then meant to publish over his own name. The printer replied that the way was clear and asked to have the manuscript at once. There were so few happenings in S. K.'s life that little things assumed immense importance:[1]

> The fact is I was a little offended by Mynster, and this feeling was enough to prompt me to do what I had earlier been so near doing.

Not till the 27th did he learn of Councillor Olsen's death, and that at once raised 'a quantity of difficulties'—by which we are to understand that it opened up the possibility of *rapprochement* with Regina and therefore prompted him to withdraw the book which might hinder the realization of this hope. He did not go so far as this, but he compromised by ascribing it to Anti-Climacus. To this final decision he was impelled by a strange and supernormal experience.[2] He relates that during the night following the 27th, when he had learnnt of the death of Regina's father,

> I was greatly overtaxed and slept rather restlessly, and strangely enough there occurred to me a word as if I were about to plunge to destruction.

In this contemporary entry the experience of that night is told so laconically that we can make little of it. But from entries made several years later we learn that what he experienced then was a vivid auditory hallucination, such as might well have frightened him into a decision. He remembered distinctly almost every word of a conversation he seemed to be carrying on with himself, but he was never able to make sure what the words meant or implied. The first entries which adequately describe this experience were written in 1852, and from them we learn what was said in this colloquy:[3]

> 'So then it is this that is required of me?'
> 'What does he imagine?'
> 'I could well wait 8 days.'
> 'See, now he wills his own destruction.'

According to S. K.'s final interpretation, it was not his better nature but his 'common sense' which tried to hold him back with the question whether so much was required of him and with the suggestion of at least a short delay. He was enough of a psychologist to understand that both voices were his own.

Not long after this, on November 19, he made a move to establish with Regina a 'sisterly relationship', believing that he had 'data' to indicate that she desired it. He was unable to do such a thing spontaneously and simply. On Sunday, July 1, Regina 'along with the whole family' was in the same church that he attended. 'She came so near that we almost touched as I passed under the pulpit. Perhaps she expected that I would greet her; I kept my eyes, however, on myself.'[1] Poor man! What he could not do simply he had to do ponderously. After he had rejected many forms of a long letter admirably expressed, he wrote a short letter to Schlegel enclosing a sealed note to Regina which the husband might give her if he thought fit. Two days later he received from Schlegel an indignant reply (not preserved) returning the note unopened.[2] This was a cruel blow, but I feel by no means assured that the triangular relationship proposed would have resulted in happiness to any of the three.

All this is to be found in her pedestal in a packet enclosed in an envelope inscribed: 'Regarding Her'.

Having dwelt so constantly in this chapter upon the problems which tormented S. K., I would not conclude without giving some notion of the deep religious thoughts which sustained him during his period. The following entry, which was made in April 1849, s described in the margin as an addendum to 'The Accounting':

Poetically about Myself

... On the other hand, should an individual say to me, 'You who have now lived for so long a time and do still daily live surrounded by these thousands with their twaddle, their grins, their bestiality, &c.—it seems to me that there is something artificial about the silence with which you suppress all reference to such a thing, or about the tranquillity with which you speak of yourself, as though you were unaffected by all such things'. To him I would make answer:

In the first place, when I speak there is an exceedingly lofty

Person who is listening. (Every man, be it said, is in the same situation, only most men do not bear it in mind.) There is an exceedingly lofty Person who is listening—God in heaven—he sits in heaven and hears what every man says. That I bear in mind. What wonder then that my speech is not without a certain solemnity? For the rest, it is not at all with these thousands I speak, but with the single individual before God—so it is rather to be wondered that my speech is not infinitely more solemn.

In the second place. Already when I was a little child it was told me, as solemnly as possible, that the crowd spat upon Christ, though He was the truth. This I have kept deeply hidden in my heart. For though there have been moments, yea, hours, when it has been as if I had forgotten it, yet I have constantly recurred to this as my first thought. I have also, the better to treasure it, hidden under the most opposite exterior the fact that I treasured this thought deepest in my soul; for I was fearful lest it might early elude me, lest it might trick me and become like a shell that fails to go off. This thought—by the help of which also I understood promptly and easily, as the least difficult thing, something I was much occupied with in my youth, namely him, the simple wise man, *intellectuality*' martyr, who was persecuted and condemned to death by 'hear say', by 'the crowd'. This thought is my life. That I am on the right way I know with the most definite assurance possible, by the fact that the twaddle, the grins, and the bestiality of th 'crowd' are the environment and the landmarks. What wonde then that my speech is not without a certain solemnity, and tha like me it has tranquillity; for the way is the right one, and I an on the right way, although far behind. Suppose that they wh after having *voluntarily* suffered for a long while the roughness ill treatment, calumny of their age (that is, being as it wer salted, for 'every sacrifice must be salted'), then after that wer derided and spat upon (that is, after having undergone the las preliminary initiation)—ended by being crucified, or beheadec or burned, or broken on the wheel; granted that these accord ing to the Christian order of precedence rank in the first class which is indeed indisputable—this being granted, I think tha without saying too much for myself I am now about the lowes in the lowest, the eighth class. Further than that I am not likel to get. But still what a teacher once wrote in his report upon a pupil fits my life exactly—and it lacked only that he had written it about me—'He goes backwards in spite of all diligence'. That was ineptly expressed by the teacher; there is only one situation where such a judgement can be said to be aptly applied, as now in the case of my life. Yet 'in spite of all diligence' is perhaps saying too little, for I use a great deal of diligence, am very diligent and industrious; and backward I go, that is perfectly certain; and the more diligent I am the more I go backward, that also is perfectly certain—so in truth with much diligence I am going more and more backward. In this way I hope to enter into eternity—and philosophically how might it be possible to enter into eternity except by going backwards; Christianly how might it be possible to enter into eternity except through the fact that everything goes backward with one? Christ was spat upon, who was the Truth—and though I were to forget all, I never forget, as hitherto I have not forgotten that they told me this when I was a child, or forgotten the impression it made upon the child. It happens sometimes that a child still in the cradle is engaged to the person who is to become his wife or her husband—religiously understood, I already when I was a child was . . . pre-engaged (*for lovet*). Alas, I have paid dearly for the fact that once I misunderstood my life and forgot . . . that I was engaged (*for lovet*)! And on the other hand, I once in my life experienced the most beautiful and blessed contentment, indescribably satisfying to me, because in the step I took on that occasion, in the danger I then voluntarily exposed myself to, I entirely understood myself and understood myself to the effect that I was engaged. Engaged! Engaged to the Love which from the very first and until this very moment (in spite of my many errors and sins) has constantly encompassed me—me of whom it can be said with perfect truth that he sinned much, and yet perhaps of whom it can also be said not altogether untruly that he loved much—engaged to a Love which infinitely surpasses my understanding, to a Fatherliness 'in comparison with which even the most loving father is only a step-father'.

And then only one thing more, upon which, as with a dying man's last will, I lay the deepest and most earnest emphasis. When I think of myself in relation to those glorious ones (to whom, however, I am related only by being at the utmost possible remove from them, below them, as the lowest in the lowest, the eighth class) I have surely a serious and sad advantage with respect to the obligation of holding out. For it seems to me that when one is himself pure, perfect and holy, the opposition of the world to the True must make one so sad that one must soon have died of sadness. I on the other hand am not a holy person, I am a penitent, to whom it may be indescribably serviceable to suffer something, and to whom, just by way of penance, it is a satisfaction to suffer. Indeed if I were contemporary with a purer one, it would be my satisfaction to divert so far as possible all the 'crowd's' jeering and ill treatment away from him to myself. This in my opinion is an advantage, that I who have the honour of serving the truth, by the fact of being a penitent, personally (for the faults I may have been guilty of at an earlier time and for the faults I now commit), find that the ill treatment I receive from men is thus far (but only thus far) rightly applied when it is directed against me—who certainly succeeded extraordinarily with the deception, the deception which possibly to a certain degree was the invention of melancholy, of making myself out the most light-minded of all.

And this is another:[1]

I arise in the morning and give thanks to God—then I begin my work. At a definite time in the evening I leave off and give thanks to God—then I sleep. And thus I live, though at single instants not without attacks of melancholy and sadness, yet essentially day in and day out in the most blessed enchantment. Alas, thus I am living in Copenhagen—and in Copenhagen I am the only one who is not serious, the only one who profits nobody and accomplishes nothing, a half-mad eccentric. So the crowd judges me, and the few who see deeper have no objection to letting this remain the common judgement about me.

But verily we need not search the Journals for proof of S. K.'s progress in becoming a Christian. The rare works written in the years 1850–2 are milestones of his progress. He felt no longer any hesitancy about publishing these books, although they became more and more express in their condemnation of the established order of things in Christendom. They became also more and more intelligible to the plain man. The poetical, the paradoxical, the humorous traits were discarded or restrained in the steady practice to attain proficiency in direct communication. There is hardly a trace left of the super-subtlety of a lonely thinker who talked predominantly with himself. No one could have any doubt what was meant by the book entitled *For Self-Examination*. Geismar recommends it as the first book of S. K.'s to be read if a man would read only one. *Judge for Yourself* is far more drastic but not less clear and convincing. This title expresses the conviction that with the New Testament in his hand every man is in a position to judge for himself whether the requirements of discipleship as S. K. states them are exorbitant or whether he has not rather presented them at a discount of 35 per cent. S. K.'s progress in direct communication is registered also in the fact that the pseudonym Anti-Climacus is discarded, and in these last books the author speaks openly in his own name. He had already ventured so far out, had assumed so fully the risk of being a Christian, that he felt at last he had the right to utter over his own name his stern reproach of established Christianity. It is true that his last book *Judge for Yourself* was not published in his lifetime, and not till twenty-one years after his death. But there is no record in the Journals of anxious deliberation about the publication of this work, and we must suppose that because this book had clearly the character of open attack its publication was delayed in expectation of the signal to launch the offensive. That signal was long delayed, and the offensive, when it began, was conducted with such mobile units (newspaper articles and tracts) that no occasion was found to bring into play such heavy artillery as this last book.

Plain as these last books were, the full force of them could not be apprehended without an understanding of the serious purpose gradually developed in the pseudonymous writings, which from the very first registered the most profound reflections, and increasingly exhibited the God-fearing satire that in the open attack became so sharp and so ruthless. But this is what no one in Denmark understood. Therefore, when the open attack was launched with the clearest possible criticism of established Christianity, all were astonished, but no one was in a condition to understand. To this there were perhaps only two or three exceptions. Professor Rasmus Nielsen, because of his private colloquies with S. K. in the privileged position of a disciple, had an inkling of what it all meant. At that moment only one of the clergy, J. N. Lange, was deeply enough acquainted with S. K.'s position to become an ardent champion. The philosopher Hans Brøchner was a champion but not a follower. He was acquainted with the whole literature S. K. had produced and understood it profoundly; he perceived that S. K.'s position was in entire agreement with the New Testament, a consistent consequence of it; he held him in high honour for the rare honesty of mind and great intellectual acumen which he had employed in the long effort to reveal the discrepancy between the New Testament and contemporary Christianity, as well as for the boldness he displayed in pressing this issue at the cost of his life; and it was probably this influence which inhibited him from bestowing the name of Christian upon the humanistic view of life which he himself represented.

I will speak of the last books in chronological order.

An Edifying Discourse was published on December 12, 1850. The theme was again 'The Woman that was a Sinner'. It was dedicated in the usual terms to his father. But the opening passage suggests that he was thinking rather of Regina. It is the most striking expression of the religious sublimation of his earthly love. At the same time it is the loftiest eulogy of woman we have from his pen. He shows how this woman was fit to be a teacher of men, and from her he passes on to the example of Mary the Mother of our Lord, extolling her as perhaps few Protestant writers have done. This is exceedingly significant in view of the tendency he displayed only a few years later to speak despitefully of woman. I do not find that what he said in disparagement of woman gives a false or an exaggerated picture of some women, of many women, but it only too evidently reflects the influence of Schopenhauer, which in his last days imparted to his Biblical pessimism a naturalistic character he was acute enough to discern in this philosopher and to condemn, but was not able altogether to resist. We see at all events how close he came at one moment to the chivalric and religious exaltation of woman which was characteristic of medieval Catholicism.

In August 1851 the little book *On My Work as an Author* was at last published. Characteristically it was 'accompanied' by *Two Discourses at the Communion on Fridays*. They dwell upon themes closely connected with that of the Discourse just mentioned: 'But of whom little is forgiven, the same loveth little'; and 'Love covereth a multitude of sins'. Love and forgiveness are the themes S. K. was most inclined to dwell upon—even when he was meditating his attack upon the Church. But the text of the first of these discourses was polemical, even in the mouth of Christ: 'Of whom little is forgiven', &c. S. K. suggested that it might well be inscribed upon the *inside* wall of the church. On the outside might be inscribed the invitation, 'Come unto me, all ye that travail and are heavy laden'; but on the inside, facing the communicant as he left the altar, should be seen this saying of Christ as 'the vindication of the altar', in case the communicant should reproach it because he left with a sense that he was unforgiven—because he loved little. I know a clergyman who had the following inscription carved upon the outside of his pulpit where it was visible to all: 'If ye know these things, happy are ye if ye do them.' But on the inside of the parapet he carved with his own hand roughly—and so secretly that no one ever knew it—the text which expressed his own discomfort as a preacher: 'How dreadful is this place!' From S. K. I have learnt how dreadful the house of God is for the hearer also—for he surely is in great peril who constantly 'hears these things' and does *not* do them.

'To one unnamed, whose name some day will be named, is dedicated, along with this little book, the author's whole production from the beginning.' So reads the dedication of the *Two Discourses*. This was S. K.'s reply to Schlegel's blunt rejection of his proffered friendship. S. K. recounts in his Journal, in an entry of May 1852, that during the last half of the year 1851 he encountered Regina every day in the street when he was taking his customary walk, and with a suspicious frequency even after he had altered his route—yet in view of the rebuff he had received from her husband he did not feel free to return her greeting except by lifting his hat.

The preface to the *Two Discourses* reveals so much that is characteristic of S. K. that I quote it in full, printing it in small type as he cautioned the printer to do:[1]

Preface

A gradually progressing work as a writer which had its beginning in *Either/Or* seeks here its definite point of rest at the foot of the altar, where the author, who personally knows best his imperfection and guilt, does not by any means call himself a witness for the truth, but only a peculiar sort of poet and thinker who, 'without authority', has nothing new to bring but would read the fundamental document of the individual, humane existence-relationship, the old, well-known, from the fathers handed down—would read it through yet once again, if possible in a more heartfelt way. (See the postscript to my 'Concluding Postscript'.)

In this direction I have nothing more to add. But let me give utterance to this which in a sense is my very life, the content of my life for me, its fullness, its happiness, its peace and contentment. There are various philosophies of life which deal with the question of human dignity and human equality—Christianly, every man (the individual), absolutely every man, once again, absolutely every man is equally near to God. And how is he near and equally near? Loved by Him. So there is equality, infinite equality between man and man. If there be any difference, Oh, this difference, if difference there be, is peaceableness itself, undisturbed it does not disturb the equality in the remotest degree. The difference is that one man bears in mind that he is loved, perhaps day in and day out, perhaps for 70 years day in and day out, perhaps having only one longing, the longing for eternity, impatient to lay hold of it and be off, he is busy with this blessed occupation of bearing in mind that he—ah, not for his virtue's sake—is loved. Another perhaps does not reflect upon the fact that he is loved, perhaps he is glad and thankful to be loved by his wife, by his children, by his friends, by his acquaintances, and does not reflect that he is loved by God; or perhaps he sighs at the thought that he is loved by nobody and does not reflect that he is loved by God. 'Yet', so might the first one say, 'I am guiltless, I cannot help it if another overlooks or disdains the love which is lavished as richly upon him as upon me.' Infinite divine love which makes no distinction! Ah—human ingratitude!—what if among us men there were likeness and equality in the sense that we are like one another, entirely alike, inasmuch as not one of us rightly reflects that he is loved.

Turning now to the other side, and expressing thanks for such sympathy and good will as have been showed me, I could wish that I might as it were present these works (as I now take the liberty of doing) and commend them to the nation whose language I am proud to have the honour of writing, feeling for it a filial devotion and an almost womanly tenderness, yet comforting myself also with the thought that it will not be disgraced by the fact that I have used it.

Copenhagen, late summer 1851. S. K.

The book which S. K. 'commended to the attention of this age *For Self-Examination*' marks a new stage of progress in the effort to break through his morbid reserve and to practise direct communication. For not only is this the most drastic criticism of the 'established' he had yet written, but he felt apparently no inhibition against publishing it on September 10, 1851, as soon as it was finished, and he proceeded at once to write (in 1851–2) a still more drastic sequel to it. We have seen why he did not immediately publish the latter. Why it was not published later S. K. himself explains in a note which he appended to the manuscript under the date of 'March 1855'. We learn that it did not correspond to his later attitude, did not attack directly and forcibly enough, and more especially (as we shall see from 'The Moral' which I am about to quote) it did not yet envisage the necessity of *external* reformation.[1]

This book dates from the time when the old Bishop was still living. For this reason it holds itself aloof [from the practical problem of reform], both because at that time I understood my relation to the Established Church in this wise, and because out of regard for the old Bishop I was fain to understand my relationship in this wise.

Now I speak much more decisively, more unreservedly, more truly, without meaning thereby to say that my earlier way of speaking was untrue.

The book concludes with[2]

The Moral

[With a note, reading:] In case it is to be used.

As loud as here is indicated (*indicated*, for I constantly tune the note down to the humble admission [I have to make with regard to myself], so loud must the note be struck if in a Christian sense there is to be any seriousness and meaning and character and truth in protesting against the Established Church or proposing to reform it.

In case any one now among us dared to assume the responsibility of stepping out ethically in character to carry out what is here indicated, and if besides this he could appeal to a direct relationship to God, I shall be instantly at his service.—So I understand myself at this present instant, but I cannot know even whether the next instant I may not be deprived of the conditions requisite for doing this, in the very next instant, perhaps while I am publishing this. [He is thinking of the possibility that the Bishop may soon make the admission he exacted.]— I shall instantly be at his service by assuming the task which I shall understand before God to be mine. This task of mine will be to follow him, the Reformer, step by step, never budging from his side, in order to see if step by step he is in character, is the Extraordinary. Should it prove to be the case that he is this, then my accompaniment will be nothing but bows and reverence before him, the Extraordinary. And truly I dare say of myself that he will find no one in these days, not a single person, who knows how to bow deeper before the Extraordinary. This is not a thing I learnt at any court, no, but higher up, in commerce with the ideals, where one learns to bow endlessly low, lower than any master of ceremonies. But . . . but if he comes short of the character—that very second I fall upon him, and I dare say of myself that in these days there is no one that deals a surer blow than I when that is my task or when one falsely gives himself out to be the Extraordinary. This sure blow I learnt in commerce with the ideals where one learns in deep humility to hate oneself, but yet because one had the courage to venture to engage with them one receives as a gift of grace the power to deal this blow.

If on the contrary there is in these days no one who ventures in character to assume the task of the 'Reformer'—then (unless the 'established order', instead of making truthfully the admission that in a Christian sense it is only a mildly modified approach to Christianity, insists upon affirming that in a strict sense it is true Christianity in accordance with the New Testament, and thereby condemns and nullifies itself)—then let the Existing exist and be upheld. Bungling efforts at reform are more pernicious than the most pernicious establishment, because reformation is the highest thing and therefore bungling at it is the most pernicious thing of all. Grant that the Established Church has faults, many of them, say what thou wilt—if thou wilt not step forth in the *character* of a true reformer, then thou shalt hold thy tongue about reformation. Oh, of all characterless exhibitions the most appalling!—to want to contrive mendaciously to look like a reformer, or to want to carry out a reform by a petty partisan pact, by balloting, &c., &c.

No, there is no such man among us, so let us hold to the Establishment; let us enter into ourselves, let each one in particular admit how far we are behind in Christianity; but thou, my God, wilt preserve me from making things all the worse by mendaciously wanting to carry out a reform.

And let it be said as loudly as possible, and would that it might be heard everywhere, and would to God that wherever it is heard it might be heeded: *the evil in our day is not the Establishment with its many faults; no, the evil in our day is just this evil inclination, this flirting with reform*, this forgery of wanting to reform without once having a conception, not to say a lofty conception, of how exceedingly lofty the thought of 'reformation' is; this hypocrisy of escaping from the consciousness of one's own incapacity by busying oneself with the diversion of wanting to reform the Church, a thing which our age has not the least capacity for. When the Church stood in need of reformation no one announced himself, there was no crowding to join the movement, all fled back, only a single man, the Reformer, was disciplined in all stillness, with fear and trembling and much trial of temptation, until in God's name he could venture to be the Extraordinary. Now it is a jumble, as if it were on a country dance-floor, with all this wanting to reform—such cannot be God's thought, but it is a swaggering device of man, and therefore instead of fear and trembling and much trial of temptation there is Hurrah, boys! Bravo!, acclamation, balloting, a spree, a racket—and a false alarm.

If this had been published, any one could have divined that the thunderstorm was approaching, but who could have guessed that the lightning would strike the Established Church rather than the dilettante reformers like Grundtvig and his followers, among whom his brother Peter was reckoned? It is evident that S. K. was prepared to venture very far out, but who could guess that he would eventually step out 'in character' to reform the Church in outward respects—indeed to make a clean sweep of it as a necessary preliminary to reform? He felt that a prophetic figure was needed, a man who 'could appeal to a direct relationship to God'. This he never claimed to have, and therefore to the very end he described himself as 'without authority' and challenged men to 'judge for themselves'. And yet this passage might prompt the presentiment that in case the right man did not appear, the true Reformer, the Missionary, the Witness for the truth, the Prophet, the Extraordinary personality—in short (for 'a darling child has many names'), the prodigious figure he had been engaged in depicting for himself in terms which were almost apocalyptic ever since his attention had been arrested by the case of Adler—in case the genuine Reformer did not appear, he would reluctantly step into the breach, though it were at the risk of his life. Yet not until the Established Church had opportunity through the mouth of its chief bishop to make the concession he required, that present-day Christianity, especially in Protestantism and more especially in Denmark, was nothing more than a mildly modified approach to

New Testament Christianity. For a long time he persisted in thinking that such an admission was not only possible but probable. For he conceived that it was the only way by which the existing order could justify its existence. For this reason he regarded his own works as the best defence of the Established Church, or rather as the only valid defence that could be made in behalf of it. But at the same time he recognized that, if such an admission was not made, his works must be regarded as the most scathing condemnation of established Christianity.

The first part of this book explains what it means 'to be sober', and I shall soon quote a long passage from it. The second part presses the obligation of imitating Christ, and the text, 'No man can serve two masters', is enough to suggest what painful reading it must be for us.

But now I return to the last book which actually was published, *For Self-Examination*. And first I quote the significant words which are printed on the back of the title-page:[1]

'Knowing the fear of the Lord, we seek to win men' (2 Cor. 5: 11). For to begin off-hand, or *first*, to want to win men is perhaps even ungodliness, at any rate worldliness, not Christianity, any more than it is the fear of God. No, let thy effort *first* express, let it express first and foremost that thou dost fear God. This has been my striving.

But thou, O God, let me never forget that though I were to win not a single man—if only my life (for the 'protestation' of the mouth is deceitful!) expresses the fact that I fear Thee—that then 'all is won!' And on the other hand, though I were to win all men—if my life (for the 'protestation' of the mouth is deceitful!) does not express the fact that I fear Thee—that then 'all is lost!'

I quote now a longer passage from the third and concluding part of this same book, selecting it chiefly because it shows what great progress S. K. had made in becoming a Christian since the days when he described so whimsically in *Fear and Trembling* the knight of infinite resignation. The Spirit had at last come to him. It had not come to him as an infant through baptism, nor as a boy with the laying on of hands by the bishop, but it came after the great renunciation. The knight of infinite resignation had received at last the accolade of the higher chivalry of faith. The passage I translate is taken from a sermon for Pentecost, and the text is the Epistle for the day (Acts 2: 1–12), but the theme is, 'It is the Spirit that giveth life.' The reader will not fail to observe how personal this account is, in spite of so impersonal a word as 'object'.[2]

So death comes first, you must first die to every earthly hope, every merely human reliance, you must die to your selfishness, or to the world; for it is only through your selfishness that the world has power over you; if you have died to your selfishness, you have died also to the world. But, naturally, there is nothing a man clings to so fast as to his selfishness—which he clings to with his whole self! Ah, when in the hour of death soul and body are separated, that is not so painful as to be obliged to separate in one's lifetime from one's own soul! And a man does not cling so fast to his physical body as a man's selfishness clings to his selfishness! Let me take an example, fashioned after those old tales of earlier times about what a man has experienced of heartfelt suffering, which these untried, sagacious times will regard as a fable possessing at the most a little poetical value. Let us take an example, and to this end let me choose a subject which we men talk so much about and which employs us so much, namely love. For love is precisely one of the strongest and deepest expressions of selfishness. So then think of a lover! He saw the object, and thereupon he fell in love. And this object then became his eyes' delight and his heart's desire. And he grasped after it—it was his eyes' delight and his heart's desire! And he grasped it, he held it in his hand—it was his eyes' delight and his heart's desire! Then (so it goes in these old tales) there was issued to him a command: 'Let go of this object!'—Ah! and it was his eyes' delight and his heart's desire! My hearer, let us take pains to apprehend rightly how deep this shaft must penetrate if selfishness is really to be slain. For in his misery he cried, 'No I will not let go, and I cannot let go of this object; Oh, have compassion upon me; if I must not retain it, well then, kill me, or at least let it be taken from me!' You can well understand him; his selfishness would be wounded very deeply indeed by being deprived of the object, but he recognized rightly that his selfishness would be still more deeply wounded if the requirement was that he should deprive himself of it. My hearer, let us go further in order to follow the suffering into its deeper recesses when selfishness must be killed even more completely. Let us take into account also the 'object'. So then this object, which he had desired, which he grasped, of which he is in possession, his eyes' delight and his heart's desire, this object which he must let go, Ah! his eyes' delight and his heart's desire, this object, let us assume for the sake of illuminating more strongly the pain of dying from it, this object is of the same opinion as he, that it would be cruel to sunder it from him—and it is he that must do this! He is to let go what no earthly power thinks of depriving him of, which now he finds it doubly difficult to let go, for (you can well think of it thus) the object resorts to tears and prayers, invokes the living and the dead, both men and God, to prevent him—and it is he that must let go this object! Here you have (if indeed he manages to get round that sharp corner without losing his senses)—here you have an example of what it is to 'die from'. For not to see his wish, his hope, fulfilled, or to be deprived of the object of his desire, the beloved—that can be painful enough, selfishness is wounded, but this does not necessarily mean to 'die from'. And even though he must deny himself, though it was his dearest wish—that can be painful enough, selfishness is wounded, but this does not necessarily mean to 'die from' (*afdø*). No, but to be obliged to deprive oneself of the object of desire which one has possession of—that is to wound selfishness at the root, as in the case of Abraham, when God required that Abraham himself, that he himself—frightful!—with his own hand—Oh, horror of madness!—must sacrifice Isaac, Isaac, the gift so long and so lovingly expected, and that from God, for which Abraham conceived that he must give thanks his whole life long and never be able to give thanks enough—Isaac, his only son, son of his old age and son of promise. Do you believe that death can smart so painfully? I do not. And in any case, when death is in question, it is then all over, but with this thing of 'dying from' it is not by any means all over, for he does not die, there lies perhaps a long life before him . . . the deceased.

. . . .

My hearer, then, then—then cometh the lifegiving Spirit. When? Why, when this has occurred, when you have 'died from'. For as it is said, 'If we are dead with Christ, we shall also live with him', so also it can be said, Would we live with him, then we must die with him. First death, then life. But when? Why, when the first has occurred. . . . That it comes in the same instant is not said. . . . But it comes, it does not delude by failing to appear. Did it not come to the Apostles? did it delude them? Did it not come later to the true believers? did it delude them by failing to appear? No it comes, and it brings the gifts of the Spirit: life and spirit. It brings faith, 'the faith'; for, in the strictest sense, faith, this gift of the Holy Spirit, only appears when death has come between. For we men are not scrupulous in the use of this word, we often speak about faith where in the stricter Christian sense it is not faith. There is inborn in every man, according to the differences of natural endowment, a stronger or a weaker spontaneity (immediacy). The stronger, the more vigorous it is, the longer it can hold out against opposition. And this power of resistance, this vital confidence in oneself, in the world, in mankind, and (among other things) in God, we call faith. But that is not using the word in a strictly Christian sense. Faith is against understanding, faith is on the other side of death. And when you died—or died from yourself, from the world—you died at the same time from the immediacy in yourself, and likewise from your understanding. That is to say, when all confidence in yourself or in human support, and also in the immediacy of faith in God, when every probability is excluded, when it is dark as in the dark night—it is indeed death we are describing—then comes the life-giving Spirit and brings faith. This faith which is stronger than the whole world has the power of eternity, it is the Spirit's gift from God, it is your victory over the world, in which you are more than conquerors.

And the Spirit next brings hope, 'hope' in the strictest Christian sense, this hope which is against hope. For in every man there is a spontaneous (immediate) hope; in the one it may be more vigorous than in another, but in death (i.e. when you 'die from') every such hope dies and transforms itself into hopelessness. Into this night of hopelessness—it is indeed death we are describing—comes then the life-giving Spirit and brings hope, the hope of eternity. It is against hope, for according to that merely natural hope there was no hope left, and so this is hope against hope. The understanding says, 'No, there is no hope.' And it will surely deride this new hope, the gift of the Spirit. As on the day of Pentecost the shrewd and understanding people there assembled derided the Apostles and said that they were full of new wine, so they will deride you and say to you, 'You must have been drunk when such a thing occurred to you, or at least you must have been out of your senses.' . . . 'It is enough to drive one to despair that there is no hope', says the understanding. 'Yet still one can understand that. But that on the farther side of this (i.e. that there is no hope) there should be a new hope, indeed *the* hope—as truly as my name is understanding, that is madness.' But the Spirit which giveth life (which the understanding does not do) declares and bears witness, 'The hope is against hope.' . . .

Finally the Spirit brings also—*love*. In other places I have endeavoured to show, what one cannot too often insist upon and can never make too plain, that what we men extol under the name of love is self-love, and that when we are not attentive to this, the whole of Christianity is brought to confusion.

Only when you are dead to the selfishness in you, and hence to the world, so that you do not love the world, neither the things that are in the world, and do not even love selfishly a single person—when in love to God you have learnt to hate yourself—only then can there be any question of the love which is Christian love. . . .

Such gifts the life-giving Spirit brought the Apostles at Pentecost—Oh that the Spirit would bring such gifts also to us. Verily there is woful need of it in these times.

'Where there are no graves', said Nietzsche, 'there can be no resurrections.'

Almost continuous with the above and at the very end of the book is the next passage I quote:[1]

My hearer, I have still one word to say; but I will clothe it in a form of presentation which may seem to thee not sufficiently solemn. Yet I do it intentionally and advisedly because I think that in this way perhaps it will make a truer impression upon thee.

Once upon a time there was a rich man; he ordered from abroad at an exorbitant price a pair of faultless and highbred horses which he would use for his own pleasure and for the pleasure of driving them himself. Then something like a year or two passed. Any one who previously had known these horses would not have been able to recognize them again. Their eyes had become dull and drowsy, their gait lacked style and decision, they couldn't bear anything, they couldn't hold out, they hardly could drive four miles without having to stop on the way, sometimes they came to a standstill while he sat and drove his best; besides that, they had acquired all sorts of vices and bad habits, and in spite of the fact that they had of course over-abundance of food, they were falling off from day to day. Then he had the King's coachman called. He drove them for a month—in the whole land there was not a pair of steeds that held their heads so proudly, whose glance was so fiery, whose gait was so handsome, no other pair of horses that could hold out so long, though it were to trot for more than a score of miles at a stretch without stopping. How came this about? It is easy to see—the owner, who without being a coachman gave himself out to be a coachman, drove them according to the horses' understanding of what it is to drive; the royal coachman drove them according to the coachman's understanding of what it is to drive.

So it is with us men. Oh, when I think of myself and of the countless men I have learnt to know, I have often said sorrowfully to myself: Here are enough talents and powers and capacities—but the coachman is lacking.

Through the course of long ages and from generation to generation we men have been driven (to stick to the figure of speech) according to the horses' understanding of what it is to drive, we have been governed, brought up, educated according to man's conception of what it is to be a man. Behold what it is we lack: loftiness, and what follows in turn from this, that we can endure so little, impatiently resort at once to the means of the instant, and in our impatience are determined to see straightway the reward of our labour, which just for this reason loses its best qualities.

Once it was otherwise. There was a time when it pleased the Deity (if I may venture to say so) to be Himself the coachman; and He drove the horses according to the coachman's understanding of what it is to drive. And what was man not capable of then! Think of the text for to-day! [This is a sermon for Pentecost.] There sat twelve men, all belonging to the class we call the common people. They had seen Him they adored as God, their Lord and Master, crucified. . . . These twelve men were required to re-create the world—and that with the most terrible handicap, viz. against its will. . . .

> It was Christianity that had to be put over. In a sense they were men like us—but they were well driven, indeed they were well driven!
>
> Then came the next generation. They put Christianity over. They were men just as we are—but they were well driven, yea, verily, they were that! It was with them as with that pair of horses when the royal coachman drove them. Never did a man ever lift his head so proudly and loftily above the world as did the first Christians in humility before God! And just as that pair of steeds could trot, even if it were for a score of miles and more, without being drawn up to give them breath, so they ran at a stretch for three score years and ten, without getting out of the harness, without being halted anywhere; no, proud as they were in humility before God, they said, 'It is not for us to lie down and dawdle on the way, we come to a stop first . . . in eternity!' It was Christianity that must be put over; they put it over, yea, that they did; but also they were well driven, yea, that indeed they were!

S. K.'s conviction was that the disciplined life was never more necessary than to-day, seeing that the task of introducing Christianity into Christendom is harder than introducing it into paganism—at least with respect to the first difficulty of overcoming 'the illusion' that all are Christians or that Christendom means a Christian world.

From *Judge for Yourself* I select a passage which matches closely the above, discovering a new parable in the King's coachman, which in this case illustrates the text (1 Pet. 5: 8) which provides the title for the first half of the book: 'To Become Sober.'

As the world views it, good sense, discretion, shrewdness, mean sobriety, whereas to venture, to let probability go, means drunkenness. As Christianity views it, the situation is exactly the reverse. 'To be sober is to come to oneself in self-knowledge before God, as nothing before Him and yet endlessly bound to Him.'[1]

> And so it is true indeed that the unconditional alone can make a man entirely sober. Let me present this to thee in figurative language, and be not disturbed if the parable does not seem sufficiently solemn, it is expressly designed to give

thee a truer impression of the matter. Ask a peasant, a cab-driver, a postilion, or a liveryman, what the driver uses the whip for, and thou wilt hear him answer, 'Naturally, to make the horse go.' Ask the King's coachman what the driver uses the whip for, and thou wilt hear him answer, 'Principally it is used to make the horse stand still.' This is the difference between an ordinary driver and a good driver. Now further. Hast thou ever observed how the King's coachman behaves? Or if thou hast not observed it, let me describe it to thee. He sits high on his box, and just because he sits so high he has the horse all the more under his control. In certain circumstances, however, he does not consider this enough. He raises himself in his seat, concentrating all his physical force in the muscular arm which wields the whip—now the lash falls. It was frightful. Generally one lash is enough, but sometimes the horse makes a desperate plunge—one more lash. That is enough. He sits down. But the horse? First a tremor passes through its whole body, actually it seems as if this fiery, powerful creature were hardly able to support itself upon its legs. That is the first. It is not so much the pain that makes it tremble as the fact that the coachman—as only the King's coachman can—has wholly concentrated himself in giving emphasis to the lash, put himself wholly into it, so that the horse is aware, not so much by reason of the pain as by something else, who it is that delivers the lash. Then this tremor decreases, there is left now only a slight shudder, but it is as if every muscle, every fibre quivered. Now that is passed—now the horse stands still, absolutely still. What was this? It got an impression of the absolute, hence it is absolutely still. When a horse which the royal coachman drives stands still, it is not at all the same thing as when a cab-horse stands still, for in the latter case this means only that it is not going, which is nothing of an art; whereas in the first case, to stand still is an act, an effort, the most strenuous effort, and also the horse's highest art, and it stands absolutely still. Absolutely still! How shall I describe this? Let me use another picture which comes to the same thing. We commonly speak of still weather—even though it blows a little or there is at least a slight breeze. But hast thou never observed another sort of stillness? Before a thunder-storm begins there is sometimes such a stillness; it is of a different sort entirely;

not a leaf stirs, not a breath of air, it is as if all nature stood still, although at the same time there is throughout all a slight and almost imperceptible shudder. What means the absolute stillness of this imperceptible shudder? It means expectancy of the absolute—of the thunder-storm which is approaching—and the absolute stillness of the horse was due to the impression it has received of the absolute.

But this is what we were speaking about when we said that the impression of the absolute, the unconditional, makes one sober, entirely sober, and at the same time alert ('watchful' is the word the Apostle uses in this text)—is not the horse a symbol of this? It got an impression of the unconditional, and it became unconditionally, absolutely still, entirely sober as it were, and alert. Perhaps it was quite a young horse which thus had need of the impression of the unconditional, perhaps it was an older horse, but one which in its advanced age had become shrewd—sober in its sense of the word—and therefore was of the opinion that things need not be carried beyond a certain point, including this thing of standing still, so that one need not stand absolutely still but might make oneself a little comfortable, because it is such an effort to stand still in this absolute sense. At all events, the royal coachman was of another opinion, he conveyed the impression of the unconditional. And that is what the King's coachman constantly does. When one is only an ordinary driver one does not crack the whip, a cab-driver or a peasant has no snap on his whip—what need of such a luxury when he prefers to belabour the beast with the butt? But the gentleman's coachman cracks the whip, especially when he is driving the gentry; and when he draws up he sits and encourages the horses by cracking the whip. He expresses the fact that he drives well, but he does not express the unconditional. The King's coachman on the other hand does not crack the whip, he expresses the unconditional, His Royal Majesty must not be made to observe in any casual way that the coachman is driving. He keeps . . . absolutely still. Then he arrives home; he throws down the reins—that very instant the horses understand that 'he' is no longer driving. Thereupon out come several grooms—and lo! the unconditional is over for the time being, and so one can cool off or make oneself comfortable according to the circumstances, one is no longer in the solemn sense altogether oneself, altogether sober—the unconditional is over for the time being.

Only the unconditional makes a man entirely sober.

But surely that is what we all are—have we not all of us received an impression of the unconditional, the absolute impression of it? For what is Christianity? Christianity is the unconditional—and surely we are all of us Christians! And what is the proclamation of Christianity? It is the proclamation of the unconditional—and we have in fact 1,000 parsons!

There follows closely upon this parable the story of the theological candidate who 'seeks'. Substantially it is the story of Ludwig From, which was published later in *The Instant* and was quoted earlier in this chapter (p. 452). But in this place S. K. expressly indicates that he himself is wounded by this satire, for he remarks, 'I am a theological candidate.' But he did not write this until he had ceased to seek a 'living' and had ventured very far out, beyond all probability of human help, seeking *first* the kingdom of God.

STATUE OF KIERKEGAARD

An old man at forty-two

PART SIX

THE CORRECTIVE—THE SACRIFICE

1852–1855

O God! God!
How weary, stale, flat and unprofitable
Seem to me all the uses of this world!
Fie on't! ah fie! 'tis an unweeded garden,
That grows to seed, things rank and gross in nature
Possess it merely.

HAMLET.

PRELUDE

We are here entering upon the last period of S. K.'s life, a period of almost three and a half years which stretches from June 1852 to November 11, 1855, the day of his death. It cannot be asserted too emphatically that the line of division between this period and the foregoing is not a formal one drawn arbitrarily by the biographer for the sake of concluding his book with a sixth part, but that it marks a real and very striking difference in comparison with the period immediately preceding it as well as with the whole previous course of S. K.'s life. Although it can be shown psychologically that the position in which we now find him is consistent with all that has gone before, is the result of his life-long effort to become a Christian, yet with the attainment of this position he seems to us to have become another man, and he himself recognized that he was fundamentally changed.

The difference we have to observe is not any change in his way of thinking, as though he had acquired a new faith or was dealing with new thoughts. In this respect there was no break in the continuity of his life. The thoughts which hitherto had chiefly engrossed him continued to engross him more and more. The clear conceptions he had attained of what Christianity essentially is he held more firmly than ever and expressed ever more sharply. His mind was so intensely concentrated upon these essential thoughts that they became his only thoughts. In a sense, therefore, he is now not so interesting a man as in any previous stage of his existence.

Only one exception must be made to the assertion that he dealt with no new thoughts. This is a glaring exception and a pitiful one. It has to do with the gross disparagement of woman, expressed in terms which in his aesthetical writings he had put in the mouth of the most repulsive characters he created, such as the Ladies' Tailor and the Seducer in 'The Banquet'.[1] This is intimately connected with his insistence upon celibacy as a requirement of the Gospel and his consequent contempt for 'parsons with a family'.[2] At the bottom of all this was a feeling of horror at the thought of perpetuating a fallen race by sexual reproduction.

S. K. believed that this could be deduced from the Christian view of life,[1] he did not reflect how dialectic the Christian view is. Solovyev's half-humorous, half-pathetic thought of 'producing more little children of God' corresponds to another aspect of the Gospel, the thought of heaven, whereas S. K. in this connexion was thinking only of hell. It is obvious enough that this whole range of thought derives from a naturalistic pessimism[2] which has nothing to do with the relative pessimism of the Bible but is a contagion he caught from Schopenhauer, whom he began to study with intense interest some time in March 1854.[3] He not only expressed a just appreciation of Schopenhauer's extraordinary talents but he found his trenchant satire peculiarly congenial to his own mood. Yet it is strange that he succumbed to the contagion of this example, for he recognized clearly Schopenhauer's moral baseness, and perceived that his pessimistic philosophy was Indian rather than Christian.

I have nothing to say in justification of this trait in S. K.'s thought. It is a flaw which the biographer cannot ignore, but I feel no need of dwelling upon it. For I regard this whole complex as a foreign body intruded into the organism of S. K.'s thought, having no integral relation to it, nor any further consequences either theoretical or practical. Certainly no practical consequences, for he continued to worship Regina. Schopenhauer's misogyny was only too practical, and because of his well-known witticism it is easier to forgive than to forget it. I am thinking of the story of his landlady whom he kicked downstairs and crippled for life so that he was compelled by the law to pay her a monthly allowance, until he was relieved of this burden by her death, and exclaimed with relief, *Obit anus, abit onus*. But S. K.'s misogyny I can forget, and in a measure I can forgive because I can explain it. Or at least I can connect it with a certain hardness of thought which is apparent during this last period and which can be referred to the fact—as evident as it is incredible—that this most dialectical man had ceased to be dialectical, was no longer willing or able to see more than one side of a question. What he says about woman—and about man, for that matter, and about parsons in particular—is only too true, and pity 'tis 'tis true, but it is not the whole truth, and hence in a higher sense it is untrue.

But this introduces a consideration so important for the understanding of S. K.'s last years that it claims particular attention. S. K. described his father as a man of iron will; a prodigious example of it. No one would think of describing Søren in such terms at any period of his life so far as we yet have followed it, from his wilful youth to the distressing abulia of the period we have just been considering. And yet now it is exactly applicable, and in an entry of September 23, 1855,[1] he is evidently thinking of himself when he says:

> Only a man of iron will can become a Christian. For only he has a will that can be broken. But a man of iron will whose will is broken by the Unconditional, i.e. by God, is a Christian. The stronger the natural will is, the more completely broken it can be and the better the Christian. . . . A Christian is a man of iron will who no longer desires his own will, but with the passion of his contrite will—fundamentally changed—desires the will of another.

This is an expression for the purity of heart he sought after: 'to will one thing'. He is no less evidently thinking of himself when he describes what he considers[2]

> The Most Beautiful Sight.
>
> If there were a man who had attained perfection in this art of being able to perceive a task, to perceive a task in every situation and at every instant (Socrates was the man who attained this in the highest degree)
>
> —if there were such a man, then to see him in relationship to God who knows how to set a task every second and in every situation—
>
> that would be the most beautiful sight.

Incredible as it may seem to the reader who has followed this story so far—and all the more to one who has read the voluminous Journals and become impatient with the endless discussions which led to no decision, and with the perpetual relapses from decisions which seemed to have been made—it is none the less true that during the whole period we are now concerned with there is no trace of indecision, no weighing of alternatives, no hint even that any decision had to be made. For S. K. had made up his mind, had clearly envisaged his task in relationship to God, and from this time forth there was no wavering. Those who were impatient at his indecision may now be offended by his resoluteness; for when once he had determined to launch an attack upon the Established Church he was neither willing nor able to see the other side. One-sidedness, he thought, and even a dose of exaggeration was necessary for the effect he desired to produce; but it is also evident from the Journals that his personal outlook was narrowed exceedingly by intensive preoccupation with his task. Hence the Journals of this period are less interesting than those that went before, and in a certain sense they make less appeal to our sympathy. Yet in a certain sense they inspire a deeper sympathy, for here we see a man whose whole nature is sharpened—even hardened in a way—by the intensity of his preoccupation with the task he looks forward to as God's appointment for him, the task of being a 'corrective', which means also, as he knows full well, to be a 'sacrifice'. This is not interesting, but it is awe-inspiring.

In the earlier Journals we have sometimes seen reason to suspect that S. K. was mentally ill when his will was unable to cope with the many possibilities his imagination suggested and the many reflections of his dialectical mind. Now we see only what most men are inclined to regard as an indubitable sign of mental soundness, namely, the clear perception of a task and the resolute will to perform it. It may be questioned which condition best exemplifies spiritual health. But at all events, those who suppose that his violent attack upon the Church must be accounted for by some sort of mental derangement occasioned by feeble health can find no support for this view in the Journals. The explosion was so unexpected that his contemporaries were naturally inclined to imagine some such thing when they wished to excuse him. But there is no such excuse for the biographers who have access to the Journals. The Journals show that for the space of almost three years he was resolved upon the duty of provoking a 'catastrophe', and was waiting with incredible patience for the signal to precipitate his attack. And all this while he was sharpening his weapons, or—to use the figure which gives the title to this chapter—he was loading the gun. He did not imagine that he might be obliged to 'hold out' so long, and several times he ejaculated the warning, 'Beware! the fuse is lit!' As I read the Journals of this period I can hear the fuse sputtering.

In one sense it might seem as if this period must be the easiest one to deal with, seeing that the literary remains which here have to be taken into account are not nearly so voluminous as for other periods of corresponding length. S. K. was true to his purpose of giving up authorship. The agitation he carried on for eight months by means of newspaper articles and tracts was not 'literature' in the stricter sense, certainly not poetry, and it amounts in all to only 370 pages in the latest publication of his *Works*. For the three years previous to this he had published absolutely nothing. The Journal for this period, as it is now printed, occupies only 960 pages and stops abruptly at about the time he began his attack. At an earlier period (November 2, 1853, to March 1, 1854) there was a gap of four months—the only conspicuous gap in the Journal since the days of his youth, at the moment when he had reached the lowest point of his moral decline. To account for this silence of four months it has been hypothetically suggested that S. K. may have relapsed into a profounder melancholy. This seems plausible enough in view of all we have learnt about him hitherto; but it must be recognized that the Journal does not afford the least support for this hypothesis, but reveals rather the astounding fact that S. K. was no longer a melancholy man. During the period we are now concerned with he was often a sad man and always essentially solitary, but, though he continues to speak of melancholy as characteristic of his nature, he shows no longer the slightest symptom of a pathological condition of mind. We have witnessed his painful struggle to realize the hope suddenly awakened in him by the Easter experience of 1848, that he might be able to conquer his reservedness and speak out. Seeing that this struggle lasted for four years and was rewarded only by partial successes, we might be disposed to doubt that it would ever be concluded by a complete victory. But, in fact, the battle issued in a decisive victory. Morbid reserve was the most tangible and the most distressing symptom of S. K.'s melancholy. When he had triumphed over this, there remained no visible sign of the old malady, no indication that he was a melancholy man. This must be pointed out here and emphasized, because this radical change was wrought slowly, there was no dramatic moment to mark its completion. But it can be said confidently that in the records we have now to deal with there is no hint that S. K. was conscious of any difficulty in speaking out clearly and decisively the rebuke against the Church which he felt it was his duty to utter. The difficulty now was to hold in until the signal to speak was given. He was several times on the point of losing patience and speaking out while the old bishop still lived. And I can imagine that his impatience made him loath to continue the Journal when the day of action was so long deferred. At this time the Journal consisted of almost nothing else but preparation for the attack, and the preparation was more than complete. It is significant that the first entry after this long silence begins with a record about Mynster: 'Now he is dead.' This means that the time for action was near, and the Journal could go on until the battle began. In fact Bishop Mynster had already been dead for a month, and the diatribe against Martensen's funeral eulogy had already been written, though it was not released for publication until many months had passed, that is, until Professor Martensen had been appointed bishop and the collection had been made for the deceased bishop's monument.

I have said that this might seem to be the easiest period to deal with, but, in fact, it is the place where it is most difficult to be fair. For S. K. has fallen as he anticipated into the hands of the professors. For the most part they are, of course, theological professors, that is, official exponents of an Establishment, and they have a natural tendency to blunt the point of his attack. This is done by affirming that it is not the consistent consequence of his whole life and thought and does not correspond to his earlier and more sober intention. I cannot say that. But even I who recognize that we have urgent need now of reformation am offended by the exaggeration which characterizes the attack and which does not seem to me to make it more effective. I am more in sympathy with the 'God-fearing satire' of the earlier works, and of that there is much in the Journals of this period. What is about to come cannot properly be called satire. It is too grim for that, too downright, too little softened by humour. It failed to produce the 'catastrophe' it aimed at. Yet it has had an immense effect. And I would not say one word to dull the point of it. We need to be wounded by it in our day.

S. K. affirmed that he had never known an honest parson. This is perhaps his most extravagant exaggeration. And yet I dare not denounce it as untrue merely because it asserts something more than the truth. I am in many respects very unlike Diogenes, but I cannot say that I have ever seen a perfectly honest man—least of all by introspection. I have no doubt that S. K. could have made out a very good case for the parsons if he had been arguing in their defence. Perhaps at the end of his life and in the heat of battle he could not say as confidently as he did in 1849:[1] 'No one can justly accuse me of being too one-sided to see the opposite side, for the opposite side has in me its warmest advocate.' But even at the end he conceded that parsons are as respectable a class as any other in the community, and he confessed that he would have joined their ranks if he had been able. On his death-bed he was as warmly attached as ever to the friend of his youth, Pastor Boesen. And when this parson rather sternly enjoined him to 'alter his statements because they did not correspond to reality', S. K. replied, as patiently as one could expect of a dying man: 'It must be thus, otherwise it cannot accomplish the purpose. It is clear enough to me that when a bomb explodes it must be thus! Do you mean to say that I should tone it down, first speak to produce an awakening, and then to put people at their ease? Why will you disturb me in this way?'

Without attempting to soften the attack which S. K. made at the cost of his life, I leave it to the reader, clerical or lay, to defend himself against it as well as he can. I have in mind a saying of Albert Schweitzer's, that 'a good conscience is an invention of the devil'.

I. LOADING THE GUN

JUNE 1852—DECEMBER 1854

§ 1. A TURNING-POINT

No one has ever had a profounder acquaintance with S. K.'s Journals than the late P. A. Heiberg, who until his recent death was editor of the new edition of his *Papers*. In an acute work, aptly described as 'psychological microscopy', he emphatically calls attention to two consecutive entries of June 1852, the second of which bears the precise date June 19. Each bears the characteristic title, 'About Myself'. According to Heiberg, they give evidence that the religious development which began with the Easter experience of 1848 culminated at this time and was complete. Having in mind these two entries in particular, he says of S. K.:[1]

> Here he succeeds in finding a simple, clear and definite expression for the thought which developed little by little from an exceedingly complicated and tangled knot, the origin of which can be traced far back in S. K.'s life. Its formation was inseparably connected with the course of his whole spiritual development, so that its solution in this clear, simple and definite thought, expressed in the concrete terms of actuality, may be regarded psychologically as the culmination of his religious development. This decisive fixed point became the ethico-religious basis for the years he had still left to live and especially for the resolute act in which it can be said with perfect truth that he accomplished in the medium of actuality what he himself regarded as his religious task, 'which he employed the whole power of his spirit to perform, for which alone he has laboured, and to which end he believed he alone was fitted'—so that his death does not come as an interruption but as the almost necessary conclusion, in full accord with the ideal claim of his life-task, and in this sense his death can be regarded as the last resolute act in the service of his life-task.

With this I heartily agree, and I am glad to be able to quote the judgement of so competent an authority, seeing that many are inclined to discount S. K.'s attack upon the Church by representing that this act was not consistent and integral with his life as a whole.

Having thus called attention to the importance of these two entries I can now quote them with the assurance that the reader will ponder them duly. I quote the whole of the first entry and the latter half of the other:[1]

> The fact that I do not make my life more comfortable, do not seek to assure myself of a livelihood, one might ascribe to pride, to arrogance.
>
> Is it that? Who indeed knows himself well enough to answer? But should it be that, or at least something like that, my thought is that just by holding out in this way it must eventually be manifest, and I must suffer my punishment.
>
> For my thought, moreover, is as follows. It seems to me that I am morally bound by the apprehension I feel that the higher principle requires me to hold out so long as there is any possibility of it. The very moment I make my life finally secure (while I have still the possibility of holding out longer) it is all over with me, and the power of worldliness will at once understand that there is no danger any more. I have constantly the impression that there is something higher stirring within me, and consequently I feel responsible for holding out as long as possible, so that I may be ready to serve it. If I have made a mistake—in God's name! this sin can be forgiven, and its punishment will come in this life; but if I should break off arbitrarily, true as it may be that I need to do something for my livelihood—if I thus break off . . . and there was something higher stirring which would have come to evidence in and through me—ah, this I shall first discover in eternity when it is too late.
>
> . . . And now I have returned to the point where I was in '48, but with a higher understanding. I understand myself in my difference from others. On the other hand, I stand to Christianity in a direct relationship, so that what I now shall have to suffer does not come under the rubric of intellectual enthusiasm for the question what Christianity is, but under that of suffering for the doctrine, so that in bearing it I have the direct support of Christianity.
>
> What must be emphasized is the following of Christ—and

I must remain as I am in my unlikeness to others. O my God, it was Thou indeed that didst hold Thy hand over me so that in the long period of my anxiety I did not set out and make a step in the direction of likeness and thereby become guilty of producing an abortion (to use the strong expression employed in one of the journals of that time to describe what I then feared), becoming entangled moreover with something in which I should discover nothing but worry, because I am not at home in it, and finally might incur a protest when I come into eternity.

'Imitation' must be insisted upon. But 'without authority' —this is and remains my category. . . .

The polemical craft which is my natural characteristic and is inseparable from my very being is here again in place. For how ironical—there are 1,000 parsons, i.e. teachers (which is something far higher than being merely a poet)—and I am only a poet.

O my God, how clearly it now all stands out before me. How endlessly much has already been done for me. It is not unlikeness I should pray myself out of, that is not the task, but alas, I shall never know the security which consists in being like others. No, I remain in unlikeness. There I remain with Thee—and verily I recognize the blessedness of it. The only thing that rendered me anxious was the thought that possibly the task was another, that I ought to get out of my unlikeness—a thought which may very well have been prompted by the wish to make my life secure.

So I am courageous and joyful—not indeed with an ebullient joy as in '48, for then anxiety about my livelihood was more remote—if at this moment I were free from it I should again exult, for all things are good. However, during the past years I have suffered so much and have been compelled to view my task so seriously that doubtless I am a good deal changed.

But even with such economic anxiety as I have, conjoined with the picture my knowledge of the world enables me to paint in advance of the rumpus which will ensue, I am calm and joyful, perhaps more definitely so, with a more tranquil confidence, than in '48.

The reader who has attentively followed S. K.'s story up to this point will hardly need the explanation that the possibility which here is so definitely discarded was the thought of securing himself by accepting an ecclesiastical living, and that the alternative which he embraced was the resolution to hold himself in readiness to respond to a call of God. He felt this was about to summon him to perform a specific task for which he alone was fitted but which he could not perform unless he preserved his independence. The task was already much clearer to him than these entries would give us to suppose, and he had no doubt that it would involve suffering and death.

The remainder of the Journal shows that this moment was decisive. The possibilities which are here so plainly discarded were never again seriously discussed, and never for an instant was the bitter task, here so calmly accepted, put in doubt. It is very significant to note that his financial distress, though it became of course more and more pressing, was hardly ever alluded to. Before the signal to act was finally given there intervened nearly three years of waiting, three years of looking forward to the task he was to accomplish as 'the corrective—the sacrifice'. It was hard waiting. S. K. illustrates it by[1]

A Picture

July 3, 1855.

Think of a big, well-trained hound. He accompanies his master who makes a visit to a family where, as all too often in our time, there is a whole assembly of ill-behaved youths. Their eyes hardly light upon the hound before they begin to maltreat it in every sort of way. The hound, which was well trained, as these youths were not, fixes at once his eye upon his master to ascertain from his expression what he is expected to do. And he understands his glance to mean that he has to put up with all the ill treatment, to accept it indeed as though it were only kindnesses they conferred upon him. Thereupon the youths became naturally still more rough, and finally they were agreed that it must be a prodigiously stupid hound which puts up with everything.

The hound meanwhile is concerned only about one thing—what the master's glance commands him to do. And, behold, this glance is suddenly changed, it signifies—and the hound understands it at once—employ your strength. That instant with a single leap he has seized the biggest lout and thrown him to the ground—and now it is only the master's glance that brings him to a stop again—and the same instant he is as he was a moment before.

Just so with me . . . .

It was hard waiting, a slow way of dying, a martyrdom terribly long deferred. Literally he was 'holding out'—and it was no certain how long his frail health and his dwindling means woul permit him to wait.

It was hard to hold out when he was deprived of the occupa tion of literary production in which he had found such keen delight:[1]

> The consequence is that there now lies stored up as it were in my head or in my thought an enormous productivity—indee I believe that at this instant several professors and poets coul be produced out of me.
>
> Oh, praise be to God, and again, praise be to God that I stil hold out, and again, praise be to God that I received strength t hold out. . .
>
> Oh, what frightful sufferings, to have to bring to birth and nc to dare to, and on the other hand to dare still less to procure a abortion.

Besides everything else there was the constant vexation thi solitary man had to put up with because of the notoriety whic had been prompted by *The Corsair* and never died down. S. K recurs again to the figure of being trampled to death by gees but now he pictures to himself the longer and more awful tortur of being exposed naked and smeared with honey to be stung t death by insects.[2] We get a more concrete notion of what he ha to suffer when we read the half-humorous reflection that he coul not instruct his shoemaker to make allowance for a swelling on th side of his foot, knowing that the man would tell his wife, 'Magis ter Kierkegaard has a deformed foot!', that this news would g into the Danish papers, and then into the Swedish, where th route of his daily promenades was already described.[3] But for a this, it would not have been so hard to hold out if he could hav withdrawn from the perilous nearness to God in which he foun himself:[4]

> I said to God: I cannot any longer endure being so close t

Thee; permit me to retire. Thou art love; and when I perceive that the close relationship to Thee (in the pain of that unlikeness of mine) will continue to be sheer suffering, Thou wilt in 'grace' permit me, yea, Thou wilt aid me to slip away a little farther from Thee; for this I understand, that the closer one comes to Thee, the more suffering there is in this life. So Thou wilt not be wroth, and in another way Thou wilt watch over me that now when this pain is taken away which day by day bound me to Thee and reminded me of Thee, that now I may not forget Thee and finally invert the whole relationship and imagine that the fact that I now feel no pain is a sign of Thy good pleasure, instead of being perhaps Thy ill pleasure with me, for as I have said, I well understand that the nearer to Thee, the more pain—Oh, but I cannot, Thou loving one, Thou must permit me to withdraw farther from Thee.

So I thought to myself. However, it did not come to pass.

Passages like this, which are not rare in the later journals, make one suspect that S. K. was not so far remote from mysticism of the specifically Catholic type as he himself was inclined to believe at a time when he was acquainted only with the more pantheizing mysticism of Jacob Boehme. The Journals give us many glimpses of his familiar talks with God, expressed with childlike simplicity. And yet once in a while we are made aware that even such self-revealing documents as these do not let us into the secret of his life with God. 'Religious thoughts', he said, 'I do not like to register.'[1] Quite casually one discovers that he was accustomed to pray constantly for his disciple Professor Rasmus Nielsen. He makes a contrite confession of a fit of petulance which had prompted him to omit this prayer, and thereupon he registers the fact that he had again 'taken him up into my God-relationship'.

We learn incidentally from an entry of October 13, 1853[2] that for a year and a half S. K. had been practising the ascetic life—'to see how much I could bear', is the expression he uses. It is significant that this secret practice was not mentioned even in the Journal until he had decided to give it up as a temptation to sophistry, and to return to 'grace'. He explains in another place that the determination what meats one may or may not eat can hardly be anything but sophistical. One might reflect that ascetic practices were obviously advisable in the case of a man whose fortune was almost gone and whose heterogeneity, as he said, rendered it very difficult to make a living. We must picture him as living in great simplicity at this time. The stench of a tannery and the barking of a dog had made him uncomfortable in the quarters he rented in 1848, and already he had moved to Nørregade, where the air of his smaller bed-chamber was unwholesome. But it is clear that he felt a strong attraction to the ascetic life and was inclined to regard it as a counsel appropriate to every Christian.[1] He remarks with interest that Pascal practised secretly a stern asceticism.[2] And the monastic life in particular had a strong fascination for him. 'Back to the cloister!' he was ready to cry. 'There is only one thing higher, and that is martyrdom.' The only fault he found in it was the temptation to spiritual pride. All this was a part of his programme for 'reforming the Reformers', but it hardly got beyond the Journals.[3] In a way he was happier as his fortune diminished, for he already had a bad conscience about his wealth. On one occasion he spoke of doing what he was accustomed to do 'with a troubled conscience'. An opponent travestied this remark by representing that in S. K.'s opinion it 's no matter what you do if you do it with a troubled conscience. S. K. replied that everybody was free to say such things about him—if they could do it with a good conscience.

§2. MONEY MATTERS

This book of mine was all but finished when there was published in Denmark a little work by Professor Frithiof Brandt and Magister Else Rammel about 'Søren Kierkegaard and Money Matters',[4] which throws a new and in many respects a novel light upon this matter. It is astonishing that in the space of only sixteen years S. K. could make away with the considerable fortune he inherited from his father. Curiosity was rife on this subject as soon as he was laid in the grave and the public learnt that he had hardly enough money left to defray his funeral expenses. The persons who might with most reason be expected to know the true explanation proceeded to give it. The explanation given by S. K.'s niece Henriette Lund and her half-brother Trols Lund (who could refer to the testimony of their father who long had had the custody of S. K.'s property) and by Hans Brøckner (who could speak from intimate personal acquaintance) was eventually summarized by Brandes and has till now been accepted (though with some reservations) by all Kierkegaardian scholars. The explanation, briefly stated, amounts to this: he was obliged to consume his capital because, according to the letter of the Old Testament, he believed usury to be a sin and regarded all interest as usury; the expense of publishing his books consumed a great part of his fortune, and works of beneficence accounted for the disappearance of the rest. The painstaking study of these diligent authors has proved that this explanation is a myth. By laborious search in the state archives, in the records of the companies in which S. K. held stock, and in the account-books of his publishers it has been possible to learn with sufficient precision the extent of his fortune, the investments in which it was held, and the dates at which he sold his securities from time to time to provide for his rather lavish expenditure.

It appears that the inheritance received from his father amounted to twice as much as the figure Trols Lund indicated and at which the last editors of the *Papers* arrived by a too careless computation.[1] The state archives contain a precise valuation of the real estate, stocks, and mortgages which were apportioned to S. K. by the executor of his father's will. The total is given as 31,355 rigsdaler, amounting in U.S. currency to $75,000—a sum which must be doubled at least if we would form an idea of its purchasing-power a hundred years ago, even if we take no account of the simpler scale of living which prevailed at that time. With such a fortune an investment at 4 per cent. would have supplied an income equal to the salary of a university professor at that time, and for a single man this would have been ample.

The notion that S. K. had conscientious scruples about receiving interest is belied by the fact that the stocks and mortgages he received as his share of his father's estate were converted into cash only when he wanted to spend a part of his principal, and that when he sold his house he accepted a mortgage for a part of the price and invested most of the remainder in national bonds. The story of his coming to Councillor Lund with his whole fortune in cash, divided into portions which he intended to withdraw from time to time for his current expenses, must be understood to refer to a very late period when he had very little money left. He was then no longer a 'capitalist', and if at that time he had begun to question the propriety of receiving interest on money, this scruple cost him no great loss. There is no reason to doubt

Henriette Lund's report that when Uncle Søren came to her father to withdraw his last portion of money 'Father gazed at him sorrowfully and questioningly, and he responded with a long and serious look'—or, as Trols Lund adjoins to this, that the two men 'shook hands in silence'.

It appears also that no case can be made out for the assumption that any considerable part of his fortune ('the greater part', as Brøckner surmised) was expended upon works of beneficence. His house was besieged by beggars and he liked to give alms in the street. His way of giving alms was evidently in accord with the New Testament—and in this day of institutional charity we are perhaps beginning to suspect that there is something to be said for it. However, the weekly accounts his servants rendered for routine expenditures of this sort do not suggest that they made any serious encroachment upon his fortune.

It has been proved that the least tenable part of the myth is the notion that S. K. spent a great part of his fortune on the publication of his many books. Brandt shows that on the most conservative estimate he earned on this score something over 5,000 rigsdaler, and he calls attention to the fact that only the first twelve books (ending with *A Literary Review* in 1846) were printed at S. K.'s expense and sold on commission. All the rest (including the nine numbers of *The Instant*) were taken by the publishers at their risk and with the obligation of paying the author the customary royalties. S. K. himself is in part responsible for the prevailing misapprehension; for in numerous passages both in the *Works* and in the *Journals* he complains that in a little land like Denmark he could earn no money by his books but had to 'lay out money on them'. We are now compelled to recognize that in his estimate of the cost of producing his books he included, reasonably enough, the living-expenses of the author. This was a fair interpretation of the maxim that 'the labourer is worthy of his hire'. His large library was obviously indispensable to an author who was producing at such a rate, and we can reckon that this cost him more than all the commissions and royalties he received from his publishers. Moreover, he was put to considerable expense for secretaries who were very necessary to him during the period of his most intense production. It is a defect of Brandt's book that it takes no account of these two major items in reckoning how S. K. spent his fortune. Brandt leaves us with the impression that

S. K. was reduced to penury chiefly by the extravagant scale of his household expenses, the elegant apartments he rented, and his insistence, up to the time of his death, upon having a man-servant as well as a maid-servant.

It is true that S. K. always required the best of everything. *The best* was his category—and it is an expensive one. The 'aesthetical' remained strong in him even after it was 'dethroned'. When everything about him was to his taste he found himself in the best mood for literary production. And the long drives in the country, which must have cost a pretty sum, were a very necessary recreation when his production was at its height. The examination of his cook's accounts convinces Brandt that S. K. lived sumptuously every day. He sometimes had broth both at luncheon and dinner! But the facts which are adduced in this connexion seem to me, measured by my bourgeois scale of consumption, to indicate that S. K. lived well but not extravagantly.

About the necessity of extravagance S. K. has this to say:[1]

> Without extravagance I never should have been able to labour on the scale I have laboured; for my extravagance has all along been reckoned with a view to keeping me in the vein of productivity on the prodigious scale.
>
> In any case it is a pious extravagance (associated with the fact that I am a penitent). If, however, it is a fault in God's sight that I had too much imagination and therefore have been so active poetically—very well, I am quite willing to admit it before God, seeing that as against Him I am always in the wrong. But that this fault, in so far as it is a fault, is forgiven me—of that I am eternally assured. And I believe really that it only then becomes a fault when in some way or another I become self-important in God's presence, as if I had done something meritorious in the whole affair—but this He will surely prevent, He the loving Father, upon whose fatherly love I meditate again and again, and will for ever meditate, as a blessed employment.

Nevertheless, in his later years S. K. himself bewailed his 'extravagance'. It is significant that he was prompted to condemn it not so much on account of the economic embarrassment it ultimately entailed as because it seemed to him inconsistent with the Christian way of life.

Brandt (p. 69) publishes for the first time a letter written by S. K. to his brother which shows how stubbornly he clung to the notion his father had impressed upon him that neither of the two sons was destined to survive his 34th year. The consumption of his inheritance was shrewdly (if not wisely) reckoned with a view to this prophecy. To his great surprise he lived nine years longer—until his 'extravagance' had reduced him to penury. Councillor Lund might well regard his death as opportune and perceive in it 'a sign of God's great goodness towards him, that he spared him from suffering want or being dependent upon the bounty of another'.

§ 3. MARTENSEN AND MYNSTER

Before I endeavour to acquaint the reader with the character of the attack which S. K. launched against the Church, something must be said about the two figures who were named as the more express objects of it, namely Martensen and Mynster, the Professor and the Bishop. But although these are the only two persons that are named, it must not be supposed that the attack was a personal one. The 'Professor' impersonated a class which included the 'docents' in the lowest grade; and the Bishop Primate impersonated the clergy in general—all the 'parsons' of every rank. We have had occasion to note that S. K. was inclined to aim his shafts only at shining marks. Only these two men were eminent enough to be named as exponents of the prevailing corruption of Christianity, 'especially in Protestantism, and more especially in Denmark'. This is enough to show that he was not interested in denouncing the baser deviations from Christian faith and practice which were obvious enough to all, but rather the glittering corruptions which were held in high repute. Both Martensen and Mynster were eminent figures and in many respects might be regarded as the best examples of their kind. Martensen was the most brilliant exponent of theological learning in Denmark, and his works were well known in England and America. Mynster was in all respects one of the most admirable bishops the Protestant churches can boast of, a man of imposing presence and persuasive eloquence, whose sermons were not only heard with acclaim but read with devotion, an orthodox theologian who at the same time was well abreast of the highest intellectual culture of his age, a wise ecclesiastical ruler, and withal a man of genuine piety. The fact that S. K. singles out such a man as the express object of his attack shows that what he was intent upon denouncing was precisely those things which in the Christendom of his day, and of ours as well, enjoy the highest repute. It is inevitable therefore that those who cannot be brought to acknowledge any flaw in the conceptions we commonly cherish of what it means to be a Christian in the most reputable sense will feel compelled to regard S. K.'s attack upon Mynster as a monstrous aberration of judgement and an outrageous injustice to the memory of a good and great man.

First I will speak about Hans Larssen Martensen and endeavour to say what needs to be said in the briefest possible space. He was born in 1808, five years before S. K., and therefore was just old enough to act as his tutor at the University. He came back from Germany with an enthusiasm for the Hegelian philosophy and yet was presumptuous enough to claim that he had 'gone beyond' Hegel in the interpretation of Christianity. This naturally did not endear him to S. K., though he was quite ready to recognize his talents and could understand Martensen much better than Martensen could understand him. It is generally recognized now that he was not a great thinker, but in his day he enjoyed a great reputation. He attained rapid advancement in his career, rising from the rank of 'docent' to the unique position of Professor of Theology, combining with that the office of Court Preacher, until as the successor of Mynster he rose to the supreme rank of Bishop Primate of the Danish Church. His works on *Ethics* and on *Dogmatics* were acclaimed even in England and America. S. K.'s fundamental opposition to the theology of Martensen is strongly expressed in his *Papers*;[1] but he showed conspicuous self-restraint in the fact that he did not openly attack it. He was even indignant with his disciple Professor Rasmus Nielsen for referring to his pseudonymous works in support of his own criticism of Martensen's *Dogmatics*. He was satisfied with indirect ways of expressing his dissent from Martensen's opinions and his contempt for his person. *Training in Christianity* was obviously directed against Martensen's views, and if the Professor was not clever enough to perceive it, Bishop Mynster was. Moreover, it may be assumed that his scornful references to 'docents' had chiefly Martensen in mind, although he commonly spoke of 'privat-docents' and remarked that, as this was a title which up to that time was used only in Germany, no one could accuse him of pointing to any one of his contemporaries in Denmark. It is certain at all events that he was thinking chiefly of teachers in the theological faculty when he ridiculed the 'docents', and his criticism was prompted by the conviction that it is clear enough what Christianity is and what it requires, but exceedingly difficult to do it. There is no need to explain Christianity, but a very natural tendency of the human heart to wish to explain it away. To defend a cause is to discredit it. The 'docents' employed themselves in proving the truth of Christianity 'on three grounds', whereas the only effectual recommendation of it is to 'reduplicate' it in one's own life.

> Divine authority is a category. In this case there is mighty little or nothing at all for privat-docents to do, or licentiates, or self-important reviewers. As little need as a young girl has of barbers to shave her beard or as a bald man has of friseurs to 'accommodate' his head of hair—just so little need is there of the assistance of these gentlemen.[1]

It is significant that when Martensen was appointed to the chair of theology S. K. began to speak of 'the professor' as the object of his scorn. 'Take away the paradox from a thinker', he said, 'and you have the professor.'[2] The professor was labelled 'Judas No. 2'.[3]

> Although everything has been done in Christendom to make Judas out as black as possible, I could imagine him a whole quality worse. As I imagine it, J. I. is not, as in reality he was, an individual who had fallen into despair and in a moment of rage sells his master for the paltry sum of 30 pieces of silver—where already there is some extenuation in the smallness of the sum, and in a sense even in his frightful end. No, J. is a much more highly cultured man, calm, and in possession of a shrewder understanding of life, of profit. So he goes to the high priests and says to them, I am willing to betray Him. But now hear my conditions. I am not so much intent upon getting a large sum all at once which I might squander in a few years. No, I want a certain fixed sum yearly. I am a young man, well and strong, having in all human probability the prospect of a long life before me—and I could wish to lead (married and

with family) an agreeable existence with rich opportunity for enjoyment. That is the price.

This according to my notion is a whole quality more abhorrent. . . . It is easy to see that I have represented J. a little *à la* professor.

But the most celebrated passage in the Journal is the following:[1]

'The Professor'

Let us take mathematics. It is very possible that a celebrated mathematician, e.g., might become a martyr to his science—hence there is nothing to hinder me from becoming a professor of the subject he lectured upon, for here the essential thing is a doctrine, science, and the personal life of the teacher is accidental.

But ethico-religiously, and Christianly in particular, there is no doctrine that can be regarded as essential while the personal life of the teacher is accidental; here the essential thing is imitation. What nonsense then that one, instead of following Christ and the Apostles, and suffering what they suffered—that one instead of this should become a professor. Of what?—Why, that Christ was crucified and the Apostles scourged.

Nothing was lacking but that on Golgotha there had been a professor present who promptly installed himself as professor . . . of theology? It is true, we know, that at that time theology had not yet emerged, so at that time it would have been clear that, if he would become professor of anything, it must have been of the fact that Christ was crucified—to become professor of . . . that somebody else was put to death.

It might be quite curious to let such a professor go through the whole campaign. So he first of all became professor of . . . that Christ was crucified. Then began the Apostles. So then Peter and James [*sic*] were brought before the Council and thereupon scourged—that immediately became a new §, and the self-same day the Professor became professor of . . . that Peter and James were scourged. Thereupon the Council forbade the Apostles to preach Christ. But what did the Apostles do? They did not let themselves be discouraged, they continued to preach, for one must obey God rather than man—and the Professor did not let himself be discouraged in the least, he became professor of . . . that Peter and James, notwithstanding they had been scourged, did not let themselves be kept back from preaching the truth—for a professor is inclined to love a new § more than God and the truth.

The 'Professor' follows steadily along—it has even become proverbial of professors that they 'follow', follow the age, not however that they follow, imitate, Christ. Suppose that there was a theological professor living at that time when theology had not yet emerged—one could go through the Acts of the Apostles and get one's bearings by observing what he now was professor of.

So it ended with the Apostles being crucified—and the Professor became professor of . . . that the Apostles were crucified. Finally the Professor departed with a quiet peaceful death.

Look you, this is the way to put a stop to all this boast of scientific method when it becomes too self-important and pretentious—one seizes the Professor and sets him down outside until he makes admissions [the admission which S. K. was urging the Church to make, that the whole thing was not really Christianity]—and then, so far as I care, the whole established order can go on.

In any case, the theological professor is a *point de vue* in Christendom: just in the degree that the professor is accounted the highest thing, in that same degree is one thoroughly disoriented in Christianity; by the way the 'professor' is judged, one can perceive the state of Christendom and the prevailing judgement about what Christianity is.

And here is another reference to the Professor:[1]

Passages are to be found in the N.T. from which one can justify bishops, presbyters, and deacons (however little the present examples resemble the original picture), but one will search in vain in the N.T. for a passage where professors of theology are mentioned. Hence one would be prompted to laugh involuntarily when in that passage where it is said that God appointed some to be prophets, others to be apostles, others to be pastors—one would be prompted to laugh involuntarily if it were added, 'some to be professors of theology'. It might just as well read, God appointed some to be privy councillors.

'The Professor' is a later Christian invention. A later

Christian invention indeed, for it was made about the time when Christianity began to go backward, and the culminating point of the 'Professor's' ascent coincides exactly with our age when Christianity is entirely abolished.

. . . .

In the 'Pseudonyms' I have used merely 'privat-docents', but the 'Professor' is the truer type, just because of the serious importance of his life . . . the Right Honourable Knight of the Order of . . . .

We cannot dispose so briefly of Mynster, for no other man was so deeply interwoven with S. K.'s adult life as a whole, and the conflict with him epitomizes the conflict with the Established Church. If all the entries expressly devoted to Mynster were to be gathered together, they would make a large volume.

Jacob Peter Mynster was born in 1775 and was therefore 38 years older than S. K., who felt himself bound to show a special devotion to the older man, not merely because of his high position, but more particularly because he had been the revered pastor of his deceased father. S. K. could say that he had 'been brought up on Mynster's sermons', for as a boy he had been paid for copying them out, and at school he had been reprimanded for imitating them in his written exercises. In his adult years he never failed to hear Mynster preach, except on the occasion of the old man's last sermon. On the Sundays when the Bishop was not preaching in Copenhagen S. K. was accustomed to read one of his printed sermons. It is likely that the numerous comments the Journal contains about preaching were most of them prompted by sermons he had just heard Mynster deliver; and perhaps by following this clue one might be able to determine the weekly intervals in the undated Journals. Against the content of these sermons S. K. found little to complain of. He remarked, 'I can convict Mynster—by his own sermons.'

S. K. preferred to date his acquaintance with Mynster, not from childhood's memories of him as a guest in his father's house, or as the pastor who prepared him for confirmation, but from the days when he himself had become an acclaimed author and could meet the older man on terms of intellectual equality.

But one must know something of the background of Mynster's life. Like S. K. he had prepared for the ministry of the Church without ever having had serious convictions about Christianity; and without any change of heart he had assumed the pastorate of a parish in the Established Church. But in 1803 he experienced a genuine and profound religious awakening, and from that time forth he was a zealous opponent of the prevailing rationalism and a staunch defender of orthodoxy. His conservatism, political and religious, constituted a positive bond between him and S. K., but he was so attached to the Established Church and came so near to deifying it that he was inclined to suppress every movement of religious awakening which occurred during his long episcopate of twenty years, and naturally he was specially fearful of so radical a return to New Testament Christianity as was advocated by S. K.

Until the old man was dead S. K. never spoke of him but in terms of the profoundest reverence—an obsequious reverence, his contemporaries thought. Yet it appears from the Journals that in conversation with the Bishop he had been quite frank in emphasizing the difference which separated them. There seems to have been a strange relationship of attraction and repulsion between these two dissimilar men:[1]

> Although Mynster has a certain goodwill towards me, and more in his secret heart than he is willing to admit, yet it is evident that he thinks of me as a suspicious or at least a dangerous person. Hence he would like to have me out in the country.

S. K. attached great significance to the fact that Mynster had described him as his 'complement':[2]

> The very first time I talked with him, repeating it later as emphatically as possible, I said to Bishop Mynster that I expressed the position exactly contrary to his, and that it was just for this reason (apart from the prompting of filial piety) that he was so important to me. He showed by his reply that he had heard me with entire attention and in the course of the conversation he admitted that he had understood me. At one point he said that we were complements to one another—which I did not follow up because it was a greater courtesy than I could expect, but I merely remarked again emphatically upon my difference. I said to him that there often was something [i.e. in his books] I knew must displease him, but that I did

indeed think of him in that connexion and thought particularly of him—yet without altering it.

So I know that my relationship to him is as pure as possible.

Although S. K. politely waived the courteous suggestion that he was the 'complement' of Mynster, he was deeply impressed by it. He was ready to believe that the Bishop would be well content to know that his own one-sided presentation of Christianity as a mild consolation was supplemented by another which represented the 'whole side of Christianity which he left out', that is, the thought of imitation, the *following* of Christ even unto death. He conceived that this side, although it was not expressed by Mynster, must surely be contained in 'the hidden inwardness' the Bishop talked so much about. But gradually he became aware that this hidden inwardness concealed nothing of the sort; and when the Bishop angrily displayed his profound distaste for his own complement, the disillusionment was complete. This whole experience is very plainly reflected in the *Papers* and the Journal.[1] It seems evident to me that this long-cherished and deluded hope, the hope that Mynster might before his death make the admission that the Christianity he stood for was not the whole of Christianity but a lenient form which needed the sterner complement, this hope which for so long a time restrained S. K. from uttering sharply his denunciation of the prevalent abuse of Christianity, making it so much harder and more bitter for him in the end when he found himself obliged to require, not only an inward change in the heart of the Established Church, but an outward change, indeed the abolition of the whole thing so as to clear the ground for starting afresh—I say that this seems to me to explain the pathetic phrase, several times repeated in the first letter of attack upon Martensen, which describes Mynster as 'my life's misfortune'.

When he thought of Mynster he envisaged him predominantly in his role as a preacher:[2]

> That warm, fresh, full eloquence, that heavenly glance, those tears, the suppressed sob, the visible tremor of the body as his hands were raised in prayer.

What a bitter disillusionment when he was compelled to recognize that 'he was great only as a declaimer—and my life's misfortune. . . . I honoured that false draft instead of protesting it.'

He reflected that the confusion of thought which regards a priest predominantly as a speaker signifies the abolition of Christianity.

The doubt about Mynster emerged occasionally as early as 1843:[1] 'Where is the boundary between prudential wisdom and religiousness?' But it was not until 1848, after the Revolution, that it became profoundly disquieting. He believed that he could discern a change in Mynster when the constitutional revolution had deprived him of the firm support he had hitherto enjoyed in the Royal Chancellery and required him now to depend upon the ballot for defining what Christianity is—consequently to solicit the support of the press. Nothing was more abhorrent to S. K.[2] He says of the press[3] that 'it ought to have this inscription on a sign-board: Here people are demoralized in the shortest possible time, in the highest possible degree, at the lowest possible price.' That 'it reduces men to a mass' is a more precise allegation against it.

In 1848 the criticisms of Mynster become very frequent in the Journal. I select a few entries, without any attempt to classify them, but simply in the order in which they come:

> Hence Mynster has always had so great a partiality for 'these quiet hours in holy places', because there he could dispense Christianity as one of life's ingredients. . . . For Mynster, however, it would be quite impossible, indeed the most impossible thing of all, to preach in the market-place. Yet it has become almost a heathenish and theatrical thing, this preaching in churches, and Luther is quite right in insisting that we should not preach in churches. In paganism the theatre was the church—in Christendom the churches have practically become theatres. How so? Why, in this way. One finds it agreeable and not devoid of a certain pleasure to hold communion through the imagination once a week with the highest thoughts. Nothing more than that. And this has actually become the norm for the sermons in Denmark. Hence this artistic remoteness—even in the clumsiest sermons.[4]
>
> Does Bishop Mynster's life give expression to this: 'Though all should fall away, yet shall I hold fast to that which I have loved with a pure devotion, as I have loved nothing else, and more zealously than has any one else; I will not let go that which I did not first put faith in for the reason that others

believed it. Why should I cease to believe because others cease to believe?' (These are all quotations.) But, some one rejoins, his life has not afforded him occasion to be so tempted; he has lived in established Christendom where all hold fast to faith. Aha! That's it! But in his sermons he asseverated again and again (quotations are not far to seek) that there are only very few Christians to be found in Christendom, that the multitude are very far backward and quite the opposite of Christians—deluded, depraved, &c.

Should not then this asseveration about devotion to Christ, together with this knowledge of the situation, should it not have resulted in a very different figure from that of the most superior and cultured gentleman, the admiration of the ladies, the much flattered, who I might almost say revels in all the pleasures of life—Bishop Mynster? True, once a week he preaches admirably. True, there has lived many a simple citizen (my father for example) who by taking his Sunday discourses literally becomes a Christian. Alas! that is almost a satire on the Bishop.[1]

S. K. early became aware that Mynster's sermons were con-ived only for Sundays—'but, alas, there are 6 days in the week'. e said in one place, 'I am Bishop Mynster's sermons on Mon-ıy.'

And yet I have loved Bishop Mynster, my only desire is to do everything to enhance his prestige; for I have admired him, and every time I am able to do something in his favour I think of my father, to whom I believe this gives joy.[2]

And yet I am so much attached to Bishop Mynster, and that not only because the memory of my father binds me to him. No, Mynster expresses the purely human ideal in a more masterly way than I have ever beheld it. On the other hand he is so alien to the decisive Christian expression that if he were to speak his mind about it he would say, It is demoniacal.[3]

Year by year the relationship between these two men became ɔre tense. Mr. Dru remarks justly that this was another case of ıhappy love'. In 1847 S. K. was fearful lest *The Works of Love* ght displease Mynster. In 1849 he had more reason to expect ıt the Bishop would be offended by *The Sickness unto Death*; d he was so grateful to him for making little fuss about it that

he proposed to dedicate to him one of the small books he designe
to publish in 1850. Several drafts of the dedication were written;
but just then something happened which exasperated the differ
ences between them.

S. K. and Mynster were accustomed to present to one anothe
all the books they wrote. Although *Training in Christianity* wa
ascribed to Anti-Climacus, it was duly presented to the Bishop b
the real author.

My Conversation with Bishop Mynster, October 22, 1850,
after he had read 'Training in Christianity'.

I had talked the day before with Pauli [Pastor Pauli, Myn
ster's son-in-law], who said to me as follows: 'The Bishop i
very angry, his words are these, as soon as he came into th
sitting-room the first day: "The book has greatly embittere
me, it is a profane game played with holy things." And whe
Pauli dutifully inquired of him whether, as he had occasion t
talk with me, he should report that to me, Mynster replie
"Yes, and let him come up here at once to visit me and I sha
tell him that myself."'

Perhaps, who knows? the last words were an invention c
Pauli's, just to keep me, if possible, from going to the Bisho

Anyhow, I had a different view of the case. When Mynst
talks like this and says, 'The next time he calls on me I sha
tell him that myself', he has practically given the book its pas
port and me with it.

The following morning I went to him. . . . I began at onc
in this wise: 'To-day I have come on a particular busines
Pastor Pauli told me yesterday that you have a mind to see m
at once to reprimand me for my last book. I beg you to regar
it as a new expression of the deference I have always showe
you that so soon as I am informed of this I instantly make m
appearance.' . . . He replied, 'No, I have no right to repriman
I have told you before that I have no objection to every bi
singing with its own beak.' Thereupon he added, 'People ca
perfectly well say what they want about me.' But this last o
servation made me suspect that there was a little sarcasm, ar
I sought instantly to save the situation. I replied that this w
not my intention, I would beg him to tell me if I had in ar
way distressed him by publishing such a book. Then h

answered, 'Yes, I really believe that it will not do any good.' With this reply I was contented; it was kindly and personal.

There was nothing remarkable about the rest of the conversation, except that at the very beginning he said, 'Yes, one half of the book is an attack on Martensen, the other half on me'; and later we talked about a passage in the 'Reflections' which he considered coined for him. The rest of the conversation was as usual. . . .[1]

S. K. was rather supinely contented with this conversation, for he reason that it did not compel him to open his full attack upon he Established Church, as he must have done had his book been ondemned by authority. He observed that no ecclesiastical uthority had condemned it, nor even the religious press. At a ater time he reproached Mynster for not doing one thing or the ther. He ought either to have recognized it as a true exposition f Christianity, or to have denounced it strongly as a gross offence gainst the Church.

It may be suspected that Mynster sought a more adroit way f paying S. K. back. In 1851 S. K. rendered him a much ppreciated service by defending the Church against a sectarian novement sponsored by Dr. Rudelbach. In a small book the Bishop himself wrote on this theme he expressly thanked S. K., ut at the same time he contrived to touch him to the quick by ssociating his name with that of Goldschmidt, saying in the same reath that Goldschmidt was a 'talented' young author and S. K. 'gifted' one. Afterwards he vainly sought to explain that 'gifted' as the higher term. S. K. suspected, I think not unreasonably, hat the Bishop meant to wound him. This must be the fact, unss it is possible to suppose that Mynster had never heard of *The orsair*. S. K. also suspected—and the Bishop subsequently onfirmed him in this—that Mynster in complimenting Goldchmidt was seeking his support as a prominent journalist.[2]

At this point we must interject an explanation of Goldchmidt's entrance upon the scene. He had returned to Copenagen and established a very reputable monthly review, *North and outh*. He was intent upon attaining an honourable position in ciety. He attained it, and a marble bust of Goldschmidt now dorns one of the city streets, while the bronze statue of S. K. is be seen in the garden in front of the Library.

[S. K. speaks of the return.] The bad boy of literature, little Goldschmidt (who, be it parenthetically observed, has become perfectly well-mannered, so that, according to what my barber tells me, almost 'every month' or 'every week' he gets good marks for conduct).[1]

S. K. was ready enough to forgive and to forget if only Goldschmidt would make a public apology and retractation for his seven years' activity as proprietor of *The Corsair*. He was not satisfiec with a nonchalant remark in the new review which spoke of the seven years in *The Corsair* as 'a transitional period in my development'. He might as well have said, thought S. K., 'my first stage of development was seven years in a reformatory—or, I became a public harlot—that was the first phase'.[2]

S. K. felt this affront he had received from the Bishop the more keenly because it indicated that Mynster repudiated his 'compliment'. He took the matter up with energy. Incidentally we may note in this case, as in the last long passage cited, how natural i had become for him to speak out bluntly. Indeed we canno find in this period a single instance of 'indirect communication'. And surely he displays astonishing intrepidity in both of thes conversations with His Excellency the Most Reverend Bisho Primate of Denmark:[3]

Conversation with Bishop Mynster, May 2[, 1851].

. . . Then I suddenly turned the conversation to his book an said bluntly that I had not come previously to thank him for m copy because there was something in it I could not approve o . . . [He insists that the Bishop should be careful of his ow reputation, which might suffer by bringing Goldschmidt for ward in that fashion, without exacting of him a retractation.]

Thereupon I said to him: 'It may seem strange that a yout should talk thus to an old man; nevertheless, will you not per mit me to do it, and let me also give you a bit of advice? If ther is something you disapprove of in me, I could wish that yo would give me a thrashing; do it, do it, I can bear it, and I sha take pains to see that you do not suffer for it; but by all mean take care not to act in a way that would injure your reputatio It is your reputation I am interested in.'

Then I repeated over and over again, 'I want to have th said, and said distinctly, I would have my conscience clear, must be noted that I have said I cannot approve of it'—and as I said this I leaned over the table and wrote as it were with my hand. To this he made reply, 'Well, it is observed.' And I saw to it that every time I said it he made a rejoinder which indicated that he had heard it.

It ended with, 'Thanks, good friend', &c., &c.

And I separated from him in as friendly a way as possible.

S. K. was glad that he had talked with Mynster, but it cannot e said that on this occasion he was contented. This seemed to im the signal for beginning his attack upon Mynster and upon ie Church which he represented. He sat down at once to write . We have numerous drafts of a polemic against Bishop Myn-ter and the Establishment, all provided with directions for the rinter, from which we can see how nearly he came to publishing .[1] It is not clear how he had the patience to withhold his hand or three more years until the old Bishop died. But while in pub-c he continued to speak of the Bishop with customary reverence, ie criticisms in his Journal become more and more caustic. I iall quote here a number of selections in chronological order. 'his will not seem a waste of time and space when it is observed iat this is a sample of the attack upon the Established Church f which Bishop Mynster was so admirable an exponent.

(1850) If on the contrary Bishop Mynster maintains that the preaching of Christianity as he represents it is genuine Christianity according to the New Testament, I shall immediately begin the attack.[2]

So while I strive with all my might to unveil [the faults of the Established Church], Bishop Mynster strives to veil them. [And yet he is patient enough to say to himself], You do your part, let him do his. . . . Bishop Mynster has a double aspect. He possesses a religious inwardness, and from this he draws his incomparable sermons, which I have read, do read, and shall continue to read, these incomparable sermons which when they are heard are peerless, for he is an orator. But then he has another aspect—and alas, the week, as is well known, has six days. Worldly shrewdness from first to last, in all shapes and forms, worldly shrewdness is his element.[3]

When a nurse wants to entice a child to take something that does not taste good she behaves thus: she raises it to her mouth, pretending to taste it, and then says, Ah! how good it tastes. She herself takes good care not to taste it, but the child doesn't see that—the child is only a child—and so the child swallows it. So it is with Mynster's Sunday ceremony, with sighs and tears: 'Ah! Christianity tastes so good.' That is to get us to accept Christianity.—And he thinks we cannot see that on Monday his life expresses something quite different.

(1851) Mynster preached to-day on the beauty of the Christian life—and very beautifully.[2]

(1852) In one of his meditations he dwells pathetically upon the fact that tears avail so little; he says that he will collect all those hypocritical tears which people have shed at hearing his sermons, whereas it was made plain later that they had not done anything to correspond with it: and with these tears I shall stand forth on the Day of Judgement and say, 'I have done my part.' —Strangely enough I had just been thinking of gathering up all the tears which Mynster had shed upon the pulpit, whereas it has been made clear that he does not act accordingly. So this agrees with the word Mynster said to me the first time we talked together: 'We are complements.' I complete his collection of hypocritical tears with my collection of his tears.[3]

When I talked with Mynster the first time after the publication of 'Training in Christianity' he said among other things that he perceived clearly enough it was him I was bent upon attacking. . . . This is a misunderstanding. I said to him expressly when I brought him the book that I had wished one of us two were dead before it was published. But if one really wants to attack a man, one hardly would wish him to be dead beforehand.[4]

At this point it is in place to warn the reader against the danger of this same 'misunderstanding' in our day. Any one who supposes that the attack ultimately launched against Martensen and Mynster was, in the odious sense of the word, a personal attack has entirely missed the point of it. They were the only two individuals he expressly named, except when he was replying to the very few signed articles which his adversaries published in the press. But it is very clear that these two men were singled out not for reasons of personal spite, but because in their different ways they were so eminently representative of the Establishment—

ıd represented it at its best. Martensen represented the dog-
atic *system*, as a thing for itself; and Mynster represented
ıietistic piety—as a thing for itself! Against rationalism,
hich had been prevalent when he was a youth, S. K. did not
:ed to waste any words—so thoroughly had Mynster succeeded
replacing it with piety on the basis of orthodoxy. S. K. did
ɔt exaggerate when he affirmed again and again that Mynster
ırried a whole generation'. If the piety which this great man
.d made to prevail deserved to be attacked as a partial, all-too-
.rtial, exposition of Christianity, it obviously could be attacked
ost effectively in the person of the eminent man who by his
ample, by his teaching, and by his use of patronage had caused
to prevail. Loath as he certainly was to attack the man who had
r so long been the object of his admiration and affection, S. K. re-
rded it as an advantage that, instead of needing to set up a straw
ure or to incur the danger of seeming to beat the air, he could
ack the evils he so much deplored in an instance so concrete and
well known. Yet he could affirm at this time with as much
ıson as at an earlier period that his attitude was 'not finitely
lemical, not polemical against any one in particular, but only
initely polemical'.

(1853) The trouble with the Mynsterish attitude and the
official attitude as a whole is that they neither know how to
apply the pattern of 'imitation', nor, in consequence of this,
to insist effectively upon the necessity of fleeing to grace. The
latter is what I have wanted and constantly want to do: I
would apply the Christian requirement, imitation, in all its
endlessness, so as to insist in the direction of grace.

March 1, 1854. Now he is dead.

If one could have moved him to end his life with the admis-
ion in behalf of Christianity that what he represented was not
properly Christianity but a softened expression of it—that
would have been so desirable, for he carried the whole genera-
ion.

The possibility of this admission had therefore to be kept
open until the last, yea, until the last, with the expectation that
n dying he might make it. Hence he must never be attacked,
ence I was compelled to put up with everything, even when
ıe did so desperate a thing as that about Goldschmidt, no one

could know whether this might not perhaps work on him s
that he still might be moved to make that admission.

Dead without that admission—everything is altered, no
all he has left behind him is the fact that he has preached Chris
tianity fast into an illusion.[1]

What I do, I do with sorrow; yet it must be done, about th
I am perfectly clear, I can find no peace until it is done.
regard it as a merciful dispensation of providence that I w
dispensed from doing it while he was alive. But even after h
death I would fain keep silence. Let no one reproach me f
doing it, or, if some one is inclined to, I must put up with i
The painful thing for me is that I must do it, for honest
speaking there are certainly not many, or rather there are ve
few, perhaps none, that have been more sincerely devoted th
I to Bishop Mynster and found more joy in admiring h
(humanly speaking) distinguished qualities—no one more th
I, who also for the sake of a deceased father felt myself bound
him.[2]

Among the scattered papers dating probably from the last ye
of S. K.'s life we have two pictures which graphically describe t
tragedy of his relationship to Mynster:

My feelings at the time when I was contemporary
with Bishop Mynster

Imagine a very great ship, greater if you will than the bi
gest ships we have at present, suppose it has room for 1,0
passengers, and naturally it is equipped on the greatest p
sible scale with conveniences, comforts, and luxuries, &c.

It is towards night. In the cabin they are having a mer
time, everything illuminated in the most resplendent mann
all is glittering, in short all is merriment and good cheer, a
the noise and tumult of their joyous abandonment to mirth c
ries out into the night.

Above on the bridge stands the captain, and beside him t
next in command. The latter takes the glass from his eye a
hands it to the captain, who replies, There is no need of it
see well enough the little white speck on the horizon—it w
be a dreadful night.

Thereupon he gives his orders with the noble and intre

composure which befits an experienced seaman: The crew will stay on deck all night; I myself will assume command.

Then he goes to his berth. It is no great library he has with him, yet he has a Bible. He opens it, and strangely enough he opens it just at the text: This night thy soul shall be required of thee. Strange!

After a moment of devotion he dresses for night duty, and now he is the practised seaman through and through.

But in the cabin the merriment goes on; song is heard there and music and noise, the clatter of dishes and flagons, champagne sparkles, and the captain's health is drunk, &c., &c.—'It will be a dreadful night', and perhaps this night thy soul shall be required of thee.

Is not this dreadful? And yet I know of a still more dreadful thing.

All is the same except that the captain is another. In the cabin all goes merrily, and the merriest of all is the captain.

The white speck on the horizon is there; it will be a dreadful night. But no one sees the white speck or divines what it means. But no (this would not be the most dreadful thing), no, there is one that sees it and also knows what it means—but he is a passenger. He has no command on the ship and cannot do anything decisive. However, to do the only thing in his power, he sends a request to the captain to come on deck for a moment. There is considerable delay; finally he comes out but will listen to nothing, and with a jest he hastens down again to the noise and the reckless joy of the society in the cabin, where the captain's health is drunk and he responds complacently.

In his anguish the poor passenger ventures once more to disturb the captain; but now the captain has even become discourteous to him. Nevertheless the white speck remains unchanged upon the horizon—'it will be a dreadful night'.

Is not this still more dreadful? It was dreadful for those thoughtless, noisy passengers, dreadful that the captain is the only one that knows what impends—ah, but the important thing is that the captain knows it. So it is more dreadful when the only one that sees and knows what impends is . . . a passenger.

That (in a Christian sense) there is to be seen a white speck on the horizon which means that a dreadful tempest impends—that I knew; but alas I was and am only a passenger.

Imagine a young officer, we can imagine him a competent young officer.

There is a battle. Our young officer commands half a battery.

He sees (and we can imagine that he sees aright), he sees 'my three cannon trained upon that spot—and the victory is ours'.

But just at that spot (or if not exactly at that spot, yet in such a position that it is impossible to train the cannon upon that spot), just there stands his own general, the old Field-marshal Friedland, with his staff.

Imagine what that young man must suffer! 'I am young', says he to himself, 'my future would be made if I could succeed in employing my cannon. . . . Oh, but this is the instant to do it!' The instant passes. 'A fig for myself,' says the young officer, 'but the battle could be decided if only I might employ my cannon. Oh, this is indeed dreadful that it is my own general who stands there so that I cannot succeed in employing my cannon.'

It needs to be remarked here (because none of the passages quoted have made it clear enough) that the criticism of the Established Church contained in the latest books, particularly in *Training in Christianity*, which the Bishop and many others regarded as an attack, S. K. himself regarded not as an attack but as a defence, and as the only possible defence. If only the admission were made that the prevailing conception and practice did not represent New Testament Christianity, then the formal constitution of the Establishment might be preserved; for at least something would be gained, the relationship to Christianity would become an honest one, and many a parson would be relieved of a bad conscience.[1] S. K. was convinced that Mynster in his heart was well aware of the discrepancy he pointed out, and that the parsons commonly suffered in conscience for 'the difficulty of their position in these times'. The question naturally has been raised whether it could be regarded as an entirely satisfactory solution to have churchmen confess honestly that they proposed to continue to live in dishonesty. It must be observed that on the one hand S. K. regarded this as a concession to human weakness (his own weakness included), and on the other hand as a transitional situation:

> I have desired this both for my own sake, so that I need not undertake a task beyond my strength, and for the sake of others whom in my melancholy I love.
>
> I meant that this movement must be made as the first step. When that was done, then perhaps we might get to see that this was no stopping-place, but that we must push right through.[1]
>
> Then I could introduce new points of view in all directions. . . . And I proposed it in such a way that it remains to refer it to God to see how He will dispose.[2]
>
> Let us above all be honest and admit the true situation.[3]

§4. PROTESTANT/CATHOLIC

Although I am very far from wishing to shield any Church or any individual from the wholesome wounds S. K. inflicts, I cannot regard the often repeated refrain, 'especially in Protestantism, and more especially in Denmark', as a mere rhetorical phrase. For it is clear that many of S. K.'s complaints apply especially if not exclusively to Protestant abuses; and to the evident disparagement of Protestantism he frequently emphasizes Catholic contrasts. It is clear enough that he was repelled by the worldly pomp and political power of the Pope;[4] 'Yet still Catholicism has a conception and presentation of Christian ideality . . . of becoming nothing in this world, whereas Protestantism is finiteness from end to end'.[5] He complains that Protestantism, which started out as a corrective, has been made a norm. Like the flying buttress which supports the cathedral wall, it is not designed to stand alone and obviously cannot do so.[6] Although Protestantism intended to attach itself closely to the New Testament and so shake off innumerable accretions which had deformed Christianity, it had in effect got infinitely far away from its source because of a fond belief in the 'perfectibility of Christianity', the notion of an ever bigger and better Christianity.[7]

S. K.'s criticism of Luther was as often as not admiring criticism in the earlier period, but in his last years we can find little but denunciation.

> By his later life Luther accredited mediocrity. One does not commonly reflect that it requires a hero to accredit mediocrity

for the first time. This hero was Luther. But the instant it is accredited nothing more is required by mediocrity . . . and with that we are blest above measure in Protestantism.[1]

'He did inestimable harm by the fact that he did not become a martyr.'[2] 'He was a confused pate, who lifted burdens off'[3] . . . and hence was 'the very opposite of an Apostle'. He expresses Christianity in man's interest, whereas the 'Apostle' expresses it in God's interest. 'He took man's part against God.'[4] Through his influence 'the Apostle Paul has been exalted at the expense of Christ'.[5] The distinction he made between the Law and the Gospel was a false distinction,[6] as Karl Barth vigorously affirms in an address which has just come to hand.[7] He expressly encouraged the marriage of priests 'as a concession to concupiscence'.[8] 'For Christianity he was an exceedingly important patient, but he was not a physician.'[9] Hence, 'Back to the cloister!'[10]

Martensen made a specious charge when he said that S. K. was an individualist without any notion of a Church. But, in the first place, this overlooks the fact that S. K. had a much more definite notion of the authority of the Church than has ever prevailed in Protestantism. He was not inclined to tolerate any authority in the Church except spiritual authority—that is to say, he repudiated all legal authority, whether it was derived from the State or arrived at by balloting within the Church. There can be no popular authority in the Church of God, but only God's authority—therefore no democratic rule, no constitutional government in the sense of political liberalism. This is primitive *and* Catholic doctrine. Spiritual authority resides only in the individual, 'the official is the impersonal'. The priest possesses authority by reason of his ordination—*ex opere operato*. It is notorious that S. K. held this notion at one time. It might be supposed that he repudiated it when he discovered that the 1,000 parsons of Denmark possessed no more authority than that which they derived from the fact that they had behind them the police and the house of correction,[11] when he denied that as employees of the State they had authority to administer the sacraments,[12] and questioned even if the chalice of the Lord's blood, which the Roman Church refused to the laity, ought to be administered to the priests of Denmark,[13] and whether as 'actors' they could claim the right of burial in consecrated ground. But remember that he is speaking 'more especially of Denmark'. He made no retraction of his belief in ordination, and it is certain that he continued to regard every ministry in the Church as dependent upon divine appointment—from the ministry of the Apostles down. A cursory glance at the titles of the entries in the Journal for the year 1852 discloses the fact that he had been reading hardly anything but the Church Fathers. He must have had some notion of the Church!

In the second place, Martensen, like many others, failed to understand what S. K. meant by stressing so much 'the individual'. It did not mean that he was what we call an individualist. It is true that he speaks of the Church as 'an abstraction'.[1] But this means only that he discarded Richard Rothe's theory of the Church as a society, prior to, and apart from, the individuals that compose it.[2] He affirms on the contrary that 'to relate oneself to God personally, as an individual, quite literally as an individual, is the formula for being a Christian'.[3]

> Every time this occurs it is always an event of incomparably greater importance than a European war or a war which involves all the corners of the earth, it is a catastrophic event which moves the universe to its deepest depths. . . . He whose life does not present relative catastrophes of this sort has never, not even in the remotest approximation, addressed himself as an individual to God—that is just as impossible as to touch an electrical machine without receiving a shock.

But who will affirm that the 'crowd', the 'flock', the 'mass', the 'numerical' constitute the Church? These words represent all that was most hateful to S. K., and together with the 'human samples', turned out all alike by the mass-production of education, they serve to define negatively what he meant by 'the individual'. The pressing need of the moment is to split the mass into individuals—as cholera does, he remarks. And then—if they become 'individuals before God'—then we may have a Christian Church again. The most shocking affirmation S. K. makes is that 'Christianity does not exist'. Yet this is perfectly true if there are no individuals who come into personal relationship to God—unless there can be Christianity and a Church where there are no Christians. Passages to this effect are too numerous to quote or even to indicate. The following passages illustrate very well what S. K. meant by all this.[1] He avails himself of the formula familiar to all in the Christmas game of

'Star-gazing'

It is not about astronomy I propose to speak. That is well enough in its place. It is about Christianity, about being a Christian; and what I refer to is the forfeit imposed in the Christmas game of 'star-gazing'.

1

So then: 'Whose pledge is this?' 'This is Mr. H—'s.' 'What shall the forfeit be?' 'He shall go into a dark room and gaze at stars.'

So he goes in. Let him now forget everything, but think passionately upon one fact, that he is not altogether alone in the dark room, but that God is present and says to him: 'Art thou a Christian? Answer me—yet it is not what thou dost answer that will decide the matter, but how thou dost answer, whether thou wilt answer with perfect sincerity. For if thou dost not answer with perfect sincerity, then I shall let thee—and thou knowest that I the Almighty am able to do all things—then I shall let thee fall down dead here upon this floor, and never again wilt thou play the game of Christmas or the game of star-gazing.' He answers: 'Thou dreadful One, never have I thought of this answer as so decisive. I go to church every time the Court Preacher Petersen preaches, that is, every 6th Sunday, which is more than several of my familiar friends do; also I sometimes read one or another religious book; I really thought that I had faith and was a Christian, and all the more because I have to put up with it that these friends of mine taunt and deride me for going to church. But if it must be taken so seriously, I admit in all sincerity that I am not really a Christian.' Thereupon we open the door and he comes out and joins the company.

2

'The next! Whose pledge is this?' 'Miss T—'s.' 'What shall the forfeit be?' 'She shall go into a dark room and gaze at stars.'

Now let her forget everything, but think passionately upon one fact, that God is present and says to her: 'I know it, thou dost treasure in thy soul a secret wish; thou hast never spoken about it to any one and dost not dare to, yet this wish is really the content of thy life, thou livest in and for this wish—well then, this wish shall be fulfilled, entirely according to thy desire, if only thou wilt answer sincerely this question: Art thou a Christian? Be not terrified, it is not what thou dost answer that shall decide the matter; no, it is the question whether thou art sincere.' She answers: 'Thou God of love, Oh, bear not too hard upon me; I am only a weak girl; I have grown up in my parents' house and become like the other girls; but about this question I have never thought so decisively—I am so much alarmed, it seems to me that surely there are hardly any grown men serious enough to take the matter so seriously. It is such a prodigious weight Thou layest upon the answer, nothing less than that the fulfilment of my wish is made to hang upon it. Yet even this, that I regard it as a prodigious weight, is indeed the proof that I am not really a Christian, for otherwise the question concerning me would be still more important than my wish.' And if it were not dark in this room, I believe that one might have seen that God's eye rested upon this girl with singular favour; for in her inexperience there was more wisdom than in many a learned man's much knowledge.

3

'The next! Whose pledge is this?' 'Pastor F—'s.' 'What shall the forfeit be?' 'He shall go into a dark room and gaze at stars.'

Let him now forget everything, especially his preoccupation with the fact that there exist the state and the diplomatists and the politicians of importance, that there is such a thing as Christianity in the land, that it is incumbent upon him to support the throne, &c.; but on the other hand let him think passionately upon the one fact that God is present and says to him: 'Art thou a Christian? As a teacher thou hast bound thyself with a sacred oath; in a solemn ceremony thou hast received the aid of the Holy Ghost—therefore great is thine accountability if thou art not a Christian. However, this shall not decide the matter, no, but rather thy sincerity. Answer sincerely! If not, then I shall let this great accountability which hangs by a mere hair over thy head—I shall let it fall upon thee crushingly with more than a ton weight.' He answers: 'Thanks, O God, thanks that Thou dost state the case for me in this way; for thus I can admit with sincerity that I am not really a Christian. Things have gone with me as with many others beside me. One becomes a parson at an early age. Then one marries—and has the responsibility of a family. Then doubts arise. But now it is too late, now one must, as we men say, hold one's ears; one is forced farther and farther into untruth, so becomes less and less a Christian, yet more and more defiantly assertive that naturally one is a Christian since one is a teacher in Christendom. Thanks, therefore, O God, that Thou dost state the case for me in this way.'

This company was composed of 25 persons. Each severally went into the dark room which was witness to the admission: 'I am not really a Christian.'—Now they are all assembled in the drawing-room. Is this a company of Christians? Yes, naturally, we are indeed all of us Christians, we are a Christian nation, &c.

Bishop Martensen ought to have remembered that 'Go into thy closet and shut the door' is a part of Christ's definition of a Christian, and hence a part of His definition of the Church.

It has commonly been claimed on behalf of Protestantism (in contrast with Catholicism) that it lays greater emphasis upon the responsibility of the single individual before God. I suspect that this was a misapprehension from the beginning. It may be said that this was the premiss of Protestantism, but it is a premiss which is not much in evidence to-day, when in the decay of all objective authority there is less and less practice of self-examination and self-discipline. However, I do not intend to quote anything more from S. K. bearing on the distinction between Protestant and Catholic—except the following picture of two worldly prelates:[1]

When Catholicism degenerates, what form of corruption will show itself? The answer is easy: Mock holiness. When Protestantism degenerates, what form of corruption will show itself? The answer is not difficult: Shallow worldliness. But in Protestantism this will show itself with a refinement which cannot occur in Catholicism.

Let us take a perfectly simple instance. Imagine a Catholic prelate who is perfectly worldly—naturally not to such an extreme that the law can punish him or that nature itself will take its revenge; no, he is altogether too worldly to be so stupid; no, the whole thing is so shrewdly calculated (and this is the worldliest thing about it) for shrewd enjoyment, and then in turn for the enjoyment of this very shrewdness—and thus his whole life is the enjoyment of all possible pleasure such as no worldly-wise Epicurean could exceed. How then will the Catholic judge him? Well, I assume that he says (quite becomingly), It is not my business to pass judgement upon the higher clergy; but none the less the Catholic will readily see that this is worldliness. And why will he readily see this? Because the Catholic sees at the same time an entirely different side of Christianity expressed—a fact which also the high prelate must put up with, that side by side with him there walks one who lives in poverty, and that the Catholic has a profound sense that this is truer than the prelate's way of life, which, alas, is mere worldliness.

Imagine now on the other hand a Protestant land where there is no thought of Catholicism, where for a long, long time people have accepted the Lutheran view, but without its original premiss; where for a long, long time they have been rid of ascetics and fasters and monks and of them that in poverty preach Christianity—and not only so, but have got so thoroughly rid of it, as of something ridiculous and foolish, that if any such figure were to turn up now, one would burst with laughter at so outlandish a beast; they have got rid of it as the lower, the imperfect conception of Christianity. Imagine now in this Protestant land a Protestant prelate who is the exact counterpart of the Catholic. What then? Why, in this case the Protestant prelate possesses a refinement of pleasure, ah, a refinement! which the Catholic prelate would suck his fingers in vain to taste, inasmuch as in the whole Protestant environment there is not a living soul that has a profound sense of the significance of renouncing the world (the sort of godliness which had its share of truth, even if it was exaggerated, in the middle ages), since the whole religiousness of the land is erected upon the upshot of Lutheranism (without its original premiss), that godliness is nothing but frank-hearted enjoyment of life (which is indeed strange when one has witnessed Luther's fear and trembling and trial of temptation). Thus the Protestant prelate possesses a refinement of pleasure —What a deuce of an advantage, the Catholic prelate may perhaps exclaim, the deuce take him!—the refinement, namely, that his contemporaries understand his worldliness and worldly enjoyment as . . . godliness! Behold, say the contemporaries one to another (and remember that in Catholicism the situation for the prelate was that one said to the other, Let us not look upon it or dwell upon it, it is just simply worldliness), behold the Lutheran frank-heartedness, behold him over the turtle soup, there is no such fine connoisseur as he, see how he can suck enjoyment from every situation, and how shrewd he is about his own advantage, and so let us admire his Lutheran frank-heartedness! High he soars in Lutheran frank-heartedness—high above this lower and imperfect ideal of entering a monastery, of fasting, of preaching Christianity in poverty high he soars above it all in freedom of spirit and Lutheran frank-heartedness! The noble thing is not to wander away from the world, to flee from it—no, genuine Lutheranism is like the prelate, for this is godliness. His contemporaries do not merely put up with this or take pains to ignore it; no, they regard it with admiration—as godliness. . . . But why cannot the same thing occur in Catholicism? Because Catholicism has the universal premiss that we men are pretty much a lot of rascals. And why can it happen in Protestantism? Because the Protestant principle is related to a very singular premiss: a man who sits in the anguish of death, in fear and trembling and much trial of temptation—and of this there are not many examples in any generation.

Here again the figure of Bishop Mynster is discernible, in spite of some exaggeration. It seems as if perhaps S. K. did not make sufficient allowance for the temptations of his position. He recognized clearly enough the peril in which the ordinary parson is placed, but he does not seem to have reflected how much more perilous is the position of a bishop—so perilous indeed that it must be almost impossible for him to be a Christian. He is peculiarly exposed to 'the lust of the flesh, the lust of the eye [if he is a cathedral-builder—and in any case to] the pride of life

Lest any one suspect that I am expressing here a vulgar prejudice against prelacy, I refer to the fact that St. Chrysostom, one of the greatest of bishops, was troubled by the doubt whether any bishop could be saved.

§ 5. THE ESTABLISHED CHURCH

In the open attack S. K.'s criticism of the abuses of Christianity were narrowed exceedingly and were directed specifically against the State Church of Denmark. 'Especially in Denmark' was not a mere phrase—but we must remember that it was Denmark of nearly a century ago. The case was not so sharply narrowed in the Journals, and this makes it plain that the pamphleteering attack did not express S. K.'s whole interest, or even his deepest interest. There he narrowed the issue as a tactical measure. It was only what had to be said first, and with 'vigorous exaggeration', in order to produce a 'catastrophe' which would very emphatically 'call attention to Christianity'.

Nevertheless the Journals of these latter years contain a good deal of criticism of the Established Church and of the clergy. English readers who are unacquainted with Lutheranism as an 'established' religion may need to be told what this is all about. For we are familiar with the fact that the Roman Church, wherever it has been established, has commonly succeeded only too well in maintaining its ascendancy in the State or over it, and that the Reformed (Calvinistic) Churches have always known how to preserve their independence. But it is notorious that Lutheranism was always subservient to the State and has shown little power of resistance to bureaucratic control. It is significant that the unexpected resistance to the totalitarian state we now witness in Germany was led by a Swiss Calvinist, Karl Barth; and there is reason to believe that S. K. injected iron into the blood of the Confessional Christians in Germany.

In this day and generation we cannot hear without amazement S. K.'s complaint that 'all are Christians'. We have got far beyond that. But so it was in his day—and even later. An admirable little book of etiquette which I found indispensable in Germany devoted its longest chapter to the thesis that 'it is a requisite of good form to have one's children baptized'. It argued cogently that they were not likely to ask to be baptized when they had reached years of discretion, and that as unbaptized persons they would not only be exposed to social embarrassment but be subjected also to civil disabilities. It was this attitude towards baptism which prompted S. K. to doubt the advisability of baptizing infants. He remarked that in the early times when baptism was understood to impose an obligation there was a tendency to defer it as long as possible, whereas now when it means only privilege it cannot be had too early.[1] Such considerations are not altogether out of place to-day. But it seems almost incredible to us that David Strauss, who was the most effective opponent of Christianity in S. K.'s day, had all his children baptized. And in our own day Ernest Haeckel did not formally separate himself from the Church until the last years of his life. It was not easy for him to do so, for the State still insisted that every one must be a Christian—or a Jew. S. K. did not hesitate to attack this situation by a *reductio ad absurdum*. The following is a passage from the Journal, but with variations it was repeated in the *Instant:*[2]

> To be or to call one's self a Christian is a condition so essential for getting on in life that I suppose no one could get permission to earn his living by keeping a whore-house unless he could produce proof that he was baptized and is (i.e. calls himself) a Christian. That is to say: to earn a living in this way is admissible, says the State, but only on the assumption and understanding and condition that you are a Christian. God in heaven!

But it is unnecessary to quote many passages when in one 'picture' S. K. graphically describes the relationship between[3]

> Christianity—the State
>
> Take a picture. When a cabman, for example, sees a perfectly splendid horse, only 5 years old and without a blemish, the very ideal of what a horse should be, a fiery, snorting steed such as never before was seen—then says the cabman, 'No, that's a horse I can't bid on, nor can I afford to pay for it, and even if I could, it wouldn't be suitable for my use.' But when some half-score years have gone by, when that splendid horse is now spavined and lame, &c., then the cabman says, 'Now I can bid on it, now I can pay for it, and I can get so much use out of it, or what is left of it, that I can really take pleasure in spending a little to feed it.'
>
> So it is with the State and Christianity. With the proud air

Christianity had when it first entered the world—'No', every state might say, 'that religion I can't buy; and not only that, but I will say, Good Lord deliver me from buying that religion, it would be certain ruin to me.' But then as Christianity in the course of some centuries had become spavined, chest-foundered, bungled, and generally made a mess of, then said the State, 'Yes, now I can bid for it; and with my cunning I perceive very well that I can have so much use and profit out of it that I can really take pleasure in spending a little to polish it up a bit.'

If only Christianity in gratitude for its polishing doesn't become itself again and polish off the State—'Ouch! Good Lord deliver us!—every state can see that this religion is my ruin'. The cabman is well secured, he has bought shrewdly, he runs no risk that the 20-year-old hackney jade can become again the fiery 5-year-old—which according to the cabman's judgement no cabman can be served by, just as little, precisely as little, as the State can be served by . . . Christianity ever young.

Naturally, the attack against the State Church was directed principally against its officers, the parsons, who were denounced as hirelings of the State, intent only upon a fat 'living' which would support them in ease 'with wife and family', with 'the prospect of steady advancement'.[1]

The Preaching of the Gospel

Parson: Thou shalt die unto the world.—The fee is $10.

Neophyte: Indeed, if I must die unto the world, I can well understand that on this account I have got to fork out much more than $10; but permit me one question: Who gets the $10?

Parson: Naturally, I get it, it is my living, for I must live, together with my family, by preaching that one must die unto the world. The price is therefore very cheap, and one might well require something more. If you will be reasonable, you can understand yourself that to preach that a man must die unto the world, if it is done seriously and with zeal, takes a lot out of a man. Hence I really have the greatest need of spending the summer in the country with my family to get some recreation, &c.

This is a terrible passage. Fortunately there is not much exaggeration of this sort in the Journal, but there is much more of it and much worse in the *Instant*.

S. K. was always interested in parsons, since he had so long intended to be one himself; and having an analytical mind he was of course not sparing of criticism. He thought of the parsons chiefly as preachers, as they also regarded themselves; and it is a pathetic thought that one who was so nearly a clergyman as S. K. was compelled all his life to hear other people preach. He had his favourite preachers. Among them was Visby, whom he often mentions in the Journal with an enthusiasm which apparently was untroubled by such reservations as commonly were mingled with his admiration for Mynster. Yet it is evident that he had to suffer much—especially from preachers who struggled to reach a religious climax and lapsed unwittingly unto the 'aesthetical'. But even if the sermon was irreproachable, there remained the disturbing suspicion that the preacher was only a . . . preacher. He remarks that as a matter of fact they had taken an oath to teach—but not to live accordingly. The following, as the context shows, was not directed exclusively at the parsons:[1]

If only men were not able to talk!

Life in the animal world is so easy to understand, so simple —because the animal has the advantage over men that it is not able to talk. In this realm of existence the only thing that speaks is its life, its actions.

'Something is better than nothing' is an adage which applies only to relative values; when it is a question of the unconditional it does not apply. The 1,000 parsons who are not unconditionally devoted to Christ are not better than nothing.[2]

The symbolical books of the Church recognize that there are various degrees of blessedness in the hereafter—why don't the preachers say anything about that? It is just possible that one or another of their hearers might wish to aspire to a higher degree.[3]

There are 1,000,000 Christians in Denmark, there are 1,000 parsons, there are deans and bishops, there are undertakers and sextons, there are hearses, baptismal clothes and shrouds, everything is Christianly O.K.—so that it is almost ridiculous when there comes a man and makes such an effort as Magister

Kierkegaard has made in a literary way, and ends by letting it be known that all he wanted to do was to call attention to Christianity.[1]

According to the New Testament, Christianity is the deepest wound that can be inflicted upon a man . . . and now the modern clergyman is trained in the art of introducing Christianity in such a way that it signifies nothing, and when he is perfect in that he is a paragon. But that is revolting. Oh, it is all very well in the case of a barber who becomes skilful enough to take off a man's beard without his noticing it; but when it comes to a matter which is expressly intended to wound, the acquisition of such skill in applying it that possibly it will not be noticed—that is disgusting.[2]

But enough of these quotations. If I were to make a collection of S. K.'s sayings about preachers and preaching, I could find more of them in the earlier Journals, and more edifying ones. He had no longer patience to discuss at any length the question of preaching when he felt that the whole thing must be done away with:[3]

And always this ambiguity that the sermon is appraised aesthetically. It is really a desperate situation. Either/Or. Let a cobbler's apprentice preach, but let his life express what he teaches—the Or is: let an actor declaim, and then we know at least where we are.

§ 6. CHRISTENDOM/CHRISTIANITY

The field of vision widens out immensely when S. K. comes to deal with the contrast 'Christendom/Christianity'. In the Journals of the last year this topic occupies far more space than all the other polemical topics put together; and this shows that the pamphleteering attack on the Established Church was only a skirmish in the great battle S. K. was waging. When he brings suit against 'Christendom' we can none of us escape with an alibi; for this term embraces us all, whether Lutherans, Calvinists, Anglicans, Catholics, or Orthodox, whether we belong to a 'free' Church or an 'established'—and not least of all if we are vague Christians of a modern sort whose religion is indistinguishable from the prevailing culture of a particular period and nation. We are reminded in these days that Ethiopia is a part of

Christendom. 'Christendom', according to S. K., is an 'illusion of the senses'. It cannot honestly be said that we have entirely recovered from that illusion, although it has become impossible to say that 'all are Christians'. It was only a generation ago that we applauded the missionary slogan, 'To win the world for Christ in our generation', which evidently assumed that our part of the world ('Christendom') was already won—and so we proceeded to carry *our* culture to less favoured lands. In this day we are not all of us so naïve; and yet (except for Russia and Mexico) there is hardly a nation in Europe or the two Americas which does not count itself a Christian nation—especially when it is at war with another.

'Christendom is a conspiracy against the Christianity of the New Testament', says S. K.[1] He does not mean to say that it is a new conspiracy in our day, for it dates at least from the Peace of the Church in the fourth century.

Christianity a Fortress

Imagine a fortress, absolutely impregnable, provisioned for an eternity.

Then there comes a new commandant. He conceives that it might be a good idea to build bridges over the moats—so as to be able to attack the besiegers.

Charmant! He transforms the fortress into a country estate—and naturally the enemy takes it.

So it is with Christianity. They changed the method—and naturally the world conquered.[2]

Christendom came about as soon as emphasis was laid upon 'extension' at the cost of 'intensity'.[3] 'True Christians/many Christians' is the way the alternative is stated in the *Instant*. In this way Christianity has been 'transformed into optimism'. The world in fact is the same old world; it has not been changed, but taking advantage of the illusion of Christendom it has conquered. 'A Christian world' is nonsense. If the world in fact were Christian, if it were true that 'all are Christians', there would be no opportunity, no possibility even, of becoming a Christian. New Testament Christianity could no longer exist. These sharp expressions are found in the *Instant*, but the thoughts they expressed were often pondered during the preceding years.

Christianity not only does not exist; no, it is non-existent to such a degree that the very thing we warn against as detestable, ungodly—precisely that is New Testament Christianity.[1]

Truly it was an injustice to Columbus that America was not named after him, but it was a much greater injustice to Jesus Christ that Christendom was named after him.[2]

Christianity has been spread too thin. The zeal for extension must be checked, in favour of a deeper intensity. It might be better if the Gospel were taken away from us until we should learn to appreciate it. And about

The New Testament

. . . This foolery with Bible societies which distribute New Testaments by the million.

No, I could be tempted to make another proposal to Christendom. Let us collect all the New Testaments there are in existence, let us carry them out to an open place or up upon a mountain, and then while we all kneel down let some one address God in this fashion: Take this book back again; we men, being such as we now are, are no good at all for dealing with a thing like this which only makes us unhappy. Such is my proposal, that like the inhabitants of Gadara we beseech Christ to 'depart out of our coasts'. This is an honest and manly way of talking, quite different from that disgusting, hypocritical, preachifying fudge about life being of no value to us apart from the inestimable blessing of Christianity.[3]

Ludicrous

A man's whole life is worldliness, all his thought and effort from morning till night, his waking and his dreaming.

—At the same time, *naturally*, he is a Christian, for doesn't he live in Christendom! and in his quality as a Christian he is 'a stranger and a pilgrim' in the world.

This is just as ludicrous as when the savages adorn themselves with a single piece of European clothing—for example, the savage who comes on board stark naked except for the epaulets of a general on his shoulders.[4]

But I need not quote more of this inexhaustible material, seeing that the reader has already been made acquainted with S. K.'s criticism of Christendom from his earlier period. It cannot be too strongly stressed that no new thoughts of importance emerge in this last period, though we find now a sharper and more direct expression of thoughts which had long been brewing.

§ 7. SUFFERING AND MARTYRDOM

Far more important than all the negative aspects of S. K.'s polemic, which we have already considered, are the positive interests denoted by the terms 'renunciation', 'dying unto the world', 'sacrifice' and 'martyrdom'—in short, 'the price of eternity'.[1] Needless to say, these are not new ideas to S. K. in this last period of his life. We have traced them from his youth when he shrank from Christianity as 'a radical cure', and we have seen that he traced the thought of martyrdom back to his early childhood. It is true that in this last period these ideas were stressed more strongly and were more frequently in evidence. But S. K. had always associated suffering with Christianity. In his congenital disposition to melancholy, in his strange upbringing, in his ill health, in his solitary life, there was reason enough for the sombre view he took of Christianity—so much more sombre than any of the Apostles give evidence of. It is not strange that the optimistic age in which he lived (and in which we live) should be inclined to dismiss his interpretation of Christianity as a morbid symptom, something pathological. And yet it is not easy to dismiss it, for he held the New Testament in his hand as he preached, and he could turn to chapter and verse. He could show that what he was urging so zealously is implied in the very notion of discipleship. It is a fact that the 'disciples' were required to 'follow' their Master, and that in the New Testament the imitation of Christ meant invariably imitation of His sufferings. There is only one expression of it more general, when St. John says that one ought to 'walk even as He also walked'. Though it is in accord with St. John's thought to say that the path in which He walked was love, yet St. Augustine justly observes that this path led Him to the cross. S. K. says:[2]

> What I have constantly aimed at is to get this problem stated (before God and man, if I may so say): Can one be a Christian without being a disciple?

It is so clear from the New Testament what is meant by 'being a disciple' that at a very early time Christians ceased to apply this title to themselves and reserved it for the immediate followers of Jesus, seeking thus to escape from the implications of this word. Here was the place where S. K. felt the need of 'calling attention to Christianity'. This is the whole side of Christianity which Mynster left out. But this side simply could not be included in a religion which had ceased to be eschatological, when men no longer sincerely welcomed the thought that 'what we suffer now is not to be compared with the glory that shall burst upon us' (Rom. 8: 18). In this situation the Christianity of the New Testament is an absurdity—as St. Paul recognized when he exclaimed that, if Christ be not risen, if we are left like the Gentiles without a heavenly hope which justifies the different tenor of our life, then 'we are of all men most pitiable' (1 Cor. 15: 19). The New Testament is so clear that it required hundreds of years and hundreds of learned commentaries to obscure it:[1]

> Suppose that in the New Testament it were written, for example (a thing which we can at least suppose), that every man shall have $100,000 . . . do you believe that then there would be any question of a commentary?—or not rather that every one would say: That is easy enough to understand, there is absolutely no need of a commentary, for God's sake, let us be delivered from any commentary. . . .
>
> But what actually is written in the New Testament (about the narrow way, about dying into the world) is not a bit more difficult to understand than that about the $100,000. The difficulty lies elsewhere, in the fact that it is not to our liking —and therefore, therefore, therefore we must have commentaries and professors and commentaries.
>
> It is to get rid of doing God's will that we have invented learning . . . we shield ourselves by hiding behind tomes.

'Christianity without the following of Christ is merely mythology, poesy.'[2] 'The enlightened 19th century treats Christianity as a myth, but lacks the courage to give it up.' If one is ever to become a Christian, he must do it now, for in eternity it will be too late; the question then is if he has *been* a Christian.[3] 'One must take the world as it is', they say:[4]

> But when an individual, not a mere sample man, but one who possessing primitive originality stands alone with the

New Testament in his hand, ready to risk all and to suffer all, and says: 'No, my good world, I have no intention of taking you as you are; here are the instructions how you ought to be' —that is an event, an event which moves the universe, is alertly observed by it—it produces an intentional change in the world, which a European war can be said to do only in a *superficial* sense in so far as it changes the political map; no, it is a change in the world, so that existence from its depths becomes attentive, hosts of angels and legions of demons set themselves in motion.

There is a false and crafty humility which serves as an excuse for not presuming to imitate Christ, claiming that it is more modest simply to adore Him. But 'I cannot' means 'I will not'.[1]

Oh, but when I read the New Testament I get the impression that in God's opinion every man is a giant. . . . There is nothing which every one is so much afraid of as getting to know how prodigiously much he is capable of. Thou art capable—wouldst thou know of what?—thou art capable of living in poverty; thou art capable of enduring almost all possible ill-treatment. . . . How ironical that every man is designed to be an Atlas, capable of bearing the weight of the world—and then to see what we men are; and, alas, how sorry a thing it is that we ourselves are to blame for what we are.[2]

In other chapters we have had so many illustrations of what S. K. means by renunciation, dying unto the world, suffering, sacrifice and martyrdom, that it is not necessary here to quote at great length from the inexhaustible material furnished by the later journals, and I cite, therefore, only a few of the more striking expressions.

The way renunciation is commonly understood has appeared to me to be an attempt to make God out a foolish pedant and God's relationship to man an eternal stinginess and perpetual pettiness. Hence it has not appealed to me in the least. But the real situation is entirely different; for renunciation, yea, the delight of renunciation, is simply a lover's understanding with God. So far as I am concerned, truth obliges me to admit that it was God that gave me the hint. I had not dreamed of it, had not even believed myself capable of it. But it was as though

God had whispered to me the secret: Renunciation is a higher relationship to God, it is really a love-relationship; and for me at least an enchantment was spread over renunciation—I have never been so enchanted.

This thought I have loved like my very life—I was on the point of reconciling myself to the notion that I must give it up, that it was my duty to submit to the humiliation of giving it up because I could no longer afford to live for it.

Now—Oh, blessed fortune!—I am again restored to this thought of mine, but in a far deeper sense. It seems as if God said to me: 'My little friend, I who am love would find the greatest joy in discovering an expedient to make thee again independent; but then thy cause will not go forward, then thou wilt hardly need to have anything to do with me, at least thou wilt not learn to love me in a higher sense. Thou art now so far developed that, were I to bestow riches upon thee, I might almost be angry with thee if thou didst not instantly give them back, saying: No, under the circumstances, I dare not. Surely thou art too much developed not to recognize thyself how unseemly it is while living in opulence to preach the blessedness of doing without, too much developed to help thyself out by saying, as thou didst say when it was well enough to have the honesty to say it, that thou art only a poet.' And so it is, even though I can say that I have been something more than a poet.[1]

The Two Ways

One is to suffer; the other is to become a professor of the fact that another suffered.

The first is 'the way'; the second goes round about (the adverb 'about' is so aptly used for lectures and sermons) and perhaps it ends by going down below.

. . . . . .

The professors and parsons live by presenting the sufferings of others, and that is regarded as religiousness, uncommonly deep religiousness even; for the religiousness of the congregation is nothing else but hearing this presented. A *charmante* religiousness, just as genuine as tea made with a bit of paper which once lay in a drawer beside another bit of paper which once had been used to wrap a few dried tea-leaves from which tea had already been made three times.

'Another dies for me in order that my life may be gay.'[1] It is the same scornful arraignment Robert Browning brings: Christ died, and

All this took place, you think,
This throe on dissolution's brink,
Only to give our life a zest
And prove our sorrows for the best?

According to the New Testament, to be a Christian properly means . . . to be sacrificed. The Apostle rushes forth to protest, testifying that one sacrifice was made once for all and that no further sacrifice is needed—and to make sure that this preaching is well understood he is . . . sacrificed. Thereupon thousands and thousands of martyrs are sacrificed to confirm the preaching that no other sacrifice is needed; the New Testament itself predicts that every true Christian will be sacrificed in one way or another.[2]

The Passion for Martyrdom

When one is able to endure the isolation involved in being a single individual, entirely without the mitigation of intermediate terms, without the alleviation of any illusion, alone in the endless world and the endless world of men—but out of a million men 999,999 will lose their senses before they attain this isolation—alone before the face of God—then the thing of loving God and being loved by God will appear to him so blessed that for sheer blessedness he must say: O my God, now I have but one wish, one prayer, one desire, one passion, that I may experience suffering, become hated, persecuted, mocked, spit upon, put to death. For if God's love for me were to be expressed in the fact that in a sensual sense I enjoyed good days, that I received this world's goods, if it were thus to be directly expressed—phew, phew, that would be disgusting to me, I should die for shame, I should loathe it like an unnatural lust, feel that it was as disgusting as fat fish with treacle.

Behold, this is the passion for martyrdom.[3]

Yet, just here, where the loftiest and most exacting ideals of Christianity are most positively expressed, a polemical note is not lacking. Indeed it cannot be lacking. Such ideals cannot but wound. 'Christianity cannot but be polemical to a certain extent.'

The adage *corruptio optimi pessima* (the corruption of the best is the worst) is true here, for it is more especially the highest ideals that receive the homage of hypocrisy. It was against hypocrisy especially that Jesus directed the shafts of His satire, assailing it with His 'whip of small cords'. The lash cannot bite too deep into the flesh of the hypocrite—to chastise, if possible to save, or in any case to save others from contagion. So S. K. evidently felt. His blows were terrible. And all the while he cried: 'I want honesty!' But he did not forget that with respect to the highest ideals we are all of us sorely tempted to be hypocrites.

Psychological

A child which obediently does the father's will which is just the opposite of the child's wish—I am far from saying that the child doubts the father's love, but still there is no trumpeting of the father's love and ingratiating talk about how loving the father is. . . . And on the other hand, the child who understands very well that it is he who gets his own way and that the father's will is not done—then indeed there is trumpeting and bassooning and ingratiating talk about what a loving father he has.

So it is with us men in relationship to God. Imagine a man who knows very well that it is God's will and that it is Christianity according to God's conception of it, to live in poverty and abasement—but that is something he cannot put up with, on the contrary he wants to possess superabundance and to attain brilliant success in life, and so he takes the liberty of representing this arbitrarily as Christianity. Then you will see or hear how he can trumpet about God's love, about how loving God is, how blessed a thing it is that God is love—all calculated as it were to hoodwink God, just as the child cunningly ingratiated itself with the father so that he perhaps might not observe that he was being made a fool of.[1]

Imagine a father. There was something he wished the child to do—and what it was the child knew. So, thought the father, I will contrive something that will please the child immensely. So he presents it to him. (Indeed it is far too much I am doing for the child!) so I am sure he will love me in return. 'He will love me in return'—by that the father meant that the child will now do the father's will. But the child—a devilish shrewd child—accepted the present but did not do the father's will.

On the other hand the child thanked and thanked him again, said, 'Many, many thanks', and said, 'It is a dear good father'; but the child had its own way.[1]

'I am not that yet, but I am making an endeavour.'

'But really it is perfectly high-handed and unjust, and at the same time it is a senseless procedure, suddenly, at 4 o'clock in the afternoon, to assail a man, confront him with the Christian requirement, and when it turns out that his life doesn't express it, then to conclude, *ergo*, thou art not a Christian. Good Lord, I may not be that, but I make an endeavour, and really, if we are not to be driven quite mad, that is the utmost there can be any question of—an endeavour.' . . .

Suppose that it was a question of running a race. In case a man comes along walking at an even pace with a cane in his hand and a pipe in his mouth and something under his arm to boot—surely he is not running a race? No, but he is making an endeavour, it comes little by little.[2]

Substantially this is what William Law so much insisted upon in the *Serious Call*: we do not fail to lead a Christian life because of the notorious difficulty of accomplishing any task up to the ideal, but simply because 'we have never had even the bare intention of pleasing God in all our actions'.

The Tame Geese

A Revivalistic Meditation

Suppose it was so that the geese could talk—then they had so arranged it that they also could have their religious worship, their divine service.

Every Sunday they came together, and one of the ganders preached.

The essential content of the sermon was: what a lofty destiny the geese had, what a high goal the Creator (and every time this word was mentioned the geese curtsied and the ganders bowed the head) had set before the geese; by the aid of wings they could fly away to distant regions, blessed climes, where properly they were at home, for here they were only strangers.

So it was every Sunday. And as soon as the assembly broke up each waddled home to his own affairs. And then the next Sunday again to divine worship and then again home—and that was the end of it, they throve and were well-liking, became plump and delicate—and then were eaten on Martinmas Eve—and that was the end of it.

That was the end of it. For though the discourse sounded so lofty on Sunday, the geese on Monday were ready to recount to one another what befell a goose that had wanted to make serious use of the wings the Creator had given him, designed for the high goal that was proposed to him—what befell him, what a terrible death he encountered. This the geese could talk about knowingly among themselves. But, naturally, to speak about it on Sundays was unseemly; for, said they, it would then become evident that our divine worship is really only making a fool of God and of ourselves.

Among the geese there were, however, some individuals which seemed suffering and grew thin. About them it was currently said among the geese: There you see what it leads to when flying is taken seriously. For because their hearts are occupied with the thought of wanting to fly, therefore they become thin, do not thrive, do not have the grace of God as we have who therefore become plump and delicate.

And so the next Sunday they went again to divine worship, and the old gander preached about the high goal the Creator (here again the geese curtsied and the ganders bowed the head) had set before the geese, whereto the wings were designed.

So with the divine worship of Christendom. Man also has wings, he has imagination....

And then when some one reads this he says, It is very pretty—and that 's the end of it, then he waddles home to his affairs, becomes (or at least endeavours with all his might to become) plump, delicate, fat—but on Sunday the parson preachifies on this wise, and he hearkens to it . . . always like the geese.[1]

A World-Change

In an author of old time I read the following observation, or something like it. When one sees a man holding the axe wrong and chopping in such a way that he is likely to chop everything but the log, one does not say how wrongly the woodsman handles the axe; but one will say, The man is not a woodsman.

Make the application. When one sees thousands and thousands and millions of Christians whose lives have not in the remotest way even the least likeness to what—and that is the decisive thing—to what the New Testament calls Christians—is it not strange and confusing, is it not to speak as one would not do in any other situation, when one says how poorly the Christians express what it is to be a Christian, how far they are from expressing it? In every other situation one would say, These men are not Christians.

Now then, take this seriously; say: These men are not Christians—and you have a world-change.[1]

The following passage deals with the same theme, but it was written about a year later, on July 2, 1855, not many months before S. K.'s death, and the tone is much sharper. We may wonder why it was not published in the *Instant*. Perhaps the reason is that it was not sharp enough. At all events it suggests what limitless resources of satire S. K. possessed.

'Yet he endeavours'

. . . Let me employ a picture. In our time they often talk about a North Pole expedition, an undertaking which is understood to imply the highest degree of difficulty and danger.

Let us suppose that mankind had got it into its head that the fact of having taken part in such a North Pole expedition was in some way of importance for its eternal blessedness—and let us suppose that the parsons had got hold of this thing and now (out of love!) would be helpful to men.

It is clear enough that in order to take part in such a North Pole expedition one must, if he lives in Europe, first leave Europe, his home.

The parsons will take advantage of this. Naturally, they wil easily see that the number of persons who really undertake th dangerous and difficult North Pole expedition will be exceed ingly small, and that so small a number will not suffice to pro vide a livelihood for a legion of parsons with their families. Th thing to do therefore is to transform the 'North Pole Expedi tion' into 'an endeavour in the direction of such a North Pol expedition', and then to jabber men into the vain belief tha all—the millions—are also endeavouring in the direction c such a North Pole expedition.

And how this can be done is not far to seek. For exampl there is a man who lives in Copenhagen. He travels with th highest degree of convenience and comfort by steamship to London and back again—'and', says the parson, 'that was his North Pole expedition; it is true that he did not attain the North Pole, yet he made an endeavour'. 'It is clear enough', so the parson expounds, 'that when one is to undertake a North Pole expedition and lives in Copenhagen, one must first leave Copenhagen. That, this man has done. On the other hand, there is in fact no one who has actually reached the North Pole, even those who went farthest, it was in any case only an endeavour. But to travel to London is also an endeavour.' Splendid! Popular in the highest degree! And on Sunday afternoon to take a hackney coach to the park, leaving one's home, is . . . also an endeavour in the direction of discovering the North Pole—*ergo* we are all making an endeavour.[1]

'The Spirit'

It is not true, as scoffers and freethinkers audaciously declare and as the common run of men, either in despair or in rebellion, affirm with sighs or else noisily, that there exists no such Spirit which when one calls upon it will entirely re-create a man, renew him, give him strength for self-denial, for all possible self-denial.

No, it is not thus. Such a Spirit really exists. But the fact is that for one who is aware of this it is so terrible a thing to call upon this Spirit that he dare not do it—especially for one who from childhood has been coddled with grace, coddled with the notion that all is sheer leniency. For in this case he must get an entirely different conception of God; and oh, his prayer also must become entirely different from that which he was accustomed to from childhood and which was his blessed delight.

Take a picture. There is a winged horse, for example—far more than winged, it has an infinite flight; the moment you mount him you are a whole world's distance away from this world and its way of thinking and its life and its conceptions and the notions of your contemporaries. The freethinkers, the scoffers, the common run of men, are all on the alert to deny that any such horse exists—all for the sake of making the hypocritical pretence that, if such a horse did exist, they would be ready enough to mount him.

Ah, here lies the difficulty for us all in Christendom, who still have some Christianity. We cannot deny that such a Spirit exists, that it is only waiting till we give ourselves up completely—then it will attend to the rest. Ah, but we dare not. And then comes the rub, that God is still concerned with us.

And so I am of the opinion that in Christendom one should apply 'grace' in the first instance, not merely 'grace' in relation to the past, but grace in relation to the bold adventure which is required of us.[1]

§ 8. THE DIVINE MAJESTY

After the cannon has been fired off there remains nothing to show for the explosion but cold cannon-balls lying about in the field. Something has vanished, namely the energy which once propelled these spent missiles, which now testify only indirectly to a force that was dissipated the instant the gun was fired. And even the exploding gases were never visible except before the gun was fired, while they were still in the form of powder.

The articles which were published in the *Instant*, though they worked havoc in their time, are now spent missiles. For this reason I propose to say little about them in the next chapter, but I linger now so much the longer upon the loading of the gun. And I call attention not so much to the balls that were rammed into it as to the powder, the charge which contained the energy stored up for explosion. We have seen that into the gun were rammed such explosive materials as the evangelical precepts of 'following', imitation, sacrifice. Yet all of these I think of as contained rather in the explosive shells that were to be launched against the enemy. The propulsive force which ejected them was something else—it was S. K.'s conception of the infinite majesty of God.

God's Majesty

. . . God is pure subjectivity, sheer, pure subjectivity; it has in it nothing at all of objective being; for that which has such objectivity is subsumed under the concept of relativities.

. . . In the Christian view God is infinite majesty in such a way that nothing can engage His attention on its own account but only in so far as His majesty may be pleased to observe it whence it follows that the most insignificant thing can concern Him just as much as what we men call the most important. . .

. . . Though there were to break out not merely a European

war, but if Europe got into a war with Asia, and if Africa, America, and Australia found themselves compelled to take part in it; in and for itself alone this need never concern God at all—but that a poor man sighs to Him, that is something that concerns Him, for so it pleases His majesty, and this moves Him subjectively.

But suppose now that all of Europe's emperors and kings issued a rescript commanding all the thousands of hired servants (I mean the parsons) OFFICIALLY to supplicate the aid of heaven. Suppose there was arranged a prodigious exhibition of united worship of God, with 100,000 musicians, 50,000 elected deputies, and a million of ordained hired servants, to supplicate *officially* the aid of heaven—that would not concern at all the heavenly majesty—but that a poor man who walked down Cheapside sighed in the sincerity of his heart unto God, *that* concerns Him, concerns Him indescribably, infinitely, for so it pleases His majesty, and it moves Him subjectively.

And wherefore is it that the other did not concern Him, the prodigious official hubbub which could be heard at a distance of several miles and must have been able to penetrate to heaven—wherefore did not that concern Him in the least, wherefore? My friend, whatever conception you may have of God, you surely do not doubt that He is what one might call a 'connoisseur', a fine connoisseur—He who is pure subjectivity, and subjectivity is related to connoisseurship. Hence it is that one generally regards women (who in comparison with men are predominantly subjective) as fine connoisseurs, connoisseurs who know immediately how to distinguish between the official and the personal, know that the official is really insolence, a ceremonious fashion of making a fool of one. What an infinite distance therefore from God—an emperor who by a rescript, which a minister of state composed, commands 10,000 ordained hired servants to bawl officially to God, what an infinite distance compared with a poor man who sighs unto God in the sincerity of his heart.[1]

The thought of God's subjectivity occasionally lapses into metaphysics—'the In-and-for-himself-existing relates himself objectively to his own subjectivity'—but generally it is ethical and religious. God has no 'cause', no 'objects' for the attainment of which He has need of man, so that a man might flatter himself by conceiving that he was a necessary instrument for the accomplishment of God's purpose. 'No, it is man who has a cause, in which God helps him.'[1]

> Hence I am suspicious of the way one uses the expression 'to serve God'; for one cannot serve God as one serves another monarch who has objects to attain. No, the only adequate way to express a sense of God's majesty is to worship Him. Generally one makes the distinction that what is involved in worshipping God is feelings, moods, and their expression in words, whereas serving God suggests actions. No, thy action is precisely the true worship, and it is that most clearly when it is free from all bustle and the notion that God has a cause. To renounce all as an act of worship offered to God, and so not because He needs to use thee as an instrument, no, not that by any means; but to renounce all and conceive of thyself in so doing it as the most insignificant superfluity and article of luxury—that means to worship. . . .[2]
>
> It is so easy to see that He to whom everything is equally important and equally a thing of naught—easy to see that there is but one thing left that can interest Him, namely, obedience.[3]
>
> . . . Certainly God is personality. Whether He will be that in relation to a particular individual depends upon whether God so pleases. It is grace on God's part that in relation to thee He will be personality; if thou dost abuse His grace, He punishes thee by relating Himself to thee objectively. And in that sense one can say (in spite of all the proofs!) that the world has not a personal God.[4]

In conformity with his notion of the divine majesty S. K. conceives that God inflicts the most terrible punishment upon a man when He ignores him.

> Therefore it is such a false comfort, almost bestial, to believe, as is so common, that when God does not intervene to hinder one or to chastise, that then one is on splendid terms with Him. One forgets that the divine Majesty has a punishment which He himself naturally regards as the most terrible—to ignore, majestically to ignore, to leave a man to himself.[5]

S. K. recognizes that through his melancholy sympathy fo

Bishop Mynster he had almost been led to represent 'what one might call Christianity in man's interest'.

But perhaps just for this reason (because it was not on egotistical grounds I wanted to represent Christianity in man's interest), perhaps just for this reason Governance took notice of me, has led me out Farther and Farther, so that it ends with my being compelled to preach Christianity in God's interest.[1]

The Point of View for the History of the Human Race

If I should deliver an utterance on this subject—although I do not ordinarily occupy myself with such themes and regard it as unethical to concern myself with the history of the race instead of my own history—I would set forth the following view.

God has only one passion—that of loving and wanting to be loved. What then it has pleased Him to do is to go through all the modes of loving and being loved.

Naturally He Himself then plays His part and arranges everything in relation to it. At one moment He would be loved as a father by his child, then as a friend by a friend, then loved only as he who gives good gifts, then as he who tempts and proves the beloved. And in Christianity the idea is, if I may say so, to be loved as a bridegroom by his bride, and in such a wise that it becomes a sheer trial of constancy. Then He transforms Himself almost into equality with man, by accommodation, so as to be loved in this way; then the idea is to be loved by a man as Spirit—the most strenuous task, &c., &c.

My thought is: God is like a poet. This is the explanation of the fact that He puts up also with evil and with all the twaddle and pitiable insignificance and mediocrity, &c. Thus is it that a poet also is related to his poetical production (which likewise is called his creation), he suffers it to emerge. But just as one errs egregiously in believing that what the individual character says and does in the work of fiction represents the poet's personal opinion, so one errs also in supposing that what happens, for the mere fact that it happens, indicates God's approving consent. Oh, no, He has His own opinion. But poetically He suffers everything possible to emerge, He Himself is everywhere at hand, looks on, poetizes further, in one sense poetically impersonal, indifferently observant of everything; in another

sense personal, positing the most frightful difference, as tha
between good and evil, between willing as He wills and no
willing as He wills, &c., &c.

The Hegelian nonsense about the actual being the real i
therefore quite on a par with the confusion which requires
poet to admit that the words and acts of his dramatis persona
are his personal words and acts.

Only it must be firmly held that what, if I may so say, deter
mines God to want to poetize thus is not, as the pagans though
a need of passing the time; no, no, right here is the seriou
thought, that to love and to be loved is God's passion, almost a
if—Oh, infinite love!—He were Himself bound by this passior
so that He could not help but love, almost as if it were a weak
ness, whereas indeed it is His strength, His infinite love, whic
to such a degree is a love not subject to change.[1]

§ 9. THE LAST EITHER/OR

For this last section of the chapter which brings us up to th
point where the public attack upon the Established Church wa
decisively launched, or, in other words, up to the very mome
when the cannon was fired, I have aimed to select passages fro
S. K.'s *Papers* which give a just view of his state of mind at th
critical juncture. The passages I have room to quote are n
numerous enough to give a full view, but at least they will serve
dispose of the suspicion that it was a personal animosity whi
prompted this attack, or that the violence of it reveals a morb
instability of temper, a super-irascibility bordering upon i
sanity. And they serve equally well to correct the presumpti
that S. K. must have lost the ardour and confidence of Christi
faith before he exploded so savage an attack upon the institutio
of Christendom, in which he did not hesitate to employ the cru
lest expedients of warfare—not only tear-gas, but also laughin
gas.

Being in possession of the Journals we are now able to see th
such suspicions are the *exact* opposite of the truth. If mode
writers do not see this, it is because they will not. But for S. K
contemporaries, since that they had no other explanation, su
suspicions were natural and inevitable. He himself shrewd
reckoned with the fact that the attack could not produce t
'catastrophe' he aimed at unless it appeared to be 'a sort

madness'. The very violence of it, its extravagance, one-sidedness and exaggeration, were tactically calculated to produce the desired effect. Consequently even those among his contemporaries who were most inclined to sympathize with his attack felt obliged to account for the drastic form of it by supposing that ill health had made him supersensitive to irritation—an explanation which was the more specious for the fact that the attack was abruptly terminated by his illness and death.

S. K. intentionally refrained from saying anything that might enlighten his contemporaries about the purpose he had in mind or the tactics he was pursuing. They could not guess that the 'catastrophe' he sought to produce was thought of as involving him first of all, so that his imprisonment, or perhaps his execution, might seal his endeavour and draw attention emphatically to the abuses he sought to correct. He reckoned that the way to bring about a catastrophe was to act suddenly and take every one by surprise, 'coming out with the conclusion without stating the premisses'. Hence he refrained from providing any 'commentary' upon his action:[1]

> If I dared to accompany my action with a commentary, throwing light upon the ingenious purposefulness of the whole, I should have a brilliant success—but totally fail to accomplish my task. One would get no impression, no sting, of the decisive character of the action, but would be enchanted by the interesting character of the reflection by which the action was supported.
>
> A man needs resignation, however, to go to work in such a way that it must look like a sort of madness (just as he reckons it will—for without that we do not get passions aroused and the fire kindled)—whereas he knows that if he were to accompany it with a copious commentary, he would be admired for his shrewdness and avoid all danger and inconvenience, for then the action would not be effective as such but as provocative of interest.

But now we possess the commentary. First of all I would call attention to the resoluteness of S. K.'s decision. In this last act he reverts again very emphatically to the slogan 'Either/Or' which he made so prominent at the beginning of his literary career. He says in the *Instant*:[2]

> For what is Either/Or?—if I am to say it, who surely must know. Either/Or is the magic word at which the folding-doors spring open and the ideals display themselves (Oh, blissful sight!); Either/Or is the token which ensures admission to the unconditional (God be praised!); yea, Either/Or is the key of heaven!
>
> I who am called 'Either/Or' cannot be at any one's service with Both—And. I am in possession of a book which is surely all but unknown in this land, and therefore I will cite the title exactly: The New Testament of our Lord and Saviour Jesus Christ. Although I have a perfectly free relationship to that book, and am not, e.g., pledged to it by an oath, it nevertheless exercises an enormous influence over me and inspires me with an indescribable horror of Both—And.

But the Either/Or we hear now has a new ring of decision. It is different, of course, from the slogan of the aesthetical youth who proclaimed: 'Either marry/Or do not marry—both of them you will regret.' But it is different from the Either/Or of Judge William, which looked no farther than morality of a rather bourgeois sort and came to repose in the snug security of matrimony. S. K.'s 'Or' was far beyond that even when his first book was published. In a passage written in 1853[1] he traces through his writings the progress of his Either/Or. In another place he recalls that in the beginning it was associated with humour:[2]

> Laughter ought to be employed—hence the last Diapsalm in *Either/Or* [see p. 106]. But laughter should first be divinely sanctified and devoutly initiated. That was accomplished on the greatest possible scale. Laughter should not get the upper hand, nor should it all end with laughter; it is merely a faculty for casting light upon the trumpery and illusion so that I might get to the point of 'moving by the help of ideals'.

The Either/Or we now hear is anything but a query; it does not propose a dilemma which prompts to reflection, but it assumes that a resolute decision has already been made, or can instantly be made, and it prompts to action. S. K. was no longer standing at the crossways; he had resolutely chosen his path, and it proved to be the 'narrow way'. His Either/Or had been resolved into the 'Or', into the final 'Or' of the Christian ideal. Hence he had a right to express his scorn of 'up to a certain point' and the other 'locutions commonly adopted: Both—And; or both this and that and that; a Christian is this and that—and at the same time a Christian'.[1]

For the very reason that his purpose was so firmly fixed, that his lively imagination had so vividly pictured what was to come, and that he had planned so long what he was to do, he needed all the more patience to wait so many years before the signal for attack was given. He recounts how earnestly and often he prayed for patience, 'Give patience'; but thereupon he was checked by the thought how sorely he had tried the patience of God, and his prayer was changed to 'Have patience'.[2]

We get some idea how much patience was needed when we observe that the two entries I am about to quote were written in 1852—and there still remained two more years to 'hold out':[3]

> Oh, praise be to God, and again, Praise be to God that I have held out, and again, Praise be to God that I had strength to hold out.
>
> Hast thou ever seen a hound—all bloody, exhausted by the effort and loss of blood incurred with the struggle within the fox's hole, yet he does not let go, he has fixed his teeth in the fox and thus dies.
>
> I too am exhausted; but I have not let go of my thought, I have not made my life more comfortable, which only would have made less evident what I required.
>
> As I have often said, 'the end must be made fast' [i.e. the end of the thread knotted if one would sew effectively—a thought which he associated with the death of an individual—first with his father's death, now with his own]. . . . The lecturing habit cannot be put a stop to by a new doctrine, but only by a personality.

Looking forward to the task he was summoned to perform, he recognized that it was such a task as had never been performed in Christendom, yet for all that he was singularly free from delusions of grandeur. Most decidedly he was not an Apostle, and he was not a prophet of any sort. Although he was in fact a 'witness for the truth' and was expecting to witness by his death, to be 'a sacrifice', a martyr, yet he never ventured to apply to himself expressly a description which he had so greatly exalted in his own thought. He spoke of himself as 'the extraordinary', expressing thereby his recognition of the fact that he had a unique work to do and was peculiarly fitted for it by all the experiences of his life; and yet this thought had no tendency to puff him up, inasmuch as these very experiences which made him the extraordinary in a good sense had first made him 'the extraordinary in a bad sense', made him heterogeneous, unlike others, 'unable to realize the universal human'—in short, denoted what was his bitterest experience from childhood on. We may wonder that up to the last he continued to describe himself as 'without authority', notwithstanding that he rebuked as boldly as the Prophet Jeremiah. But we may observe that against the legal authority of the Established Church he set the authority of the New Testament and not his own authority. His summons was, 'Judge for yourself!' He claimed no direct commission from God, no delegated authority, but only such authority as every individual before God was responsible for exercising, the responsible authority of thinking clearly, as he for a whole lifetime had thought clearly, about what Christianity is and what it means to be a Christian. The only title he appropriated to himself was 'the Corrective'—and this, as he understood it, was far from being a proud title. For he recognized, as we have seen, that the corrective as such was obliged to insist upon a 'vigorously one-sided' aspect of the truth, and therefore was himself in need of correction and never should be treated as a norm. 'The next generation will always need an opposition to the corrective.'[1] With the thought of the corrective he constantly associated the thought of suffering and 'sacrifice', even to the sacrifice of life (see p. 587), and he had many ways of expressing his expectation of being sacrificed to his task:[2]

> Christianity in these parts simply does not exist; but before there can be any question of its being restored again, 'first a poet's heart must break, and this poet am I'—these words of mine about myself are only too true. . . . Denmark has need of a dead man.

Yet even in the expectation of martyrdom he found no reason for exalting himself above the common run of Christians, for he thought of his death as 'only a little pinch of spice' which was meant to give flavour to the whole and be lost in the whole; and he conceived that readiness to be sacrificed belonged to the common definition of a Christian, that sacrifice in one way or another was sure to be the Christian's lot, and that even the martyr dare not glory in the thought that he was a sacrifice 'for others':[1]

> Without being a sacrifice for others, the Christian is [inevitably] sacrificed—sacrificed, namely, by the unconditional relationship to the unconditional.

The following is one of the many entries in which S. K. reflects upon his task:[2]

> The task of an Apostle is to spread Christianity, to win men to it.
>
> My task is to liberate men from the conceit that they are Christians—and yet I too am serving Christianity.
>
> Take an example. Imagine a concourse of people in the street, 20,000 men who are making a tumultuous noise and disturbance. The policeman in command says to his subordinates: If only we can get them to keep calm, walk quietly and refrain from acts of violence, then it will be all right. Accordingly the personnel of the force seek to attain this end by dispersing themselves amongst the multitude and trying to make them listen to reason. Let us suppose that this succeeds. Now let the real policeman come upon the scene and pronounce his opinion. He will say: No, that doesn't help any, at bottom it only makes the matter worse to give more importance to a popular movement just for the fact that the people keep calm and are well behaved. No, the question whether a concourse of people makes a noise or is quiet isn't decisive—20,000 persons on the street *en masse*, even if they are as still as a mouse, is nothing else but mutiny, rebellion—the ground must be cleared. So it is with letting all the illusions persist, and then wanting to bring in new life. Yes, into what? It would be bringing new life into the illusions. No, it is the illusions that must be got rid of, the ground must be cleared, and instead of bringing new life into the illusions, the little life they have in them must be starved out, so as to make it manifest that Christianity simply does not exist.

S. K. recognized humbly that the peculiar talents which fitted him for his task were not the most exalted qualities:[3]

> A Christian Auditing
>
> . . . An auditing of the account is needed—and with every decade more and more.

So Governance must get hold of an individual who is fit to be employed for this purpose.

The auditor is of course something quite different from the whole gang of parsons and professors—yet he is nothing at all of an Apostle, but rather quite the opposite.

The auditor requires precisely the quality which the Apostle has no need of—intellectuality, an eminent intellectuality, and besides that a prodigious acquaintance with all possible knavish tricks and falsifications, almost as if he himself were the most accomplished of all knaves. His business especially is to recognize counterfeits.

Since all this knowledge of his is of such a prodigiously equivocal sort that there might issue from it the greatest possible confusion, the auditor is not treated like an Apostle. Ah, no; the Apostle is a trusted man, the auditor is subjected to the sharpest supervision. I constantly have in mind only one analogy for the situation, but that is so indicative. Suppose that the Bank of England became aware that there were false notes in circulation—so well made that it was a desperation to make sure of detecting them and to make sure that the counterfeiting would not continue in the future. For all the talent there was among the personnel of the bank and the police force, there was not one to be found who had a decided talent in this direction, but there was just one man who had decided talent precisely in this direction—only he was a condemned criminal. So he had to be employed, but he was not employed as a trusted man. He was subjected to the most frightful *surveillance*, with death hanging over his head he must sit down and deal with this immense pile of money, and every time he is searched from head to toe, &c., &c.

So it is with the Christian auditor: if the Apostle has the task of proclaiming the truth, the auditor has the task of detecting falsifications, of making them known as such, and thereby making them impossible; if the Apostle's personal qualification is noble and pure simplicity (which is the condition for being an instrument of the Holy Ghost), the auditor is in possession of an ambiguous knowledge; if the Apostle is in the power of Governance in one sense only, and that a good sense, the auditor is in the power of Governance in an ambiguous sense. . . .

Apostles can never again return to us, any more than Christ might return in another sense than that of His Second Advent. Christ's life upon earth is Christianity. The significance of the Apostle is: Now it has been called to your attention, and from now on it is for you men yourselves to carry it on, but under accountability.

So mankind undertook it. And though it is an eternal lie that Christianity is perfectible, it is certain that mankind displayed a crescendo of perfectibility in the art of . . . falsifying Christianity.

In the face of this falsification even God (if He would and there were nothing else to hinder) cannot employ an Apostle, for the reason that Christianity by its falsification has put itself at such a distance from God that there can be no question, if I may say so, of trustful approach to man. No, since Christendom is a forgery, and since the sin nowadays is principally cunning, so on the part of Governance (which man by his forgery has put at a distance) the relationship is altogether one of mistrust—there are no more joyous messengers to come from God (any more than the police are hailed as such), no, there come only virtuosi in dishonesty, and even these, inasmuch as they essentially pertain to the universal dishonesty, even these are treated by Governance as ambiguous characters.

The situation of Christendom which S. K. felt called upon to denounce really seemed to him so horrible that no words were too strong to describe it:[1]

. . . When one who is not a physician is present at the dissection of a cadaver he feels qualmish, and likewise a student the first time he has to dissect—but the same thing does not happen to an old anatomist. And yet it sometimes occurs that the cadaver is so disgusting that it makes even him sick. When a man in the ordinary walks of life gets such an insight into criminal life as the police detective has, he will be dumbfounded—the old police detective finds nothing dumbfounding in crime . . . and yet it can sometimes happen that the case is so frightful, so dreadfully thrilling, that he also is dumbfounded.—I can truly say that I have an inborn talent for criminal affairs; also I am now elderly and hardened—but verily this thing of Christendom overwhelms me with horror.

To tell the truth, when S. K. directs my attention to the horror of the situation, which has not essentially changed since his day, and in some respects has grown far worse, I cannot but feel as he does. No wonder he wanted to set fire to it. He remarks that Christ expressly said that He had come 'to set fire to the earth'—and that Christendom has been steadily engaged in quenching it. He observes that it is not only with water it can be quenched, but it can be smothered with mattresses and all sorts of things:[1]

> It meant setting fire to things. Now forget this. Forget that this was Christ's own interpretation of Christianity. Then take Protestantism, especially in Denmark, and say if from what you see of Christianity it would in the remotest way occur to you that it was to kindle a fire the Founder of Christianity came into the world. Will you not everywhere and in every instance get the impression that it was to quench the fire He came into the world?

In another passage the question is about how men behave at a fire:[2]

> Have you ever seen people at a conflagration? How do they appear? Is it not true that every one thinks only in deadly anguish of saving himself?
>
> But according to the opinion of Christianity, every instant a man lives he is in far greater danger than in the most violent conflagration, danger of forfeiting an eternity—do men appear like that?

In view of all this S. K. naturally felt that his duty was pressing and precise. The following was written in 1853:[3]

> ... I have something on my conscience as a writer. Let me indicate precisely how I feel about it. There is something quite definite I have to say, and I have it so much upon my conscience that (as I feel) I dare not die without having uttered it. For the instant I die and thus leave this world (so I understand it) I shall in the very same second (so frightfully fast it goes!), in the very same second I shall be infinitely far away, in a different place where still within the same second (frightful speed!) the question will be put to me: Hast thou uttered the definite message *quite definitely*? And if I have not done so, what then? ...

There is something quite definite I have to say. But verily I am not eager to say it. On the contrary, I would so infinitely prefer that another should say it—which, however, would not help me, since (as I understand it) it was and remains my task. But eager to say it I am not; on the contrary, I have wished and desired and sometimes almost hoped that I might be dispensed from saying it. For it is not a cheerful message, this definite thing, and there are several persons dear to me to whom I cannot but think it would be unwelcome to hear it said. Above all there is among us a right reverend old man, one consideration which has constantly held me back, laid restraint upon my tongue and upon my pen, a consideration for the Church's highest dignitary, a man to whom by the memory of a deceased father I felt myself drawn with an almost melancholy affection—and I must think that to him especially it will be very unwelcome that this is said.

[Thereupon S. K. reviews all his writings, which evince his reluctance to 'say it', his eagerness to put it as mildly as possible, to weaken the effect by saying it pseudonymously, seeking in various ways to divert attention from the decisive expression, even by the device of hiding it in big books which few would read, and all this with the hope that it might 'pass off quietly', so that he could say to his soul, 'Rejoice and be glad'. This hope was fulfilled time and again, but conscience continued to upbraid him. And now finally], 'it must be said, short and distinct, no more big books, it must be said briefly, distinctly. Professor Martensen found that I was too diffuse—if only I am not now too short with him! Bishop Mynster taunted me, though good-humouredly, with being too artful—if only now I do not attack him too bluntly!

The following passage will show with how much reason S. K. has been regarded as a signal instance of the sublimation of Eros:[1]

. . . It is only too true as people say of me, the practical people, that I am good for nothing, that I am a perfectly unpractical man, out of place in this practical world.

Ah, yes, I am in fact good for only one thing—yet in this respect I have perhaps quite an eminent talent—the only thing I am good for is to love. So I am always a superfluity, a mere article of luxury, in this practical world, in fact I may even be an article of luxury which is also felt to be in the way, so that it may end by my being kicked out of this world.

Yet I am good at loving! Ye women, come unto me—or, to say the same thing in another way: Come ye not unto me, what good am I for loving you, ye Misses and Mesdames of this miserable race! No, I am good at loving, even if this were my only talent—it was raised to the second power and hidden under the incognito that I was the most selfish of all.

Yes, to love was the one thing I was good for. An object, Oh for an object! But like an archer whose bow is tight-strung as seldom a bow was strung, when one offers him an object at 5 yards distance and requires him to shoot at it, just as he may say, Nay, at that distance I cannot shoot; put it at 200 or 300 yards, and then it is right for me—so it is with me. In order to be able to love I must put the object at a distance.

That was my school in which I was perfected more and more in that which is my only talent—to love.

An object, therefore, an object! That was what I sought and continued to seek.

Yea, and I found it. For Thou, Thou the eternal Love, thou infinite Rich Man, thou, naturally, like all rich men, hast no use for articles of utility, but on the other hand, like all rich men, hast use only for articles of luxury. So Thou didst find use for me who am the officially recognized article of luxury in this practical world, Thou didst find use for me—and I did find the Object.

In spite of S. K.'s vigorous repudiation of mysticism, there are some that persist in calling him a mystic. This may mean no more than a recognition of the fact that he believed in God, was a man of prayer, was aware of providential guidance, and even experienced the comfort of the Holy Ghost. But that, of course, is not sufficient to distinguish him from other Christians and to characterize him as a mystic. I would say that he never became a mystic—but that he seemed to be headed in that direction. Przywara regards the following passage as an approach to the experience of St. John of the Cross. It would certainly be a gross misapprehension to regard it as an expression of a morbid melancholy:[1]

The Night of the Unconditional

Man has a natural dread of walking in the gloom—what wonder then that he naturally has a dread of the unconditional, of having to do with the unconditional, of which it holds good that no night and 'no deepest gloom is half so dark' as this gloom and this night, where all relative ends (the common milestones and signposts), where all relative considerations (the lanterns which else are a help to us), where even the tenderest and sincerest feelings of devotion—are quenched . . . for otherwise it is not unconditionally the unconditional.

I conclude this chapter with a passage (written in 1853) which shows clearly enough that this long process of loading the gun was not prompted by hatred but by love:[1]

I am only a poet who moves men by means of ideals. . . . To move, only to move, is what I desire. Oh, may this succeed! Thou poor man—it is true, 'silver and gold have I none', but if thou art not already mindful of it to thine advantage, if thou dost not already know, thou couldst not even wish to know how endlessly thou art loved. Thou sick man—it is true, I do not dispose of medical skill, least of all when I know that only a miracle could restore thy health, but if thou art not already mindful of it to thine advantage, if thou dost not already know, thou couldst not even wish to know how endlessly thou art loved. Thou who art wronged, the victim of prejudice, the offended, the forsaken—it is true that to get justice done thee, to create society for thee or restore it to thee, is beyond my power, but if thou art not already mindful of it to thine advantage, if thou dost not already know, thou couldst not even wish to know how endlessly thou art loved. Thou mighty man, rich and highly placed—it is true that to insure thee against the plots of envy is beyond my power, but if thou art not already mindful of it to thine advantage, if thou dost not already know, thou couldst not even wish to know how endlessly thou art loved. And thou, O woman, thou of whom it may well be said in general that in comparison with man thou dost always choose the better part because what doth concern thee most is to be loved, if thou art not already mindful of it to thine advantage, if thou dost not already know, thou couldst not even wish to know how endlessly thou art loved. And this I am both able and ardently desirous to declare unto thee, thou poor man, thou sick man, thou who art a servant, thou who art wronged, offended, forsaken, the victim of prejudice, thou who art mighty, rich and highly placed, and thou, O woman. But that I may be able to do this I must first show the endless greatness of the Christian requirement, for otherwise thou canst not perceive how far thou art behind, the endless greatness of the distance, and so canst not at all perceive the endless greatness of thy debt, and so not at all the endless greatness of grace—and consequently not at all the endless greatness of love. For so it is hid from thee, thou dost not get to know that which perhaps thou art so eager to know, which also will be so good for thee to know—how endlessly thou art loved. Couldst thou desire that the Christian requirement should be pared down, reduced to the common market price? Couldst thou desire that one should flatter thee and tell thee that thou art well advanced—perhaps even (according to the scale of 'the common market price'), perhaps even something quite extraordinary? Look well to it, for by desiring that (as perhaps thou dost not reflect) thou wilt prevent thyself from getting to know how endlessly thou art loved. Let us indeed beware of that!

II. THE EXPLOSION

DECEMBER 18, 1854—OCTOBER 2, 1855

EXPLOSIONS are sudden and generally do not last long. Yet the explosion of S. K.'s pent-up indignation, once it found vent, continued for more than nine months to resound throughout Denmark and the whole of Scandinavia, with frequent detonations; and seeing what a prodigious mass of explosive material was stored up in the Journals of the three preceding years, there is no telling when it might have ended had not the gunner died at his post.

The first gun was fired against Martensen, and through him it made havoc of the deceased Bishop's fame for godliness. It took the form of a letter published on December 18, 1854, in the *Fatherland*, the conservative political daily to which S. K. had for many years occasionally contributed, and which numbered among its editors Gjødvod, the only journalist S. K. regarded as a friend. But this letter was dated significantly 'In February 1854'. That is to say, it was written immediately after the panegyric which Professor Martensen pronounced upon the deceased Bishop on the Sunday preceding his burial, which occurred on February 7. This oration was delivered on February 5, the 5th Sunday after Epiphany, and in it the Professor proclaimed that the 'irreplaceable' prelate (whom he expected to replace) was 'a genuine witness for the truth', 'not only in word and profession, but in deed and in truth', vindicating to him a place in 'the holy chain of witnesses which stretches from the days of the Apostles'. Although Professor Martensen was supercilious enough to say that he had not been able to read through all of S. K.'s 'prolix' books, he had surely read enough to know with what reverence the notion of a 'witness for the truth' was treated, and it is probable that in applying this inappropriate term to Mynster he was not unaware that he would pique S. K. In fact S. K. regarded it as a monstrous offence against his cause and therefore accepted it as the signal to begin his attack. He sat down forthwith and wrote the most scathing denunciation of Martensen, in which he exposed the serious shortcomings of the late Bishop and asked the question whether the Professor was telling the *truth*.

S. K. was true to his principles in proposing to open his attack in a political daily,[1] conformably to his conviction that the Gospel ought not to be preached in churches but in the street. In my opinion this action was not inconsistent with his disparaging opinion of the press. He had never felt any scruple about writing for the newspapers. In fact, it was in a newspaper that one of his earliest attacks upon the press was made. He surely did not make himself *particeps criminis* with the mendacity and cowardly anonymity which he deplored in the press when he spoke the truth courageously over his own name, without the least expectation of winning the mob to his side, or the faintest intention of submitting the truth of Christianity to the ballot. Martensen had provided him with a good opening, too good to be ignored, although he reflected upon the tactical disadvantage of beginning with a personal attack and keeping attention fixed for a considerable time upon one narrow issue. Gradually the issue was widened to include the clergy of the Established Church, all of whom were presumably 'witnesses for the truth'; the attack was then directed against the Church Establishment as a whole; and it was immensely widened by the fact that this public controversy drew attention to his later books where the positive grounds for his position could be apprehended.

But although this first letter was so promptly written, it was not possible to begin the attack at once, unless he would interfere with Martensen's prospect of advancement to the episcopate, and also, as he reflected, with the effort that was being made to raise a fund for a monument to Mynster. Having already been compelled to wait so long in order that Mynster might be 'buried with full music', he had to face another period of grim waiting—another ten months, until Martensen was appointed, consecrated, and enthroned in the primatial see of Denmark.

This delay is enough to prove that S. K. was not actuated merely by personal rancour. But it must be well understood that it did not imply hesitation. Of that there is not the slightest trace. When the letter against Martensen had been lying in his desk for a month, S. K. wrote the following:[2]

My Christian Plea.

In March 1854. S. Kierkegaard.

But now Bishop Mynster is dead, and this is significant for

me, I am now developed for it, and now I can and will say quite directly what hitherto I have only aimed at rather indirectly, and therewith enter my Christian plea that (as doubtless the majority knows inwardly with greater or less clarity or at least suspects, although no one will come out with it)—that Christianity actually does not exist, or exists only in a very unreal sense, that here in this country, under the name of Christianity, we have instead of Christianity an aggregate of words and phrases (well-intentioned enough), or an aggregate of (well-intentioned) illusions and delusions and confused vision and ambiguity and plausibility and half-measures and characterlessness, &c., &c., for which undeniably the long and worldly-wise rule of the deceased Bishop is in part to blame. Although now with the death of Bishop Mynster others may understand their life to the effect that now is the time for them to take advantage of the headway produced by his work, I understand my life in my own way, to the effect that just now is the time to apply the check, and hence, to enter my Christian plea as a *check*.—For though I, alas, am only a poet, and 'only a poet who desires if possible to move by the help of ideals', yet I am a check. If, kindly intentioned as I am, they will meet me in a kindly spirit, all may be mild and moving. If they will oppose me, it may go hard with me, but still I am a check; if they will oppose me violently, with the utmost violence, it may be frightful for me, but still I am a check. I am not a power of any sort, but a weakness, I am not at the head of any party, only a solitary man, and yet I have a power, a duplex power: a tender melancholy capable of moving, if you will; and satire, if you will. This one and only duplicity is my power, and it is just the power needed as a check. But this power of checking I possess in such weakness that, whether I will or not, I am constrained and for this reason I am a check.

Even at this moment he did not know clearly what he might be called upon to do. He said to God:[1]

Thou knowest that it has not been made quite clear to me what I must do. Only so much have I understood, that I must hold out.

The waiting was all the harder because he was more and more

isolated from the world. 'Alone in my kayak' was an expression he had used in student years.

> It is as if God said to me: My little friend, only be calm, wheresoever thou art, that is thy place—alone in thy kayak. Where I go along, all is well, a nut-shell is as safe as an admiral's ship. But woe unto thee if thou dost become indolent, impatient, worldly-wise, and hast the notion that it would be better to have a somewhat bigger ship and the help of a small crew—for at that instant I leave the boat.[1]

Mynster being dead, he had relinquished the fond hope that the whole thing might be quietly arranged by persuading the rulers of the Church to make some concession or admission:[2]

> No, that one dare not do, for—the misfortune in fact is that one can be sure that however strongly one expresses oneself, it all resolves itself into an 'up to a certain point'—and so one has failed of accomplishing one's task of introducing the unconditional. No, like the spring of a beast of prey, and like the thud with which a bird of prey strikes its quarry—so must the unconditional be introduced.

At this moment he was thinking of something far more 'catastrophic' than the attack upon Martensen which was lying in his desk, he was thinking of 'the midnight cry' which was also written long beforehand, and which he launched when the battle was hottest under the title 'This Must be Said'.[3]

> If a catastrophic effect is to be produced [he means his arrest, imprisonment, and possibly his execution], what I have thought of doing was, unexpectedly, after a period of complete silence, to utter 'the cry': that the public divine worship is a mockery of God and to take part in it is criminal.

As a matter of fact, when S. K. commenced the attack he did not plunge at once *in medias res* by uttering 'the cry', but he began with the thin edge of the wedge, the letter against Martensen, which, as we have seen, was published on December 18. That indeed was astonishing enough to his contemporaries, and it was followed by twenty more letters in the *Fatherland* which appeared at irregular intervals until May 26, 1855, when the last one appeared and again singled out Martensen for attack. The intervals decreased towards the end, and the tone became ever more vehement. Whereas the first letters resolutely held the discussion to the initial question whether Mynster was a witness to the truth, the issue, as I have said, gradually broadened.

On May 16, just before the last newspaper article appeared, and coincident with the publication of the second edition of *Training in Christianity*, S. K. broadcast a little pamphlet entitled '*This Must be Said*—so let it be said'. On the back of the title-page appeared the name he best knew it by: 'But at midnight there was a cry. Mt. 26: 6.' To show that it had long been held in leash, the date of its writing was printed above it: 'Dec. 1854.' I quote only the nucleus of it:[1]

This must be said—so let it be said:

Whosoever thou art, whatever thy life may be, my friend—by ceasing to take part (if in fact thou dost) in the public function of divine worship as it now is, thou hast one guilt the less, and a great one, that thou dost not take part in treating God as a fool, and in calling that the Christianity of the New Testament which is not the Christianity of the New Testament.

This was the beginning of the pamphleteering crusade. Soon after, on May 24, appeared the first number of the *Instant*. This was a pamphlet which was issued every little while up to the time of his death. It consisted on the average of 24 pages containing seven or more short and pithy articles on a great variety of subjects. By this time the discussion had widened considerably, although the Established Church was always the object of attack. People were encouraged to subscribe to the *Instant*, and the circulation proved to be as large as that of the daily paper he had previously used—with the advantage that the author could be sure it would be bought only by persons who were interested in his 'plea'. In this way also he had a greater freedom of utterance, and he could feel that through these tracts he was more than ever preaching in the street.[2] The ninth number was published on September 24. The tenth was ready to be printed when he died. Some idea of the character of the articles may be got from the titles in Appendix IV.

The effect of these tracts was enormous in Denmark, and they were promptly translated in the Swedish papers. S. K. had become again a popular figure. Goldschmidt, in an appreciative obituary dedicated to him, remarked quite justly that it was time for him to die, since popularity was the last thing he could endure. It was a matter of course that free-thinkers and sectaries should hail S. K.'s attack upon the Established Church, but the sequel proved that it was welcomed by many within the Church, even among the pastors. The effect of S. K.'s writings at that time, as it has been ever since, was to persuade some that they did not properly belong in the Church, to stimulate others to be better Protestants, and induce still others to take refuge in the Roman Church. Trols Lund in his Reminiscences gives a vivid picture of the keen interest aroused among the youth of the land. He was then a schoolboy, but he filched each number of the *Instant* from his elder brother's study and felt that he was walking in a new world, breathing a freer air. The boys were thrilled when one of their teachers proclaimed to his class that he was on S. K.'s side.

But the parsons in the main were only embittered. Most of them did not know S. K.'s books, and so could not understand what it was all about and how serious a basis there was for this attack. Still less could they answer it. After a lame attempt on the part of Bishop Martensen to answer the charge made against him, he thought it more dignified to preserve complete silence, and the subordinate clergy did not know what to say. It is significant that most of the replies made to S. K. were anonymous. 'The human bite', said S. K., 'isolates an individual in such a way that he can become idea-bearer.'[1]

> Ah, so I understood it, I thought I should have Thee, O God, as a help in loving men. Thou didst understand it differently, Thou didst use men against me to help me to love Thee.[2]

With all this there was no external change in the Established Church. It must not be supposed that S. K. had expected it to collapse. He entertained no such illusions—the 'catastrophe' he had in mind was to involve him alone, and only by dying for the cause did he expect it to prevail. He knew that the Established Church was 'a machine' which would 'go buzzing on' undisturbed.[3]

> Let us try a thought-experiment. If one could establish the fact that Christ had never existed, nor the Apostles either, that the whole thing was a poetical invention—in case nothing was done on the part of the State or the congregations, no hint that

they would suppress the livings, I should like to see how many parsons would resign their posts.

Dean Swift said almost exactly the same thing (I quote from memory): 'If it could be proved conclusively to the satisfaction of every one that such a person as Jesus Christ never existed, it might cause a momentary embarrassment even to the Established Church.'

But also the personal catastrophe did not occur in any of the ways that S. K. had pictured to himself. The crowd was far from being inflamed against him, and though some of the parsons cried out that he ought to be imprisoned, the higher authorities did nothing at all. The Cultus-Minister happened to be a wise man, and it is said that the Prime Minister gave notice that if an author who had shed such lustre upon Denmark were to be arrested, he would at once release him.

S. K. found opportunity during this time of strife to bid farewell to the two persons he had loved most. He contrived the farewell to his father by publishing, between the 7th and 8th numbers of the *Instant*, another 'Edifying Discourse', which he dedicated as usual 'to the deceased Michael Petersen Kierkegaard, sometime hosier in this town'. The title of it is 'God's Unchangeableness', and the text (Jas. 1: 17) was the first one he ever preached upon. This sermon had been actually preached, in 1851, and it betrays the date of its composition by the fact that, unlike the utterances of the last year of his life, it is thoroughly dialectical: it dwells not only upon the sombre side of the consideration that God is unchangeable, but also upon the comfort of this thought.

The farewell to Regina was not of his contriving. Just before she left for the West Indies they passed one another in the street. She said in a low voice, 'God bless thee. May it go well with thee.' S. K. raised his hat. On his death-bed he remarked half-humorously that he was glad his 'little Governess' was away from Denmark when the strife was hottest.

In these days S. K. received no visitors, answered no letters, and commonly conversed with no one in the street. But Hans Brøchner relates that he encountered him several times and was amazed at the confidence and peace expressed by his countenance and his speech.[1]

I conclude this chapter with brief selections from the polemical tracts. I cite them in chronological order, so that they give some notion of the progress of the attack. I recognize that they are neither numerous enough nor complete enough to give a just idea of S. K.'s last writings, yet it will be evident that the author who for so many years had written expressly for a limited class of thinkers had become past master in the art of speaking to the man in the street. No political tracts have ever been couched in a more popular and telling form, and yet the intellectual superiority of the writer is everywhere evident.

It is evident also that in spite of the exaggeration S. K. intentionally employed, and the holy zeal he manifests, he never gives the impression of being a fanatic.

I begin with the letters published in the *Fatherland*. Even while S. K. was still insisting upon his initial objection to Martensen's eulogy of the late Bishop, it was easy for him to involve Martensen himself and all his clergy in the ridiculous situation of being 'witnesses for the truth':[1]

> This is the point—and it can be shown that the new Bishop by thus canonizing Bishop Mynster makes the whole Church Establishment an impudent indecency.
>
> For if Bishop Mynster is a witness for the truth, so—as even the blindest can see—so likewise is every parson in the land a witness for the truth. For what was aesthetically distinguished and extraordinary in Bishop Mynster had nothing at all to do with the question whether or not he was a witness for the truth, a question which pertains to character, life, existence, and in this respect Bishop Mynster was completely homogeneous with every other priest in the land who does not offend against the requirements of civil justice. Hence every priest in the land is also a witness for the truth.
>
> It is quite true that I am acquainted with several men who are in the highest degree respectable, capable, remarkably capable clergymen, but I venture to assert that in the whole realm there is not one who regarded as a 'witness for the truth' would not be comical.[2]
>
> We have, if you will, a complete garrison of bishops, deans, and parsons, learned men, eminently learned, talented, gifted, with well-intentioned zeal they all declaim—do it well, very

well, exceedingly well, or fairly well, indifferently well, badly—but not one of them is in the character of the Christianity of the New Testament, and not even in the character of endeavouring in the direction of the Christianity of the New Testament. But when such is the case, the existence of the Christian garrison is so far from being advantageous to Christianity that it is actually a peril, because it so very easily occasions the misunderstanding and the erroneous inference that when we have such a complete garrison we naturally have Christianity also. A geographer, for example, when he had assured himself of the existence of this garrison would consider that he was completely justified in introducing in his geography the statement that the Christian religion prevails in the land.

We have what one might call a complete inventory of churches, bells, organs, foot-warmers, alms-boxes, hearses, &c. But when Christianity does not exist, the existence of this inventory, Christianly considered, is so far from being advantageous to Christianity that it is actually a peril, because it so very easily occasions the misunderstanding and the erroneous inference that when we have such a complete Christian inventory we naturally have Christianity also. A statistician, for example, when he had assured himself of the existence of this Christian inventory would consider that he was completely justified in introducing into his statistics the statement that the Christian religion is the prevailing one in the land.[1]

A Thesis

only a single one

Oh, Luther, thou hadst 95 theses—terrible! And yet, in a deeper sense, the more theses there are, the less terrible it is. The situation is far more terrible—there is only one thesis. [He means the thesis that Christianity does not exist.[2]]

An article published on March 31, entitled 'What I Want', expresses his position clearly and justly:[3]

Quite simply: I want honesty. I am not, as one with the best intentions has wished to represent me, I am not Christian severity contrasted with Christian leniency.

By no means; I am neither severity nor leniency—I am: mere human honesty. . . .

I want honesty. If that is what this race and this generation wants, if it will uprightly, honestly, frankly, openly, directly rebel against Christianity and say to God, 'We can but we will not subject ourselves to this authority'—but observe that it must be done uprightly, honestly, frankly, openly, directly—well then, strange as it may seem, I am for it; for honesty is what I want. And wherever there is honesty I can join in. An honest rebellion against Christianity can only be made when one honestly admits what Christianity is and how he himself is related to it.

And what have the clergy done for their part? They have (and I am sorry to be compelled to be so courteous, but it is true), they have preserved a significant silence. It is curious: if they had replied, something very fatuous was sure to come out, perhaps the whole of it would have been fatuous; now on the other hand how significant the whole thing has become by reason of this significant silence!

What then does this significant silence signify? It signifies that what concerns the clergy is their livings. In any case it signifies that the clergy are not witnesses for the truth, for in that case it would be inconceivable that the clergy as a whole—especially after the Right Reverend Bishop Martensen had made such a luckless attempt at speaking—could want to preserve silence while it was openly made obvious that official Christianity is both aesthetically and intellectually ludicrous and indecent, a scandal in the Christian sense.

Assuming on the other hand that a living is what concerns the clergy, this silence is perfectly understandable. For it was not the livings in a finite sense I was aiming at with my attack, and well known as I am to the clergy they must know very well that such a thing could never occur to me, that not only am I not a politician but I hate politics, indeed that I might even be disposed to fight for the clergy were any one to attack the livings in a finite sense.

Hence this complete silence—my attack did not really concern the clergy, i.e. it has nothing to do with what does concern them. Take an example from—I had almost by a slip of the tongue said, 'another world'—take an example then from the same world, from the shopman's world. If it were possible to make an attack upon a merchant in such a way as to show that his wares were bad but without this having the least effect upon the usual turnover of his wares—then he will say: 'Such an attack is perfectly indifferent to me; whether my wares are good or bad does not concern me at all in and for itself; remember that I am a merchant, what concerns me is the turnover. In fact I am a merchant to such a degree that if one could show, not only that the coffee I sell is damaged and spoiled, but that what I sell under the name of coffee is not coffee at all—if only one assures me that the attack will have no effect whatever upon the turnover, such an attack is perfectly indifferent to me. What does it matter to me what sort of thing it is people guzzle under the name of coffee? What concerns me is only the turnover.'[1]

S. K.'s observations about 'livings' reminds me that a few years ago an irreproachable clergyman of the Church of England proposed a 'voluntary ministry', as he called it, recommending that the bishops ordain to the priesthood men who were earning their own living in a secular calling (as undeniably the earliest Catholic presbyters and bishops did) and had not been ruined morally and intellectually by going through a theological seminary.—No, this last was not what he said: he did not complain that Christianity had been made a learned science; he uttered no reproach against the existing order, but urged only that in places where there was no money to pay a 'hired minister' (again, this is not his phrase, it is the well-known Quaker reproach)—he urged that in such a case some man who was known as an earnest Christian and who so lived in this world as to be an example to his neighbours should be chosen and ordained (as St. Paul proposed) to administer the sacraments and exhort his brethren to live conformably to the Gospel. I have wondered that this suggestion was not everywhere welcomed. It has puzzled me a good deal to observe that it has been met only by silence. I cannot repress the suspicion that this is a 'significant silence'—significant of the fact that the established order feels that its economic position is threatened if in practice a 'volunteer ministry' is admitted even as a rare exception.

The last newspaper article which appeared before the issue of the 'midnight cry' explains that the new edition of *Training in Christianity* is unrevised because it is to be regarded as an historical document, but that if it were to be published now for the first time it would have been altered in the following particulars:[1]

> It would not have been by a pseudonym but by me, and the Preface thrice repeated would have been omitted, and consequently also the Moral to Part I.

This retraction concerns me personally, for I find comfort in the Preface and the Moral (see pp. 434 and 435). S. K. explains in this context that in the Preface and the Moral he had treated 'grace' as if it were available not only for the forgiveness of sins past but also as 'a sort of dispensation from the actual following of Christ and the actual exertion of being a Christian'. I think he puts the case against himself too strongly. I would say rather that the Preface and the Moral, which offer the grace I so much need, might too easily be twisted into an indulgence or a dispensation. This means, as S. K. often affirmed, that 'in a certain sense it is so frightfully easy to fool God'.[2]

Grace is a subject S. K. deals with very often in the later journals, and I would seek his real meaning there rather than in a controversial article written under the smart of 'the human bite'. No writer I am acquainted with meditates so deeply upon 'the contradiction which is really a completion' involved in the Apostle's word: 'Work out your own salvation with fear and trembling; for it is God that worketh in you both to will and to work for his good pleasure.' God's action here is grace; but it is what S. K. calls 'grace in the first instance',[3] with reference to the future, whereas 'grace in the second instance' means the forgiveness of past sins. When S. K. affirms, 'The Spirit is the Comforter', he rightly understands this word to mean, not a consoler, but one who strengthens exceedingly. 'No man is saved without grace—not even an Apostle.' But he saw that ('in Protestantism') grace was so much talked about because it was regarded as a dispensation to sin, or at least an excuse to give up striving. Grace can be abused like the sacraments, 'by which men relieve themselves of the duty of loving God'.[4] Hence:[5]

> Severity first—i.e. the severity of ideality—and then gentleness. I myself have as much need as anybody of being spoken to gently, my soul is much disposed to speak gently—but in a time of confused thinking the first must be put first, lest gentleness be an occasion for slothful indulgence.

With this understanding I can still apply to myself the comfort of the Preface and the Moral—but with fear and trembling.

The first number of the *Instant* was published on May 24, 1855. It may be remarked here by the way that often in the manuscript and sometimes in the printed text the individual articles bear a date anterior, often far anterior, to the date of the number in which they are contained—which shows that an abundance of ammunition had been stored up in the magazines and was ready to be used at a moment's notice. Knowing what significance S. K. attached to 'the instant'—an atom of eternity in time—we cannot wonder that he gave this name to his tracts. But 'working in the instant' was very far from being to his taste. It meant abandoning the agreeable detachment of authorship, that 'remoteness in which like a lover I can dally with thought, and like an artist in love with his instrument entertain myself with language, coaxing out of the expressions everything that thought requires'. He recalls that Plato affirmed, somewhere in the *Republic*, that the state was not likely to be ruled well except by a ruler who had no desire to rule. Hence he concluded that he was the right man for the job of working in the instant, 'for God knows, nothing is more distasteful to my soul'.[1]

> Why then do I want to work in the instant? I want to do it because I shall eternally regret not having done it, and eternally regret it if I let myself be deterred from it by the fear that the generation which now lives will at the most be inclined to regard a true account of what Christianity is as something interesting and remarkable, and then remain quite calmly where it is, in the illusion of being Christians and the belief that the parsons' game of Christianity is Christianity.

One of the articles in the second number is entitled, 'If we are really Christians—what then is God?'[2]

> He is the most ludicrous being that ever has lived, His Word the most ludicrous book that ever has come to light—to set (as He does in His Word) heaven and earth in commotion, to threaten with hell, with eternal punishment—in order to attain what we understand by being Christians (and surely we are true Christians). No, nothing so ludicrous has ever been met with. Suppose that a man with a loaded gun advanced

upon a person and said, 'I will shoot you dead', or imagine something still more dreadful, that he said, 'I will seize you and torture you with the most agonizing death if you do not (be attentive now, for here it comes), if you do not make your life here on earth as advantageous and as rich in enjoyment as possible.'

I quote one short passage from a pamphlet which was issued between the second and third numbers of the *Instant*, entitled, 'What Christ's Judgement is upon Official Christianity':[1]

So time passed. I was on perfectly good terms with these perjured men—and in all quietness I managed to get the ideals presented and became acquainted with the persons I had to deal with.

But at last these good men became impatient with the poet, he became too impertinent for them. This occurred with the publication of the letter against Bishop Martensen about Bishop Mynster. Completely secure as they were they then made a great outcry (as will be remembered from that period) that it was 'much too great a scale that was applied' &c.—comfortably secure.

Then this poet suddenly transformed himself—he cast aside the guitar, if I may so speak—and brought out a book which is called 'The New Testament of our Lord and Saviour Jesus Christ', and with a glance—indeed it was the glance of a detective—he put it up to these good perjured teachers, these 'witnesses for the truth', whether this is not the book to which they were bound by oath, this book whose scale is a good deal greater than that which he had used?

One of the best-known passages is that about Frederick and Juliana:[2]

A living—and then Juliana—that Frederick and Juliana can come together. Oh, these proofs that are produced for the truth of Christianity, these devilish learned and profound and entirely convincing proofs, what do they all amount to in comparison with Juliana and the fact that in this way Frederick and Juliana can come together! If at any moment the thought should struggle in Frederick, 'I myself do not really believe this doctrine, and then to have to preach it to others. . . .' If such thoughts should struggle in Frederick, go to Juliana, she can drive such thoughts away. 'Sweet Frederick,' she says, 'only let us manage to come together. Why do you go and torment yourself with such thoughts? There are surely 1,000 parsons like you; in short, you are a parson like the others.'

Juliana, indeed, plays a great role in procuring clergy for the state. And hence they should have been wary about introducing Juliana, and also about introducing livings. For it is possible, as Don Juan says to Zerline, that only in the soft arms of a blameless wife does true felicity reside, and possibly it is true as both poets and prose writers have testified, that in these soft arms one forgets the world's alarms; but the question is whether there is not also something else one can only too easily forget in these soft arms—namely, what Christianity is. And the older I grow, the clearer it becomes to me that the prattle into which Christianity has sunk, especially in Protestantism, and more especially in Denmark, is due in great part to the fact that these soft arms have come to interfere a little too much, so that for Christianity's sake one might require the respective proprietors of these soft arms to retire a little further into the background.

Suppose that no God exists, no eternity, no accounting, then official Christianity is a perfectly charming and elegant invention for making this life in a thoroughly sensible way as rich in pleasure as is possible, far richer than the pagan could have it. For it is notorious that what constantly troubled the pleasure-loving pagan was this thing about eternity; but to this thing about eternity official Christianity has given such a slant that eternity just exists for giving us relish and inclination for rejoicing in and enjoying this life.

An article entitled 'What Says the Fire-Chief?' shows that S. K. was not so much worried by his enemies as by the well-intentioned people who were eager to bring his attack to an end by adjusting things nicely:[1]

So also in case of a conflagration. Hardly is the cry of Fire! heard before a crowd of people rush to the spot, nice, cordial, sympathetic, helpful people; one has a pitcher, another a basin, the third a squirt, &c., all of them nice, cordial, sympathetic, helpful people, eager to help put out the fire.

But what says the Fire-Chief? The Fire-Chief he says—to be sure, on other occasions the Fire-Chief is a very agreeable and cultured man; but at a fire he is what one might call coarse-mouthed—he says, or rather he bawls out, 'Go to hell with all your pitchers and squirts.' And then when these well-intentioned people are perhaps offended, regard it as highly improper that they should be treated in this way, and require at least that they should be treated with respect—what says the Fire-Chief then? Well, on other occasions the Fire-Chief is a very agreeable and cultured man who knows how to show to every one the respect that is his due, but at a fire he is rather different, he says, 'Where the deuce is the police force?' And then when some policemen arrive he says to them, 'Rid me of these damn people with their pitchers and squirts; and if they won't yield to fair words, smear them a few on their backs, so that we can be rid of them—and get to work.'

The Bible-Interpretation of Mediocrity

interprets and interprets Christ's Word for so long a time that it gets its own meaning out of it, the prosaic (the trivial)—and now after it has removed all difficulties it is reassured and appeals to Christ's Word.

It quite escapes the attention of mediocrity that thereby a new difficulty is created, a difficulty which surely is one of the most ludicrous it is possible to think of, that God should let Himself be *born*, that 'the Truth' should have come into the world—to make trivial remarks. And likewise a new difficulty, the difficulty of explaining how it came about that Christ was crucified; for it is not usual in this trivial world to apply the death-penalty for making trivial remarks.[1]

S. K. recounts with satisfaction a conversation he once had with Bishop Mynster:[2]

I said to him that it would be about as well if the parsons were to give up preaching, that all their preaching had no effect whatsoever, because quietly in the back of their heads the congregation thought: Well, this is his means of livelihood. To this Bishop Mynster replied, to my surprise, There is something in that. I had really not expected this reply, for though this was said under four eyes, yet Bishop Mynster was usually discretion itself on this point.

S. K. not only inveighed against the lukewarm Christians, but in the last number of the *Instant* (the number which was not published till long after his death) he paid his respects to the Grundtvigians, the most fervent sect in the Danish Church. The caption is 'Convent Beer', which contains an allusion unintelligible to the uninitiated. In his journals he had a great deal to say about this party, in which his brother was a leader. This party is still strong in the Danish Church—and magnanimous enough to forgive S. K. I have been struck by a passage[1] in which he refers to the distasteful 'odour of heartiness' he scented in them. I am struck with this because this phenomenon has been observed in a more modern sect.

It would not be fair to S. K. were I to conclude this chapter without quoting a part of his address to the 'plain man', which in fact was the last word of his controversy, although it was written in that number of the *Instant* which was suppressed by his death:[2]

> Thou plain man! The Christianity of the New Testament is something endlessly high, but note that it is not high in such a sense that it has to do with the difference between man and man with respect to intellectual capacity, &c. No, it is for all. Every one, unconditionally every one, if he unconditionally wills it, if he will unconditionally hate himself, will unconditionally put up with everything, suffer everything (and this every man can if he will)—then is this endless height attainable to him.
>
> Thou plain man! I have not separated my life from thine; thou knowest it, I have lived in the street, am known to all; moreover I have not attained any importance, I do not belong to any class-egoism, so if I belong anywhere, I must belong to thee, thou plain man, thou who once (when one profiting by thy money pretended to wish thee well), thou who once wast too willing to find me and my existence ludicrous, thou who least of all hast reason to be impatient over or ungrateful for the fact that I am of your company, which the superior people rather have reason for, seeing that I have never decisively united myself to them but merely maintained a loose relationship to them.
>
> Thou plain man! I do not hide from thee that, according to my notion, the thing of being a Christian is endlessly high, that

at no time are there more than a few that attain it—as Christ's own life attests when one considers the age in which He lived, and also His preaching indicates if one takes it literally. Yet nevertheless it is possible for all. But one thing I adjure thee for the sake of God in heaven and by all that is holy, flee the parsons. . . .

III. HALLELUJAH!

OCTOBER 2—NOVEMBER 11, 1855

On October 2, 1855, as he was carrying home from the bank the last slender sum that remained of the considerable fortune he had inherited, S. K. sank unconscious upon the street and was carried to the Frederick's Hospital, where he died on November 11. No adequate diagnosis is recorded in the hospital journal, but it appears that he was paralysed from the waist down. At all events he was not able to walk. It may be that this was due to the deformity of the spine which he himself attributed to a fall from a tree in his childhood. He believed that he might recover if he would return to his home, but he evidently had not the will to live, and he who had all his life been the exception was content to die like a common man in a hospital. He was tenderly treated there. The head nurse was not only attentive to his comfort but was careful to provide him with flowers of her own choosing, and his nephew Henrik Lund was serving his apprenticeship there as physician. But for physicians as such he had no use. He affirmed that his illness was psychical (associating it with his thorn in the flesh), whereas they wanted to treat it by the usual medical methods. When he entered the hospital he said that he had come there to die.

He received few visitors—would not admit his brother Peter—nd among these few the most frequent visitor was the friend of is youth, Pastor Boesen. In spite of the bitter things he had been aying about parsons he welcomed this friend with warm affection nd gave him his confidence more freely than he had ever done efore in all his life. The Pastor seems to have been a stern atechist, but we have reason to be grateful to him for preserving record of S. K.'s conversation. He continued to visit him almost aily until about a fortnight before his death, when he could no onger raise his head and could hardly speak. Then Boesen had to o on a journey, and when he returned S. K. was dead. His eport, which is published by Gottsched in the last volume of the *apers*,[1] is the only direct testimony we have to the confidence and eace S. K. gave evidence of in his last days of suffering; although is niece Henriette Lund[2] recounts that on her first visit to her beloved uncle she perceived that there was mingled with his pain and sadness a blessed feeling of triumph. 'I got an impression of it on entering his little room and encountering a glow of light, as it were, radiating from his face. Never have I beheld in such a way the spirit break through the bodily frame and communicate to it a splendour as if it were the transfigured body at the dawn of the resurrection.'

In reply to Boesen's first question, 'How goes it?' his answer was, 'Badly, it is death; pray for me that it come quick and well.' He confided at once to Boesen that he was 'ruined' and had only enough money left for his burial. This he had never confided to any one before—least of all to the parsons he was upbraiding for their worldliness. We have seen that he was not disposed to let any one know 'how good he was'; but we can be certain that he would not have been able to denounce so boldly the worldliness of the Church if he himself had not renounced the possibility of earning a livelihood as a parson in the Established Church and thereby been brought to complete destitution. From all that we know of S. K. we can be sure that he was glad the 'catastrophe had come about in such a way that it involved no one in the guil of occasioning his death. He recognized that the end of his lif was a signal example of the intervention of 'Governance', and h had never been so much at peace. He declined to receive th Sacrament from the hands of an employee of the state, and a Boesen was firm that no layman could administer it, he had t die without the viaticum, though he died in faith.

It appears from Boesen's own narrative that he attended th sick man rather as a parson than as the friend of his youth—no withstanding he was so gently welcomed. Boesen had in fact n sympathy with S. K.'s position and no comprehension of the sig nificance of his writings. A year after S. K.'s death he rejecte Peter Kierkegaard's suggestion that he might undertake the tas of editing his friend's books and journals. This was so far fro him that in 1869 he tried to restrain Barfod from publishin passages from the Journals which would be distasteful to Bisho Martensen. By that time Boesen had attained ecclesiastical pr ferment. He was Dean of Aarhus. We can understand that, spite of the visits of the old friend which were so gratefully w comed by the dying man, S. K. was alone.

I can understand now that he would not have been less alone

he had permitted his brother to visit him. That he should deny to his only brother access to the chamber where he lay dying has seemed to me and to many a sign of an unregenerate heart, spiteful and unforgiving. But Weltzer's recent book[1] has relieved me of the painful feeling that S. K. treated his brother unjustly or unkindly. He was easily prevailed upon to send his brother a message of goodwill. But in his weakness he felt unable to face the situation of being in company with his nearest relative while he knew that in sympathy he was far from him. The documents published by Weltzer show that Peter was a very difficult man to have as a brother, and for the first time they make it clear how totally he failed to comprehend Søren's position. Even after Søren was dead this only brother manifested (unconsciously, I suppose) a sour hostility to him and to all he had endeavoured to accomplish. As head of the family he resisted all attempts to mark with a stone the spot where Søren's body lay in the family burial lot—yielding only in 1875, when it was too late to identify the precise place. Hence the pilgrims of to-day are puzzled at seeing Søren's name on a marble slab which marks no grave but is loosely leaning against the family monument. Peter had taken possession of his brother's literary remains by no other right than the reverent submission of his nephews and nieces. For it will be remembered that in his will Søren had left Regina heir to all that he possessed, which in fact consisted chiefly of his writings. Peter made a good deal of money by the sale of the books previously published and those which he tardily gave to the printer. But for a long time he turned a deaf ear to the indignant appeals of his nephew, Henrik Lund, and Rasmus Nielsen that he should permit the publication of the Journals. The first volume of them was not published till 1869. Moreover, in 1875, when there was a public clamour for a portrait of S. K., Peter vetoed the proposal of Chr. Kierkegaard that he should publish one or both of the portraits he had sketched. The following year, when the well-known full-face was published (by Trols Lund?) in spite of his prohibition, he indignantly protested—on the ground that his brother had been averse to having a portrait made.

On his death-bed S. K. showed no interest in the controversy he had been so zealous to stir up—except in resenting Boesen's stern suggestion that he had said what was not true about the parsons and might wish to retract it. He rejoiced that God had deigned to use him as an instrument, but now he was laid aside and had no more responsibility. 'Have you been angry and bitter?' asked Boesen. 'No,' he replied, 'but afflicted, grieved, and indignant in the highest degree.' Boesen asked if he could pray to God in peace. The answer was, 'Yes, that I can; and so I pray first for the forgiveness of sins, that they all may be forgiven; then I pray that I may be free from despair in death . . . and that I may know a little before when death is coming.' On that day, says Boesen, the weather was fair, and I said, 'When you sit up and talk like that you look so well it seems as if you should get up and go out with me.' The reply was, 'Yes, there is only one objection, that I cannot walk. But there is another way of conveyance, by means of which I can be lifted up; I have had a feeling of becoming an angel, getting wings—and that indeed is what will come to pass, to sit upon the clouds and sing: Hallelujah, hallelujah, hallelujah! All the rest is evil. I do not mean that what I said was evil, but I said it to do away with the evil, and so get to Hallelujah, hallelujah, hallelujah!' 'And this is all because you believe on and take refuge in divine grace?' asked the persistent catechist. 'Naturally, what else?' said S. K. 'I am glad to die, so that I am certain I have accomplished my task. What comes from a deceased man people will often listen to more readily than to what comes from a living man.' Boesen asked if he had still something he wanted to say to the public. 'No.—Yes, my greeting to all; I have cared for them all a great deal; and tell them my life was one great suffering, unknown to others and misunderstood; it all seemed like pride and vanity, but it was not. I am not a bit better than others, I have always said that and said nothing else.'

S. K. died on a Sunday, and he was buried on the Sunday following, the funeral service being read by the Dean in the Cathedral Church of Our Lady. Some one had blundered, but it is not clear who was to blame. The dean was aware that it was dangerous to have the funeral in the largest church and on a Sunday when a crowd could more easily gather. S. K.'s brother Peter found it too late to make any change when he arrived from his distant parish of Petersborg. In fact, the church was crowded by sympathizers and opponents, while many were obliged to remain on the street. A crowd of students had fought their way in to act as guard of honour. In this perilous situation Peter

Kierkegaard made the funeral oration and managed by marvellous tact to preserve the peace. He succeeded in making even the opponents understand that at the bottom of his brother's extravagant assertions there was something very serious which it behoved them all to heed. But at the cemetery, where S. K. was buried beside his father, it did not prove possible to suppress the excitement. S. K.'s nephew, Henrik Lund, interrupted the Dean as he was about to begin the committal service. He inveighed against the dishonesty of the Church in appropriating a man who had so decisively rejected it. He read from the Revelation the passage which refers to the Church of the Laodiceans which God would 'spew out of his mouth', and this he matched with passages from the *Instant*.

It was very shocking, no doubt—but S. K. was at peace, and I cannot think that his peace would be disturbed by knowing that the fire he had kindled continued to burn.

I conclude this chapter—and this book—with a passage which clearly belongs here, although it was written (prophetically) in the Journal three years before this time:[1]

'The Sacrifice', the Corrective

As a skilful cook says with regard to a dish in which already a great many ingredients are mingled: 'It needs still just a little pinch of cinnamon' (and we perhaps could hardly tell by the taste that this little pinch of spice had entered into it, but she knew precisely why and precisely how it affected the taste of the whole mixture); as an artist says with a view to the colour effect of a whole painting which is composed of many, many colours: 'There and there, at that little point, there must be applied a little touch of red' (and we perhaps could hardly even discover that the red is there, so carefully has the artist suppressed it, although he knows exactly why it should be introduced). So it is with Governance.

Oh, the Governance of the world is an immense housekeeping and a grandiose painting. Yet He, the Master, God in heaven, behaves like the cook and the artist. He says: Now there must be introduced a little pinch of spice, a little touch of red. We do not comprehend why, we are hardly aware of it, since that little bit is so thoroughly absorbed in the whole. But God knows why.

A little pinch of spice! That is to say: Here a man must be sacrificed, he is needed to impart a particular taste to the rest.

These are the correctives. It is a woful error if he who is used for applying the corrective becomes impatient and would make the corrective normative for others. That is the temptation to bring everything to confusion.

A little pinch of spice! Humanly speaking, what a painful thing, thus to be sacrificed, to be the little pinch of spice! But on the other hand, God knows well him whom he elects to use in this way, and then he knows also how, in the inward understanding of it, to make it so blessed a thing for him to be sacrificed, that among the thousands of divers voices which express, each in its own way, the same thing, his also will be heard, and perhaps especially his which is truly *de profundis*, proclaiming: God is love. The birds on the branches, the lilies in the field, the deer in the forest, the fishes in the sea, countless hosts of happy men exultantly proclaim: God is love. But beneath all these sopranos, supporting them as it were, as the bass part does, is audible the *de profundis* which issues from the sacrificed one: God is love.

APPENDIXES

APPENDIX I

NOTES TO THE TEXT

THE references to S. K.'s *Works* and *Papers* are given here in the form which is now usual on the Continent. They refer to the most recent edition of the *Works*, in 15 volumes, and to the first complete edition of the *Papers*, which has now reached 20 volumes with 3 more to come. The *Works* are indicated by a Roman numeral followed immediately by the number of the page, whereas a Roman numeral followed by A, B, or C indicates the Papers ('A' indicates the Journal), and the number which follows indicates the section, the page being mentioned only when the section is long. *EP* indicates the earlier and less voluminous edition of S. K.'s *Papers* (*Efterladte Papirer*), and the number following indicates the page. Only the last volume needs to be referred to frequently, and that is meant when another is not expressly designated. *Forl.* indicates Meyer's edition of the entries in the Journal which relate to S. K.'s engagement (*Forlovelsen*).

These notes will seem superfluous to most readers, yet some may complain that I have not always indicated the source of my quotations. There are in fact a dozen or more cases where I have lost the reference to the Journal, and to find it again in the 18 volumes would be as difficult as finding a needle in a haystack.

Page

xii. **1** X⁴. A. 628 f.

2. **1** *EP* I. 159. **2** I. 9.

4. **1** *Die Bedeutung der ästhetischen Schriften S. K.'s*, 1879.

6. **1** *S. K. als Philosoph*, German ed. trans. by Schrempf, 1892–1922. **2** p. 172. **3** *Das Geheimnis Kierkegaards*, 1929. Cf. his *Polarity*, 'A German Catholic's Interpretation of Religion', trans. by A. C. Bouquet, Oxford Univ. Press, 1935. It is a detailed defence of the doctrine of the *anologia entis* against the attacks of Karl Barth. Przywara was editor of *Stimmen der Zeit*, the Roman Catholic rejoinder to Barth's *Zwischen den Zeiten*. He makes too much, it seems to me, of the *analogia entis* as the distinction of Catholic theology.

7. **1** *Sein und Zeit*, 3rd ed. 1931. **2** *Philosophie*, 3 vols., 1932. **3** VIII. A. 18. **4** *Die geistige Situation der Zeit*, 1st ed. 1931, Eng. trans.: *Man in the Modern Age*, 1933.

8. **1** X¹. A. 34. **2** X². A. 299. Fechner: *Leben nach dem Tode*, p. 52, 'You have asked me whether, and I have answered with the how. Faith can do without the whether, but if it is asked, the only way it can be answered is with the how; and so long as the how is not established the whether will not cease to come and go.' **3** Werner Brock: *An Introduction to Contemporary German Philosophy*, Cambridge Univ. Press, 1935. Cf. the reference to S. K. in Aubrey: *Present Trends in Theology*. **4** *Del sentimiento trágico de la vida*, 1st ed. 1921, 4th ed. 1931, Eng. trans. 1931.

9. **1** *Nein! Antwort an Emil Brunner*, p. 51. It is No. 14 of *Theologische Existenz Heute*. **2** X¹. A. 59.

19. **1** IV. A. 144. **2** IX. A. 411.

21. **1** III. A. 66. **2** III. A. 75. **3** III. A. 78.
22. **1** VII. A. 5.
25. **1** *Erindringer fra Hjemmet*, p. 195.
26. **1** IX. A. 68. **2** IX. A. 119. **3** VIII. A. 25.
28. **1** VIII. A. 424. **2** IV. A. 173.
29. **1** IX. A. 48. **2** IV. B. 1, pp. 103–82.
37. **1** II. 288 ff.
39. **1** XII. 197 ff.
41. **1** X¹. A. 272.
42. **1** XI. 71 ff.
45. **1** V. A. 33. **2** III. A. 123.
46. **1** IX. A. 70. **2** VIII. A. 126.
47. **1** XIII. 604 ff.
50. **1** X². A. 454.
51. **1** VII. 579 ff.
56. **1** *EP* I. xlvii ff.
58. **1** II. A. 557.
59. **1** *EP* I. 3-6. **2** II. A. 802-807.
66. **1** XIII. 605 ff.
68. **1** II. A. 66. **2** II. A. 804.
70. **1** IV. A. 85. **2** VI. 265 f.
72. **1** IV. A. 114.
73. **1** I. 151 f. **2** The French translators use *angoisse*.
74. **1** X. 95.
75. **1** II. A. 803, 806.
78. **1** *Den unge S. K.*, 1929.
79. **1** II. 171–83.
86. **1** II. 183. **2** 209 ff.
88. **1** II. 211 ff.
90. **1** II. 215–18. **2** II. 231. **3** I. B. 2.
91. **1** I. A. 181; cf. Brandt, *Den unge S. K.*, p. 69 f.
92. **1** II. B. 1–21. **2** XIII. 45 ff. **3** XI. A. 590.
93. **1** II. A. 520. **2** *Det 19 Aarhundrede: Erindringer an S. K.*, p. 243.
95. **1** *Livs Erindringer og Resultater*, p. 214.
96. **1** *Stemninger og Tilstander*, 1838.
97. **1** III. 197. **2** III. 171. **3** Cf. IV. A. 148.
98. **1** *S. K. en Psykiatrisk-Psykologisk Studie*, 1933.
99. **1** III. 198. **2** III. 250.
100. **1** I. A. 8 (Sept. 11, 1843). **2** I. A. 333.
106. **1** I. 4, 6, 10 f., 14 ff., 20 f., 25, 28 ff.
107. **1** I. A. 72.
109. **1** I. A. 75.
111. **1** VI. A. 81 (1843). **2** I. A. 94.
112. **1** I. A. 99.
114. **1** XIII. 564. **2** XIII. 607.
117. **1** I. A. 75, p. 56. **2** I. A. 179, 165, 166. **3** II. 210 ff. **4** *Den unge S. K.*
121. **1** II. 194, 199, 217.

122. **1** I. A. 89, also 99, p. 70. **2** I. A. 75, p. 58. **3** II. A. 97. **4** IV. A. 144. **5** X². A. 455.
123. **1** Cf. II. A. 596. **2** XI. 201 ff.
124. **1** XI. 207.
125. **1** VI. 340 ff. **2** VI. 245 ff.
126. **1** XI. 207 f.
127. **1** III. A. 233. **2** II. A. 18.
128. **1** Probably II. A. 584. **2** IV. 417.
129. **1** X². A. 493. **2** IV. 346 ff., 366, 377.
131. **1** II. 204.
132. **1** *Kierkegaard Studier*, I and II; *En Episode i S. Ks Ungdomsliv*, 1912; *En Segment af S. Ks religiøse Udvikling*, 1918.
133. **1** III. A. 245. **2** IV. A. 65, 68, 132, 147. **3** IV. A. 132.
134. **1** IV. A. 68. **2** VI. A. 55. **3** VII. A. 6.
135. **1** IV. 436 f. **2** IV. 437.
136. **1** *Livserindringer*, I, p. 412. **2** IV. A. 107.
137. **1** II. A. 19. **2** II. A. 20.
138. **1** VI. A. 105. **2** VIII. A. 550.
139. **1** I. A. 254. **2** III. A. 242.
140. **1** I. 51 f.
141. **1** XI. 207. **2** X³. A. 413. **3** IV. 426 ff. **4** I. A. 326. **5** I. A. 282. **6** II. A. 605. **7** II. A. 603.
142. **1** I. A. 163. **2** II. 351 ff.
143. **1** V. B. 46. **2** II. A. 116.
144. **1** I. A. 167. **2** I. A. 156, 157, 158.
145. **1** I. A. 330. **2** II. 265 f.
146. **1** I. A. 162–66.
147. **1** I. A. 161.
148. **1** *EP* 108. **2** I. A. 279.
149. **1** II. A. 209. **2** II. A. 216.
151. **1** II. A. 118, 119.
152. **1** I. A. 640. **2** II. A. 63.
155. **1** I. A. 174. **2** I. A. 177. **3** I. A. 178. **4** I. A. 179. **5** I. A. 182, 191. **6** I. A. 196.
156. **1** I. A. 333. **2** I. A. 334. **3** I. A. 335. **4** I. A. 336. **5** I. A. 339. **6** I. A. 32.
157. **1** II. A. 328. **2** II. A. 745. **3** II. A. 11. **4** II. A. 24. **5** II. A. 30.
158. **1** II. A. 67. **2** II. A. 68. **3** II. A. 617.
159. **1** II. A. 34. **2** II. A. 76. **3** II. A. 62, 63, 64. **4** II. A. 65. **5** II. A. 73. **6** II. A. 127–30. **7** II. A. 132. **8** II. A. 662. **9** II. A. 83. **10** II. A. 84.
160. **1** II. A. 622. **2** II. A. 168. **3** II. A. 171. **4** II. A. 172. **5** II. A. 190. **6** II. A. 201. **7** II. 202. **8** II. A. 643. **9** I. A. 325.
161. **1** II. A. 682. **2** II. A. 702. **3** II. A. 745. **4** II. A. 750. **5** II. A. 752.
162. **1** II. A. 730. **2** I. A. 100. **3** II. A. 110. **4** II. A. 223, cf. VIII. A. 465.

163. **1** I. A. 94.
164. **1** II. A. 152. **2** I. A. 302. **3** I. A. 305. **4** I. A. 273. **5** I. A. 317. **6** I. A. 2, 105.
165. **1** I. A. 234 (Sept. 10, 1836). **2** II. A. 75. **3** I. A. 237.
166. **1** II. A. 239.
167. **1** II. A. 786. **2** II. A. 790.
168. **1** II. A. 230, 756, 231–5, 757–9. **2** S. K. had in mind the hero of an Icelandic saga. Cf. III. 234.
170. **1** II. A. 212. **2** II. A. 228.
171. **1** IV. 453 n.
172. **1** X^5. A. 96. **2** XIII. 609.
173. **1** XIII. 561.
175. **1** III. 236 f.
176. **1** *S. K. en Psykiatrisk-Psykologisk Studie*, 1933. **2** *EP* 300 (Nov. 24, 1854).
177. **1** *Jesus der Herr*, pp. 15 ff.
179. **1** II. A. 211. **2** IV. 452 n. **3** Such a cramp is described in Gertrude Le Fort's novel, *The Veil of Veronica*, cap. V, German ed. 1928, English ed. 1933.
180. **1** X^2. A. 325. **2** II. A. 243.
181. **1** *Erindringer fra Hjemmet*, pp. 105 ff.
182. **1** Emanuel Hirsch: *Kierkegaard-Studien*, pp. 46 ff.
183. **1** II. A. 73.
184. **1** XIII. 607. For the context see p. 115. **2** e.g. XIII. 574 ff. **3** II. 234 ff.
185. **1** II. A. 557. **2** IX. A. 71.
186. **1** II. A. 804, 807.
187. **1** VIII. A. 7, 414.
191. **1** *Forl.* 135. **2** *Forl.* 115. **3** *Forl.* 92. **4** XII. 311.
192. **1** X^2. A. 3 (1849).
194. **1** X^2. A. 149. **2** *Forl.* 139. **3** *Forl.* 140 f.
195. **1** Mourier, 388 ff. **2** Raphael Meyer: *Kierkegaardisk Papirer, Forlovelsen*. Henriette Lund: *Mit Forhold til Hende*. **3** *S. K. en Psykiatrisk-Psykologisk Studie*, 1933. **4** IV. A. 142.
196. **1** IV. A. 161. **2** X^5. A. 149.
197. **1** I. 452 ff.
198. **1** X^1. A. 280, p. 191.
199. **1** IX. A. 130.
200. **1** III. A. 62. **2** X^5. A. 149. **3** VI. 213 f.
201. **1** II. A. 273. **2** II. A. 347.
202. **1** II. A. 422.
203. **1** IX. A. 69. **2** X^5. A. 150. **3** III. A. 90.
204. **1** VI. 214 f.
206. **1** III. A. 64. **2** IV. A. 215. **3** *Forl.* 59. **4** X^5. A. 149, p. 160.
207. **1** Mourier.
208. **1** III. A. 142. **2** *Erindringer fra Hjemmet*, p. 172.
209. **1** VI. 223 f.
210. **1** III. A. 95. **2** Henriette Lund: *Mit Forhold til Hende*, p. 34 f.

212. **1** III. 198 f.
213. **1** IX. A. 18.
214. **1** III. A. 96.
215. **1** IV. A. 215. **2** III. A. 103. **3** III. A. 105. **4** III. A. 133.
216. **1** X^1. A. 667.
217. **1** III. A. 161.
218. **1** X^5. A. 149, p. 162; *Forl.* 79. **2** VI. 347. **3** X^5. A. 149, p. 163.
219. **1** IV. A. 107.
220. **1** X^2. A. 3.
222. **1** X^5. A. 149.
224. **1** V. A. 88. **2** III. A. 147 f., 150 f., 159 f., 166, 172, 176, 178, 229.
228. **1** *Forl.* 43–66. **2** VIII. A. 100.
230. **1** XIV. 369 ff.
233. **1** *Forl.* 69.
234. **1** III. A. 176. **2** I. 19. **3** II. A. 122.
235. **1** *Forl.* 69. **2** *EP* I. 314. **3** *Forl.* 60. **4** *Forl.* 68. **5** IV. A. 42.
236. **1** IV. A. 70. **2** X^5. A. 153.
237. **1** IV. B. 45, p. 202 f. **2** VII. 237 f.
238. **1** IV. A. 70 (1843). **2** X^1. A. 266, p. 177.
239. **1** X^3. A. 413.
240. **1** IV. B. 59, pp. 217 ff.
241. **1** IV. A. 215. **2** IV. A. 223. **3** *Forl.* 51.
242. **1** IV. A. 314. **2** III. B. 177.
243. **1** II. 188. **2** I. 26. **3** III. B. 199, 22.
244. **1** I. 25. **2** III. B. 177, cf. 179, 60. **3** II. 279.
245. **1** IV. A. 216. **2** I. 23 f., cf. IV. A. 217.
246. **1** IV. A. 43. **2** X^1. A. 266, p. 176.
248. **1** XIII. 577. **2** III. B. 182.
249. **1** XIII. 610. **2** I. 37, cf. IV. A. 224.
250. **1** I. 49.
252. **1** IV. A. 97. **2** X^5. A. 149, 20. **3** V. B. 153 f.
253. **1** IV. A. 101. **2** IV. A. 107. **3** IV. A. 108. **4** Especially III. A. 262 f.
254. **1** IV. A. 110 f., 119, 132, 135, 137 ff., 147. **2** *EP* I. 415.
256. **1** III. 187, cf. IV. B. 96, 4; 117, 4. **2** III. A. 203, IV. A. 126. **3** IV. B. 97, 30. **4** X^5. A. 149, 20.
257. **1** IV. A. 169. **2** II. 292.
258. **1** IV. 322 n. **2** Cf. VII. 248 f. **3** IV. 459 n., 461 n.
259. **1** IV. B. 111, p. 277. **2** Cf. VII. 249 f. **3** IV. B. 120, p. 308, cf. 117, p. 282.
260. **1** III. 274, IV. B. 117, p. 284. **2** IV. B. 111, p. 372, IV. 396 n. **3** IV. 39 ff. **4** IV. A. 166.
261. **1** IV. 468 f., cf. IV. A. 92.
262. **1** II. 65, cf. I. A. 75, p. 58 (1835); VI. 466.
263. **1** XIII. 609 f.
264. **1** Cf. VII. 253 f. **2** III. 133. **3** I. A. 273. **4** III. 132. **5** III. 145. **6** VIII. A. 650, p. 298.
265. **1** III. 109. **2** III. 174. **3** II. 228. **4** X^2. A. 163, p. 130. **5** X^2. A. 185 f.

266. **1** III. 135. **2** IV. B. 67. **3** IV. A. 76.
267. **1** III. 100 ff.
271. **1** I. 380 f.
273. **1** IV. A. 83.
274. **1** IV. B. 143. **2** IV. A. 234. **3** VIII. A. 6.
277. **1** III. A. 6, cf. IX. 204 ff., X. 117 f.
278. **1** VII. 242, 257 f.
279. **1** VI. 486 ff.
280. **1** Cf. VII. 425 f., 455 f., VI. A. 147–56, VI. B. 10–12.
283. **1** VI. A. 78.
284. **1** VI. B. 41, 10.
285. **1** V. A. 110. **2** Cf. VII. 270 ff., 275. **3** VI. 70.
286. **1** VII. 516 f.
288. **1** V. A. 34. **2** XIII. 530.
289. **1** VII. A. 27. **2** III. 218.
293. **1** VII. 522 n. **2** VII. 359. **3** VII. 145 f., 156 n., 165 f., 168, 213 f., 598, VIII. 154.
295. **1** VII. 170 ff.
296. **1** VI. B. 41, 6; cf. VII. 256.
297. **1** VI. B. 194–235, 271–95. **2** VII. 220–9.
302. **1** VII. 266. **2** VI. 24, 34, 60 f., 179, 602 ff., VII. B. 19, 7. **3** e.g. VI. 469.
303. **1** VI. 295 ff.
304. **1** Cf. X[1]. A. 50, IX. A. 75.
308. **1** I would not have it thought that in using this title I wantonly differ from Professor Swenson. The fact is, he deliberately differed from me; for when finally, after a long and excruciating debate with himself, he adopted a title (*Fragments*) which is at least not obviously better than the word Bain and Dru and I had agreed to use, he knew that I had written *Scraps* throughout my manuscript and was pledged to use it. Thus my effort (in which Swenson had collaborated) to ensure substantial uniformity of nomenclature was rendered vain. **2** VII, last page.
309. **1** VI. 10. **2** VII. 7. **3** VII. 7 f.
310. **1** IV. 273 f., VII. 21, &c. **2** VII. 265 f. **3** VII. 212. **4** IV. 448 f., cf. 450.
311. **1** IX. A. 118. **2** V. B. 194. **3** IV. A. 121. **4** IV. 237.
312. **1** IV. 212. **2** IV. 388–99. **3** IV. 236, 252. **4** VII. 412.
314. **1** VII. 185.
316. **1** I. A. 36. **2** IV. B. 87, 2; cf. 84, 4; 94, 4. **3** VI. 233. **4** IV. 273 ff., 279, XII. 420. **5** X[2]. A. 354, X[5]. A. 635 f. **6** VIII. A. 650, p. 298; V. A. 28, X[2]. A. 279. **7** VII. 336 n. **8** IV. 275. **9** VII. 368 n. **10** IV. B. 19, 8. **11** IV. 251, VII. 602. **12** VII. 24, 34, 116, 340.
317. **1** VI. 466 f., cf. IV. 275 n. **2** VII. 218.
318. **1** VII. 189. **2** VII. 210 n.
319. **1** VII. 193 f.
320. **1** VII. 605.
322. **1** X. 192.
323. **1** VII. 546 ff., 561 f., 564 ff.

325. **1** VII. 490–515, 551 f.
326. **1** VII. 214, 219. **2** VII. 357.
327. **1** IV. 237 ff.
329. **1** Cf. V. 210 f.
330. **1** VII. 390.
333. **1** *Gesammelte Aufsätze zur Religionssoziologie*, 1921, vol. i, pp. 62–206. Eng. trans. by Parsons: *The Protestant Ethic and the Spirit of Capitalism*, 1930. **2** Southey: *Life of Wesley*, cap. 29.
335. **1** VII. 515 ff. **2** VII. 210 ff. **3** VII. 448. **4** VII. 524, IV. 266 f., 416, 420. **5** VII. 244 f. **6** VII. 390 ff. **7** IV. 258 ff. **8** IX. A. 72. **9** VII. 468 ff. **10** V. A. 77. **11** VII. 357 ff. **12** IV. 230. **13** IV. 241. **14** VII. 196 f.
336. **1** VII. 196 f.
337. **1** X². A. 592.
338. **1** VII. 27. **2** VII. 19 ff.
340. **1** VII. 146, 213, cf. 154.
341. **1** VII. 151–62.
347. **1** VII. B. 32, p. 203.
348. **1** X¹. A. 98, p. 77; 623, cf. VII. B. 22, X². A. 620.
350. **1** XII. 459 ff. **2** XIII. 467, cf. X³. A. 88.
351. **1** VII. B. 72, p. 262. **2** *EP* (1846), 297.
352. **1** *Livs Erindringer og Resultater*, p. 429. **2** VII. A. 107. **3** X¹. A. 131, 135.
353. **1** VII. B. 37, p. 213. **2** VIII. A. 515. **3** VIII. A. 544.
354. **1** VII. A. 163. **2** IX. A. 370. **3** VII. A. 456, 458, VIII. A. 458.
355. **1** VII. A. 107. **2** VII. A. 120 (1846).
356. **1** VII. A. 103. **2** VIII. A. 44. **3** VII. B. 37, p. 313. **4** VII. A. 50.
358. **1** VII. B. 55, pp. 234 ff. **2** VII. A. 90. **3** VII. A. 125. **4** VIII. A. 99 (May 1847). **5** IX. A. 64 (1848), cf. X². A. 588, 612, 616, X³. A. 90.
359. **1** X¹. A. 40–3.
360. **1** VII. A. 222. **2** *EP* (1854), 76 f.
363. **1** VII. B. 235, pp. 14 ff.
364. **1** VIII. A. 128. **2** X¹. A. 138, X². A. 251 (5). **3** VIII. A. 62, 143 f.
366. **1** VII. A. 4. **2** VII. A. 221.
367. **1** VII. A. 229. **2** X¹. A. 138.
370. **1** VIII. A. 20 f. **2** VIII. A. 15 f.
371. **1** VIII. A. 235 ff., cf. VI. A. 106.
372. **1** VIII. 300 ff.
376. **1** VIII. A. 390. **2** X. 241 ff.
378. **1** VIII. A. 358. **2** X⁶. B. 249, p. 412.
379. **1** VIII. A. 250. **2** VIII. A. 229.
381. **1** VIII. A. 82, 120. **2** e.g. IX. A. 260, X¹. A. 122, X². A. 375.
383. **1** VIII. B. 26.
384. **1** VII. B, pp. 218 f.
385. **1** X². A. 578.
386. **1** X². A. 475.

387. **1** VIII. A. 250.
392. **1** p. 357. **2** X^{2}. A. 66.
393. **1** X^{6}. B. 249, p. 412.
394. **1** X. 277 ff.
397. **1** VIII. A. 649 (May 11, 1848).
398. **1** VIII. A. 675.
399. **1** IX. A. 74, cf. 25, 55. **2** X. 215 f., 219 f.
400. **1** VIII. A. 640 f.
402. **1** IX. A. 177 (July 1848). **2** VIII. A. 645.
403. **1** VIII. A. 646, cf. 647. **2** VIII. A. 673.
404. **1** VIII. A. 650. **2** VIII. A. 185. **3** *EP* 297, VIII. A. 156.
405. **1** VIII. A. 126.
406. **1** X^{6}. B. 145, pp. 204 ff.; 151, pp. 229 ff.
409. **1** VIII. B. 186, cf. 187. **2** VIII. B. 188.
410. **1** IX. 272. **2** X. 143.
411. **1** XI. 133 f.
412. **1** XI. 164. **2** XI. 226 f., 233, 237.
413. **1** XI. 264. **2** XI. 240 ff.
415. **1** XI. 213 ff.
416. **1** X^{1}. A. 11. **2** X^{1}. A. 281.
417. **1** IX. A. 161.
418. **1** IX. A. 222. **2** IX. A. 213. **3** VIII. A. 347. **4** VIII. A. 643.
419. **1** XI. 15–20.
423. **1** IV. 296. **2** XI. 111.
424. **1** IX. 83.
425. **1** VIII. A. 637–9. **2** University of Texas Bulletin, No. 2326, 239 pages. It can be had for 25 cents.
426. **1** X^{1}. A. 351.
427. **1** XII. 224.
429. **1** XI. 256. **2** XI. 254. **3** X^{1}. A. 440.
430. **1** XII. 250 ff.
432. **1** X^{6}. B. 253, 2 (1849).
433. **1** XII. 165 f.
434. **1** XII. 17. **2** IX. A. 232. **3** X^{1}. A. 425.
435. **1** XII. 87 ff.
438. **1** IX. A. 224, cf. 222 f. (1848).
439. **1** IX. A. 265. **2** IX. A. 223 f., X^{1}. A. 266.
440. **1** IX. A. 173, 185, X^{1}. A. 266. **2** XIII. 580. **3** XIII. 535. **4** XIII. 528.
441. **1** XIII. 595 ff.
444. **1** XIII. 621 ff.
445. **1** IX. B. 57.
446. **1** X^{5}. B. 107–10, cf. IX. B. 64 f. **2** II. A. 770. **3** IX. A. 512. **4** IX. A. 221.
447. **1** IX. A. 221.
448. **1** X^{2}. A. 587.
449. **1** X^{2}. A. 525. **2** X^{3}. A. 72.
450. **1** IX. A. 414.

451. **1** IX. A. 365. **2** IX. A. 216.
452. **1** X^{1}. A. 494, cf. 499. **2** XIV. 256 ff., cf. XII. 450 ff.
453. **1** X^{1}. A. 56. **2** X^{1}. A. 162.
454. **1** X^{1}. A. 167. **2** X^{1}. A. 497, 511.
455. **1** IX. A. 483. **2** IX. A. 79. **3** X^{1}. A. 115–18.
456. **1** The most important are: X.^{1} A. 56, 94, 97, 223, 421–4, 435, 509; X^{2}. A. 147, 177; X^{3}. A. 265. **2** X^{1}. A. 510.
457. **1** IX. A. 9, X^{1}. A. 74, 78, 117, 121, 510, 517, X^{6}. B. 45, X^{2}. A. 147, 177, X^{3}. A. 265.
458. **1** IX. A. 218, X^{1}. A. 94, 97. **2** X^{1}. A. 513. **3** X^{1}. A. 115.
459. **1** X^{1}. A. 136. **2** X^{1}. A. 133 f., cf. X^{6}. B. 241. **3** XIII. 606.
460. **1** IX. A. 419. **2** X^{6}. B. 246.
462. **1** X^{1}. A. 511. **2** X^{2}. A. 177, cf. 147. **3** X^{4}. A. 587, cf. 302 f.
463. **1** X^{1}. A. 542. **2** X^{2}. A. 210, *Forl.* 131 ff., cf. X^{1}. A. 648, 661, 668, X^{2}. A. 4, 18, 68, 210–17.
466. **1** IX. A. 72.
469. **1** XII. 313.
471. **1** XII. 556. **2** XII. 552.
474. **1** XII. 342. **2** XII. 416 ff.
478. **1** XII. 423 ff.
487. **1** *EP* 46 f., 64, 88 f., 91 f., 94, 103, 110, 153, 374. **2** *EP* 308 f., 314, 357 f., 374, &c.—not to speak of the *Instant*.
488. **1** *EP* 304 f., 310, 337 f., 361. **2** *EP* 56 ff., 79 ff., 85 f., 102, 114 f. **3** *EP* 49 ff., 65, 68, 191 f., 250.
489. **1** *EP* 562. **2** *EP* 166 f.
493. **1** X^{2}. A. 61, p. 48.
494. **1** *S.K.'s religiøse Udvikling*, 1925, p. 7 f.
495. **1** X^{4}. A. 559 f.
497. **1** *EP* 506.
498. **1** X^{5}. A. 105. **2** *EP* 176. **3** *EP* 217. **4** X^{4}. A. 600.
499. **1** X^{5}. A. 146 (Oct. 13, 1853). **2** X^{5}. A. 146.
500. **1** X^{4}. A. 150, X^{5}. A. 89, 94, *EP* 191. **2** X^{4}. A. 537. **3** X^{6}. B. 235, pp. 288 ff.; *EP* 7, 29, 42, 77, 161, 432. **4** *S. K. og Pengene*, 1935.
501. **1** *Papirer, Tidstavlen*, date Aug. 29, 1839.
503. **1** X^{2}. A. 511, cf. X^{1}. A. 177.
505. **1** X^{6}. B. 103–43, cf. X^{2}. A. 495, 596.
506. **1** VIII. B. 15, p. 66. **2** X^{1}. A. 609. **3** XI. 224, *EP* 138 f.
507. **1** X^{3}. A. 122.
508. **1** X^{2}. A. 633, cf. 637, VI. B. 133 f., pp. 225 f.
510. **1** VII. A. 221. **2** VIII. A. 332 (1847).
511. **1** *EP* 417–31, 494, cf. X^{4}. A. 566, X^{6}. B. 226. **2** *EP* 450.
512. **1** IV. A. 71. **2** X^{5}. A. 138, *EP* 262 f. **3** X^{5}. B. 111, p. 304. **4** IX A. 39.
513. **1** IX. A. 84. **2** IX. A. 85. **3** IX. A. 240.
514. **1** X^{6}. B. 162–70.
515. **1** X^{3}. A. 563, cf. 56, 59. **2** X^{4}. A. 271.
516. **1** X^{6}. B. 125 (1849). **2** IX. A. 494. **3** X^{4}. A. 270.
517. **1** X^{6}. B. 171–236, i.e. 142 pages. **2** X^{6}. B. 112. **3** X^{6}. B. 218.

518. **1** X^6. B. 224. **2** X^3. A. 782. **3** X^4. A. 566. **4** X^4. A. 604.
520. **1** *EP* 1. **2** *EP* 411. **3** *EP* 496 ff.
522. **1** *EP* 426.
523. **1** X^4. A. 457 end. **2** *EP* 141. **3** X^6. B. 235, p. 393. **4** *EP* 121. **5** *EP* 284. **6** *EP* 337. **7** X^5. A. 98, 100 f.
524. **1** *EP* 19. **2** *EP* 18 f. **3** X^1. A. 154. **4** *EP* 119. **5** *EP* 311. **6** *EP* 204 f. **7** 'The Gospel and the Law', *Theologische Existenz Heute*, No. 23. **8** *EP* 398. **9** *EP* 75. **10** *EP* 42. **11** X^4. A. 644. **12** XIV. 67. **13** *EP* 2 f.
525. **1** *EP* 353. **2** X^4. A. 226. **3** *EP* 296 f.
526. **1** *EP* 381–4.
528. **1** *EP* 337–41, cf. X^4. A. 510, 521.
532. **1** X^5. A. 114, X^4. A. 617, *EP* 194, 225, 360. **2** *EP* 136 f.
533. **1** X^4. A. 627.
534. **1** *EP* 350. **2** X^5. A. 118. **3** *EP* 387.
535. **1** X^6. B. 145, p. 212. **2** *EP* 23. **3** X^5. A. 128.
536. **1** *EP* 318. **2** *EP* 131. **3** X^5. A. 26, *EP* 252.
537. **1** *EP* 24. **2** *EP* 59. **3** *EP* 131. **4** *EP* 181.
538. **1** *EP* 255. **2** *EP* 26.
539. **1** *EP* 389. **2** X^4. A. 626. **3** X^5. A. 18, p. 22. **4** *EP* 240 ff.
540. **1** X^4. A. 656, X^5. A. 5, 14.
541. **1** X^4. A. 673, p. 484; cf. 117, 121.
542. **1** *EP* 205 f. **2** X^5. A. 81, p. 92. **3** X^5. A. 81, p. 92.
543. **1** X^4. A. 655.
544. **1** X^4. A. 624, pp. 441 f. **2** *EP* 391 f.
545. **1** *EP* 345 f.
546. **1** *EP* 394 f.
547. **1** *EP* 502 f., cf. X^5. A. 143.
548. **1** X^4. A. 43, cf. 44.
549. **1** *EP* 247 f.
550. **1** X^4. A. 640, cf. *EP* 295, 341. **2** *EP* 295 f. **3** *EP* 3. **4** *EP* 319. **5** *EP* 239.
551. **1** *EP* 242, cf. 119, X^3. A. 658.
552. **1** *EP* 271.
553. **1** *EP* 367 f. **2** XIV. 106, 115.
554. **1** X^6. B. 236. **2** *EP* 410.
555. **1** X^4. A. 665. **2** X^4. A. 665, p. 477. **3** X^4. A. 666, cf. 557.
556. **1** X^5. A. 106. **2** X^4. A. 586 (Aug. 1852), 664.
557. **1** *EP* 5. **2** *EP* 222 f. **3** *EP* 232.
559. **1** *EP* 259.
560. **1** *EP* 342. **2** *EP* 390. **3** X^6. B. 232, p. 371.
561. **1** X^6. B. 232, p. 371.
562. **1** *EP* 31 f.
563. X^6. B. 235, pp 394 ff.
566 **1** *EP* 469 (April 1854). **2** *EP* 412.
567. **1** *EP* 231 (Oct. 1854).
568. **1** *EP* 488. **2** *EP* 187 f., cf. XIV. 185. **3** *EP* 370, cf. XIV. 83 ff.
569. IV. 83, cf. X.^{5} A. 127. **2** *EP* 487 n.

570. 1 *EP* 549. 2 *EP* 183. 3 X.[4] A. 571.
571. 1 *Det 19 Aarhundrede*, p. 373.
572. 1 XIV. 28. 2 XIV. 36.
573. 1 XIV. 44. 2 XIV. 48. 3 XIV. 45.
575. 1 XIV. 69 ff.
576. 1 XIV. 78. 2 X[3]. A. 784, p. 495; XIV. 331 f. 3 X[4]. A. 466, X[5]. A. 44, 99, 101, 103. 4 *EP* 199. 5 IX. A. 413 (1848).
577. 1 XIV. 103 f. 2 XIV. 135.
578. 1 XIV. 144. 2 XIV. 177 f.
579. 1 XIV. 239 f.
580. 1 XIV. 243. 2 XIV. 283.
581. 1 *EP* 544. 2 XIV. 371 f.
583. 1 *EP* 593 ff. 2 *EP* 609.
585. 1 *Peter og S. K.*, 1936.
587. 1 X[4]. A. 596.
623. 1 *Erindringer*, p. 25.

APPENDIX II

QUOTATIONS FROM THE *WORKS*

THEY are arranged consecutively, to give the reader a faint notion of the character of the books from which they are taken—a fairer notion at all events than can be got from the dry bones of the Synopsis which is given in Appendix IV. Many long passages equally important have been quoted from the *Papers*, but they need not be included in this list because the sequence is not so important.

The page-numbers show how widely the quotations are dispersed in this book, and the figures in parentheses, which refer to the latest Danish edition, show how sparsely they illustrate S. K.'s *Works*.

Either/Or, Vol. I. vi (3), 102 ff. (4 ff.), 249 f. (37), 250 (49), 140 (51 f.), 74 (151).
— — Vol. II. 79 ff. (171 ff.), 131 (204), 86 f. (209 ff.), 87 f. (211 ff.), 184 (234 ff.), 145 (266 f.), 244 (279), 37 ff. (288 ff.), 142 (252).
Two Edifying Discourses (1843), Vol. III. 272 f. (15).
Johannes Climacus, Vol. IV. B. 29 ff. (103 ff.).
Repetition, Vol. III. 99 (198), 212 f. (198 ff.), 175 (236 f.), 99 (250), 257 f. (292).
Philosophical Scraps, Vol. IV. 273 ff. (327 ff.).
The Concept of Dread, Vol. IV. 129 ff. (346 ff., 377), 135 (436 f.), 310 f. (448 f.), 261 f. (468).
Stages on Life's Road, Vol. VI. 285 (70), 45 f. (212), 200 f. (213 f.), 204 ff. (214 f.), 209 f. (223 f.), 70 f. (265 f.), 218 (347), 317 (466 f.), 279 f. (486 ff.).
Unscientific Postscript, Vol. VII. 309 f. (7), 338 ff. (19 ff.), 341 ff. (151 ff.), 295 f. (170 ff.), 314 (185 and note), 319 (193 f.), 336 (196 f.), 318 f. (210 n.), 340 f. (213), 317 (218 f.), 297 ff. (220 ff.), 303 ff. (229 ff.), 330 (390 f.), 335 f. (536), 51 ff. (579 ff.), 309 (last page).
Discourses in Various Spirits, Vol. VIII. 371 f. (235 ff.), 372 ff. (300 ff.).
Christian Discourses, Vol. X. 376 ff. (241 ff.), 394 ff. (277 ff.).
Lilies of the Field, Vol. XI. 419 ff. (15 ff.).
Two Minor Treatises, Vol. XI. 42 ff. (71 f.), 424 f. (83), 423 (111).
The Sickness unto Death, Vol. XI. 124 f. (209), 126 f. (209 f.).
Training in Christianity, Vol. VII. 434 (17), 435 f. (87 f.), 433 (165 f.), 39 ff. (197 ff.), 430 ff. (250 ff.).
For Self Examination, Vol. XII. 475 (342), 475 ff. (416 f.), 478 ff. (423).
Judge for Yourself, Vol. XII. 480 ff. (447 ff.), 471 ff. (552).
The Point of View, Vol. XIII. 173 (561), 248 (577), 441 f. (595 ff.), 47 (604 f.), 459 (606), 115 (607), 49 f. (607 f.), 263 f. (609 f.), 444 f. (621 f.).
About My Work as an Author, Vol. XIII. 440 (528, 535).
Articles in 'The Fatherland', Vol. XIV. 572 (28), 572 (36), 573 (44), 573 (45), 574 f. (69 f.), 576 (78).
This Must Be Said, Vol. XIV. 569 (83).
The *Instant*, Vol. XIV. 577 (103), 577 f. (135), 578 (144), 578 f. (177 f.), 579 (239 f.), 452 (256 ff.), 580 (283), 230 (369 f.), 581 (371 f.).

APPENDIX III

LIST OF DATES

1813, May 5. S. K. born in Copenhagen.
June 3. Baptized in the Church of the Holy Ghost.
1821. Entered the School of Civic Virtue.
1823, Jan. 23. Regina Olsen born.
1828, Apr. 20. S. K. confirmed in the Church of Our Lady.
1830, Oct. 30. Matriculated in the University.
Nov. 1. Enrolled in the Royal Life Guards.
4. Discharged as physically unfit.
1831, Apr. 25/7. Takes 1st and 2nd part of the 'Second Examination'.
1837, May (between 8 and 16). Visit to the Rørdams' where he sees Regina for the first time.
1837/8. Teaches Latin in the School of Civic Virtue.
1838, Apr. 22. Regina confirmed.
May 19, 10:30 a.m. Entry: 'An indescribable joy'.
Aug. 8/9. His father died.
14. His father buried in the Assistants' Cemetery.
Sept. 7. Pub. of *From the Manuscripts of One Still Living*.
1840, June 2. Applies for his examination in theology.
July 3. Takes his examination.
19–Aug. 6. Tour in Jutland.
Sept. 8/10. Woos Regina and becomes engaged.
Nov. 17. Enters the Pastoral Seminary.
1841, July 16. His dissertation on 'The Concept of Irony' accepted by the Faculty for the Master's degree.
Aug. 11 (*circa*). Sends back the ring to Regina.
Sept. 16. His dissertation printed.
29. Defence of his thesis.
Oct. 11. Final breach with Regina.
25–Mar. 6. Visit to Berlin.
1843, Feb. 20. Pub. of *Either/Or*.
Apr. 16. At evensong at Easter Regina nods.
May 16. Pub. of *Two Edifying Discourses*.
May?–June? Short visit to Berlin.
Oct. 16. Pub. of *Repetition*, *Fear and Trembling*, and *Three Edifying Discourses*.
Dec. 6. Pub. of *Four Edifying Discourses*.
1844, Mar. 5. Pub. of *Two Edifying Discourses*.
June 8. Pub. of *Three Edifying Discourses*.
13. Pub. of *Philosophical Scraps*.
17. Pub. of *The Concept of Dread*, *Prefaces*.
Aug. 31. Pub. of *Four Edifying Discourses*.
Oct. 16. Moves from Nørregade to the house on the Nytorv.

1845, Apr. 29. Pub. of *Three Discourses on Imagined Occasions.*
30. Pub. of *Stages on Life's Road.*
May 13–24. Visit to Berlin.
Dec. 20. Criticism in *Gæa* of 'Guilty?/Not Guilty?'
27. S. K.'s reply in *The Fatherland.*
29. P. L. Møller's reply in *The Fatherland.*
1846, Jan. 2. First article against S. K. in *The Corsair.*
10. S. K.'s reply in *The Fatherland.*
Feb. 27. Pub. of *The Concluding Unscientific Postscript.*
Mar. 9. S. K. begins his 'Report' in the 1st NB Journal.
Mar. 30. Pub. of *A Literary Review.*
May 2–16. Visit to Berlin.
July 12. Buys Magister Adler's books.
Oct. 2. Goldschmidt retires from *The Corsair.*
1846/7. *The Book on Adler* written.
1847, Mar. 13. Pub. of *Edifying Discourses in Various Spirits.*
Sept. 29. Pub. of *The Works of Love.*
Nov. 3. Regina married to Schlegel.
Dec. 23. Goldschmidt begins publication of *North and South.*
24. S. K. sells his house on the Nytorv.
1848, Jan. 20. Death of King Christian VIII.
Apr. 19. Entry: 'My whole nature is changed!'
26. Pub. of *Christian Discourses.*
Mar./Apr. War with Germany and constitutional revolution.
July 24/7. Pub. of *A Crisis and the Crisis in the Life of an Actress.*
1848/9. *The Point of View for My Work as an Author* written.
1849, May 14. Pub. of Second Edition of *Either/Or, The Lilies of the Field.*
19. Pub. of *Two Minor Ethico-Religious Treatises.*
June 25/6. Councillor Olsen died and S. K. decided to publish *The Sickness unto Death.*
July 30. Pub. of *The Sickness unto Death.*
Nov. 13. Pub. of *The High Priest—The Publican,* &c.
19. S. K. writes to Regina through Schlegel.
1850, Apr. 30. Moves to chambers in Nørregade.
Sept. 27. Pub. of *Training in Christianity.*
Dec. 20. Pub. of *An Edifying Discourse.*
1851, Aug. 7. Pub. of *About my Work as an Author* and *Two Discourses at the Communion.*
Sept. 10. Pub. of *For Self-Examination.*
1851/2. *Judge for Yourself* written.
1854, Jan. 30. Bishop Mynster died.
Feb. Article against Martensen written.
Dec. 18. Article against Martensen pub. in *The Fatherland.*
1855, Jan.–May. Polemic in *The Fatherland.*
May–Sept. The 9 numbers of the *Instant* issued.
Oct. 2. S. K. taken to the hospital.
Nov. 4, 11. His death and burial.

APPENDIX IV

SYNOPSIS OF KIERKEGAARD'S WORKS

1. FROM THE PAPERS OF ONE STILL LIVING.
   Published *against his will* by S. Kierkegaard. Sept. 7, 1838.
   About Andersen as a Novelist, with constant reference to his last work, *Only a Fiddler*.
2. THE CONCEPT OF IRONY with constant reference to Socrates. By S. A. Kierkegaard. Sept. 16, 1841. Dissertation for the Master's Degree.
3. EITHER/OR, A Fragment of Life. By Victor Eremita. Feb. 20, 1843.
   Vol. 1 containing the papers of 'A' (the aesthetical stadium). *Diapsalmata—ad se ipsum*; the unreflective erotic stages or the musical-erotic (1st stage illustrated by the Page in *Figaro*, the 2nd by Papageno in *The Magic Flute*, the 3rd by Don Juan in Mozart's opera); the reflection of classical tragedy in modern tragedy; Shadow Pictures (Marie Beaumarchais, Donna Elvira, Marguerite); The Unhappiest Man; *The First Love*, by Scribe; Rotation of Crops, an essay in social sagacity; The Diary of the Seducer.
   Vol. 2, containing the papers of 'B' (the ethical stage). Judge William's letters to his 'young friend' (i.e. 'A') on The Aesthetical Value of Marriage, and on The Equilibrium between the Aesthetical and the Ethical in the Composition of Personality. Ultimatum: sermon by a country parson on 'The edification in the thought that before God we are always in the wrong'.
4. JOHANNES CLIMACUS or DE OMNIBUS DUBITANDUM EST. 1842/3. (Not completed.)
5. TWO EDIFYING DISCOURSES. By S. Kierkegaard. May 16, 1843.
   (1) Faith's Expectation. (2) Every good gift, &c. is from above. Jas. 1: 17.
6. REPETITION. An essay in experimental psychology. By Constantine Constantius. Oct. 16, 1843. (The first 48 pages describe humorously the author's futile attempt to accomplish 'repetition' in an aesthetical sense. The remainder of the book deals with 'repetition' as a religious category and a young man's struggle to attain it.)
7. FEAR AND TREMBLING. Oct. 16, 1843. A dialectical lyric. By Johannes de silentio. Oct. 16, 1843. Preface. Prelude. (Four conceptions of Abraham's trial.) Eulogy of Abraham. Problemata: I. Is there such a thing as a teleological suspension of the ethical? II. Is there an absolute duty to God? Was Abraham ethically justified in concealing his intention from Sarah, from Eliezer, and from Isaac? Agnes and the merman. Epilogue.
8. THREE EDIFYING DISCOURSES. By S. Kierkegaard. Oct. 16, 1843.
   (1) Love covereth a multitude of sins. 1 Pet. 4 : 8. (2) The same theme. (3) Strengthened in the inward man. Eph. 3 : 13 ff.
9. FOUR EDIFYING DISCOURSES. By S. Kierkegaard. Dec. 6, 1843.
   (1) The Lord gave, the Lord hath taken away, &c. Job 1 : 21 f. (2) Every good gift, &c. Jas. 1 : 17. (3) The same theme. (4) To win one's soul in patience. Lk. 21 : 19.
10. TWO EDIFYING DISCOURSES. By S. Kierkegaard. March 5, 1844.

(1) To preserve one's soul in patience. Lk. 21 : 19. (2) Sunday after Christmas. Patience in expectation. Lk. 2 : 33–40.

11. THREE EDIFYING DISCOURSES. By S. Kierkegaard. June 8, 1844.
(1) Remember now thy Creator in the days of thy youth. Eccl. 12 : 1. (2) Expectation of an eternal blessedness. 2 Cor. 4 : 17 f. (3) 'He must increase, I must decrease.' Jn. 3 : 30.

12. PHILOSOPHICAL SCRAPS or A Scrap of Philosophy. By Johannes Climacus. Published by S. Kierkegaard. June 13, 1844. Is an historical point of departure possible for an eternal consciousness? How can such a thing have more than historical interest? Is it possible to base an eternal blessedness upon historical knowledge?

Proposition: The question is asked in ignorance by one who does not even know what can have prompted him to ask such a question.

Chapter I. A Thought-Project. (A) A Socratic Question: How far does the truth admit of being learned? (B) In case the Instant in Time has decisive significance: (*a*) The antecedent condition; (*b*) The teacher; (*c*) The disciple.

Chapter II. God as Teacher and Saviour (an imaginative essay).

Chapter III. The Absolute Paradox (a metaphysical crotchet). Supplement: Offence at the Paradox (an acoustical illusion).

Chapter IV. The Case of the Contemporary Disciple.

Interlude: Is the past more necessary than the future? When the past becomes actual, does it thereby become more necessary than it was?

Supplement: The application.

Chapter V. The Disciple at Second Hand.

13. THE CONCEPT OF DREAD. A simple deliberation on psychological lines in the direction of the dogmatic problem of original sin. By Vigilius Haufniensis. June 17, 1844.

Introduction: In what sense is the subject of this deliberation a problem of interest for psychology? And in what sense, after being a problem of interest for psychology, does it point precisely to dogmatics?

Chapter I. *Dread as the Presupposition of Original Sin.*

Chapter II. *Dread as Original Sin in Progressive Experience.*

Chapter III. *Dread as the Consequence of that Sin which consists in the default of the Consciousness of Sin.* (1) Due to the default of spirit. (2) Dialectically qualified with reference to fate. (3) With reference to guilt.

Chapter IV. *Sin's Dread* or *Dread as the Consequence of Sin in the Individual.* (1) Dread of the evil. (2) Dread of the good (daimonia). (*a*) Freedom lost somatic-psychically. (*b*) Freedom lost pneumatically.

Chapter V. *Dread as a means of Salvation in conjunction with Faith.*

14. PREFACES. Light reading for particular classes according to season and circumstance. By Nicholas Notabene. June 17, 1844.

Preface: About prefaces in general, and how it comes about that the author can write only a preface. I. The pleasure of having written a book . . . such as the age demands, and which is suitable as a gift. II. The reading public—especially in Denmark—and the reviewers. III. Books as New Year's presents. IV. Professor Heiberg: *littérateur*, philosopher, theologian, and astronomer. V. But how much better a speech before an applauding assembly—especially our Society for Total Abstinence. VI. Books for the cultured, e.g. Bishop Mynster's 'Sermons'. Christianity properly addresses itself to the cultured classes. VII. About writing a System/and about real writing, for a real reader. VIII. About the publication of a philosophical review: The difficulty in general; The purpose of this review; My expectation.

15. FOUR EDIFYING DISCOURSES. By S. Kierkegaard. Aug. 31, 1844. (1) To have need of God is man's highest perfection. (2) The thorn in the flesh. 2 Cor. 12 : 7. (3) Against cowardice. 2 Tim. 1 : 7. (4) The true man of prayer strives in prayer and prevails—in that God prevails.

(Note. The EIGHTEEN EDIFYING DISCOURSES were soon after published in one volume.)

16. THREE DISCOURSES ON IMAGINED OCCASIONS. By S. Kierkegaard. April 29, 1845. (1) On the occasion of a confession. (2) On the occasion of a wedding. (3) Beside a grave.

17. STAGES ON LIFE'S ROAD. Studies by various writers, collected, prepared for the press and edited by Hilarius Bookbinder. April 30, 1845. Preface: *Lectori benevolo!*

'In Vino Veritas.' A reminiscence related subsequently by William Afham (*af ham* means *by him*). Prefatory note. Preparation of the banquet. Speeches by 'the young man', by Constantine Constantius, Victor Eremita, the Ladies' Tailor, and John the Seducer. Termination of the banquet. Various remarks about marriage in reply to objections, by a married man (i.e. Judge William).

'Guilty?'/'Not Guilty?' A story of suffering. Psychological experiment by Frater Taciturnus.

Part I. Quidam's Diary.

Part II. Communication to the reader.

1. What is unfortunate love? and what is its particular character in the experiment? 2. Misunderstanding as a tragic and comi-tragic principle employed in the experiment. 3. The tragic tends more to the historical than does the comic. 4. How the attainment of repentance is dialectically hindered. Supplement: A side-glance at Shakespeare's *Hamlet*. 5. Heroes. Suffering. The aim of tragedy. Supplement: Self-induced suffering—self-torture. 6. To repent of nothing is the highest wisdom. The forgiveness of sin. A word in conclusion.

18. CONCLUDING UNSCIENTIFIC POSTSCRIPT TO THE PHILOSOPHICAL SCRAPS. A mimic-pathetic-dialectic composition, an existential contribution. By Johannes Climacus. Published by S. Kierkegaard. Feb. 27, 1846.

Part First: The Objective Problem of the Truth of Christianity.

Chapter I. The Historical point of View. (1) The Holy Scriptures. (2) The Church. (3) The witness of the centuries.

Chapter II. The Speculative Point of View.

Part Second: The Subjective Problem: the relationship of the subject to the truth of Christianity, or the problem of becoming a Christian.

SECTION ONE: Something about Lessing

Chapter I. An Expression of Gratitude to Lessing.

Chapter II. Some theses possibly or actually attributable to Lessing.

1. The subjective existing thinker is attentive to the dialectic of communication.
2. The existing subjective thinker is as negative as he is positive in his existential relation to the truth, has just as much the sense of the comic as he has essential pathos, and is constantly in the process of becoming, i.e. is engaged in an endeavour.
3. Lessing has said that contingent historical truths can never constitute proof of eternal truths of the reason, and that the transition wherewith one would base an eternal blessedness upon historical testimony is a leap.
4. Lessing has said that if God held in his right hand the whole truth, and in his left the constant endeavour after truth, he would choose the latter. (*a*) A logical system is possible. (*b*) A system of existence is impossible.

Section Two: The Subjective Problem, or how the subjectivity of the individual must be qualified in order that the problem may present itself to him

Chapter I. About Becoming Subjective.

Chapter II. The Subjective Truth, Inwardness. Truth is Subjectivity.

Supplement: Reference to a contemporary movement in Danish literature.

Chapter III. The Real, i.e. the Ethical Subjectivity. The subjective thinker.

1. What it means to exist; actuality.
2. Possibility as higher than actuality; actuality as higher than possibility; the poetic and intellectual ideality; the ethical ideality.
3. The simultaneity of the individual factors entering into the subjectivity of the individual; this simultaneity viewed in opposition to the succession posited in the speculative process.
4. The subjective thinker; his task; his form, i.e. his style.

Chapter IV. The Problem of the *Scraps*: How can an eternal blessedness be based on historical knowledge?

Section I. By way of orientation in the plan of the *Scraps*.

1. That the point of departure is taken in paganism, and why.
2. The importance of a preliminary agreement with respect to what Christianity is, before there can be any question of mediation between Christianity and Speculation. The absence of such an agreement favours mediation, at the same time that it renders mediation illusory. The presence of such an agreement makes mediation impossible.
3. The problem of the *Scraps* as a problem introductory, not to Christianity, but to becoming a Christian.

Section II. The problem itself.

The eternal blessedness of the individual is decided in time, by means of a relationship to something historical, whose historical nature is so constituted as to include in its composition that which according to its nature cannot become historical, and so must become such by virtue of the absurd.

A. The Pathetic Aspect of the Problem.

1. The *initial* expression for existential pathos: the absolute direction (respect) towards the absolute *telos* expressed in action through the transformation of existence.—Aesthetic pathos.—The deceptiveness of mediation.—Medieval monasticism.—Simultaneously to relate oneself absolutely to the absolute *telos* and relatively to relative ends.
2. The essential expression for existential pathos: Suffering. Fortune and misfortune as principles for an aesthetic view of life, contrasted with suffering as the principle for a religious view of life (illustrated by reference to the religious address). The reality of the suffering (humour). The reality of the suffering in the last analysis as the sign that an existing individual is related to an eternal blessedness.—The illusion of the religious life.—Trial.—The ground and significance of suffering in the first instance as involved in dying away from immediacy while still remaining in the finite.—An edifying digression.—Humour as the incognito of religiousness.
3. The *decisive* expression for existential pathos: Guilt. That the inquiry goes backward instead of forward.—The eternal remembrance of one's guilt is the highest expression for the relation between a consciousness of guilt and an eternal blessedness.—Lower expressions for the consciousness of guilt and corresponding forms of atonement.—Self-imposed penance.—Humour.—The religion of secret inwardness.

Remarks intermediate to A and B.

B. The Dialectic Aspect of the Problem.

1. The dialectical contradiction, which constitutes the breach of continuity: to expect an eternal blessedness in time through a relationship to something else in time.
2. The dialectical contradiction that an eternal blessedness is based on a relationship to something historical.
3. The dialectical contradiction that the historical fact in question is not a simple historical fact, but is constituted by that which can become historical only against its nature, and so by virtue of the absurd.

Supplement to B. The retro-active effect of the dialectical upon the pathetic, leading to an intensification of the pathos; the factors simultaneously present in this pathos.

1. The consciousness of sin.
2. The possibility of offence.
3. The smart of sympathy.

Chapter V. Conclusion.

Supplement: An Understanding with the Reader.

19. THE BOOK ON ADLER. (Written and twice rewritten in 1846/7, but not published. Vol. VII[1] of the *Papers*.)

Introduction.

Chapter I. The Historical Situation.

Magister Adler's collision with the established order as a teacher in the State

Church; the State Church entirely justified in deposing him; about the particular individual in particular and what may be required of him.

Chapter II. The so-called factor of revelation considered in terms of the whole modern development.

Chapter III. Adler's own abandonment of his essential standpoint, or that he does not understand himself, does not himself believe that he experienced a revelation. This is illuminated *directly-indirectly* by a little brochure which contains the documents of the case of his deposition, and *indirectly* by his four last books.

Recapitulation.

Chapter IV. A Psychological Interpretation of Adler as a phenomenon and as a satire upon the Hegelian philosophy and the present age.

1. Psychological exposition.
2. The catastrophe of Mag. Adler's life.
3. Mag. Adler's merit.
4. The fundamental fault in Mag. Adler which accounts for the incongruity of his position.
5. Mag. Adler as an epigram upon Christendom of to-day.

20. A LITERARY REVIEW. By S. Kierkegaard. March 30, 1846. (A review of an anonymous novel, 'Two Ages'; but the latter part is a clear exposition of S. K.'s social philosophy.)

21. EDIFYING DISCOURSES IN VARIOUS SPIRITS. By S. Kierkegaard. March 13, 1847.

Part First. An Occasional Discourse (dedicated to 'that individual'). Purity of heart is to will one thing.

Part Second. What is to be learnt from the lilies of the field and the birds of the air? (Three discourses on Mt. 6 : 24 ff.)

Part Third. The Gospel of Sufferings. Christian Discourses.

1. The joyfulness of following Christ. Lk. 14 : 27.
2. But how can the burden be light when the suffering is heavy? Mt. 11 : 30.
3. The joyfulness of the thought that the school of suffering educates for eternity.
4. The joyfulness of the thought that man in relation to God always is guilty when he suffers.
5. The joyfulness of the thought that it is not the way which is straight, but the straightening itself is the way.
6. The joyfulness of the thought that even when temporal sufferings press heaviest, the blessedness of eternity outweighs them.
7. The joyfulness of the thought that courage enables the sufferer to overcome the world, and that there is a victory which transforms insult into honour and defeat into triumph.

22. THE WORKS OF LOVE. By S. Kierkegaard. Sept. 29, 1847.

Some Christian Reflections in the form of Discourses.

I. Love's hidden life and the discovery of it by its fruits.

II. (A) Thou *shalt* love. (B) Thou shalt love thy *neighbour*. (C) *Thou* shalt love thy neighbour.

III. (A) Love is the fulfilment of the Law. Rom. 13 : 10.
(B) Love is a matter of conscience. 1 Tim. 1 : 5.

IV. Our duty to love the men we see. 1 Jn. 4 : 20.
V. Our duty to remain in love's debt to one another. Rom. 8 : 8.

Second Part.

I. Love edifieth. 1 Cor. 8 : 1.
II. Love believeth all things—and yet is never deceived. 1 Cor. 13 : 7.
III. Love hopeth all things—and yet is never put to shame. 1 Cor. 13 : 7.
IV. Love seeketh not her own. 1 Cor. 13 : 5.
V. Love covereth a multitude of sins. 1 Pet. 4 : 8.
VI. Love abideth. 1 Cor. 13 : 13.
VII. Compassion is a work of love, even if it can give nothing and is unable to do anything.
VIII. The victory of forgiveness through love, which wins the defeated.
IX. It is a work of love to remember the deceased.
X. It is a work of love to sing the praise of love.

23. THE DIALECTIC OF ETHICAL AND ETHICO-RELIGIOUS COMMUNICATION 1847. (Notes for a book which was never finished. It occupies 47 pages in the *Papers*, viii, B 79–89.)

24. CHRISTIAN DISCOURSES. By S. Kierkegaard. April 26, 1848.

Part I. *The Anxieties of the Heathen.*

1. The anxiety of poverty. Mt. 6 : 31 f.
2. The anxiety of abundance. Mt. 6 : 31 f.
3. The anxiety of lowliness. Mt. 6 : 25, 32.
4. The anxiety of high place. Mt. 6 : 25, 32.
5. The anxiety of pride. Mt. 6 : 27.
6. The anxiety of self-torture. Mt. 6 : 32, 34.
7. The anxiety of irresolution, fickleness, disconsolateness. Mt. 6 : 24, 32.

Part II. *Exultant notes in the Conflict of Suffering.*

1. The joyfulness of the thought that a man suffers but once and triumphs eternally.
2. The joyfulness of the thought that affliction does not destroy hope but increases it.
3. The joyfulness of the thought that the poorer you become the more you can make others rich.
4. The joyfulness of the thought that the weaker you become so much the stronger does God become in you.
5. The joyfulness of the thought that what you lose temporally you gain eternally.
6. The joyfulness of the thought that when I 'gain all' I lose nothing at all.
7. The joyfulness of the thought that adversity (*Modgang*) is success (*Medgang*).

Part III. *Thoughts which Wound from Behind—for Edification.*

Christian Addresses. Motto on the back of the title-page:

The Christian cause needs no *defence*—it is not really served by any *defence*; it is aggressive; to defend it is of all perversities the most indefensible, the most *preposterous*, and the most dangerous—unconsciously it is the insidious betrayal. The Christian attitude is aggressive, within Christendom, as a matter of course, it assails from behind.

1. Watch thy foot when thou goest to the house of the Lord. Eccl. 5 : 1.
2. 'Behold, we have left all and followed thee; what shall we have therefore?' (Mt. 19 : 27)—and what shall *we* have?
3. All things must work together for our good—'when' we love God.
4. The resurrection of the dead is at hand, of the just—and of the unjust.
5. Our salvation is now nearer—than when we first believed.
6. It is blessed indeed—to suffer derision in a good cause.
7. He is believed on in the world.

Part IV. *Discourses at the Communion on Fridays. Christian Discourses.*

1. Lk. 22 : 15. 'I have heartily desired to eat this Passover with you.'
2. Mt. 11 : 28. 'Come unto me, all ye that labour and are heavy laden.'
3. Jn. 10 : 27. 'My sheep hear my voice, and I know them, and they follow me.'
4. 1 Cor. 11 : 23. 'The Lord Jesus in the night in which he was betrayed.'
5. 2 Tim. 2 : 12 f. 'If we deny him, he will also deny us.'
6. 1 Jn. 3 : 20. 'If our heart condemn us, God is greater than our heart.
7. Lk. 24 : 51. 'And it came to pass, while he blessed them he was parted from them.'

25. THE CRISIS AND A CRISIS IN THE LIFE OF AN ACTRESS. Signed: *Inter et inter.*
(S. K.'s last aesthetical work. In 1848, July 24–7, it appeared in four parts as *feuilleton* in 'The Fatherland'. In 1855, after S. K.'s death, it was published as a whole, Prof. Heiberg being editor, whose wife is this actress.)

26. THE LILIES OF THE FIELD AND THE BIRDS OF THE AIR. Three Godly Discourses. By S. Kierkegaard. May 14, 1849. (Same day as the 2nd ed. of *E/O*. Mt. 6 : 24–34.)
1. 'Behold the birds of the air; consider the lilies of the field.'
2. 'No man can serve two masters.'
3. 'Behold the birds of the air; they sow not neither do they reap.'

27. TWO MINOR ETHICO-RELIGIOUS TREATISES. By H. H. May 19, 1849.
I. Has a man a right to let himself be put to death for the truth?
II. About the difference between a genius and an Apostle.

28. THE SICKNESS UNTO DEATH. A Christian psychological exposition for edification and awakening. By Anti-Climacus. Edited by S. Kierkegaard. July 30, 1849.—Preface.—Introduction.

First Section: *The Sickness unto Death is Despair.*

I. That Despair is the Sickness unto Death.
A. Despair is a sickness in the spirit, the self—and so it can be a triple thing: despair at not being conscious of having a self; despair at not willing to be one's self; despair at willing to be one's self.
B. The possibility and the actuality of despair.
C. Despair is 'the sickness unto death'.
II. The universal presence of this sickness (despair).
III. The forms of this sickness (despair).
A. Despair so regarded as to ignore the consideration whether it is conscious or not, so that only the factors of the synthesis need to be considered.

1. Despair viewed under the aspects: finiteness/infinity.
   (*a*) Infinity's despair is due to a lack of finitude.
   (*b*) Finitude's despair is due to a lack of infinitude.
2. Despair viewed under the aspects: possibility/necessity.
   (*a*) Possibility's despair is due to a lack of necessity.
   (*b*) Necessity's despair is due to a lack of possibility.

B. Despair viewed under the aspect: consciousness.
1. The despair which is ignorant of the fact that it is despair, or the despairing ignorance of the fact of having a self and an eternal self.
2. The despair which is conscious of being despair, which therefore is conscious of having a self in which indeed there is something eternal, and now is either in despair at not willing to be one's self, or in despair at willing to be one's self.
   (*a*) In despair at not willing to be one's self. The despair of weakness.
      1. Despair about the earthly or about something earthly.
      2. Despair about the eternal or about one's self.
   (*b*) In despair at willing to be one's self, Defiance.

Second Section: Despair is Sin.

A. Despair is Sin.

Chapter I. Gradations of consciousness of self (the determinant: Before God).

Supplement: That the definition of sin has in it the possibility of the offence; a general remark about offence.

Chapter II. The Socratic Definition of Sin.

Chapter III. That Sin is not a Negation but a Position.

Supplement to A: But would not sin then in a certain sense be a great rarity? (The Moral.)

B. Sin's Continuation.
1. The sin of despairing over one's sin.
2. The sin of despairing of the sinner's forgiveness (offence).
3. The sin of giving up Christianity *modo ponendo*, of declaring it untruth.

29. 'THE HIGH PRIEST'—'THE PUBLICAN'—'THE WOMAN THAT WAS A SINNER.' Three discourses at the Communion on Fridays. By S. Kierkegaard. Nov. 13, 1849.

I. Heb. 4 : 15. II. Lk. 18 : 13. III. Lk. 7 : 47.

30. THE POINT OF VIEW FOR MY WORK AS AN AUTHOR. A Direct communication. Report to History. By S. Kierkegaard. Written in 1848. Published in 1859.

Part I. The Ambiguity or Duplicity in the whole Literary Production:
A. As to whether the Author is an Aesthetical or a Religious Author.
B. Evidence that the Author is and was a Religious Author.

Part II. The Whole Literary Production Construed, and from this point of view, that the Author is a Religious Author.

Chapter I.

A. *The Aesthetical Production.* Why the beginning was made with aesthetical production, or what this production signifies, integrally understood.

1. That 'Christendom' is a prodigious illusion of the senses.
2. That if real success is to attend the effort to bring a man to a definite position, one must first of all take pains to find him there where *he* is, and begin there.
3. The illusion that religion and Christianity are something one first has recourse to when one becomes old.
4. That even if a man will not follow where one endeavours to lead him, one thing it is still possible to do for him—compel him to take notice.
5. That the whole aesthetical productivity viewed as an integral part of the whole is a deceit, yet understood in a particular sense.

B. 'Concluding Postscript.'
C. The Religious Productivity.
Conclusion.

Chapter II. The Difference in my Personal Mode of Existence Corresponding to the essential difference of my productivity.
A. The personal mode of existence in relation to the aesthetical productivity.
B. The personal mode of existence in relation to the religious productivity.

Chapter III. The Share Governance had in my Writings.
Epilogue.

31. 'THE INDIVIDUAL.' Two 'notes' concerning my Work as an Author. By S. Kierkegaard. Published posthumously with the above in 1859. Preface.
1. About the Dedication to 'that Individual'. (Dated 1846.)
2. A Word about the Relation of my Literary Activity to 'the Individual'. (The first draft written in 1847.)
Postscript. (Dated 1849.)
A Postscript to the 'Two Notes'. (Dated 1855.)

32. ARMED NEUTRALITY or My Position as a Christian Author in 'Christendom'. (Notes for a book of that name written in 1849.)

33. ABOUT MY WORK AS AN AUTHOR. By S. Kierkegaard. (1849) 1851, before Aug. 7.

34. TRAINING IN CHRISTIANITY by Anti-Climacus. Edited by S. Kierkegaard. Sept. 27, 1850. *Procul, O procul este profani!* Preface by the Editor, S. K. Invocation.

NO. I

The Invitation: 'Come unto me, all ye that labour and are heavy laden, and I will give you rest.' For revival and increase of inwardness. Three interpretations.

I. *Pause.*
(*a*) Who uttered that word of invitation?
(*b*) Can one learn from history to know anything about Christ?
(*c*) Can one prove from history that Christ was God?
(*d*) Are the consequences of Christ's life more important than his life?
(*e*) A comparison between Christ and a man who in his time suffered at the hands of his contemporaries the same treatment Christ suffered.
(*f*) The misfortune of Christendom.

II. *The Inviter*. A. The first period of his life. B. The second period.

III. *The Invitation and the Inviter.*
IV. *Christianity as the Absolute; Contemporaneousness with Christ.*

The Moral

NO. II

'Blessed is he who is not offended in me.'

A Biblical statement and a Christian definition of concepts. Prelude. The content of this statement in a brief summary.

A. The possibility of offence which has not to do with Christ as Christ (the God-Man) but with him as a mere individual man who comes into collision with the established order.

B. The possibility of essential offence in the direction of loftiness, that an individual man speaks and acts as if he were God, says of himself that he is God, therefore tending towards the definition of God in the composite term God-Man.

C. The possibility of essential offence in the direction of lowliness, that he who gives himself out to be God shows himself to be the lowly, poor, suffering, and finally impotent man.

Conceptual qualifications of 'the offence', i.e. the essential offence.

1. The God-Man is a 'sign'.
2. The form of a servant is unrecognizableness (the incognito).
3. The impossibility of direct communication.
4. The impossibility of direct communication was in Christ the secret of his sufferings.
5. The possibility of the offence lies in the refusal to employ direct communication.
6. To refuse to employ direct communication is to require faith.
7. The object of faith is the God-Man, precisely because the God-Man is the possibility of the offence.

NO. III

Lifted up on high he will draw all men unto himself
(Seven Christian Reflections).

35. AN EDIFYING DISCOURSE. By S. Kierkegaard. Dec. 20, 1850. The woman that was a sinner.

36. TWO DISCOURSES AT THE COMMUNION ON FRIDAYS, by S. Kierkegaard. 1851. Dedicated to 'One unnamed' (i.e. Regina). Preface (new and important).
    1. 'But to whom little is forgiven, the same loveth little.' Lk. 7 : 47.
    2. 'Love covereth a multitude of sins.' 1 Pet. 4 : 7.

37. FOR SELF-EXAMINATION commended to this age. By S. Kierkegaard. Sept. 10, 1851. 'Seek to win men.'
    Preface: Exhortation to read the book aloud.
    1. What is required in order to behold one's self with real blessing in the mirror of the Word? James 1 : 22 ff. 5th Sunday after Easter.
    II. Christ is the Way. Acts 1 : 1–12. Festival of the Ascension.
    III. It is the Spirit that giveth life. Acts 2 : 1–12. Whit-Sunday.

38. JUDGE FOR YOURSELF! For Self-Examination Commended to this Age.

Second Series. Written in 1851/2. Published posthumously 1876. Preface (it is important).

I. *To become Sober.* 1 Pet. 4 : 7. 'Be ye therefore sober.'

II. *Christ as Example, or No Man can Serve Two Masters.*

The Moral. A note dated March 1855.

39. 21 ARTICLES IN THE *FATHERLAND*. By S. Kierkegaard. Dec. 18, 1854–May 26, 1855. (In parentheses are the dates when the several articles were written.)

1. Was Bishop Mynster, a 'witness for the truth', one of the 'genuine witnesses for the truth', is this truth? (Feb., 1854) Dec. 18, 1854.
2. There the case rests! Dec. 30, 1854.
3. A challenge to me from Pastor Paludan-Müller. Jan. 12, 1855.
4. The point at issue with Bishop Martensen. Jan. 29, 1855.
5. Two new witnesses for the truth. Jan. 29, 1855.
6. On the occasion of Bishop Mynster's death. 'Seest thou these great buildings?' (March 31, 1854) March 20, 1855.
7. Is this Christian worship, or is it making a fool of God? (May 1854) March 21, 1855.
8. What has to be done—whether by me or by another. (Whit Monday 1854) March 22, 1855.
9. The religious situation. March 26, 1855.
10. A thesis—just one only. March 28, 1855.
11. 'Salt': for 'Christendom' is—the corruption of Christianity; a 'Christian world' is—apostasy from Christianity. March 30, 1855.
12. What do I want? March 31, 1855.
13. In reference to an *anonymous* proposal to me. April 7, 1855.
14. Would it be right now to 'stop clanging the alarm'? April 11, 1855.
15. Christianity by royal commission/or Christianity without royal commission. April 11, 1855.
16. What a horrible punishment! April 27, 1855.
17. A result. May 10, 1855.
18. A monologue. May 10, 1855.
19. Concerning an absurd assumption of importance in opposition to me and the interpretation of Christianity which I maintain. May 15, 1855.
20. About the new edition of 'Training in Christianity'. May 16, 1855.
21. That Bishop Martensen's silence is: (1) Unpardonable in a Christian sense; (2) Ridiculous; (3) All too shrewd; (4) And in more than one respect despicable. May 26.

40. THIS MUST BE SAID; SO LET IT NOW BE SAID. By S. Kierkegaard. May 16, 1855.

41. THE INSTANT, Numbers 1 to 10. May 24–Oct. 1855.

The Instant, No. 1. May 24, 1855. (1) Prelude (April 20). (2) With regard to 'This must be said'; or how is the decisive thing to be accomplished? (3) Is the State justified—the Christian State!—in making Christianity impossible if that were possible! (4) 'Take an emetic!' (April 2).

The Instant, No. 2. June 4, 1855. (1) To 'my reader'! (April 27). (2) That the task is twofold (May 17). (3) Bodily ease / and concern about an eternal blessedness. (4) The human protects (patronizes) the divine (April). (5) A eulogy upon the human race, or proof that the New Testament is no longer truth. (6) We are all of us Christians. (7) One difficulty about the New Testament. (8) Granted we are Christians, what then is God? (9) Granting that we really are Christians, supposing that, Christianly speaking, it is all right with 'Christendom' and 'a Christian world'—then the New Testament is *eo ipso* no longer a guide for the Christians, cannot be that. (10) What luck we are not all of us parsons! (May 11).

42. WHAT CHRIST'S JUDGEMENT IS UPON OFFICIAL CHRISTIANITY. By S. Kierkegaard. June, 1855.

The Instant, No. 3. June 27, 1855. (1) State/Christianity. (2) Is the State justified, Christianly speaking, in seducing a part of the studious youth? (3) Is the State justified, Christianly speaking, in receiving an oath which not only is not kept but the taking of which is a self-contradiction? (4) Is the State justified, Christianly speaking, in misleading the people, or in misleading their judgement as to what Christianity is? (5) Let the State examine the account, and it will at once be evident that the account is radically wrong. (6) If the State verily wishes to serve Christianity, let it abolish the 1,000 benefices (May 12).

The Instant, No. 4. July 7, 1855. (1) Medical diagnosis. (2) What really is shocking (April 10). (3) Truth and livings (April 13). (4) True Christians / many Christians (April 9). (5) In 'Christendom' all are Christians; where all are Christians the Christianity of the New Testament *eo ipso* no longer exists, indeed is impossible (April). (6) The difficulty of my task (April 18). (7) The official / the personal.

The Instant, No. 5. July 27, 1855. (1) We are all Christians, without once having the vaguest idea what Christianity is (April 29). (2) A genius / a Christian (April 29). (3) The Christianity of the spiritual man / the Christianity of us men (April 19). (4) New Testament Christianity / 'Christendom's' Christianity (May 19). (5) Where all are Christians Christianity *eo ipso* does not exist (May 23). (6) A revolt in defiance / a revolt in hypocrisy—or about the apostasy from Christianity. (7) The taking of an oath—or the official / the personal (May 28). (8) Newfangled religious securities (guarantees) (June 10). (9) Beware of them that walk in long robes. Lk. 20 : 46.

The Instant, No. 6. Aug. 23, 1855. (1) Short and Sharp (May 29). (2) The measure of our apostasy—and therewith again about the peculiar difficulties I have to contend with (May 30). (3) Fear most of all to be in error. (4) That we—'Christendom'—are not in the place where Christ and the New Testament require one to be in order to be a Christian (May 12). (5) What says the Fire-Chief? (July 24). Little remarks (June 26): (*a*) The common sort of Bible interpretation. (*b*) The theatre / the church. (*c*) God / the world.

The Instant, No. 7. Aug. 30, 1855. (1) Why does 'man' love above all things the 'poet'—and why, from a godly point of view, is it precisely the 'poet' that is the most dangerous of all? (2) Fishing for men. (3) What sort of person one calls a Christian (July 3). (4) 'First the kingdom of God'—a kind of short story (July 13). (5) That 'Christendom' from generation to generation is a fellowship of non-Christians; and the formula according to which this comes about (July 25). (6) Confirmation and the marriage ceremony; a Christian comedy or something still worse (July 28). (7) That (especially in Protestantism) the so much lauded Christian education of children in the Christian family is, Christianly speaking, based upon a lie, a sheer lie (Aug. 3). (8) The truth about the parson's significance for society (July 30). (9) About the interest shown in my cause (July 25).

43. GOD'S UNCHANGEABLENESS. A Discourse. By S. Kierkegaard. Aug. 1, 1855 (Dedication to his father bears the above date. It was preached May 18, 1851).

The Instant, No. 8, Sept. 11, 1855. (1) Contemporaneousness; what you do in contemporaneousness is the decisive thing (1853). (2) Man lives but once. (3) An eternity to repent in. (4) What can be remembered eternally? (June 8). (5) A picture of life and a picture from life. (6) The divine righteousness. (7) Tremble—for in a certain sense it is infinitely easy to make a fool of God (June 16).

The Instant, No. 9. Sept. 24, 1855. (1) So thus the case stands. (2) The ideal must be proclaimed—or else Christianity in its deepest foundation is falsified. (3) A dose of disgust with life. (4) Become a prattler—and you shall see that all difficulties vanish (Aug.). (5) The parsons are cannibals, and that in the cruellest way (Aug. 23?). (6) The parson not only proves the truth of Christianity, but he disproves it at the same time (Sept. 8).

The Instant, No. 10. (Not published. Found on his desk when he died.) (1) I call it optical illusion (Aug. 25). (2) 'How can ye believe, ye who receive honour from men?' (July 15). (3) What the echo answers (July 9). (4) The crime of 'Christendom' is comparable to that of wishing to appropriate an inheritance unjustly (Aug. 24). (5) When is 'the Instant'? (May 29). (6) My task (Sept. 1). (7) Little remarks (Aug. 2): The divine worship of the parsons; Parsons / actors; The parson as a screen; Paganism / 'Christendom's' Christianity; A frightful situation; Heartiness / heartlessness; The refinement of meanness; 'This is for the sake of the successor'; Convent beer; The higher wisdom in the idea that there is a predecessor and a successor.

APPENDIX V

SELECTED BIBLIOGRAPHY

BY LEE M. CAPEL

A. DANISH EDITIONS

1 *Søren Kierkegaards Samlede Værker*. 2nd edition, edited by A. B. Drachmann, J. L. Heiberg, and H. O. Lange. Vols. I–XV (vol. XV contains a subject and author index by A. Ibsen, and a terminological dictionary by J. Himmelstrup). Copenhagen: Gyldendalske Boghandel, Nordisk Forlag, 1920–1936.

2 *Søren Kierkegaards Papirer*. 2nd edition, edited by P. A. Heiberg, V. Kuhr, and E. Torsting. Vols. I–XI [3] (in twenty parts individually bound). Copenhagen: Gyldendalske Boghandel, Nordisk Forlag, 1909–1948.

3 *Breve og Aktstykker vedrørende Søren Kierkegaard*. A critical text edition, published by the Søren Kierkegaard Selskabet, edited with a commentary by Niels Thulstrup. Vols. I–II. Copenhagen: Munksgaard, 1953, 1954.

B. ENGLISH TRANSLATIONS

4 *Either / Or. A Fragment of Life*. [1843].* Vol. I translated by David F. Swenson and Lillian Marvin Swenson; vol. II translated by Walter Lowrie. Princeton: Princeton University Press, 1944.

5 *Either / Or. A Fragment of Life*. Translated by David F. and Lillian Marvin Swenson and Walter Lowrie. Translation and notes revised together with a foreword by Howard A. Johnson. Garden City: Doubleday, 1959; Anchor paperback A 181 a-b.

6 *Fear and Trembling. A Dialectical Lyric*. [1843]. Translated by Walter Lowrie. Princeton: Princeton University Press, 1941.

7 *The Sickness unto Death*. [1849]. Translated by Walter Lowrie. Princeton: Princeton University Press, 1941.

8 *Fear and Trembling & The Sickness unto Death*. Translated by Walter Lowrie. Translation revised by Howard A. Johnson. Garden City: Doubleday, 1954; Anchor paperback A 30.

9 *Repetition. An Essay in Experimental Psychology*. [1843]. Translated by Walter Lowrie. Princeton: Princeton University Press, 1941.

* The year in brackets after the first appearance of a title indicates the original publication date.

10 *Edifying Discourses.* [1843–1844]. Translated by David F. and Lillian Marvin Swenson. Vols. I–IV. Minneapolis: Augsburg Publishing House, 1948.

11 *Edifying Discourses. A Selection.* Edited with an introduction by Paul L. Holmer. Translated by David F. and Lillian Marvin Swenson. New York: Harper & Brothers, 1958; Torchbook paperback TB 32.

12 *Philosophical Fragments Or A Fragment of Philosophy.* [1844]. Translated by David F. Swenson. Published for the American Scandinavian Foundation. Princeton: Princeton University Press, 1941.

13 *Philosophical Fragments.* Translated by David F. Swenson; with an introduction and commentary by Niels Thulstrup, translated by Howard Hong. Princeton: Princeton University Press, *forthcoming.*

14 *The Concept of Dread.* [1844]. Translated by Walter Lowrie. Princeton: Princeton University Press, 1944. 2nd edition, translation revised by Howard A. Johnson, 1957.

15 *Stages On Life's Way.* [1845]. Translated by Walter Lowrie. Princeton: Princeton University Press, 1940.

16 *Thoughts On Crucial Situations in Human Life.* Three discourses on imagined occasions. [1845]. Translated by David F. Swenson, edited by Lillian Marvin Swenson. Minneapolis: Augsburg Publishing House, 1941.

17 *Concluding Unscientific Postscript to the Philosophical Fragments.* [1846]. Translated by David F. Swenson and Walter Lowrie. Published for the American Scandinavian Foundation. Princeton: Princeton University Press, 1941.

18 *The Present Age & Two Ethico-Religious Treatises.* [1846 & 1859]. Translated by Alexander Dru and Walter Lowrie. London: Oxford University Press, 1940.

19 *Works of Love.* [1847]. Translated by David F. and Lillian Marvin Swenson. Princeton: Princeton University Press, 1946.

20 *Works of Love.* Translated with an introduction and notes by Edna and Howard Hong. New York: Harper & Brothers, 1962.

21 *Purity of Heart.* [1847].* Translated by Douglas V. Steere. New York: Harper & Brothers, 1938; revised edition, 1948; Torchbook paperback TB 4, 1956.

22 *Purify Your Hearts!* Translated by A. S. Aldworth and W. S. Ferrie. London: C. W. Daniel Co., 1937.

* Nos. 21–25 are various translations of the three parts of *Edifying Discourses in Various Spirits.* [1847]. Unfortunately, the three parts of this work have never been restored to their original unity in one volume.

23 *Consider the Lilies*. Translated by A. S. Aldworth and W. S. Ferrie. London: C. W. Daniel Co., 1940.

24 *The Gospel of Suffering & The Lilies of the Field*. Translated by David F. and Lillian Marvin Swenson. Minneapolis: Augsburg Publishing House, 1948.

25 *Gospel of Sufferings*. Translated by A. S. Aldworth and W. S. Ferrie. London: J. Clarke, 1955.

26 *Christian Discourses*. [1948]. Translated by Walter Lowrie. This volume also contains: *The Lilies of the Field and the Birds of the Air* [1849], and *'The High Priest'—'The Publican'—'The Woman that was a Sinner'* [1849]. New York: Oxford University Press, 1939; Galaxy paperback 49.

27 *Training in Christianity*. [1850]. Translated by Walter Lowrie. This volume also contains: *An Edifying Discourse* [1850]. New York: Oxford University Press, 1941.

28 *For Self-Examination & Judge for Yourselves!* [1851 & 1876]. Translated by Edna and Howard Hong. Minneapolis: Augsburg Publishing House, 1940.

29 *For Self-Examination & Judge for Yourselves!* Translated by Walter Lowrie. This volume also contains: *Two Discourses at the Communion on Fridays* [1851], and *The Unchangeableness of God* [1855]. New York: Oxford University Press, 1941.

30 *Attack upon "Christendom."* [1854–1855]. Translated by Walter Lowrie. Princeton: Princeton University Press, 1944; Boston: Beacon Press paperback, 1956.

31 *The Point of View for My Work as an Author*. [1859]. Translated by Walter Lowrie. This volume also contains: *'The Individual,' Two 'Notes' concerning My Work as an Author* [1859], and *On My Work as an Author* [1851]. New York: Oxford University Press, 1939; newly edited with a Preface by Benjamin Nelson, Harper & Brothers, 1962; Torchbook paperback TB 88.

32 *On Authority and Revelation: The Book on Adler;* or a cycle of ethico-religious essays.* Translated with an introduction and notes by Walter Lowrie. Princeton: Princeton University Press, 1955.

33 *Johannes Climacus, or De Omnibus Dubitandum Est.** Translated with an assessment by T. H. Croxall. Stanford: Stanford University Press, 1958.

34 *The Concept of Irony*. [1841]. Translated with an introduction and notes by Lee M. Capel. New York: Harper & Brothers, *forthcoming*.

* Nos. 32 and 33 were never completed for publication by Kierkegaard; they have been translated into English because they contain his views on two important themes. The drafts and manuscripts of these works were published in the Danish edition of the collected papers (cf. No. 2 above).

SELECTIONS AND ANTHOLOGIES

35 *The Journals of Kierkegaard*. Edited and translated by Alexander Dru. New York: Oxford University Press, 1938.

36 *The Journals of Kierkegaard*. Edited and translated by Alexander Dru (an abridgement of No. 35). New York: Harper & Brothers, 1959; Torchbook paperback TB 52.

37 *Kierkegaard's Diary*. Edited by Peter P. Rohde, translated by Gerda M. Andersen. New York: Philosophical Library, 1960.

38 *A Kierkegaard Anthology*. Edited by Robert Bretall. Princeton: Princeton University Press, 1946; New York: Random House, 1959. (Modern Library).

39 *Kierkegaard*. Selected and introduced by W. H. Auden. London: Cassell, 1955.

40 *The Living Thoughts of Kierkegaard*. Edited by W. H. Auden. New York: David Mc Kay, 1952.

41 *Selections from the Writings of Kierkegaard*. Edited and translated by Lee M. Hollander. Austin, Texas: The University of Texas Bulletin, No. 2326, 1923; revised edition, Garden City: Doubleday, 1960; Anchor paperback A 210.

42 *The Prayers of Kierkegaard*. Edited by Perry D. Le Fevre. Chicago: University of Chicago Press, 1956.

43 *The Witness of Kierkegaard*. Edited by Carl Michalson. New York: Association Press, 1960.

44 *Meditations from Kierkegaard*. Edited and translated by T. H. Croxall. Philadelphia: Westminster Press, 1955.

C. BIOGRAPHICAL MATERIAL

45 Ammundsen, V. *Søren Kierkegaards Ungdom*. Copenhagen, 1912.

46 Brøchner, H. "Erindringer om Søren Kierkegaard," in *Det nittende Aarhundrede*. Vol. I, pp. 337–374. Copenhagen, 1877. (For an English translation of this material see No. 49 below).

47 Brandt, F. *Den Unge Søren Kierkegaard*. Copenhagen, 1929.

48 Brandt, F. and Else Rammel. *Søren Kierkegaard og Pengene*. Copenhagen, 1935.

49 Croxall, T. H. *Glimpses and Impressions of Kierkegaard*. Translated by T. H. Croxall. Welwyn. Herts: J. Nesbit, 1959.

50 Heiberg, P. A. *Søren Kierkegaards religiøse Udvikling*. Copenhagen, 1925.

51 Heiberg, P. A. and V. Kuhr. *Kierkegaard Studier*. Pts. I–III. Copenhagen, 1912–1918.

52 Koch, Carl. *Søren Kierkegaard og Emil Boesen*. Copenhagen, 1901.

53 Kühle, Sejer. *Søren Kierkegaard. Barndom og Ungdom.* Copenhagen, 1950.

54 Lowrie, Walter. *A Short Life of Kierkegaard.* Princeton: Princeton University Press, 1942. Garden City: Doubleday, 1961; Anchor paperback, A 273.

55 Lund, Henriette. *Mit Forhold til Hende.* 2nd edition, Copenhagen, 1904.

56 Lund, Henriette. *Erindringer fra Hjemmet.* Copenhagen, 1909.

57 Meyer, Raphael. *Kierkegaardiske Papirer. Forlovelsen.* Udgivne for Fru Regine Schlegel af Raphael Meyer. Copenhagen, 1904.

58 Thulstrup, Niels. *Katalog over Søren Kierkegaards Bibliotek.* Published by the Søren Kierkegaard Selskabet, edited with an introduction by Niels Thulstrup. Copenhagen, 1957.

59 Weltzer, Carl. *Peter og Søren Kierkegaard.* Vols. I–II. Copenhagen, 1936.

D. SECONDARY LITERATURE

English Studies

60 Collins, James. *The Mind of Kierkegaard.* Chicago: Henry Regnery Co., 1953.

61 Croxall, T. H. *Kierkegaard Studies.* London: Lutterworth Press, 1948.

62 Croxall, T. H. *Kierkegaard Commentary.* New York: Harper & Brothers, 1956.

63 Diem, Hermann. *Kierkegaard's Dialectic of Existence.* Translated by Harold Knight. London: Oliver and Boyd, 1959.

64 Heinecken, Martin J. *The Moment Before God.* Philadelphia: Muhlenberg Press, 1956.

65 Henriksen, Aage. *Kierkegaard Studies in Scandinavia.* Publications of the Kierkegaard Society, Copenhagen. Vol. 1. Copenhagen: Munksgaard, 1951.

66 Johnson, Howard A. and Niels Thulstrup. *The Kierkegaard Critique.* An international round-up of essays interpreting Kierkegaard. Edited by Howard A. Johnson and Niels Thulstrup. New York: Harper & Brothers, 1962.

67 Jolivet, R. *An Introduction to Kierkegaard.* Translated by W. H. Barber. New York: E. P. Dutton, 1952.

68 Roos, Heinrich. *Søren Kierkegaard and Catholicism.* Translated by Richard M. Brackett. Westminster, Md.: Newman Press, 1954.

69 Swenson, David F. *Something About Kierkegaard.* 2nd edition, revised and enlarged by Lillian Marvin Swenson. Minneapolis: Augsburg Publishing House, 1945.

70 Thomas, John Heywood. *Subjectivity and Paradox*. New York: Macmillan, 1957.

71 Thomte, Reidar. *Kierkegaard's Philosophy of Religion*. Princeton: Princeton University Press, 1948.

SCANDINAVIAN STUDIES

72 Beyer, H. *Søren Kierkegaard og Norge*. Christiania, 1924.

73 Bohlin, Torsten. *Sören Kierkegaards etiska äskädning*. Stockholm, 1918.

74 Bohlin, Torsten. *Kierkegaards dogmatiska äskädning i dess historiska sammanhang*. Uppsala, 1925.

75 Bohlin, Torsten. *Sören Kierkegaard. Mannen och verket*. Stockholm, 1939.

76 Brandes, Georg. *Søren Kierkegaard. En kritisk Fremstilling i Grundrids*. Copenhagen, 1877.

77 Drachmann, A. B. *Hedenskab og Christendom hos Soren Kierkegaard*. In *Udvalgte Afhandlinger*. Copenhagen, 1911.

78 Geismar, Eduard. *Søren Kierkegaard. Livsudvikling og Forfattervirksomhed*. Pts. I–VI in 2 vols. Copenhagen, 1926–1928.

79 Henriksen, Aage. *Kierkegaards Romaner*. Copenhagen, 1954.

80 Himmelstrup, Jens. *Søren Kierkegaards Opfattelse af Sokrates*. Copenhagen, 1923.

81 Høffding, Harold, *Søren Kierkegaard som Filosof*. Copenhagen, 1892.

82 Jansen, F. J. Billeskov. *Studier i Søren Kierkegaards Literære Kunst*. Copenhagen, 1951.

83 Lindström, Valter. *Stadiernas teologi*. Lund, 1943.

84 Lindström, Valter. *Efterföljelsens Theologi hos Sören Kierkegaard*. Stockholm, 1956.

85 Lønning, Per. *Samtidighetens Situation*. Oslo, 1954.

86 Roos, Carl. *Kierkegaard og Goethe*. Copenhagen, 1955.

87 Sjöstedt, N. A. *Sören Kierkegaard och svensk litteratur*. Göteborg, 1950.

88 Thulstrup, Niels. *Kierkegaardiana*. Vols. I, 1955; II, 1957; III, 1959. Publication of the Soren Kierkegaard Selskabet, edited by Niels Thulstrup. Copenhagen: Munksgaard.

GERMAN STUDIES

89 Diem, Hermann. *Philosophie und Christentum bei Sören Kierkegaard*. Munich, 1929.

90 Diem, Hermann. *Die Existenzdialektik von Sören Kierkegaard*. Zollikon-Zurich: Evangelischer Verlag A. G., 1950.

91 Hirsch, E. *Kierkegaard-Studien*. Vols. I–II. Gütersloh, 1930–1933.

92 Radermacher, Hans, *Kierkegaards Hegelverständnis*. Cologne, 1956.
93 Rest, Walter. *Indirekte Mitteilung als bildendes Verfahren dargestellt am Leben und Werk Sören Kierkegaards*. Münster, 1937.
94 Ruttenbeck, W. *Sören Kierkegaard. Der christliche Denker und sein Werk*. Berlin, 1929.
95 Sløk, Johannes. *Die Anthropologie Kierkegaards*. Copenhagen, 1954.
96 Thust, M. *Kierkegaard, der Dichter des Religiösen*. Munich, 1931.

FRENCH STUDIES

97 Jolivet, R. *Introduction à Kierkegaard*, éditions de Fontenelle, abbaye de Saint-Wandrille, 1946.
98 Mesnard, Pierre. *Le vrai visage de Kierkegaard*, bibliothèque des archives de philosophie, Paris, 1948.
99 Mesnard, Pierre. *Kierkegaard, sa vie, son œuvre, avec un exposé de sa philosophie*, P. U. F., Paris, 1954.
100 Steffensen, Steffen, and Hans Sörensen. *Symposion Kierkegaardianum. Orbis Literarum*, tome X fasc. 1–2. Edited by Steffen Steffensen and Hans Sörensen. Copenhagen: Munksgaard, 1955.
101 Wahl, J. *Etudes Kierkegaardiennes*, deuxième édition, bibliothèque d'histoire de la philosophie, Paris, 1949.

Although this bibliography has concentrated on the English editions of Kierkegaard's writings, special attention is called to the following foreign language editions.

102 Kierkegaard, Søren. *Philosophiske Smuler*. Udgivet med Indledning og Kommentar af Niels Thulstrup. Copenhagen: Munksgaard, 1955.
103 Kierkegaard, Søren. *Afsluttende Uvidenskabelig Efterskrift*. Udgivet med Indledning og Kommentar af Niels Thulstrup. Vols. I–II. Copenhagen: Gyldendal, 1961.
104 Kierkegaard, Søren. *Frygt og Baeven*. Udgivet med Indledning og Kommentar af Niels Thulstrup. Copenhagen: Gyldendal, 1961.
105 Kierkegaard, Sören. *Philosophisch-Theologische Schriften*, (complete in three volumes); *Poetisch-Philosophische Schriften*, (one volume thus far). This compact German edition, still in progress, is under the general editorship of Hermann Diem, and includes the excellent notes of Niels Thulstrup, Secretary of Søren Kierkegaard Selskabet, Copenhagen. This edition is being published by the Jakob Hegner Verlag, Cologne and Olten, 1951 ff.
106 Kierkegaard, Søren. *Journal. Extraits*. Edited and translated into French by K. Ferlov and J.-J. Gateau. Vols. I–IV. Paris: Gallimard, 1941–1957.
107 Kierkegaard, Søren. *Diario*. Edited and translated into Italian by Cornelio Fabro, C.P.S. Vols. I–III. Brescia: Ediziono Morcelliana, 1948–1951.

APPENDIX VI

NOTES ON KIERKEGAARD'S PORTRAITS

THE six illustrations contained in this book present an occasion for discussing briefly the problem of S. K.'s portraits. They even require some explanation, and I avail myself of this occasion the more willingly because the subject is one which has hitherto been neglected. The only serious contribution to the study of it was made by the Danish sculptor Rikkard Magnussen in the art review *Sameleren*, in the May number for 1927. I am told that he is preparing to publish a monograph on this subject. So far as I am aware, no other reference has been made to it, except by Brandt in a few pages of his *Den unge S. K.*, 1927, pp. 42–7, where he reaches conclusions very unsatisfactory to me.

Although there exist no pictures of S. K. more reliable than the six I present here, the reader needs to be informed that only the first two of them were drawn from life. The first of these (facing the first title-page) is the full-face portrait of S. K. as a youth, which was sketched hastily in pencil by Chr. Kierkegaard, a second cousin of S. K.'s, who by profession was a drawing-master. It was probably made in 1839 when Søren was 26 years of age, and before it was published in 1876 (that is, posthumously) it was carefully finished, with an evident tendency to idealize the subject. In 1838 the same artist made a hasty sketch of S. K.'s head in profile, which was reproduced much later in a woodcut without any change or improvement. It is not to be wondered at that many are inclined to think neither of these portraits trustworthy.

The question has been raised whether we possess any reliable likeness of S. K. It is notorious that he was resolutely opposed to having his portrait made, and we may suppose that any artist who essayed to do such a thing must have been compelled to do it almost instantaneously.

Such an instantaneous sketch we have in the second illustration—opposite the title-page of Part II. It is now in the possession of the Frederiksborg Museum. It was drawn by David Jacobsen, and represents S. K. seated at table in the room he occupied as a university student. Magnussen has twice published it, with reasons persuasive enough to convince me that it is really a portrait of S. K. Indeed I am inclined to think that it is the best portrait we have of him. All the artist's care was concentrated upon the well-drawn line of the profile. He roughly indicated the furniture of the room, with the long pipes hanging on the wall, pipe-lighters in a jar, and a book flung upon the floor—traits characteristic of S. K.

I have more to say about the third illustration, which faces the title-page of Part III. It is a plaster medallion, 16½ inches (42 cm.) in diameter, which was made about the year 1875 by Carl Aarsleff, Professor of Art in the University, at the order of Madame Julie Thomsen, *née* Kierkegaard (or Kirkegaard). The same artist later superintended the execution of the large bronze statue of S. K. in front of the Royal Library in Copenhagen. No copy was made of this plaster relief. I bought it from Mr. Roby-Thomsen when I was visiting Copenhagen. At that time neither he nor I supposed that it had any great value as a portrait, seeing that it was made some twenty years after S. K.'s death. It struck me, however, that it seemed to mediate in a remarkable way between the idealized full-face drawn by Chr. Kierkegaard and the hateful caricature (not reproduced here) which Brandt perversely prefers as a likeness of the sarcastic young Kierkegaard. Without such a middle term it would not be easy to believe that these two pictures, drawn by love and hate, represent the same person. Brandt justly remarks that S. K.'s physiognomy 'invited caricature' as well as idealization. In part this was due to the fact that his features were exceedingly mobile. His niece Henrietta Lund says of him,[1] 'His mouth was large, but in compensation for that, what a whole gamut of different moods it was capable of expressing with its flexible lines, all the way from sweet sadness and tenderness to bold defiance and subtle irony—this last being not the least observable trait.' I have a painful suspicion that this cruel sketch which Brandt makes so much of did in fact represent young Søren only too faithfully ... at his worst, at the instant when he was launching a sarcastic retort. If the full-face by Chr. Kierkegaard may be thought to depict him some degrees better than his best, this posthumous portrait by Aarsleff may be supposed to represent fairly his normal expression. To me this seems good enough, even if it is not so good as the profile so sympathetically sketched by David Jacobsen.

Prompted by hints in Weltzer's recent book on *Peter og Søren Kierkegaard*, which reached me in May of this current year, I began to suspect that this relief might have real value as a portrait, notwithstanding the late date of its execution. I learned that Julie Thomsen was a daughter of Michael Andersen Kierkegaard, that cousin of Søren's father to whom he turned over his lucrative business when he retired, and who then adopted the surname of his benefactor. At the time in question surnames were so far from being fixed that his father bore the name of Gade, notwithstanding that he was a brother of Michael Pedersen Kierkegaard's father. Thus Julie was only second cousin to Søren; but their intimacy, as I learn, was so close and affectionate that Weltzer (p. 96) ventures to suppose that Julie's marriage in 1835 to Quartermaster Alfred Thomsen was 'something of a disillusionment to Søren'. However that may be, he maintained a close friendship with her until his death. It is known that she possessed a collection of his letters which she declined to deliver to Barfod, the first editor of S. K.'s papers, on the ground that they were 'too personal'. What chiefly interests us here, however, is Weltzer's remark that 'she was the only one who was allowed to have a portrait of him'. Nothing more is known about that unique portrait, though one might be tempted to suppose that it was made by her cousin Chr. Kierkegaard. Twenty years after Søren's death, at the time when the public was clamouring for the publication of his portrait, Julie had this medallion made by Professor Aarsleff, and if she had in her possession a contemporary sketch which represented S. K. at the very age she required Aarsleff to represent him, it is not probable that she failed to furnish the artist with this very necessary help. If this consideration has weight, if the plaster relief is copied from a contemporary portrait, it has of course a peculiar value. In any case, we cannot suppose that Julie Thomsen would have been satisfied with a portrait which did not faithfully depict her favourite cousin.

This plaster medallion when I received it was covered with a coat of yellowish oil paint which very much obscured its significance, and also rendered photography impossible because it had become tarnished and mottled with age. When I discovered its value I removed the paint so far as possible and covered it with water-colour in two contrasted tints, which enabled me to make a photograph in which the modelling is more evident than in the original. Professor Geismar took back with him to

Denmark a copy of this photograph with the purpose of writing a brief monograph on it. As he has not yet done this, I have to compose these notes without the aid I might have expected from such a study.

The other three illustrations are very far from being contemporary portraits, and yet the artists have spared no pains to make them as faithful as possible, employing all the material at their disposal, including not only all the sketches which are in existence, but also the verbal descriptions of S. K. which have been left us by his contemporaries.

Facing the title-page of Part IV is a photograph of the oil painting in the Frederiksborg Museum which was made by Luplau Janssen in 1902. It represents S. K. engaged in lively conversation with the artist Laurenz Frølich in the course of one of his customary promenades on the street. The place is the Nytorv (New Market), the public square on which S. K. lived a great part of his life. Immediately behind him, alongside of the City Hall, is the great house he inherited from his father.

Facing the title-page of Part V is the photograph of another oil painting in the Frederiksborg Museum, made by the same artist and in the same year. It represents S. K. doing his writing by standing at a high desk. I suppose that the artist, with an antiquarian interest, had discovered that such a piece of furniture had been preserved or was described as belonging to the household effects which he left. The tradition is that every room in his house had a table or desk, with pens, ink, and paper, so that he might be able to jot down his thoughts wherever he was.

Facing the title-page of Part VI is a photograph of the plaster model for the large bronze statue in front of the Royal Library in Copenhagen. Because a photograph of the plaster reproduces the effect of the modelling more perfectly, I have preferred this to a picture of the exquisite bronze statuette in the Frederiksborg Museum which was made in Rome by L. Hasselriis, and from which the large statue was copied, not very perfectly. I rejoice to have on my desk a replica of the statuette, which seems to me the most endearing monument to S. K.

I have not reproduced here a famous picture of S. K. taking his customary promenade on the street, drawn from memory by a famous artist, W. Marstrand, at the moment when the news reached him of the great man's death. It represents S. K. as he was familiarly known to the populace of Copenhagen. It is justly regarded as a caricature, and yet it probably depicts faithfully enough the effect which S. K.'s spinal curvature had upon his figure and gait. It evidently influenced profoundly not only Luplau Janssen's comical picture of S. K. on the street but also the tender conception of the statuette. So much depends upon the personal equation in one's judgement of S. K.'s outward appearance. The judgements men form of the inward man, on the basis of his literary production, are quite as personal, and they will always differ as widely.

APPENDIX VII

A GLOSSARY OF SOME OF THE TERMS USED CHARACTERISTICALLY BY KIERKEGAARD

PRELIMINARY REMARK

Almost all of the terms dealt with here can best be defined by contrasting them with their opposites. We can understand why S. K. uses them with so much emphasis when we apprehend that any of these pairs of opposites must logically comprise the whole universe in their scope. We understand, for example, why he speaks with such deep disparagement of being 'close' when we are made aware that being 'open' expresses a universal ethical maxim. I print here at the outset a list of contrasted terms arranged in parallel columns; and I call attention to the fact that, although the more express contraries are printed opposite one another, there is some degree of contrast between almost any term in the one column and every term in the other, whereas there is essential congruity between all the terms in the same column. It is hardly necessary to say that the author of *Either/Or* deals predominantly with pairs of contrary terms.

Open.	Close.
Direct.	Indirect communication. Maieutic, double reflection, reduplication.
Objectivity.	Subjectivity, inwardness, pathos.
Immanence.	Transcendence.
Necessity.	Freedom.
Actuality.	Possibility.
'The System'.	Paradox.
Speculation.	Existence.
Mediation.	'The leap'.
The universal.	The particular, the individual.
'Recollection'.	'The repetition'.
Immediacy.	Reflection ('mediacy').

Such a list may be more useful than the following definitions, and yet no sooner is it formulated than doubts suggest themselves. For example, S. K. discovers that 'actuality' is permeated by 'possibility' (by contingency and freedom); and on the other hand, he discovers opposites where we might not think of looking for them—as when he says, 'the contrary of sin is not virtue but faith', and in another place, that the opposite of faith is not unbelief but defiance. Hence the reader must reconsider this list in the light of the definitions which follow.

The Absurd—*see* Paradox.

Actuality (*Virkelighed*) would be well defined by observing that its antithesis is Possibility—were it not that S. K. (in opposition to Hegel) regards actuality as something that has *become* (following Aristotle), hence something into which there enters contingency, freedom, i.e. Possibility. Hence in the *Philosophical Scraps* he can raise such a question as 'When the past becomes actual does it become more necessary than it was?' (the title of the Interlude following Chapter IV. Cf. iv. 314).

AESTHETICAL, aesthetics. It suffices to remark that the word is not limited to the appreciation of the beautiful as it appeals to the senses of sight and hearing, but that it is used here broadly (as by philosophers generally) with reference to the satisfaction of all the senses. It means a eudaimonistic view of life and the pursuit of pleasure, as opposed to a serious ethical view. And yet the ethical is not a complete opposite, for the aesthetical is contrasted even more expressly with the religious. Even in the religious stage, however, the aesthetical (according to S. K.) is 'not abolished, it is dethroned'.

For *examples* of S. K.'s use of any of the words which are here briefly defined, the reader is referred to the Index which concludes this book. In the definitions which follow I print generally in capital letters all the words explained in this list, wherever they recur, to call attention to the fact that they explain one another reciprocally (either by contrast or by resemblance) and to refer the reader to the place where they are defined.

CLOSE (*indesluttet*)—*see* OPEN.

COMMUNICATION, INDIRECT. S. K. maintained that 'direct communication', which seeks to impart truth by simply communicating 'results', is not possible with regard to such truths as most deeply concern a man (viz. ethical and religious truths); for in this case not only *what* one learns but *how* one appropriates it is of importance. Such truths must be appropriated subjectively and by one's own effort. He had learned from Socrates to employ the maieutic method (the method of midwifery) to bring to birth thoughts which the learner already obscurely possessed. His use of 'indirect communication' had therefore to do with his notion of INWARDNESS, SUBJECTIVITY, and EXISTENCE, q.v. In its highest expression it takes the form of REDUPLICATION and DOUBLE REFLECTION, q.v. But it also had to do with the fact that his melancholy made him CLOSE, and when he learned to regard his closeness as a daimonia, sinister light fell upon 'indirect communication' as he had used it to obscure his thought.

DESPAIR (*Fortvivlelse*). It is recognized as 'the sickness unto death', and yet it may be the beginning of the new life. Only when a man in the cruel grip of NECESSITY has lost the POSSIBILITY is he driven to 'chose his own self' and make the desperate 'leap' of faith—and with that he recovers the POSSIBILITY and is assured of the REPETITION.

DIALECTICS. Since S. K. criticizes sharply Hegel's 'dialectical method', it must not be supposed that the dialectics he so much insisted upon is the same thing. Both deal with opposites, but the difference is that, whereas Hegel 'mediates' between them and thus reaches a point of repose, S. K.'s thought continually vibrates between the opposite poles, recognizing that contradiction and PARADOX are inherent in EXISTENCE, which because it resists the effort of the reason to regiment it into a system is denounced by reason as 'the absurd'. S. K.'s use of the word 'dialectics' is not remote from its etymological meaning: dialogue, involving question and answer, the enunciation of different points of view. The pseudonyms, and the characters which they in turn invent, serve this end at least as well as the characters Plato introduces in the Socratic dialogues.

DOUBLE REFLECTION (*Dobbelt-Reflexion*). An instance of INDIRECT COMMUNICATION requiring artful suppression of the communicator, who as a 'subjective existing thinker' becomes aware on second reflection that the truth he has acquired 'interests' his EXISTENCE, and that it cannot simply be appropriated by another without being acquired by the same process of reflection, which the indirect method is designed to stimulate. REDUPLICATION means 'to exist in what one understands', i.e. to reflect the truth in one's life.

DREAD. It has been pointed out in the text (p. 73) that this word does not adequately render the Danish *Angest* (German and modern Danish *Angst*). The French translators use the word *angoisse*; and in fact *Angest* as used by S. K. implies an agonizing premonition prompted by nothing concrete, but by horror at . . . nothingness—like the dizziness one may experience on the brink of an abyss. This Dread when it is realized as entanglement in the toils of NECESSITY becomes DESPAIR, q.v.

EXISTENCE, existential. A word used pregnantly by S. K. to denote the paradoxical character of *human* existence, qualified as it is by the fact that it is 'a synthesis of the infinite and the finite, of the eternal and the temporal'. SPECULATION does not do justice to the facts of human existence when it attempts to regiment them in a system. Therefore S. K. insists upon the importance of 'existential thinking', which in the nature of the case must be dialectical and paradoxical.

FREEDOM (*Frihed*). 'Freedom of the will', in the sense of *liberum arbitrium* about which philosophers have quarrelled, S. K. discards as a nonentity—and nevertheless he is a champion of human freedom as against determinism. He champions even a sort of freedom (contingency) in nature itself. And above all he vindicates the freedom of God. Man has definite limits to his freedom; but 'with God all things are possible'. This is affirmed in face of the persistent effort of the philosophers to subject God as well as men (like the ancient Greeks) to NECESSITY (ἀνάγκη)—necessity which is exemplified not only by the laws of nature but also by the moral law. It is enough for man if, under whatever straitening of necessity, he be free, as he is, to 'chose his own self'; for with that all possibilities open to him, even 'the true repetition' which is eternity, a participation in the infinite possibility of God.

GOVERNANCE (*Styrelsen*). It means divine providence—not, however, the providence which *provides* (*Forsyn*), but the providence which guides. Yet I have to reject the word guidance because it is commonly understood to mean guidance from *within*, in a mystical sense, whereas S. K. thought of providence as ruling and overruling the outward circumstances and tenor of his life as well as his inward thought and disposition—and doing this always *from* without, a transcendent providence, 'a divinity that shapes our ends, rough-hew them how we will'.

IMMANENCE—*see* TRANSCENDENCE.

IMMEDIACY (*Umiddelbarhed*). The significance S. K. attaches to this word, in opposition to REFLECTION, is explained by Hegel's use of it in his *Logic*, the first half of which is devoted to 'immediacy' as the sphere in which one apprehends 'being'. He means by this word what is apprehended in nature directly (i.e. without REFLECTION), either by the senses or by intuition. Hegel's next stage is REFLECTION, by which one attains the concept of 'substance'. S. K. uses this word also to describe the sensuous life, relatively untroubled by reflection.

The INDIVIDUAL (*det Enkelte*)—*see the* PARTICULAR.

INWARDNESS (*Inderligheden*)—*see* SUBJECTIVE.

'The LEAP' (*Springet*). It is by this metaphor that S. K. expresses his passionate repudiation of the smooth transition Hegel sought to effect by means of MEDIATION. S. K. protests that there is no real MOVEMENT in logic, no genuine *becoming*, and that in EXISTENCE every movement which effects a real change is a 'leap', an act of FREEDOM. This applies especially to faith, which is not attained by continuous and gradual approximations but by a resolution of the will, in 'the Instant'.

MAIEUTIC—*see* COMMUNICATION, INDIRECT.

MEDIATION—the *deus ex machina* by which Hegel sought to reconcile opposites and introduce movement into logic, thereby arriving at new concepts by a continuous process of thought. *See* DIALECTICS.

MOVEMENT (*κίνησις*). Following Aristotle, who used this word to denote the change from POSSIBILITY (*κατὰ δύναμιν*) to ACTUALITY, S. K. protests, against Hegel, that movement is not a *logical* transition but a real *becoming*. Hence the emphasis he lays upon 'becoming'.

NECESSITY (*Nødvendighed*). Like most philosophers, Hegel identified the necessary and the ACTUAL, thus subjecting to necessity all reality, including God. Against this S. K. protested passionately in the interest of FREEDOM; and in defence of his paradoxical philosophy of freedom and contingency he reverted to Aristotle's definition which distinguishes sharply between necessity and ACTUALITY and associates the latter with POSSIBILITY. S. K. regarded necessity, i.e. the loss of possibility, as the occasion of DESPAIR. One is delivered from necessity and despair by an act of freedom, the 'choice of one's own self'—beyond that lies the REPETITION.

OFFENCE (*Forargelse*). It is the word commonly used in the English Bible to translate *πειρασμός*, though sometimes it uses 'stumbling-block'. It is therefore a TEMPTATION in the sense of trial which might deter one from faith. S. K. speaks of it most frequently in connexion with 'the martyrdom of believing in opposition to the understanding'. Every PARADOX of faith is a stumbling-block to the understanding, but the greatest 'offence' is the incognito of the God-Man.

OPEN (*aabenbar*). S. K. had learnt from Hegel to regard the UNIVERSAL as an expression of the ethical maxim and to understand that this required OPENNESS on the part of the individual. Accordingly, CLOSENESS must be regarded as unethical. But S. K. had a secret he could not reveal, even to his fiancée. So for him the question was pressing, whether there be such a thing as 'a teleological *suspension* of the ethical', i.e. of the *universal* maxim. That is to say, is there any place for the individual who finds himself impeded by a sense of *duty* from 'realizing the universal'? Is he necessarily guilty in pursuing the aim (*telos*) which he feels himself bound to pursue? 'Is there such a thing as an absolute duty towards God?' It was the thought of the individual's relation to God which liberated him from the tyranny of ethical theory. For this he found the paradigm in Abraham, who at God's express command was ready to slay his son (thus putting himself outside the pale of ethical law), and who, because of the peculiar situation had God placed him in, was unable to be 'open', i.e. could not impart his secret either to Sarah or to Isaac or to Eleazar. In this instance the vice of closeness was seen to be a duty, yet S. K. never regarded it as a virtue, and in the end he recognized that his closeness was a daimonia. Yet in the end Abraham was justified, for like Job he received the REPETITION.

PARADOX, paradoxical. It means contrary to appearance, plausibility, or probability. Faith as such can find an appropriate object only in paradox; for if faith is reached, or subsequently justified, by demonstration, or by plausible argument, it is no longer faith but knowledge. Paradox emerges in the ethical sphere so soon as interest is centred in the individual. Hegel's system is then found to be inapplicable, for it is concerned only with the universal. It emerges in the intellectual sphere as the 'absolute paradox' of the God-Man. But, in general, 'religion B' is paradox religiousness.

The PARTICULAR (*det saerlige, Enkelthed, det ejendommelige*). It is the opposite of the UNIVERSAL, q.v. 'That particular individual' (*hiin Enkelte*) S. K. often spoke of as 'my category'. But a philosophical theory of ethics is interested only in the universal: the individual and his particular personal griefs are ignored. The comfort Job's friends offered the afflicted man was perfectly good ethics, but it contained no comfort for his particular griefs, and Job refused to be *resigned*, as ethical theory requires one to be. So he became another paradigm for S. K. in his struggle against the thraldom of ethical theory. Reason is as cruel to the individual in the formulation of its ethical system as in the formulation of a deterministic world-view; and in the struggle of the individual against NECESSITY and to recover the POSSIBILITY, to regain FREEDOM, it is just as important to vindicate a 'suspension of the ethical' (not its abolition), for the sake of *duty*, as to be assured that the 'laws of nature' are suspended by the will.

PATHOS. The Greek word πάθος denotes first, passivity; then, suffering (passion in the passive sense); and then, passion in an active sense. This last is the pathos of the 'subjective existential thinker', who is passionately interested in his thinking because the theme of it so deeply concerns him. The first expression of his pathos is enthusiasm for an absolute aim (*telos*); the essential expression of his pathos, however, is suffering. But S. K. often uses this word in the commoner sense of the pathetic.

POSSIBILITY (*Mulighed*). We can understand the PATHOS with which S. K. uses this word when we reflect that it is the opposite of NECESSITY, that it means room for FREEDOM, and therefore is like breath to a drowning man, a man 'lost to the possibility', as S. K. puts it. The possibility is necessary for man—but also for God. If God is imprisoned in necessity, man's possibility is an illusion, there is no justification for faith, no ground for the hope of REPETITION, and the beginning and end of wisdom for man is the philosophical (stoical) resignation which 'accepts the universe'. But Job was justified in his belief in the infinite possibility of God—he received the REPETITION.

POTENCY (*Potenz*). Generally, I have *interpreted* this word as a mathematical term (1st to *n*th power), because not every reader can be expected to recognize it as a term peculiar to Schelling's philosophy.

PROVIDENCE—*see* GOVERNANCE.

RECOLLECTION (*Erindring*)—*see* REPETITION.

REDUPLICATION—*see* DOUBLE REFLECTION.

REFLECTION (*Reflexion*), in the sense of cogitation, is contrasted with IMMEDIACY, q.v. As an eminently reflective mind, S. K. would naturally make much use of this word; but he hardly would have used it with so much emphasis and in so many senses if it had not been employed by Hegel as his special device for arriving at the concept of substance (*Wesen*).

REPETITION (*Gjentagelsen*). No term in S. K.'s vocabulary is more important, and none so baffling. At the outset, in the book which bears this title, he cunningly contrived to make it difficult for the reader to understand what he meant. Consequently, one of the most astute men of his time had no suspicion that it might mean more than the regular recurrence of seasons, &c., in the natural world. In fact, even its pseudonymous author, Constantine Constantius, hardly conceived of it as more than that, although 'the young man' whom he was studying could go farther because he was religious. The repetition was associated first of all with the story of Job, who received everything back again manyfold—and with the case of Abraham, who received his son back. But in the end we are apprised that this physical restitution does not constitute the essence of the matter: 'Repetition is a religious category . . . it is a movement in virtue of the absurd . . . eternity is the true repetition.' In the stricter sense this is not eschatology; for eternity is already in the possession of the man who by faith is delivered from the servitude which is represented by the universal ethical maxim, by the dead hand of dogmatics, as well as by the laws of nature, and has thereby recovered his POSSIBILITY, or rather has attained, in the 'immediacy after reflection', a far fuller possibility than he had before. It is characteristic that S. K. expressly contrasts REPETITION with the Platonic RECOLLECTION (*Erindring*) by which one can retreat from the too real world into the eternal world of ideas, which is the Greek immortality: 'Repetition is a decisive expression for what recollection was to the Greeks. Just as the ancients taught that knowledge is recollection, so will the new philosophy teach that all life is repetition. . . . Repetition and recollection are the same movement, only in a different direction; for what is remembered has been, and it is remembered backward, whereas repetition is a forward-looking recollection' (iii. 193). Although in this there is not a trace of *apocalyptic* eschatology, the forward orientation is the same—and nothing is more essential to Christianity than this orientation.

SPECULATION (or 'the System'). S. K.'s drastic criticism of 'Speculation' was aimed expressly at Hegel because at that time he was the latest and most triumphant impersonation of the perennial effort of the reason to give a complete and coherent account of reality; but in attacking 'the System' he denounces in general the presumption and futility of such an effort. He himself offers only 'scraps of philosophy', being convinced that a 'system' is impossible for a finite mind (cf. DIALECTICS). He objects that speculation not only fails to give an exhaustive account of reality (and especially of human reality or EXISTENCE), but does not give a true account of it as far as it goes; for reality (and more especially existence) always contains elements of contingency, of FREEDOM, which is a PARADOX to the reason. Among the many points of resemblance between S. K. and Hamlet, Prince of Denmark, not the least striking is the saying, 'There are more things in heaven and earth, Horatio, than are dreamt of in your philosophy.'

SUBJECTIVE, subjectivity. First of all the suspicion must be eliminated that by his insistence upon this word S. K. means to applaud what we commonly call subjective thinking, viz. distortion of reality by the personal equation. He meant in fact a deeper and truer apprehension of reality. By Hegel's claim to objectivity of thought (by which he meant personal disinterestedness in the results of speculation) S. K. was prompted to emphasize the importance of subjectivity, i.e. passionate personal *interest* in thought and its result. 'The subjective existential thinker' is concerned only with what *matters* to him (*interesse*), and the philosophy which has to do with this he counts the only true philosophy. Such philosophy must permeate the life of the thinker and profoundly modify his EXISTENCE. Hence only ethical and ethico-religious knowledge is essential knowledge. In this sense of subjectivity S. K. uses even more commonly the word INWARDNESS (*Inderlighed*).

'The SYSTEM'—*see* SPECULATION.

TEMPTATION. It has often been a cause of complaint that the English language makes no distinction between temptation and temptation, i.e. between the temptation which seduces by the bait of pleasure (*Fristelse*), and that which works deterrently by the threat of suffering (*Anfaeglelse*), this latter being the meaning the word has in the Lord's Prayer. To discriminate between these two very different senses of the word 'temptation' one must use the word 'trial' or 'trial of temptation'.

TRANSCENDENT, transcendence, transcendental. It is the opposite of IMMANENT. The point of departure for S. K.'s use of this word, so far as it is peculiar to him or peculiarly emphasized, was his protest against Hegel's affirmation that thought and being are one, that the outward is the inward, that thought permeates all things, and that this doctrine of immanence excludes all notion of transcendence in any form. In opposition to this he denies that the doctrine of immanence fairly describes reality, especially the reality of human EXISTENCE, which contains PARADOXES which thought does *not* permeate, and transitions in the process of *becoming* which are not continuous but are effected by the 'leap'.

The UNIVERSAL (*det Almene*). S. K. inherited this term from Hegel as a characterization of the ethical. In his earlier works he accepted it without criticism, notwithstanding that it condemned him personally for the fact that by reason of his peculiar fate he was unable to 'realize the universal', more especially in the matter of marriage, and was compelled to reflect persistently upon the rights of the INDIVIDUAL, and also upon his duties, in contrast with the universal precept. Such reflections did not lead him to discard the ethical theory, or even this definition of ethics, but only to vindicate to the individual the right and the duty to 'suspend' it upon due occasion. Cf. 'the teleological suspension of the ethical'. *See* FREEDOM, NECESSITY, OPEN.

INDEX

THIS index seeks to be discriminating rather than complete, useful rather than perfect—if there be such a thing as a perfect index. It may be a mark of its imperfection that it refers rather to the thing than to the word, and its incompleteness is most strikingly evidenced by the omission of the divine names. But how would it help the reader if he were pointed to every page of the book for S. K.'s thoughts about God? The newly published index to S. K.'s *Works* (not including the Journal) contains 40 closely printed columns referring to God and Christ, &c.—and all of this might as well have been omitted—if the object were to help the reader to find his way.